Step by Step

XML
STEP BY STEP
SECOND EDITION

Michael J. Yo

PUBLISHED BY
Microsoft Press
A Division of Microsoft Corporation
One Microsoft Way
Redmond, Washington 98052-6399

Library of Congress Cataloging-in-Publication Data
Young, Michael J.
    XML Step By Step / Michael J. Young.--2nd ed.
       p. cm.
    Includes index.
    ISBN 0-7356-1465-2
    1. XML (Document markup language)   I. Title.

  QA76.76.H94 Y68 2001
  005.7'2--dc21   2001044924

Printed and bound in the United States of America.

1 2 3 4 5 6 7 8 9   QWT   6 5 4 3 2

Distributed in Canada by Penguin Books Canada Limited.

A CIP catalogue record for this book is available from the British Library.

Microsoft Press books are available through booksellers and distributors worldwide. For further informa-
tion about international editions, contact your local Microsoft Corporation office or contact Microsoft
Press International directly at fax (425) 936-7329. Visit our Web site at www.microsoft.com/mspress.
Send comments to *mspinput@microsoft.com*.

Acquisitions Editor: David J. Clark
Project Editor: Jean Cockburn

Body Part No. X08-24444

Contents

Preface to the Second Edition

I finished writing the first edition of *XML Step by Step* around the time of the final snowfall over the southern Rockies in the spring of 2000. Less than a year later, I was once again witnessing the last snowfalls of the season and working on *XML Step by Step*, this time starting the second edition. I wrote this preface to discuss my goals in writing the second edition, to describe what's new in this edition, and to explain why Microsoft Press and I decided to create a second edition so soon after the first.

My first goal in writing the second edition was to bring the book up-to-date with the many changes in XML technologies that had occurred since the book was originally published. The current version of the XML specification is still 1.0, as it was when I wrote the first edition. However, since I wrote that edition, the technologies used to display and work with XML have undergone many changes, and even the XML 1.0 specification itself has appeared in a second edition that includes error corrections and clarifications. The following are some of the important updates to the book. (Don't worry if you haven't heard of the XML technologies mentioned in this preface. They're all explained in the book.)

- To reflect the explosive growth of XML applications, I added 16 more XML applications to the list in Chapter 1. (Even with these additions, the list still represents only a small sampling of the current uses for XML.)

- I wrote a new chapter (Chapter 7) covering XML schemas as defined by the World Wide Web Consortium (W3C) XML Schema specification, which achieved the status of recommendation in May 2001. An XML schema is used to define the content and structure of a class of XML documents. I also added several sections to Chapter 11 to explain how to check the validity of an XML document using an XML schema.

■ I completely revamped the final chapter in the book, which formerly covered XSL style sheets (based on the W3C's December 1998 Extensible Stylesheet Language (XSL) Version 1.0 working draft), to cover the newer XSLT style sheets (based on the W3C's November 1999 XSL Transformations (XSLT) Version 1.0 recommendation). I also covered many more style sheet features than before.

■ I updated the book to cover the XML features of Microsoft Internet Explorer versions 5.0 through 6.0, as well as MSXML 2.0 through 4.0. (MSXML is the software module that provides basic XML services for Internet Explorer. The first edition covered Internet Explorer versions 5.0 through 5.5, and MSXML 2.0 through 2.5.) Also, I recaptured each of the figures that shows a Windows element, such as a message box or the Internet Explorer window, using the Microsoft Windows XP Professional operating system.

My second goal in revising the book was to provide new or expanded coverage on important technologies and techniques that were already available when I wrote the first edition, but that I was unable to include—or to fully cover—due to space limitations. The second edition is about 100 pages longer than the first. The following are some of the important new topics you'll find in these additional pages:

■ I added coverage to Chapter 3 on the often confusing topic of how white space (sequences of space, tab, or line break characters) is handled in XML documents.

■ I greatly expanded the coverage on the increasingly important topic of namespaces. Namespaces are used to qualify names in XML documents so that naming conflicts can be avoided. Chapter 3 now includes a general discussion on namespaces (in the section "Using Namespaces"), and later chapters (Chapters 5, 8, 10, 11, and 12) now include information on using namespaces with specific XML technologies.

■ I added a sidebar to Chapter 3 covering the new all-inclusive URI Internet addressing scheme ("URIs, URLs, and URNs").

- In response to the many messages I received from readers working with non-English languages in XML, I added a lengthy sidebar to Chapter 3 covering XML language encoding ("Characters, Encoding, and Languages").

- Because of the importance of cascading style sheet (CSS) properties for formatting XML, regardless of the method used to display the document, I covered quite a few additional properties and property settings. These include properties and settings first supported by Internet Explorer version 6.0, such as the *list-item* setting of the *display* property for creating a bulleted or numbered list. I also added coverage of some of the more advanced properties defined in the CSS Level 2 specification, such as the *position* property for placing an element's content at a specific position on the page, outside of the normal flow of text.

- In Chapter 11 I added coverage on an alternative method for loading an XML document into an HTML page using a script. (The first edition covered only the data island method for loading an XML document. A data island is an XML document or a reference to an XML document embedded within an element in an HTML page.)

My third goal for the second edition was to clarify and correct the text of the first edition wherever necessary. I am grateful to the readers who took the time to e-mail me about parts of the book they found confusing or that they suspected were in error. Their feedback was a great help in revising this book.

One reason that Microsoft Press and I were motivated to invest our resources in this second edition is that it has now become abundantly clear that XML is truly a pivotal technology, and one that is here to stay. Those who are cynical enough to say that the computer industry generates new technologies as if it were throwing mud at a wall to see what will stick, would have to say that XML has stuck.

We were also motivated to revise this book because of the tremendous positive feedback we received from readers and reviewers of the first edition. We were especially gratified when the first edition of *XML Step by Step* won the top award, "Distinguished Technical Communication," in the 2000-2001 International Technical Publications Competition of the Society for Technical Communication (STC).

Acknowledgments

I would like to express my gratitude to the team of talented and dedicated professionals who produced and supported the second edition of *XML Step by Step*. In particular, I would like to offer a warm thank you:

To David J. Clark (acquisitions editor at Microsoft Press) for arranging the contract, for providing ongoing support, and for making this second edition possible.

To Jean Cockburn (project editor at Microsoft Press) for skillfully coordinating the entire project and for her continuing help, support, and patience. It was a pleasure working with you!

To the team at WASSER Studios for its huge role in editing and producing the book: Susan Carlson (project lead), Avon Murphy (technical editor), Sharon Baerny (copy editor), Britton Steel (production project manager), Kreg Hasegawa (proofer), and Andrea Heuston (desktop publisher).

To the World Wide Web Consortium and to the Internet Explorer and MSXML developers at Microsoft Corporation for creating and supporting XML. In particular, I'd like to thank Eldar Musayev at Microsoft for kindly providing me with timely insights on MSXML.

Michael J. Young
Taos, New Mexico
October, 2001

Introduction

Extensible Markup Language, or XML, is currently the most promising language for storing and exchanging information on the World Wide Web.

Although Hypertext Markup Language (HTML) is presently the most common language used to create Web pages, HTML has a limited capacity for storing information. In contrast, because XML allows you to create your own elements, attributes, and document structure, you can use it to describe virtually any kind of information—from a simple recipe to a complex database. And an XML document—in conjunction with a style sheet or a conventional HTML page—can be easily displayed in a Web browser. Because an XML document so effectively organizes and labels the information it contains, the browser can find, extract, sort, filter, arrange, and manipulate that information in highly flexible ways.

XML thus provides an ideal solution for handling the rapidly expanding quantity and complexity of information that needs to be delivered on the Web.

Why Another XML Book?

XML can be confusing. XML applications are appearing at an astounding rate, and XML is intimately tied to an ever-increasing number of related standards and technologies used to format, display, process, and enhance XML documents. Many of these related standards and technologies are still in their infant stages, and are rapidly changing and evolving.

Most of the XML books that I have read attempt a comprehensive coverage of these technologies but get a bit lost in the maze. I believe that the typical XML book tries to survey too many XML technologies too superficially, without discriminating between the important and the unimportant, the practical and the impractical, the current and the future.

I wrote *XML Step by Step* to answer the most fundamental XML questions—what XML is, why it's needed, and how it can be used—and to teach the most important, practical XML technologies available *now*.

Although I was quite selective in choosing the topics to include in this book, I cover each of them in depth, and avoid partial solutions. (For example, because I tell you how to define XML attributes in Part 2, in Part 3 I show you how to access these attributes when you display the document.)

I never truly understood XML until I started actually writing and displaying XML documents. Consequently, I gave this book a hands-on approach, including many step-by-step instructions, practical examples, and tutorial exercises. I avoided theoretical and abstract discussions that can be so difficult to understand with a topic like XML.

The book and companion CD are also unique in providing a complete XML learning kit. This kit provides all the information, instruction, and software that you need to learn the practical basics of creating and displaying XML documents. The book also includes a comprehensive set of links to a wealth of XML information on the Web, which you can explore if you want to go beyond the basics.

What You'll Learn in This Book

Part 1 of this book (Chapters 1 and 2) provides a gentle introduction to XML and prepares you for the detailed information that comes later. Chapter 1 answers the basic questions I mentioned earlier—what XML is, why it's needed, and how it's being used to solve real-world problems. Chapter 2 provides a hands-on exercise that gives you a quick overview of the entire process of creating an XML document and displaying it in a Web browser.

Part 2 (Chapters 3 through 7) focuses on the rules and techniques for creating XML documents. Chapters 3 and 4 show you how to create well-formed XML documents—documents that conform to the basic syntactical rules of XML. Chapters 5, 6, and 7 tell you how to create valid XML documents—documents that not only conform to the basic syntactical rules, but also match a specific document structure that you define either in the document itself or in a separate file. The chapters in Part 2 are based primarily on version 1.0 of the official XML specification developed by the World Wide Web Consortium (W3C).

Part 3 (Chapters 8 through 12) teaches you the most important of the current techniques for displaying XML documents in Web browsers. Chapters 8, 9, and 12 explain how to display an XML document by linking a style sheet that provides the browser with formatting and other display instructions. Chapters 8 and 9 cover cascading style sheets. A cascading style sheet (CSS) is a simple type of style sheet that allows you to precisely control the way the document content is formatted, but doesn't allow you to modify that content. Chapter 12 explains style sheets created with XSLT (Extensible Stylesheet Language Transformations). An XSLT style sheet is a more advanced type of style sheet that allows you not only to format the document content (using CSS properties), but also to select and modify the content, giving you complete control over the displayed output.

Chapters 10 and 11 teach you how to display an XML document by linking the document to a conventional HTML Web page that contains instructions for selecting and presenting the XML data. Chapter 10 explains how to do this using data binding, a straightforward technique that is suitable primarily for simple, symmetrically structured XML documents. Chapter 11 shows you how to display an XML document from an HTML page by writing a script that uses the XML Document Object Model (DOM), a much more flexible technique that allows you to display any type of XML document and any document component.

note

Throughout this book, I use the term *page* to refer to HTML source and the term *document* to refer to XML source. I chose this convention to help clearly distinguish these two markup languages, which are often used in conjunction.

Part 3 focuses specifically on using the Microsoft Internet Explorer Web browser for displaying XML documents. (You'll see more details on Internet Explorer in the following section of the Introduction.)

Finally, the Appendix provides the addresses of Web sites containing an abundance of further information on most of the topics covered in this book. I also include all of these addresses in the chapters, each in the appropriate context. You'll find a copy of the Appendix on the companion CD in the Resource Links folder, under the filename Appendix.htm. (Instructions for installing the companion CD files are given later in the Introduction.) You can visit any of these Web sites by opening Appendix.htm in your Web browser and simply clicking a link, rather than typing the address into the browser.

tip

You might want to explore the following general XML information sites on the Web to supplement your reading of this book. The W3C offers a wide variety of information, standards, and services for Web authors at *http://www.w3.org/*, and it provides a diverse collection of XML resources at *http://www.w3.org/XML/*. The Microsoft Developer Network (MSDN) Library furnishes extensive documentation on XML as supported by Microsoft products under the topic "XML and Web Services" at *http://msdn.microsoft.com/library/*. And the online reference work *The XML Cover Pages* includes comprehensive information on XML and other markup languages at *http://www.oasis-open.org/cover/*.

note

The preceding Tip contains several references to topics found in the MSDN Library on the Web, and you'll find similar references throughout the chapters in this book. Once you've used your browser to connect to the MSDN Library at *http://msdn.microsoft.com/library/*, you can locate the specific referenced topic either by browsing through the hierarchical table of contents in the left frame, or by using the MSDN Library's Search feature. The reason this book doesn't provide the exact topic URLs, or the precise locations of the topics in the table of contents, is that Microsoft periodically reorganizes the MSDN site, changing the URLs of topics and their organization.

XML Step by Step, Internet Explorer, and MSXML

Although XML documents can be processed and displayed by many different types of software applications, the primary purpose of the language is to provide a universal format for storing, exchanging, and displaying information *on the Web*. Accordingly, this book teaches you how to display and work with XML documents using Web browsers, which are the most ubiquitous applications for accessing and displaying Web documents. Although most of the display techniques given in this book are based on public standards, and many of them will work with a variety of browsers, I wrote the book specifically for Microsoft Internet Explorer versions 5.0 through 6.0.

Internet Explorer uses the services of a separate software module to process and work with XML documents. This module is known as Microsoft XML Core Services, or just MSXML. (The product was formerly known as the Microsoft XML Parser.) When you set up Internet Explorer on a computer, it automatically installs a particular version of MSXML. For instance, Internet Explorer 6.0 automatically installs MSXML version 3.0. If you wish, you can also install a later version of MSXML so that the more advanced XML services it provides are available to the browser (in addition to the features provided by the originally installed MSXML version). For example, if you want to be able to check the validity of XML documents using the latest implementation of XML schemas (described in Chapter 7), you need to install MSXML version 4.0, which is the first version of MSXML to support this type of schema. This book covers MSXML versions 2.0 through 4.0.

Because the companion CD provided with this book includes both Internet Explorer 6.0 and MSXML 4.0, you have everything you need to display the XML documents that you create using the techniques in the book. (See the next section for a description of the companion CD and for installation instructions.)

note

You can download the latest version of Internet Explorer at *http://www.microsoft.com/windows/ie/*. You can download the latest version of MSXML through the MSDN Library on the Web at *http://msdn.microsoft.com/library/*.

Throughout this book, the unqualified expression *Internet Explorer* refers to Internet Explorer versions 5.0 through 6.0. Most of the techniques given in the book will work using any of these Internet Explorer versions, together with the version of MSXML that ships with the browser. If the book doesn't include a reference to a specific required version, you can assume that the technique described will work with any of these versions. A few techniques, however, require Internet Explorer 5.5 through 6.0 (namely, some of the CSS properties given in Chapters 8 and 9). A few other techniques require Internet Explorer 6.0 (several of the CSS properties, plus the technique for using XSLT style sheets explained in Chapter 12). And one important technique requires that you install MSXML 4.0 (using the XML schemas described in Chapter 7 to validate XML documents). Whenever a technique requires a specific version of Internet Explorer or MSXML, the book clearly states the version requirement.

> **note**
>
> When the book states a version requirement, it refers to specific Internet Explorer or MSXML versions. For example, next to a feature it might state "Internet Explorer 6.0 only." Almost certainly, a *later* version will also work. However, I've taken the conservative approach of mentioning only the versions I've actually tested.

Using the Companion CD

The companion CD included in the back of *XML Step by Step* provides the following valuable resources to complement the information in the book:

- **Copies of the source files given in the numbered listings in the book.** These listings (for example, Listing 2-1 in Chapter 2) provide example XML documents, style sheets, XML schema files, and HTML pages that display XML documents. Whenever I introduce a numbered listing, I also give the name of the file that contains that listing on the CD. (For example, Listing 2-1 is contained in the CD file Inventory.xml.) You'll find all these files on the companion CD in the Example Source folder.

- **All the graphics files displayed by the example source files.** These files are contained in the same CD folder as the source files, Example Source.

- **A copy of the Appendix in the Web page file Appendix.htm.** This file is located in the Resource Links folder on the CD.

- **Internet Explorer version 6.0.** You can use Internet Explorer 6.0 to display any of the XML documents and HTML pages provided on the companion CD. When you install Internet Explorer 6.0, it automatically installs MSXML version 3.0. (As explained earlier, MSXML is a separate software module that contains the XML processor and provides other core XML services for Internet Explorer.)

- **MSXML 4.0.** You'll need to install MSXML 4.0 in order to use the XML schemas presented in Chapter 7.

- **Microsoft XML SDK 4.0.** This software development kit (SDK) provides several tools for working with XML and MSXML 4.0.

Most importantly, it includes a help file (xmlsdk.chm) with comprehensive information on the XML technologies implemented by MSXML 4.0. You'll see many references to this help file throughout the book. (It's referred to as "the Microsoft XML SDK 4.0 help file.") When you install the XML SDK, the setup program places an icon on your desktop (labeled "Microsoft XML 4.0 Parser SDK"), which you can double-click to display the help file. Once the help file is opened, you can use the tabs in the navigation pane at the left of the window to browse through, search for, or save specific topics, as shown here:

Hide or show navigation pane

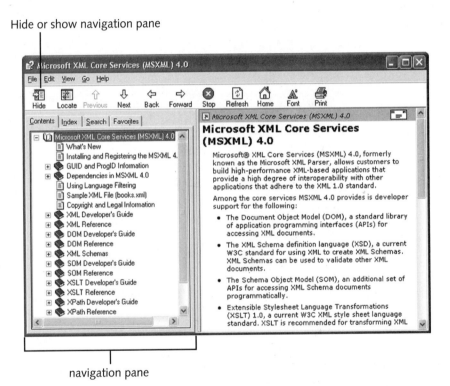

navigation pane

The menu interface on the companion CD is set up to start automatically when you insert the CD-ROM into your drive. If your computer doesn't support AutoPlay, however, you'll need to open the menu interface by using Windows Explorer to display the contents of the CD and then double-clicking the StartCD.exe file in the root folder.

The menu interface presents options for viewing the Readme.txt file, browsing the content of the companion CD, installing the example source files and the resource links (in the file Appendix.htm), installing Internet Explorer 6.0, installing MSXML 4.0 and the Microsoft XML SDK 4.0, installing Windows Installer 2.0 (which is required for installing MSXML and the XML SDK), visiting the Microsoft Press support Web site, and registering your book online with Microsoft Press. Select an option by clicking it and then simply follow the on-screen instructions.

> ## caution
>
> To install MSXML 4.0 and the Microsoft XML SDK 4.0, you need to have Windows Installer 2.0 on your computer. If you havent previously installed Windows Installer 2.0 and you arent running Microsoft Windows XP (which includes Windows Installer 2.0), you must first use the CD installation program to install Windows Installer 2.0 before you can install MSXML 4.0 and the Microsoft XML SDK 4.0. Otherwise, when you attempt to install MSXML 4.0 and the Microsoft XML SDK 4.0, you will receive an error message indicating that the proper version of Microsoft Installer isnt present on your computer.

Requirements

The following are the basic hardware and software requirements for using *XML Step by Step* and its companion CD:

- To access the companion CD and to install the software that's included on the CD, you need a computer that runs Microsoft Windows and has a CD-ROM drive and at least a 486/66-megahertz (MHz) processor (a Pentium processor is recommended). You can use Windows 98, Windows ME, Windows NT 4.0 (with Service Pack 6a or higher), Windows 2000, Windows XP, or a later version of Windows. You also need a Super VGA (800 × 600) or higher resolution monitor with 256 colors, as well as a mouse or other pointing device.

- To view the Web sites referenced in the book, you need a connection to the Internet. However, viewing these sites isn't required for successfully using the book; therefore, an Internet connection is optional.

This book is meant to introduce you to XML, so you aren't required to have prior knowledge of XML itself. However, several of the techniques that the book teaches for displaying XML documents use one or more of the following Web-authoring languages: HTML, Dynamic HTML (DHTML), and Microsoft JScript (the Microsoft version of the generic JavaScript scripting language).

Although the book explains the features of these languages used in the examples, some general knowledge of the languages would be helpful.

tip

For information on working with HTML and DHTML as implemented in Internet Explorer, see the topic "HTML and Dynamic HTML" in the MSDN Library on the Web at *http://msdn.microsoft.com/library/*. To read the official specification for the latest version of HTML 4, see the following Web site, provided by the W3C: *http://www.w3.org/TR/html4/*. For information on JScript and other Microsoft Web scripting technologies, see the topic "Scripting" in the MSDN Library on the Web at *http://msdn.microsoft.com/library/*.

How to Contact the Author

You can contact me through my Web site at *http://www.mjyOnline.com*. At this site, you'll also find book corrections, reader questions and answers on XML, links to XML resources on the Web, a list of recommended books on XML and related technologies, and information on my background and some of my other books.

Microsoft Press Support Information

Every effort has been made to ensure the accuracy of this book and the contents of the companion CD. Microsoft Press provides corrections for books through the World Wide Web at

http://www.microsoft.com/mspress/support/

If you have comments, questions, or ideas regarding the book or this companion CD, please send them to Microsoft Press via e-mail to:

MSPInput@Microsoft.com

or via postal mail to:

Microsoft Press
Attn: XML Step by Step Editor
One Microsoft Way
Redmond, WA 98052-6399

Please note that product support is not offered through the above addresses.

PART 1
Getting Started

1

Why XML?

XML, which stands for Extensible Markup Language, was defined by the XML Working Group of the World Wide Web Consortium (W3C). This group described the language as follows:

> The Extensible Markup Language (XML) is a subset of SGML...Its goal is to enable generic SGML to be served, received, and processed on the Web in the way that is now possible with HTML. XML has been designed for ease of implementation and for interoperability with both SGML and HTML.

This is a quotation from version 1.0 of the official XML specification. You can read the entire document at *http://www.w3.org/TR/REC-xml* on the W3C Web site.

note

As this book goes to press, the current version of the XML specification is still 1.0. The first edition of this specification was published in February 1998. The second edition, which merely incorporates error corrections and clarifications and does *not* represent a new XML version, was published in October 2000. You'll find the text of the second edition at the URL given above (*http://www.w3.org/TR/REC-xml*). The XML specification has the W3C status of Recommendation. Although this status might sound a bit tentative, it actually refers to the final, approved specification. (The role of the W3C is to recommend standards, not to enforce them.)

As you can see, XML is a markup language designed specifically for delivering information over the World Wide Web, just like HTML (Hypertext Markup Language), which has been the standard language used to create Web pages since the inception of the Web. Since we already have HTML, which continues to evolve to meet additional needs, you might wonder why we require a completely new language for the Web. What is new and different about XML? What are its unique advantages and strengths? What is its relationship to HTML? Is it intended to replace HTML or to enhance it? And finally, what is this SGML that XML is a subset of, and why can't we just use SGML for Web pages? In this chapter, I'll attempt to answer all of these questions.

The Need for XML

HTML provides a fixed set of predefined *elements* that you can use to mark the components of a typical, general-purpose Web page. Examples of elements are headings, paragraphs, lists, tables, images, and hyperlinks. For instance, HTML works fine for creating a personal home page, as in the following example HTML page:

```
<HTML>
<HEAD>
<TITLE>Home Page</TITLE>
</HEAD>

<BODY>
<H1><IMG SRC="MainLogo.gif">   Michael J. Young's Home Page</H1>
<P><EM>Welcome to my Web site!</EM></P>

<H2>Web Site Contents</H2>
<P>Please choose one of the following topics:</P>
<UL>
    <LI><A HREF="writing.htm"><B>Writing</B></A></LI>
    <LI><A HREF="family.htm"><B>Family</B></A></LI>
    <LI><A HREF="photos.htm"><B>Photo Gallery</B></A></LI>
</UL>

<H2>Other Interesting Web Sites</H2>
<P>Click one of the following to explore another Web site:</P>
<UL>
    <LI>
       <A HREF="http://www.yahoo.com/">Yahoo Search Engine</A>
    </LI>
    <LI>
       <A HREF="http://www.amazon.com/">Amazon Bookstore</A>
    </LI>
    <LI>
       <A HREF="http://www.microsoft.com/mspress/">
         Microsoft Press
       </A>
```

```
      </LI>
  </UL>
  </BODY>
  </HTML>
```

Microsoft Internet Explorer displays this page as shown in the following figure:

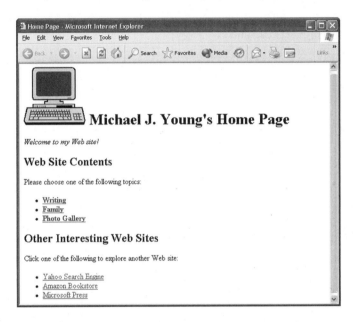

Each element begins with a *start-tag*: a block of text preceded with a left angle bracket (<) and followed with a right angle bracket (>) that contains the element name and possibly other information. Most elements end with an *end-tag*, which is like its corresponding start-tag except that it includes only a slash (/) character followed by the element name. The element's *content* is the text—if any—between the start-tag and end-tag. Notice that many of the elements in the preceding example page contain nested elements (that is, elements within other elements).

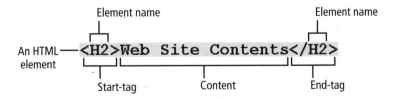

The example HTML page contains the following elements:

HTML element	Page component marked
HTML	The entire page
HEAD	Heading information, such as the page title
TITLE	The page title, which appears in the browser's title bar
BODY	The main body of text that the browser displays
H1	A top-level heading
H2	A second-level heading
P	A paragraph of text
UL	A bulleted list (Unordered List)
LI	An individual item within a list (List Item)
IMG	An image
A	A hyperlink to another location or page (an Anchor element)
EM	A block of italicized (EMphasized) text
B	A block of bold text

The browser that displays the HTML page recognizes each of these standard elements and knows how to format and display them. For example, the browser typically displays an H1 heading in a large font, an H2 heading in a smaller font, and a P element in an even smaller font. It displays an LI element within an unordered list as a bulleted, indented paragraph. And it converts an A element into an underlined hyperlink that the user can click to go to a different location or page.

Although the set of predefined HTML elements has expanded considerably since the first HTML version, HTML is still unsuitable for defining many types of documents. The following are examples of documents that can't adequately be described using HTML:

- **A document that doesn't consist of typical components (headings, paragraphs, lists, tables, and so on).** For instance, HTML lacks the elements necessary to mark a musical score or a set of mathematical equations.

- **A database, such as an inventory of books.** You could use an HTML page to store and display static database information (such as a list of book descriptions). However, if you wanted to sort, filter, find, and work with the information in other ways, each individual piece of information would need to be labeled (as it is in a database program such as Microsoft Access). HTML lacks the elements necessary to do this.

■ **A document that you want to organize in a treelike hierarchical structure.** Say, for example, that you're writing a book and you want to mark it up into parts, chapters, A sections, B sections, C sections, and so on. A program could then use this structured document to generate a table of contents, to produce outlines with various levels of detail, to extract specific sections, and to work with the information in other ways. An HTML heading element, however, marks only the text of the heading itself to indicate how the text should be formatted. For example:

```
<H2>Web Site Contents</H2>
```

Because you don't nest the actual text and elements that belong to a document section within a heading element, these elements can't be used to clearly indicate the hierarchical structure of a document.

The solution to these limitations is XML.

The XML Solution

The XML definition consists of only a bare-bones syntax. When you create an XML document, rather than use a limited set of predefined elements, you create your own elements and you assign them any names you like—hence the term *extensible* in Extensible Markup Language. You can therefore use XML to describe virtually any type of document, from a musical score to a database. For example, you could describe a list of books, as in the following XML document:

```
<?xml version="1.0"?>

<INVENTORY>
    <BOOK>
        <TITLE>The Adventures of Huckleberry Finn</TITLE>
        <AUTHOR>Mark Twain</AUTHOR>
        <BINDING>mass market paperback</BINDING>
        <PAGES>298</PAGES>
        <PRICE>$5.49</PRICE>
    </BOOK>
    <BOOK>
        <TITLE>Moby-Dick</TITLE>
        <AUTHOR>Herman Melville</AUTHOR>
        <BINDING>trade paperback</BINDING>
        <PAGES>605</PAGES>
        <PRICE>$4.95</PRICE>
    </BOOK>
```

```
<BOOK>
    <TITLE>The Scarlet Letter</TITLE>
    <AUTHOR>Nathaniel Hawthorne</AUTHOR>
    <BINDING>trade paperback</BINDING>
    <PAGES>253</PAGES>
    <PRICE>$4.25</PRICE>
</BOOK>
</INVENTORY>
```

note

When used to describe a database, XML has two advantages over proprietary formats (such as the Access .mdb or dBase .dbf format): XML is humanly readable, and it is based on a public, open standard.

It's important to understand that the element names in an XML document (such as INVENTORY, BOOK, and TITLE, in this example) are *not* part of the XML definition. Rather, you make up the names when you create a particular document. And you can choose any legal names for your elements (such as LIST rather than INVENTORY, or ITEM rather than BOOK).

tip

When you name elements in an XML document, try to choose descriptive names—for example, BOOK or ITEM rather than FOO or BAR. One of the advantages of an XML document is that it can be self-describing—that is, each piece of information can have a descriptive label attached.

As you can see from the previous example, an XML document is structured in a treelike hierarchy, with elements completely nested within other elements and with a single top-level element (INVENTORY in this example)—known as the *document element* or *root element*—that contains all other elements. The structure of the example XML document can be drawn like this:

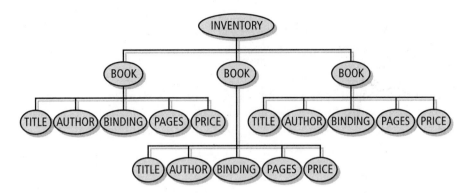

You can thus readily use XML to define a hierarchically structured document, such as a book with parts, chapters, and various levels of sections, as mentioned previously.

Writing XML Documents

Because XML doesn't include predefined elements, it might seem to be a relatively casual standard. XML does, however, have a strictly defined syntax. For example, unlike HTML, every XML element must have both a start-tag and an end-tag (or a special *empty-element* tag, which I'll describe in later chapters). And any nested element must be completely contained within the element that encloses it.

In fact, the very flexibility of creating your own elements demands a strict syntax. That's because the custom nature of XML documents demands custom software (for example, Web page scripts or freestanding programs) to handle and display the information these documents contain. The strict XML syntax gives XML documents a predictable form and makes this software easier to write. Recall from the quotation at the beginning of the chapter that "ease of implementation" is one of the chief goals of the language.

Part 2 of this book discusses creating XML documents that conform to the rules of syntax. As you'll learn, you can write an XML document to conform to either of two different levels of syntactical strictness. A document is known as either *well-formed* or *valid* depending on which level of the standard it meets.

Displaying XML Documents

In an HTML page, a browser knows that an H1 element, for example, is a top-level heading and will format and display it accordingly. This is possible because this element is part of the HTML standard. But how can a browser or other program know how to handle and display the elements in an XML document you create (such as BOOK or BINDING in the example document), since you invent those elements yourself?

There are three basic ways to tell a browser (specifically, Microsoft Internet Explorer) how to handle and display each of your XML elements. I'll cover these techniques in detail in Part 3 of the book.

- **Style sheet linking.** With this technique, you link a style sheet to the XML document. A style sheet is a separate file that contains instructions for formatting the individual XML elements. You can use either a cascading style sheet (CSS)—which is also used for HTML pages—or an Extensible Stylesheet Language Transformations (XSLT) style sheet—which is considerably more powerful than a CSS and is designed specifically for XML documents. I'll cover these techniques in Chapters 2, 8, 9, and 12.

- **Data binding.** This option requires you to create an HTML page, link the XML document to it, and bind standard HTML elements in the page, such as SPAN or TABLE elements, to the XML elements. The HTML elements then automatically display the information from the XML elements they are bound to. You'll learn this technique in Chapter 10.

- **XML DOM Scripting.** With this technique, you create an HTML page, link the XML document to it, and access and display individual XML elements by writing script code (JavaScript or Microsoft Visual Basic Scripting Edition [VBScript]). The browser exposes the XML document as an XML Document Object Model (DOM), which provides a large set of objects, properties, and methods that the script code can use to access, manipulate, and display the XML elements. I'll discuss this technique in Chapter 11.

SGML, HTML, and XML

SGML, which stands for Structured Generalized Markup Language, is the mother of all markup languages. Both HTML and XML are derived from SGML, although in fundamentally different ways. SGML defines a basic syntax, but allows you to create your own elements (hence the term *generalized*). To use SGML to describe a particular document, you must invent an appropriate set of elements and a document structure. For example, to describe a book, you might use elements that you name BOOK, PART, CHAPTER, INTRODUCTION, A-SECTION, B-SECTION, C-SECTION, and so on.

A general-purpose set of elements used to describe a particular type of document is known as an *SGML application*. (An SGML application also includes rules that specify the ways the elements can be arranged—as well as other features—using techniques similar to those I'll discuss in Chapter 5.) You can define your own SGML application to describe a specific type of document that you work with, or a standards body can define an SGML application to describe a widely used document type. The most famous example of this latter type of application is HTML, which is an SGML application developed in 1991 to describe Web pages.

SGML might seem to be the perfect extensible language for describing information that's delivered and processed on the Web. However, the W3C members who contemplate these matters deemed SGML too complex to be a universal language for the Web. The flexibility and superfluity of features provided by SGML would make it difficult to write the software needed to process and display the SGML information in Web browsers. What was needed was a streamlined subset of SGML designed specifically for delivering information on the Web. In 1996, the XML Working Group of the W3C began to develop that subset, which they named Extensible Markup Language. As the quotation at the beginning of the chapter states, XML was designed for "ease of implementation," a feature clearly lacking in SGML.

XML is thus a simplified version of SGML optimized for the Web. As with SGML, XML lets you devise your own set of elements when you describe a particular document. Also like SGML, an individual or a standards body can define an *XML application*, which is a general-purpose set of elements and attributes and a document structure that can be used to describe documents of a particular type (for example, documents containing mathematical formulas or vector graphics). You'll learn more about XML applications later in this chapter.

The XML syntax offers fewer features and alternatives than SGML, making it easier for humans to read and write XML documents and for programmers to write browsers, Web page scripts, and other programs that access and display the document information.

Does XML Replace HTML?

Currently, the answer to that question is no. HTML is still the primary language used to tell browsers how to display information on the Web.

With Internet Explorer, the only practical way to dispense entirely with HTML when you display XML is to attach a cascading style sheet to the XML document and then open the document directly in the browser. However, using a cascading style sheet is a relatively restrictive method for displaying and working with XML. All the other methods you'll learn in this book involve HTML. Data binding and XML DOM scripts both use HTML Web pages as vehicles for displaying XML documents. And with XSLT style sheets, you create templates that transform the XML document into HTML that tells the browser how to format and display the XML data.

Rather than replacing HTML, XML is currently used in conjunction with HTML and vastly extends the capability of Web pages to:

- Deliver virtually any type of document

- Sort, filter, rearrange, find, and manipulate the information in other ways

- Present highly structured information

As the quotation at the beginning of the chapter states, XML was designed for *interoperability* with HTML.

The Official Goals of XML

The following are the 10 design goals for XML as stated in the official XML specification posted on the W3C Web site (*http://www.w3.org/TR/REC-xml*).

"1   XML shall be straightforwardly usable over the Internet."

XML was designed primarily for storing and delivering information on the Web, as explained earlier in this chapter, and for supporting distributed applications on the Internet.

"2   XML shall support a wide variety of applications."

Although its primary use is for exchanging information over the Internet, XML was also designed for use by programs that aren't on the Internet, such as software tools for creating documents and for filtering, translating, or formatting information.

"3 XML shall be compatible with SGML."

XML was designed to be a subset of SGML, so that every valid XML document would also be a conformant SGML document, and to have essentially the same expressive capability as SGML. A benefit of achieving this goal is that programmers can easily adapt SGML software tools for working with XML documents.

"4 It shall be easy to write programs which process XML documents."

If a markup language for the Web is to be practical and gain universal acceptance, it must be easy to write the browsers and other programs that process the documents. In fact, the primary reason for defining the XML subset of SGML was the unwieldiness of writing programs to process SGML documents.

"5 The number of optional features in XML is to be kept to the absolute minimum, ideally zero."

Having a minimal number of optional features in XML facilitates writing processors that can handle virtually any XML document, making XML documents universally interchangeable. The abundance of optional features in SGML was a primary reason why it was deemed impractical for defining Web documents. Optional SGML features include redefining the delimiting characters in tags (normally the < and > characters) and the omission of the end-tag when the processor can figure out where an element ends. A universal processor for SGML documents would be difficult to write because it would have to account for all optional features, even those that are seldom used.

"6 XML documents should be human-legible and reasonably clear."

XML was designed to be a *lingua franca* for exchanging information among users and programs the world over. Human readability supports this goal by allowing people—as well as specialized software programs—to read XML documents and to write them using simple text editors. A benefit of human legibility is that users can easily work around limitations and bugs in their software tools by simply opening an XML document in a text editor and taking a look at it. Its human legibility distinguishes XML from most proprietary formats used for databases and word-processing documents.

Humans can easily read an XML document because it's written in plain text and has a logical treelike structure. You can enhance XML's legibility by choosing meaningful names for your document's elements, attributes, and entities; by carefully arranging and indenting the text to clearly show the logical structure of the document at a glance; and by adding useful comments. (I'll explain elements, attributes, entities, and comments in later chapters.)

"**7**   The XML design should be prepared quickly."

A standard such as XML can, of course, be viable only if the community of pro-grammers and users adopts it. The XML standard therefore needed to be com-pleted before this community began to adopt alternative standards, which software companies tend to produce at a rapid pace.

"**8**   The design of XML shall be formal and concise."

The XML specification includes a formal XML grammar, which uses a notation known as Extended Backus-Naur Form (EBNF). This notation, although diffi-cult to read casually, resolves ambiguities and ultimately makes it easier to write XML documents and especially XML software tools, further encouraging XML's adoption.

"**9**   XML documents shall be easy to create."

For XML to be a practical markup language for Web documents, not only must the software for handling XML be easy to write, but also XML documents themselves must be easy to create.

"**10**   Terseness in XML markup is of minimal importance."

In keeping with goal 6, intelligibility of XML is more important than brevity. Part of the problem in using SGML as a universal Web markup language is the excessive terseness it fosters by allowing you to omit markup in certain situations.

As you learn XML, you'll be able to judge how fully these goals have been realized. After reading Chapter 6 on using entities, you might possibly question the success of the standard in achieving clarity and ease of use, but I hope Part 2 of this book will help you over that possible hurdle.

Standard XML Applications

As you've seen, not only can you use XML to describe an individual document, but also a person, company, or standards committee can define a general-purpose set of XML elements and attributes, together with a document structure, to be used for describing a particular class of documents. The definition of the elements, attributes, and structure is known as an *XML application* or *XML vocabulary*.

For example, an organization could define an XML application for creating documents that depict molecular structures, documents that describe human re-sources, documents that choreograph multimedia presentations, or documents that store vector graphics.

note

Don't confuse the expression *XML application* that is defined here with the general term *application*, which refers to any type of software program.

An XML application is usually defined by creating a *document type definition (DTD)*, which is an optional component of an XML document, or an *XML schema*, which is contained in a separate file. A DTD or an XML schema defines and names the elements that can be used in the document, the order in which the elements can appear, the element attributes that can be used, and other document features. To use a particular XML application, you usually include its DTD in your XML document or employ its XML schema in processing your document. Using a DTD or XML schema restricts the elements, attributes, and structure that you can use so that your document is forced to conform to the XML application standard. (The example XML document you saw earlier in the chapter doesn't include a DTD.) You'll learn how to define DTDs in Chapter 5 and how to create XML schemas in Chapter 7.

An important advantage of using a standard XML application to develop documents is that an application promotes consistency, both within a single document and among separate documents of the same type. Consistency in the document elements, attributes, structure, and other features is critical in a group of documents that are all going to be processed and displayed using a particular software tool (for example, a Web page script) that is designed for that type of document.

In the next two sections, I discuss specific XML applications that have been proposed or that have already been created.

Real-World Uses for XML

Although XML might be an interesting concept, you may be wondering what you can actually do with it in the real world. In this section, I've listed a sampling of practical uses for XML. I've included ways that XML is currently used, as well as uses that various organizations have proposed. For most of these uses, I've listed in parentheses one or more standard XML applications that have been defined. For example, I've listed MathML (Mathematical Markup Language) as a specific XML application for formatting mathematical formulas and scientific content on the Web.

tip

For a much more comprehensive list of current and proposed XML applications with detailed descriptions of each application (including the ones listed here), go to *http://www.oasis-open.org/cover/xml.html#applications* on *The XML Cover Pages* Web site.

- **Storing databases.** Like proprietary database formats, XML can be used to label each field of information within each database record. (For example, it could label each name, address, and phone number within the records of an address database.) Labeling each piece of information lets you display the data in a variety of ways and search, sort, filter, and process the data in other ways.

note

Several of the Microsoft Office XP programs now use XML as one of the standard document formats. For example, Microsoft Excel 2002 lets you open or save workbooks in XML format, as an alternative to the standard .xls Excel workbook format. And Microsoft Access 2002 allows you to create a database table by importing an XML document, or to export a database table or other object to an XML document.

- **Structuring documents.** The treelike structure of XML documents makes XML ideal for marking the structure of documents such as novels, nonfiction books, and plays. For example, you could use XML to mark a play into acts, scenes, speakers, lines, stage directions, and so on. The XML marking allows software tools (such as style sheets or Web page scripts) to display or print the document with proper formatting; to find, extract, or manipulate document information; to generate tables of contents, outlines, and synopses; and to handle the information in other ways. (For instance, Jon Bosak, who chaired the XML Working Group, has created XML versions of the complete works of William Shakespeare, as well as the Old Testament, New Testament, Koran, and Book of Mormon. Go to *http://www.ibiblio.org/bosak/* to download these documents.)

- **Storing vector graphics.** (VML, or Vector Markup Language)

- **Describing multimedia presentations.** (SMIL, or Synchronized Multimedia Integration Language)

- **Creating voice interfaces for Internet programs.** (VoxML, or Voice Markup Language)

- **Defining channels.** Channels are Web pages that are pushed (sent automatically) to subscribers. (CDF, or Channel Definition Format)

- **Describing software packages and their interdependencies.** These descriptions allow software to be distributed and updated over networks. (OSD, or Open Software Description Format)

- **Communicating among programs over the Web in an open and extensible way, using XML-based messages.** These messages are independent of the operating systems, object models, and computer languages used. (SOAP, or Simple Object Access Protocol)

- **Exchanging financial information.** The information is exchanged in an open, humanly readable format, among financial programs (such as Quicken and Microsoft Money) and financial institutions (such as banks and mutual funds). (OFX, or Open Financial Exchange)

- **Creating, managing, and using complex digital forms for Internet commerce transactions.** These forms can include digital signatures that make the forms legally binding. (XFDL, or Extensible Forms Description Language)

- **Exchanging job descriptions and résumés.** (HRMML, or Human Resource Management Markup Language)

- **Exchanging information between printing companies and their customers.** (PrintML, or Printing Industry Markup Language, and XPP, or XML for Publishers and Printers)

- **Filing legal documents and exchanging legal information electronically.** (OXCI, or Open XML Court Interface)

- **Exchanging insurance-related data.** (iLingo)

- **Exchanging real estate transaction information.** (RETML, or Real Estate Transaction Markup Language)

- **Exchanging news articles on the Internet.** (NML, or News Markup Language)

- **Storing tracking information by courier services.** Federal Express, for example, currently uses XML for this purpose.

- **Formatting mathematical formulas and scientific content on the Web.** (MathML, or Mathematical Markup Language)

- **Describing molecular structures.** (CML, or Chemical Markup Language)

- **Encoding and displaying DNA, RNA, and protein sequence information.** (BSML, or Bioinformatic Sequence Markup Language)

- **Exchanging astronomical data.** (AML, or Astronomical Markup Language)

- **Encoding weather observation reports.** (OMF, or Weather Observation Markup Format)

- **Storing and exchanging geographic information.** (GML, or Geography Markup Language)

- **Encoding genealogical data.** (GedML, or Genealogical Data in XML)

- **Formatting theses and dissertations for electronic submission.** (ETD-ML, or Electronic Thesis and Dissertation Markup Language)

- **Storing theological information and marking up liturgical texts.** (ThML, or Theological Markup Language, and LitML, or Liturgical Markup Language)

- **Representing musical scores.** (MusicXML)

- **Sending electronic business cards via e-mail.** (XML version of vCard)

- **Storing and exchanging information on chess.** (ChessML, or Chess Markup Language)

- **Recording recipes on computers.** (DESSERT, or Document Encoding and Structuring Specification for Electronic Recipe Transfer)

■ **Creating HTML Web pages that are valid XML documents.**
(XHTML. If you write HTML Web pages that conform to the
XHTML application of XML, you can validate, display, and work
with the pages using standard XML tools, such as XML DOM
scripts, which are discussed in Chapter 11. See *http://www.w3.org/
TR/xhtml1.*)

XML Applications for Enhancing XML Documents

In addition to XML applications for describing specific classes of documents,
several XML applications have been defined that you can use in conjunction
with any type of XML document to facilitate the document's creation or to enhance it in some way. Several examples are:

■ **Extensible Stylesheet Language Transformations (XSLT)** allows you
to create powerful document style sheets using XML syntax. XSLT
is used in conjunction with XML Path Language (XPath), which lets
you select specific parts of an XML document. XPath uses a location
path notation—similar to file paths or URLs—to address locations
within the hierarchical XML document structure.

■ **XML Schema Definition Language** lets you write detailed schemas
for your XML documents using standard XML syntax. It provides a
more powerful alternative to writing DTDs.

■ **XML Linking Language (XLink)** lets you link your XML documents. It allows multiple link targets and other advanced features,
and is considerably more powerful than the HTML hyperlink
mechanism. XLink is used in conjunction with XML Pointer Language (XPointer), which lets you define flexible link targets. You can
use XPointer to link to any location in a target document, not just to
a specially marked link target as in HTML.

I'll discuss the XML Schema definition language in Chapter 7, and XSLT and
XPath in Chapter 12. XLink and XPointer are still evolving and aren't currently
supported by Internet Explorer; these applications are beyond the scope of
the book.

As you can see, XML is not only an immediately useful tool for defining documents, but is also serving as the framework for building the applications and
XML enhancements that will be needed as the Internet evolves.

2

Creating and Displaying Your First XML Document

In this chapter, you'll gain an overview of the entire process of creating and displaying an XML document in a Web browser. First you'll create a simple XML document, explore the document's structure, and learn some of the fundamental rules for creating a well-formed XML document. Then you'll discover how to display that document in the Microsoft Internet Explorer Web browser by creating and attaching a simple style sheet that tells the browser how to format the elements in the document.

This chapter provides a brief preview of the topics that I'll address in depth throughout the remainder of the book.

Creating an XML Document

Because an XML document is written in plain text, you can create one using your favorite text editor. For example, you can use the Notepad editor that comes with Microsoft Windows. Or, better yet, you can use a programming editor with features that make it easier to type in XML and related source files. Useful features include automatic tab insertion (the next line is indented automatically when you press the Enter key) and the ability to select and indent, or decrease the indent of, multiple lines of text. The Microsoft Visual Studio programming editor, the text editor that comes with Microsoft Visual Studio or Visual Studio .NET, is one example of an editor with these features.

note

The Visual Studio .NET editor offers many special features for working with XML. For instance, when you type a start-tag, it automatically inserts a matching end-tag; when you enter an attribute, it automatically inserts quote characters for the attribute value; and it color-codes different XML components. The editor also provides a Data view, which displays the XML data in a table format that allows you to view and quickly edit the contents of the document.

caution

If you use a word-processing program—such as Microsoft Word or WordPad—to create an XML document, a style sheet, or other source file, you must save the file in a plain text format. If you save the file in a word-processor format (such as native Word .doc format or Rich Text Format) the file will contain extraneous characters that make it unsuitable for processing in a browser or other XML program. For information on using various text file encodings, see the sidebar "Characters, Encoding, and Languages" on page 77.

Create the XML Document

1   Open a new, empty text file in your text editor, and type in the XML document shown in Listing 2-1. (You'll find a copy of this listing on this book's companion CD under the filename Inventory.xml.)

   If you want, you can omit some of the BOOK elements. You don't need to type in all eight of them—three or four will do. (A BOOK element consists of the <BOOK> and </BOOK> tags plus all text between them.)

2   Use your text editor's Save command to save the document on your hard disk, assigning it the filename Inventory.xml.

tip

Notepad normally assigns the .txt extension to a file you save. To assign a different extension (such as .xml for an XML document or .css for a cascading style sheet), you might need to put quotation marks around the entire filename and extension. For example, to save a file as Inventory.xml, you might need to type **"Inventory.xml"** (including the quotation marks) in the File Name text box of Notepad's Save As dialog box. If you omit the quotation marks, Notepad will save the file as Inventory.xml.txt if the .xml extension isn't registered on your computer. In general, if you type an extension that isn't registered, Notepad will append the .txt extension.

To open a file in Notepad that has an extension other than .txt, you need to run the Notepad program and use the Open command on the File menu. Or, once Notepad is running, you can drag a file from Windows Explorer and drop it on the Notepad window. Because the file doesn't have the .txt extension, you can't open it by double-clicking it as you can with a .txt file.

Inventory.xml

```xml
<?xml version="1.0"?>

<!-- File Name: Inventory.xml -->

<INVENTORY>
    <BOOK>
        <TITLE>The Adventures of Huckleberry Finn</TITLE>
        <AUTHOR>Mark Twain</AUTHOR>
        <BINDING>mass market paperback</BINDING>
        <PAGES>298</PAGES>
        <PRICE>$5.49</PRICE>
    </BOOK>
    <BOOK>
        <TITLE>Leaves of Grass</TITLE>
        <AUTHOR>Walt Whitman</AUTHOR>
        <BINDING>hardcover</BINDING>
        <PAGES>462</PAGES>
        <PRICE>$7.75</PRICE>
    </BOOK>
    <BOOK>
        <TITLE>The Legend of Sleepy Hollow</TITLE>
        <AUTHOR>Washington Irving</AUTHOR>
```

```
            <BINDING>mass market paperback</BINDING>
            <PAGES>98</PAGES>
            <PRICE>$2.95</PRICE>
        </BOOK>
        <BOOK>
            <TITLE>The Marble Faun</TITLE>
            <AUTHOR>Nathaniel Hawthorne</AUTHOR>
            <BINDING>trade paperback</BINDING>
            <PAGES>473</PAGES>
            <PRICE>$10.95</PRICE>
        </BOOK>
        <BOOK>
            <TITLE>Moby-Dick</TITLE>
            <AUTHOR>Herman Melville</AUTHOR>
            <BINDING>hardcover</BINDING>
            <PAGES>724</PAGES>
            <PRICE>$9.95</PRICE>
        </BOOK>
        <BOOK>
            <TITLE>The Portrait of a Lady</TITLE>
            <AUTHOR>Henry James</AUTHOR>
            <BINDING>mass market paperback</BINDING>
            <PAGES>256</PAGES>
            <PRICE>$4.95</PRICE>
        </BOOK>
        <BOOK>
            <TITLE>The Scarlet Letter</TITLE>
            <AUTHOR>Nathaniel Hawthorne</AUTHOR>
            <BINDING>trade paperback</BINDING>
            <PAGES>253</PAGES>
            <PRICE>$4.25</PRICE>
        </BOOK>
        <BOOK>
            <TITLE>The Turn of the Screw</TITLE>
            <AUTHOR>Henry James</AUTHOR>
            <BINDING>trade paperback</BINDING>
            <PAGES>384</PAGES>
            <PRICE>$3.35</PRICE>
        </BOOK>
    </INVENTORY>
```

Listing 2-1.

The Anatomy of an XML Document

An XML document, such as the example document you just typed, consists of two main parts: the *prolog* and the *document element*. (The document element is also known as the *root element*.)

```
                ┌─ <?xml version="1.0"?> ──────────────────── XML declaration
Prolog ─────────┤
                └─ <!-- File Name: Inventory.xml --> ───────── Comment
                ┌─ <INVENTORY>
                │    <BOOK>
                │      <TITLE>The Adventures of Huckleberry Finn</TITLE>
                │      <AUTHOR>Mark Twain</AUTHOR>
                │      <BINDING>mass market paperback</BINDING>
                │      <PAGES>298</PAGES>
                │      <PRICE>$5.49</PRICE>
                │    </BOOK>
Document ───────┤      .
element         │      .                                        Elements nested
(Root element)  │      .                                        within document
                │    <BOOK>                                     element
                │      <TITLE>The Turn of the Screw</TITLE>
                │      <AUTHOR>Henry James</AUTHOR>
                │      <BINDING>trade paperback</BINDING>
                │      <PAGES>384</PAGES>
                │      <PRICE>$3.35</PRICE>
                │    </BOOK>
                └─ </INVENTORY>
```

The Prolog

The prolog of the example document consists of three lines:

```
<?xml version="1.0"?>

<!-- File Name: Inventory.xml -->
```

The first line is the *XML declaration*, which states that this is an XML document and gives the XML version number. (At the time of this writing, the latest XML version was 1.0.) The XML declaration is optional, although the specification states that it should be included. If you do include an XML declaration, it must appear at the very beginning of the document.

The second line of the prolog consists of white space. To enhance readability, you can insert any amount of white space (spaces, tabs, or line breaks) between the components of the prolog. The XML processor ignores it.

The third line of the prolog is a comment. Adding comments to an XML document is optional, but doing so can increase the document's readability. A comment begins with the <!-- characters and it ends with the --> characters. You can type any text you want (except --) between these two groups of characters. The XML processor ignores comment text, although it can pass the text on to the application. (As explained in Chapter 11, the Internet Explorer XML processor makes comment text available to Web page scripts, and as explained in Chapter 12, it also makes comments available to XSLT style sheets.)

note

The *XML processor* is the software module that reads the XML document and provides access to the document's contents and structure. It provides this access to another software module called the *application*, which manipulates and displays the document's contents. When you display an XML document in Internet Explorer, the browser provides both the XML processor and at least part of the application. (If you write HTML or script code to display an XML document, you supply part of the application yourself.) The distinction is more than academic because the XML specification governs the behavior of the processor but not that of the application. An XML processor that conforms to the specification provides a predictable body of data to the application, which can do whatever it wants with this data. Note that the term *application* as used here is not the same thing as an *XML application* (or *XML vocabulary*), which I defined in Chapter 1 as a general-purpose set of elements and attributes, along with a document structure, that can be used to describe documents of a particular type.

The prolog can also contain the following optional components:

- A *document type declaration*, which defines the type, content, and structure of the document. If used, the document type declaration must come after the XML declaration. (The definition of the document's content and structure is contained in a subcomponent of the document type declaration known as a *document type definition* or DTD.)

- One or more *processing instructions*, which provide information that the XML processor passes on to the application. Later in this chapter, you'll see a processing instruction for linking a style sheet to the XML document.

note

All of the prolog components mentioned in this section are described in detail in later chapters.

The Document Element

The second main part of an XML document is a single element known as the document element or root element, which can contain additional nested elements.

In an XML document, the elements indicate the logical structure of the document and contain the document's information content (which in the example document is the book information, such as the titles, author names, and prices). A typical element consists of a start-tag, the element's content, and an end-tag. The element's content can be character data, other (nested) elements, or a combination of both.

> ### note
> The text in an XML document consists of intermingled markup and character data. *Markup* is delimited text that describes the storage layout and logical structure of the document. The following are the different kinds of markup: element start-tags, element end-tags, empty-element tags, comments, document type declarations, processing instructions, XML declarations, text declarations, CDATA section delimiters, entity references, character references, and any white space that is at the top level of the document (that is, outside the document element and outside other markup). You'll learn about each of these types of markup in later chapters. All other text is *character data*—the actual information content of the document (in the example document, the titles, author names, prices, and other book information).

In the example document, the document element is INVENTORY. Its start-tag is <INVENTORY>, its end-tag is </INVENTORY>, and its content is eight nested BOOK elements.

> ### note
> The document element in an XML document is similar to the BODY element in an HTML page, except that you can assign it any legal name.

Each BOOK element likewise contains a series of nested elements:

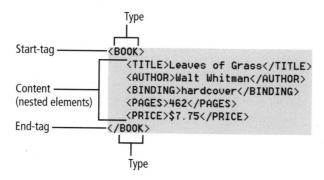

note

The name that appears at the beginning of the start-tag and in the end-tag identifies the element's *type*.

Each of the elements nested in a BOOK element, such as a TITLE element, contains only character data:

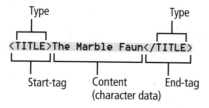

In Part 2 of the book, you'll learn all about adding elements to your XML documents and including attributes in an element's start-tag.

Some Basic XML Rules

The following are a few of the basic rules for creating a well-formed XML document. A well-formed document is one that conforms to the minimal set of rules that allow the document to be processed by a browser or other XML program. The document you typed earlier in the chapter (Listing 2-1) is an example of a well-formed XML document that conforms to these rules.

- **The document must have exactly one top-level element (the document element or root element).** All other elements must be nested within it.

- **Elements must be properly nested.** That is, if an element starts within another element, it must also end within that same element.

- **Each element must have both a start-tag and an end-tag.** Unlike HTML, XML doesn't let you omit the end-tag—not even in situations where the browser would be able to figure out where the element ends. (In Chapter 3, however, you'll learn a shortcut notation you can use for an empty element—that is, an element with no content.)

- **The element-type name in a start-tag must exactly match the name in the corresponding end-tag.**

- **Element-type names are case-sensitive.** In fact, all text within XML markup is case-sensitive. For example, the following element is illegal because the type name in the start-tag doesn't match the type name in the end-tag:

```
<TITLE>Leaves of Grass</Title>  <!-- illegal element -->
```

tip

In Part 2 of the book, you'll find detailed instructions for writing not only well-formed XML documents but also *valid* XML documents, which meet a more stringent set of requirements.

Displaying the XML Document

You can open an XML document directly within the Internet Explorer browser, just like you'd open an HTML Web page.

If the XML document doesn't contain a link to a style sheet, Internet Explorer will simply display the text of the complete document, including both the markup (the tags and comments, for example) and the character data. Internet Explorer color-codes the different document components to help you identify them, and it displays the document element as a collapsible/expandable tree to clearly indicate the document's logical structure and to allow you to view various levels of detail.

If, however, the XML document contains a link to a style sheet, Internet Explorer will display only the character data from the document's elements, and it will format this data according to the rules you have specified in the style sheet.

You can use either a cascading style sheet (CSS)—the same type of style sheet used for HTML pages—or an Extensible Stylesheet Language Transformations (XSLT) style sheet—a more powerful type of style sheet that employs XML syntax and can be used only for XML documents. (An XSLT style sheet lets you display attribute values and other information contained in an XML document, in addition to character data from elements.)

Display the XML Document Without a Style Sheet

1   In Windows Explorer or in a folder window, double-click the name of the file, Inventory.xml, that you saved in the previous exercise. Inventory.xml

Internet Explorer will display the document as shown here:

2   Experiment with changing the level of detail shown within the document element. Clicking the minus symbol (-) to the left of a start-tag collapses the element, while clicking the plus symbol (+) next to a collapsed element expands it. For instance, if you click the minus symbol next to the INVENTORY element, as shown here:

```
<?xml version="1.0" ?>
<!-- File Name: Inventory.xml  -->
<INVENTORY>
- <BOOK>
    <TITLE>The Adventures of Huckleberry Finn</TITLE>
    <AUTHOR>Mark Twain</AUTHOR>
```

the entire document element will be collapsed, as shown here:

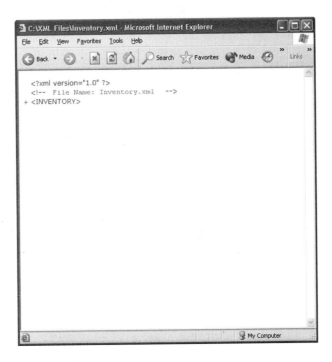

Catch XML Errors in Internet Explorer

Before Internet Explorer displays your XML document, its XML parser component analyzes the document contents. If the parser detects an error, Internet Explorer displays a page with an error message rather than attempting to display the document. Internet Explorer will display the error page whether or not the XML document is linked to a style sheet.

note

The *XML parser* is the part of the XML processor that scans the XML document, analyzes its structure, and detects any errors in syntax. See the Note on page 26 for a definition of XML processor.

In the following exercise, you'll investigate the Internet Explorer error-checking feature by purposely introducing an error into the Inventory.xml document.

1   In your text editor, open the Inventory.xml document that you created in a previous exercise. Change the first TITLE element from

```
<TITLE>The Adventures of Huckleberry Finn</TITLE>
```
to

```
<TITLE>The Adventures of Huckleberry Finn</Title>
```
The element-type name in the end-tag now no longer matches the element-type name in the start-tag. Remember that element-type names are case-sensitive!

2   Save the changed document.

3   In Windows Explorer or in a folder window, double-click the document filename Inventory.xml. Inventory.xml

Rather than displaying the XML document, Internet Explorer will now display the following error-message page:

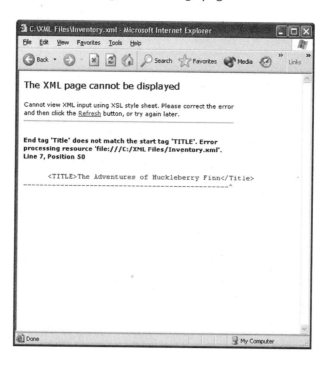

note

When you open an XML document directly in Internet Explorer, as you do in this chapter, the parser checks only whether the document is well-formed and then displays a message if it finds an error. It doesn't check whether the document is valid.

4   Because you'll work with Inventory.xml again in later chapters, you should now restore the end-tag in the first TITLE element to its original form (</TITLE>) and then resave the document.

note

If an XML document contains more than one well-formedness error, Internet Explorer displays only the first one it encounters. You'll need to fix the errors one at a time. After you fix each error, you'll need to save the document and reopen it in Internet Explorer to check for additional errors. (You can quickly reopen the document or page that's currently displayed in Internet Explorer by clicking the Refresh toolbar button or by pressing F5.)

Even though you didn't link a style sheet to the XML document, Internet Explorer uses a default style sheet to display the document; hence the error page refers to "using XSL style sheet." (XSL style sheets are similar to the more recent XSLT style sheets, which are covered in Chapter 12.)

tip

As you work through the chapters in this book, keep in mind that you can quickly check whether an XML document is well-formed by simply opening it directly in Internet Explorer. (If you display an XML document through an HTML page, as described in Part 3, an XML document with an error will fail to display, but you won't see an error message unless you explicitly write script code to show one.)

Display the XML Document Using a Cascading Style Sheet

1   Open a new, empty text file in your text editor, and type in the cascading style sheet (CSS) shown in Listing 2-2. (You'll find a copy of this listing on the companion CD under the filename Inventory01.css.)

2   Use your text editor's Save command to save the style sheet on your hard disk, assigning it the filename Inventory01.css.

The CSS you just created tells Internet Explorer to format the elements' character data as follows:

■   Display each BOOK element with 12 points of space above it (*margin-top:12pt*) and a line break above and below it (*display:block*), using a 10-point font (*font-size:10pt*).

■   Display each TITLE element in italic (*font-style:italic*).

■   Display each AUTHOR element in bold (*font-weight:bold*).

Inventory01.css

```
/* File Name: Inventory01.css */

BOOK
    {display:block;
     margin-top:12pt;
     font-size:10pt}

TITLE
    {font-style:italic}

AUTHOR
    {font-weight:bold}
```

Listing 2-2.

3   In your text editor, open the Inventory.xml document that you created in a previous exercise. Add the following processing instruction to the end of the document prolog, directly above the INVENTORY element:

```
<?xml-stylesheet type="text/css" href="Inventory01.css"?>
```

This processing instruction links the CSS you just created to the XML document. As a result, when you open the document in Internet Explorer, the browser displays the document content according to the instructions in the style sheet.

4   To reflect the new filename you're going to assign, change the comment near the beginning of the document from

```
<!-- File Name: Inventory.xml -->
```

to

```
<!-- File Name: Inventory01.xml -->
```

Listing 2-3 shows the complete XML document. (You'll find a copy of this listing on the companion CD under the filename Inventory01.xml.)

5   Use your text editor's Save As command to save a copy of the modified document under the filename Inventory01.xml. Be sure to save it in the same file folder in which you saved Inventory01.css.

Inventory01.xml

```xml
<?xml version="1.0"?>

<!-- File Name: Inventory01.xml -->

<?xml-stylesheet type="text/css" href="Inventory01.css"?>

<INVENTORY>
    <BOOK>
        <TITLE>The Adventures of Huckleberry Finn</TITLE>
        <AUTHOR>Mark Twain</AUTHOR>
        <BINDING>mass market paperback</BINDING>
        <PAGES>298</PAGES>
        <PRICE>$5.49</PRICE>
    </BOOK>
    <BOOK>
        <TITLE>Leaves of Grass</TITLE>
        <AUTHOR>Walt Whitman</AUTHOR>
        <BINDING>hardcover</BINDING>
        <PAGES>462</PAGES>
        <PRICE>$7.75</PRICE>
    </BOOK>
    <BOOK>
        <TITLE>The Legend of Sleepy Hollow</TITLE>
        <AUTHOR>Washington Irving</AUTHOR>
        <BINDING>mass market paperback</BINDING>
        <PAGES>98</PAGES>
        <PRICE>$2.95</PRICE>
    </BOOK>
```

```
<BOOK>
   <TITLE>The Marble Faun</TITLE>
   <AUTHOR>Nathaniel Hawthorne</AUTHOR>
   <BINDING>trade paperback</BINDING>
   <PAGES>473</PAGES>
   <PRICE>$10.95</PRICE>
</BOOK>
<BOOK>
   <TITLE>Moby-Dick</TITLE>
   <AUTHOR>Herman Melville</AUTHOR>
   <BINDING>hardcover</BINDING>
   <PAGES>724</PAGES>
   <PRICE>$9.95</PRICE>
</BOOK>
<BOOK>
   <TITLE>The Portrait of a Lady</TITLE>
   <AUTHOR>Henry James</AUTHOR>
   <BINDING>mass market paperback</BINDING>
   <PAGES>256</PAGES>
   <PRICE>$4.95</PRICE>
</BOOK>
<BOOK>
   <TITLE>The Scarlet Letter</TITLE>
   <AUTHOR>Nathaniel Hawthorne</AUTHOR>
   <BINDING>trade paperback</BINDING>
   <PAGES>253</PAGES>
   <PRICE>$4.25</PRICE>
</BOOK>
<BOOK>
   <TITLE>The Turn of the Screw</TITLE>
   <AUTHOR>Henry James</AUTHOR>
   <BINDING>trade paperback</BINDING>
   <PAGES>384</PAGES>
   <PRICE>$3.35</PRICE>
</BOOK>
</INVENTORY>
```

Listing 2-3.

6 In Windows Explorer or in a folder window, double-click the Inventory01.xml filename to open the document. 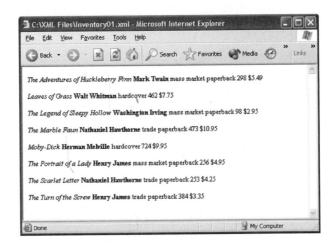Inventory01.xml

Internet Explorer will open the Inventory01.xml document and display it according to the rules in the linked Inventory01.css style sheet, as shown here:

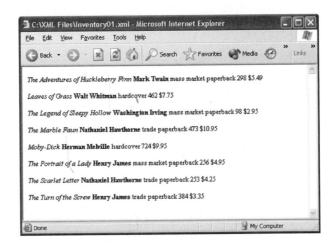

7 To get a feel for how you can change the XML document's appearance by modifying the linked style sheet, open a new, empty text file in your text editor, and type in the modified CSS shown in Listing 2-4. (You'll find a copy of this listing on the companion CD under the filename Inventory02.css.)

8 Use your text editor's Save command to save the new style sheet on your hard disk, assigning it the filename Inventory02.css.

The modified style sheet you just typed tells Internet Explorer to format the elements' character data as follows:

- Display each BOOK element with 12 points of space above it (*margin-top:12pt*) and a line break above and below it (*display:block*), using a 10-point font (*font-size:10pt*).

- Display the TITLE, AUTHOR, BINDING, and PRICE elements each on a separate line (*display:block*).

- Display the TITLE element in a 12-point (*font-size:12pt*), bold (*font-weight:bold*), italic (*font-style:italic*) font. (Note that the 12-point font-size specification made for the TITLE element overrides the 10-point specification made for the element's parent, BOOK.)

- Indent the AUTHOR, BINDING, and PRICE elements each by 15 points (*margin-left:15pt*).

■ Display the AUTHOR element in bold (*font-weight:bold*).

■ Do not display the PAGES element (*display:none*).

Inventory02.css

```
/* File Name: Inventory02.css */

BOOK
    {display:block;
     margin-top:12pt;
     font-size:10pt}

TITLE
    {display:block;
     font-size:12pt;
     font-weight:bold;
     font-style:italic}

AUTHOR
    {display:block;
     margin-left:15pt;
     font-weight:bold}

BINDING
    {display:block;
     margin-left:15pt}

PAGES
    {display:none}

PRICE
    {display:block;
     margin-left:15pt}
```

Listing 2-4.

9 In your text editor, open the Inventory.xml document. Add the following processing instruction to the end of the document prolog, directly above the INVENTORY element:

```
<?xml-stylesheet type="text/css" href="Inventory02.css"?>
```
This processing instruction links the new CSS you just created to the XML document.

10   To reflect the new filename you're going to assign, change the comment near the beginning of the document from

```
<!-- File Name: Inventory.xml -->
```
to

```
<!-- File Name: Inventory02.xml -->
```
Listing 2-5 shows the complete XML document. (You'll find a copy of this listing on the companion CD under the filename Inventory02.xml.)

11   Use your text editor's Save As command to save a copy of the modified document under the filename Inventory02.xml. Be sure to save it in the same file folder in which you saved Inventory02.css.

Inventory02.xml

```
<?xml version="1.0"?>

<!-- File Name: Inventory02.xml -->

<?xml-stylesheet type="text/css" href="Inventory02.css"?>

<INVENTORY>
    <BOOK>
        <TITLE>The Adventures of Huckleberry Finn</TITLE>
        <AUTHOR>Mark Twain</AUTHOR>
        <BINDING>mass market paperback</BINDING>
        <PAGES>298</PAGES>
        <PRICE>$5.49</PRICE>
    </BOOK>
    <BOOK>
        <TITLE>Leaves of Grass</TITLE>
        <AUTHOR>Walt Whitman</AUTHOR>
        <BINDING>hardcover</BINDING>
        <PAGES>462</PAGES>
        <PRICE>$7.75</PRICE>
    </BOOK>
    <BOOK>
        <TITLE>The Legend of Sleepy Hollow</TITLE>
        <AUTHOR>Washington Irving</AUTHOR>
        <BINDING>mass market paperback</BINDING>
```

```
      <PAGES>98</PAGES>
      <PRICE>$2.95</PRICE>
   </BOOK>
   <BOOK>
      <TITLE>The Marble Faun</TITLE>
      <AUTHOR>Nathaniel Hawthorne</AUTHOR>
      <BINDING>trade paperback</BINDING>
      <PAGES>473</PAGES>
      <PRICE>$10.95</PRICE>
   </BOOK>
   <BOOK>
      <TITLE>Moby-Dick</TITLE>
      <AUTHOR>Herman Melville</AUTHOR>
      <BINDING>hardcover</BINDING>
      <PAGES>724</PAGES>
      <PRICE>$9.95</PRICE>
   </BOOK>
   <BOOK>
      <TITLE>The Portrait of a Lady</TITLE>
      <AUTHOR>Henry James</AUTHOR>
      <BINDING>mass market paperback</BINDING>
      <PAGES>256</PAGES>
      <PRICE>$4.95</PRICE>
   </BOOK>
   <BOOK>
      <TITLE>The Scarlet Letter</TITLE>
      <AUTHOR>Nathaniel Hawthorne</AUTHOR>
      <BINDING>trade paperback</BINDING>
      <PAGES>253</PAGES>
      <PRICE>$4.25</PRICE>
   </BOOK>
   <BOOK>
      <TITLE>The Turn of the Screw</TITLE>
      <AUTHOR>Henry James</AUTHOR>
      <BINDING>trade paperback</BINDING>
      <PAGES>384</PAGES>
      <PRICE>$3.35</PRICE>
   </BOOK>
</INVENTORY>
```

Listing 2-5.

12 In Windows Explorer or in a folder window, double-click the Inventory02.xml filename to open it.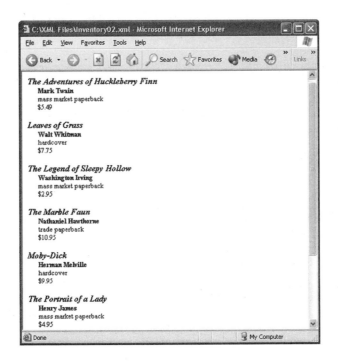

Internet Explorer will open the Inventory02.xml document and display it according to the rules in the linked Inventory02.css style sheet, as shown here (only the first six books are shown; scrolling down would reveal the last two books):

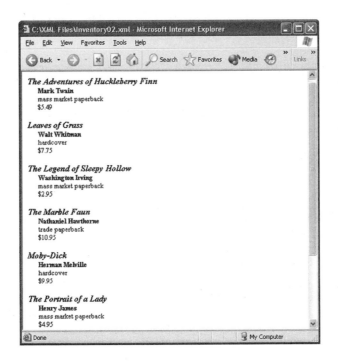

tip

Part 3 of the book provides complete instructions for displaying XML documents on the Web. I'll cover cascading style sheets, such as the one you created here, in Chapters 8 and 9. I'll cover XSLT style sheets in Chapter 12. You'll learn alternative methods for displaying XML documents on the Web in Chapters 10 and 11.

PART 2

Creating XML Documents

3

Creating Well-Formed XML Documents

In this chapter, you'll learn the basic techniques for creating a *well-formed* XML document. A well-formed document is one that meets the minimal set of criteria for a conforming XML document. When you create a well-formed XML document, you can pitch right in and begin adding elements as you need them and entering your document's data, just as you do when you create an HTML Web page. (Although, as you learned in the previous chapters, in an XML document you invent your own elements rather than use predefined ones.) And you'll have no problem handling and displaying any well-formed XML document in Microsoft Internet Explorer.

In Chapters 5 through 7, you'll learn how to create a *valid* XML document: a document that is not only well-formed but that also conforms to a more rigid set of constraints. When you create a valid XML document, in addition to adding the elements and data, you must formally define the document's content and structure, either in a document type definition (DTD) or in an XML schema file.

> **note**
>
> Permitting XML documents to be merely well-formed, rather than requiring them to be valid, is an important concession that the XML specification makes to enhance XML as a universal markup language for the Web. Merely well-formed documents are simpler to create than valid ones, making XML as easy for Web developers to use as the more familiar HTML. Also, merely well-formed documents are often easier to transmit over the Web than valid documents because they are less likely to rely on external files; and a non-validating processor can often ignore external files, making the document more suitable for Web browsing. Finally, because an XML processor isn't required to check for validity, writing a conforming XML processor that can handle any XML document is simpler, encouraging the proliferation of universal XML processors on the Web.
>
> In Chapter 5, however, you'll learn that there are some important advantages to making documents valid, especially for creating a group of similar documents.

In this chapter, you'll first learn about all the required and optional parts of a well-formed XML document. Next you'll discover how to add information to an XML document by defining the document's elements. You'll then learn how to supply additional document information by adding attributes to the elements.

The Parts of a Well-Formed XML Document

As you learned in Chapter 2, an XML document consists of two main parts: the prolog and the document element (which is also known as the root element). In addition, following the document element, a well-formed XML document can include comments, processing instructions, and white space (spaces, tabs, or line breaks). Here's an example of a well-formed XML document that shows the different document parts and the items you can add to each part:

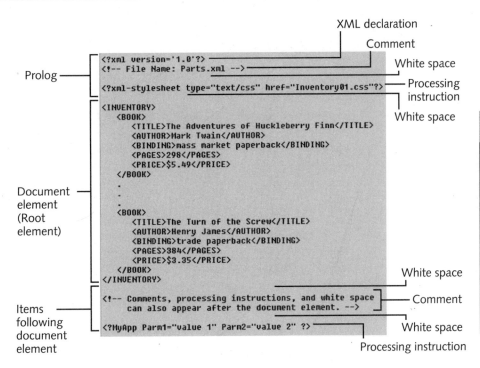

Listing 3-1 shows the complete version of this example document. (You'll find a copy of this listing on the companion CD under the filename Parts.xml.)

Parts.xml

```
<?xml version='1.0'?>
<!-- File Name: Parts.xml -->

<?xml-stylesheet type="text/css" href="Inventory01.css"?>

<INVENTORY>
   <BOOK>
      <TITLE>The Adventures of Huckleberry Finn</TITLE>
      <AUTHOR>Mark Twain</AUTHOR>
      <BINDING>mass market paperback</BINDING>
      <PAGES>298</PAGES>
      <PRICE>$5.49</PRICE>
   </BOOK>
   <BOOK>
      <TITLE>Leaves of Grass</TITLE>
      <AUTHOR>Walt Whitman</AUTHOR>
```

```
      <BINDING>hardcover</BINDING>
      <PAGES>462</PAGES>
      <PRICE>$7.75</PRICE>
   </BOOK>
   <BOOK>
      <TITLE>The Legend of Sleepy Hollow</TITLE>
      <AUTHOR>Washington Irving</AUTHOR>
      <BINDING>mass market paperback</BINDING>
      <PAGES>98</PAGES>
      <PRICE>$2.95</PRICE>
   </BOOK>
   <BOOK>
      <TITLE>The Marble Faun</TITLE>
      <AUTHOR>Nathaniel Hawthorne</AUTHOR>
      <BINDING>trade paperback</BINDING>
      <PAGES>473</PAGES>
      <PRICE>$10.95</PRICE>
   </BOOK>
   <BOOK>
      <TITLE>Moby-Dick</TITLE>
      <AUTHOR>Herman Melville</AUTHOR>
      <BINDING>hardcover</BINDING>
      <PAGES>724</PAGES>
      <PRICE>$9.95</PRICE>
   </BOOK>
   <BOOK>
      <TITLE>The Portrait of a Lady</TITLE>
      <AUTHOR>Henry James</AUTHOR>
      <BINDING>mass market paperback</BINDING>
      <PAGES>256</PAGES>
      <PRICE>$4.95</PRICE>
   </BOOK>
   <BOOK>
      <TITLE>The Scarlet Letter</TITLE>
      <AUTHOR>Nathaniel Hawthorne</AUTHOR>
      <BINDING>trade paperback</BINDING>
      <PAGES>253</PAGES>
      <PRICE>$4.25</PRICE>
   </BOOK>
   <BOOK>
```

```
      <TITLE>The Turn of the Screw</TITLE>
      <AUTHOR>Henry James</AUTHOR>
      <BINDING>trade paperback</BINDING>
      <PAGES>384</PAGES>
      <PRICE>$3.35</PRICE>
   </BOOK>
</INVENTORY>


<!-- Comments, processing instructions, and white space
     can also appear after the document element. -->

<?MyApp Parm1="value 1" Parm2="value 2" ?>
```

Listing 3-1.

The first line of the example document consists of the *XML declaration*. Although technically the XML declaration is optional, the XML specification recommends including it. In addition to making the document self-identifying as XML and specifying the XML version number (which will become important if later versions are developed), it provides a place for including two optional pieces of information: the *encoding declaration* and the *standalone document declaration*. The encoding declaration specifies the encoding scheme used for the characters in the document, and is discussed in the sidebar "Characters, Encoding, and Languages" on page 77. The *standalone* document declaration indicates whether the document contains external markup declarations (explained in Chapter 5) that affect the content of the document. It's covered in the sidebar "The *standalone* Document Declaration" on page 159. If you include an XML declaration, it must appear at the very beginning of the document. (You're not permitted to include even white space characters before the XML declaration.)

The version number in the XML declaration can be delimited with either single or double quotes. In general, quoted strings in XML markup—known as *literals*—can use either single or double quotes. Thus, both of the following are legal:

```
<?xml version='1.0'?>

<?xml version="1.0"?>
```

The example document includes a comment in the prolog and another comment following the document element. You'll learn more about comments in Chapter 4.

The document also contains two blank lines in the prolog and two more blank lines that follow the document element, each labeled "White space." White space consists of one or more space, tab, carriage-return, or line feed characters.

To make an XML document more readable to humans, you can freely add white space between XML markup—such as start-tags, end-tags, comments, and processing instructions—and also in many places within markup—for instance, the space between *xml* and *version* at the beginning of the XML declaration in the example document. The processor simply ignores white space unless it's within an element (that is, between an element start-tag and a matching end-tag, but not within markup). In that case, the processor passes the white space to the application as part of the character data of the element that contains the white space. For details on the way white space is handled in elements, see the sidebar "White Space in Elements" on page 56.

The example document has a processing instruction in the prolog and another that follows the document element. I'll discuss processing instructions in Chapter 4.

Finally, the example document includes the *sine qua non* of an XML document: the document element. Creating the document element and the nested elements that it contains is the focus of this chapter.

> **note**
>
> As you'll learn in Chapter 5, a valid XML document must either contain a document type declaration or be processed using a separate XML schema file. A document type declaration is an additional component, not included in the example document in Listing 3-1, which you can place anywhere in the prolog (outside other markup) following the XML declaration. A document type declaration contains a document type definition (DTD) that defines the content and structure of a valid XML document.

Adding Elements to the Document

The elements in an XML document contain the actual document information (in Listing 3-1, for example, the titles, authors, prices, and other information on the books in the inventory), and they indicate the logical structure of this information.

The elements are arranged in a treelike hierarchy, with elements nested within other elements. The document must have exactly one top-level element—the document element or root element—with all other elements nested within it. Hence, the following is a well-formed XML document:

```
<?xml version="1.0"?>
<!-- A well-formed XML document. -->
```

```
<INVENTORY>
    <BOOK>
        <TITLE>The Adventures of Huckleberry Finn</TITLE>
        <AUTHOR>Mark Twain</AUTHOR>
        <BINDING>mass market paperback</BINDING>
        <PAGES>298</PAGES>
        <PRICE>$5.49</PRICE>
    </BOOK>
    <BOOK>
        <TITLE>Leaves of Grass</TITLE>
        <AUTHOR>Walt Whitman</AUTHOR>
        <BINDING>hardcover</BINDING>
        <PAGES>462</PAGES>
        <PRICE>$7.75</PRICE>
    </BOOK>
</INVENTORY>
```

A Minimalist XML Document

The prolog in the XML document in Listing 3-1 contains an example of each of the items allowed within a prolog. Note, however, that these items are all optional (although the XML specification states that you "should" include the XML declaration). Hence, the prolog itself is optional, and the following minimalist document, which contains only a simple document element, conforms to the XML standard for a well-formed document:

```
<minimal>A minimalist document.</minimal>
```

This document would be displayed in Internet Explorer as shown here:

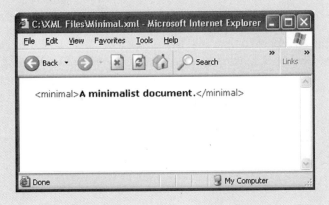

The following document, however, is not well-formed because it has two elements, rather than one, at the top level:

```
<?xml version="1.0"?>
<!-- This document is NOT well-formed. -->
<BOOK>
    <TITLE>The Adventures of Huckleberry Finn</TITLE>
    <AUTHOR>Mark Twain</AUTHOR>
    <BINDING>mass market paperback</BINDING>
    <PAGES>298</PAGES>
    <PRICE>$5.49</PRICE>
</BOOK>
<BOOK>
    <TITLE>Leaves of Grass</TITLE>
    <AUTHOR>Walt Whitman</AUTHOR>
    <BINDING>hardcover</BINDING>
    <PAGES>462</PAGES>
    <PRICE>$7.75</PRICE>
</BOOK>
```

Elements must also be properly nested. That is, if an element (delimited by a start-tag and an end-tag, as I'll explain later) begins within another element, it must also end within that same element. In other words, you can't overlap elements as you sometimes can in HTML. For example, the following elements would be allowed in HTML but would be illegal in an XML document:

```
<!-- NOT well-formed in XML: -->
<EM>italic <B>bold and italic </EM>bold</B>
```

note

An element that contains one or more nested elements (such as BOOK in Listing 3-1) is known as the *parent element* of the nested elements. An element contained directly within the parent (such as TITLE within BOOK) is known as a *child element, subelement,* or *nested element* of the parent.

The Anatomy of an Element

As you've seen, an element usually consists of a start-tag, content, and an end-tag.

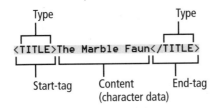

Unlike HTML, XML requires you to always include both the start-tag and the end-tag. The only exception is an element without content, for which you can use the special empty-element tag that I'll describe later in this chapter.

The name that appears at the beginning of the start-tag and in the end-tag (TITLE in the above example) identifies the element's *type*, not the specific element. A document can thus contain more than one element that has the same name (such as the BOOK or TITLE elements in Listing 3-1), all of which are considered to be of the same type.

When you add an element to your XML document, you can select any type name you want, provided that you follow these guidelines:

- The name must begin with a letter or underscore (_), followed by zero or more letters, digits, periods (.), hyphens (-), or underscores.

- The XML specification states that names beginning with the letters *xml* (in any combination of uppercase or lowercase letters) are "reserved for standardization." Although Internet Explorer doesn't enforce this restriction, it's better not to begin names with *xml* to avoid future problems.

- You can assign the element name to a namespace by placing a namespace prefix followed by a colon (:) in front of the element name, as explained in "Using Namespaces" on page 69. The element name itself must still conform to the first two rules, even if you place a namespace prefix and colon in front of it. That is, it must begin with a letter or underscore and it shouldn't start with *xml*.

Well-Formed Documents

The following are legal element-type names:

```
Part
_1stPlace
A
B-SECTION
Street.Address.1
books:TITLE <!-- Allowed only if the 'books' namespace prefix
                has been properly declared. -->
```

The following, however, are illegal element-type names:

```
1stPlace   <!-- Digit not allowed as first character. -->
B Section  <!-- Space not allowed within a name. -->
B/Section  <!-- Slash not allowed within a name. -->
:Chapter   <!-- Colon not allowed as first character. -->
```

Also, the name in the start-tag must exactly match the name in the end-tag, including the case of all letters. Thus, the following element is not well-formed:

```
<Title>Chapter One</title>  <!-- NOT well-formed. -->
```

Case is significant in element names, as it is in all text within markup. Thus, an element type named *Ace* is not the same element type as *ace* or *ACE*.

Types of Content in an Element

An element's content is the text between the start-tag and the end-tag. You can include the following types of items in the content of an element:

▨ **Nested elements.** In Listing 3-1, both the INVENTORY element and the BOOK elements contain nested elements as their content:

```
<BOOK>
   <TITLE>The Scarlet Letter</TITLE>
   <AUTHOR>Nathaniel Hawthorne</AUTHOR>
   <BINDING>trade paperback</BINDING>
   <PAGES>253</PAGES>
   <PRICE>$4.25</PRICE>
</BOOK>
```

Content of BOOK element = five nested elements

▨ **Character data.** Character data is text that expresses the information content of an element, such as a specific book title in a TITLE element:

Content of TITLE element = character data

```
<TITLE>The Scarlet Letter</TITLE>
```

Here's an example of content in an element that consists of both character data and a nested element:

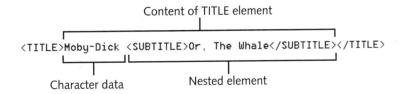

Content of TITLE element

```
<TITLE>Moby-Dick <SUBTITLE>Or, The Whale</SUBTITLE></TITLE>
```

Character data   Nested element

When adding character data to an element, you can insert any characters as part of the character data except the left angle bracket (<), the ampersand (&), or the string]]>.

note

The XML parser scans an element's character data looking for XML markup. You therefore cannot insert a left angle bracket (<), an ampersand (&), or the string *]]>* as a part of the character data because the parser would interpret each of these characters or strings as markup or the start of markup. If you want to insert < or & as an integral part of the character data, you can use a CDATA section (discussed later in the list). You can also insert <, &, or any other character—including one not on your keyboard—by using a character reference, and you can insert certain characters by using predefined general entity references (such as *<* or *&* for inserting < or &). General entity and character references are discussed next.

■ **General entity references or character references.** Here's an element containing one of each:

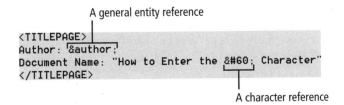

A general entity reference

```
<TITLEPAGE>
Author: &author;
Document Name: "How to Enter the &#60; Character"
</TITLEPAGE>
```

A character reference

Entity and character references are covered in Chapter 6.

■ **CDATA sections.** A CDATA section is a block of text in which you can freely insert any characters except the string]]>. Here's an example of a CDATA section in an element:

Well-Formed Documents

```
                     <TITLEPAGE>
                        Author: Mike
                      ┌ <![CDATA[
A CDATA section ──────┤  Document Name: "How to Enter the < and & Characters"
                      └ ]]>
                     </TITLEPAGE>
```

CDATA sections are covered in Chapter 4.

- **Processing instructions.** A processing instruction provides information to the XML application. Processing instructions are covered in Chapter 4.

- **Comments.** A comment is an annotation to your XML document that people can read but that the XML processor ignores and (optionally) passes on to the application. Comments are covered in Chapter 4.

Here's an element containing both a processing instruction and a comment:

```
                       <BOOK>
A processing ───────── <?MyApp Parm1="value 1" Parm2="value 2" ?>
instruction            <TITLE>The Legend of Sleepy Hollow</TITLE>
                       <AUTHOR>Washington Irving</AUTHOR>
A comment ──────────── <!-- You can put a comment inside an element. -->
                       <BINDING>mass market paperback</BINDING>
                       <PAGES>98</PAGES>
                       <PRICE>$2.95</PRICE>
                       </BOOK>
```

White Space in Elements

White space consists of one or more space, tab, carriage-return, or line feed characters. (These characters are represented, respectively, by the decimal values 32, 9, 13, and 10, or by the equivalent hexadecimal values 20, 09, 0D, and 0A.) Sometimes you insert white space into an element because you want it to be an actual part of the element's character data. For example, the leading white space in the last of the VERSE elements shown here is an integral part of the content of the poem:

```
<VERSE>For the rare and radiant maiden<VERSE>
<VERSE>whom the angels name Lenore--</VERSE>
<VERSE>     Nameless here for evermore.</VERSE>
```

Other times, you insert white space into an element merely to make the XML source easy to read and understand (often a good idea). For instance, in the following source, the line breaks inserted after the <BOOK>, </TITLE>, and </AUTHOR> tags, and the space characters before the <TITLE> and <AUTHOR> tags, make the structure of the elements easier to see and aren't intended to be part of the BOOK element's actual character content:

```
<BOOK>
    <TITLE>The Adventures of Huckleberry Finn</TITLE>
    <AUTHOR>Mark Twain</AUTHOR>
</BOOK>
```

According to the XML specification, however, the XML processor should not try to guess the purpose of various blocks of white space, but rather it must always preserve all white space characters and pass them on to the application. (The one exception is that in all text it passes to the application, the processor must convert a carriage-return and line feed character pair, or a carriage-return without a following line feed, to a single line feed character.)

XML provides a reserved attribute, named *xml:space*, that you can include in any element to tell the application how you would like it to handle white space contained in that element. (Attributes are discussed later in this chapter.) The *xml:* indicates that this attribute belongs to the *xml* namespace. Because this namespace is predefined, you don't have to declare it. (See "Using Namespaces" on page 69.) Keep in mind that this attribute has no effect on the XML processor, which always passes on all white space in elements to the application, and the application can use this information in any way, even ignoring it if appropriate.

The two standard values you can assign to this attribute are *default*, which signals the application that it should use its default way of handling white space, and *preserve*, which informs the application that it should preserve all white space. The *xml:space* attribute specification applies to the element in which it occurs and to any nested elements, unless it is overridden by an *xml:space* attribute specification in a nested element. For example, the *xml:space* attribute in the following STANZA element tells the application that it should preserve all white space in the STANZA and nested VERSE elements:

```
<STANZA xml:space="preserve">
<VERSE>For the rare and radiant maiden<VERSE>
<VERSE>whom the angels name Lenore--</VERSE>
<VERSE>     Nameless here for evermore.</VERSE>
</STANZA>
```

continued

continued

If the application abides by this example *xml:space* specification, it will preserve the leading spaces in the last VERSE element as well as the line breaks before and after each VERSE element.

When you get to Chapters 5 and 7 on creating valid documents, keep in mind that in a valid document the *xml:space* attribute must be declared just like any other attribute. (This will make sense when you read those chapters.) In a document type definition (DTD), you must declare the attribute as an enumerated type, as shown in the following example attribute-list declaration:

```
<!ATTLIST STANZA   xml:space (default|preserve) 'preserve'>
```

Remember that when you use the methods for displaying and working with XML discussed in this book, Internet Explorer provides the application, or at least the front end of the application. So you also need to know what the XML application component of Internet Explorer does with the white space that it receives from Internet Explorer's XML processor. This will tell you whether the white space will be displayed in the browser, or whether it will be available to the Web pages you write to display XML. The way Internet Explorer handles white space depends on which method you use for displaying and working with XML documents:

- **CSS.** If you display an XML document using a cascading style sheet (CSS), as explained in Chapters 8 and 9, Internet Explorer handles white space just as it does in an HTML page (regardless of any *xml:space* settings included in the document). That is, it replaces sequences of white space characters within an element's text with a single space character, and it discards leading or trailing white space. To format the text the way you want it, you can use CSS properties.

- **Data Binding.** If you use data binding to display an XML document, as explained in Chapter 10, Internet Explorer automatically preserves all the white space within an XML element to which an HTML element is bound, regardless of any *xml:space* settings included in the document. An exception is an HTML element with the DATAFORMATAS="HTML" attribute specification, as explained in Chapter 10.

- **XML DOM or XSLT Style Sheets.** If you use an XML Document Object Model (DOM) script to display an XML document following the instructions in Chapter 11, Internet Explorer preserves most white space within an element. If, however, you use an XSLT style sheet as directed in Chapter 12, Internet Explorer handles white space as it does in HTML (described in the first list item). With both display methods, the exact handling of white space depends upon how you load and access the XML document, and follows fairly complex rules. For details, search for "white space" in the topic titles of the Microsoft XML SDK 4.0 help file.

Empty Elements

You can also enter an *empty element*—that is, one without content—into your document. You can create an empty element by placing the end-tag immediately after the start-tag, as in this example:

`<HR></HR>`

Or, you can save typing by using an *empty-element tag*, as shown here:

`<HR/>`

These two notations have the same meaning.

Because an empty element has no content, you might question its usefulness. Here are two possible uses:

- You can use an empty element to tell the XML application to perform an action or display an object. Examples from HTML are the BR empty element, which tells the browser to insert a line break, and the HR empty element, which tells it to add a horizontal dividing line. In other words, the mere presence of an element with a particular name—without any content—can provide important information to the application.

- An empty element can store information through attributes, which you'll learn about later in this chapter. An example from HTML is the IMG (image) empty element, which contains attributes that tell the processor where to find the graphics file and how to display it.

tip

As you'll learn in Chapter 8, a cascading style sheet can use an empty element to display an image. In Chapter 10, you'll learn how to use data binding to access the attributes belonging to an empty or non-empty element. And in Chapters 11 and 12, you'll learn how to use HTML scripts (Chapter 11) and XSLT style sheets (Chapter 12) to access elements (empty or non-empty) and their attributes and then perform appropriate actions.

Create Different Types of Elements

1   Open a new, empty text file in your text editor, and type in the XML document shown in Listing 3-2. (You'll find a copy of this listing on the companion CD under the filename Inventory03.xml.) If you want, you can use the

Inventory.xml document you created in Chapter 2 (given in Listing 2-1 and included on the companion CD) as a starting point.

2   Use your text editor's Save command to save the document on your hard disk, assigning the filename Inventory03.xml.

Inventory03.xml

```xml
<?xml version="1.0"?>

<!-- File Name: Inventory03.xml -->

<?xml-stylesheet type="text/css" href="Inventory02.css"?>

<INVENTORY> <!-- Inventory of selected 19th Century
                American Literature -->
    <BOOK>
        <COVER_IMAGE Source="Huck.gif" />
        <TITLE>The Adventures of Huckleberry Finn</TITLE>
        <AUTHOR>Mark Twain</AUTHOR>
        <BINDING>mass market paperback</BINDING>
        <PAGES>298</PAGES>
        <PRICE>$5.49</PRICE>
    </BOOK>
    <BOOK>
        <COVER_IMAGE Source="Leaves.gif" />
        <TITLE>Leaves of Grass</TITLE>
        <AUTHOR>Walt Whitman</AUTHOR>
        <BINDING>hardcover</BINDING>
        <PAGES>462</PAGES>
        <PRICE>$7.75</PRICE>
    </BOOK>
    <BOOK>
        <COVER_IMAGE Source="Faun.gif" />
        <TITLE>The Marble Faun</TITLE>
        <AUTHOR>Nathaniel Hawthorne</AUTHOR>
        <BINDING>trade paperback</BINDING>
        <PAGES>473</PAGES>
        <PRICE>$10.95</PRICE>
    </BOOK>
    <BOOK>
        <COVER_IMAGE Source="Moby.gif" />
        <TITLE>Moby-Dick <SUBTITLE>Or, The Whale</SUBTITLE></TITLE>
```

```
        <AUTHOR>Herman Melville</AUTHOR>
        <BINDING>hardcover</BINDING>
        <PAGES>724</PAGES>
        <PRICE>$9.95</PRICE>
    </BOOK>
</INVENTORY>
```

Listing 3-2.

note

The document you typed uses the cascading style sheet (CSS) named Inventory02.css that you created in a previous exercise. (It's given in Listing 2-4 and is on the companion CD.) Make sure that this style sheet file is in the same folder as Inventory03.xml.

3   In Windows Explorer or in a folder window, double-click the name of the file that you saved, Inventory03.xml:

Internet Explorer will now display the document as shown here:

3

Well-Formed Documents

The document you entered contains the following types of elements:

- An element with a comment as part of its content (INVENTORY). Notice that the browser doesn't display the comment text.

- An empty element named COVER_IMAGE at the beginning of each BOOK element. The purpose of this element is to tell the XML application to display the specified image of the book's cover. (The *Source* attribute contains the name of the image file.) To be able to actually show the image, however, you would need to display the XML document using one of the methods discussed in Chapters 10 through 12, rather than using a simple CSS as in this example.

- An element (the TITLE element for *Moby-Dick*) that contains both character data and a child element (SUBTITLE). Notice that the browser displays both the character data and the child element on a single line, using the same format. (The CSS format assigned to the TITLE element is inherited by the SUBTITLE element.)

Adding Attributes to Elements

In the start-tag of an element, or in an empty-element tag, you can include one or more *attribute specifications*. An attribute specification is a name-value pair that is associated with the element. For example, the following PRICE element includes an attribute named *Type*, which is assigned the value *retail*:

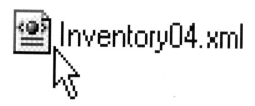

For other books, this attribute might, for example, be set to *wholesale*.

The following BOOK element includes two attributes, *Category* and *Display*:

```
<BOOK Category="fiction" Display="emphasize">
    <TITLE>The Marble Faun</TITLE>
    <AUTHOR>Nathaniel Hawthorne</AUTHOR>
    <BINDING>trade paperback</BINDING>
    <PAGES>473</PAGES>
    <PRICE>$10.95</PRICE>
</BOOK>
```

The following empty element includes an attribute named *Source*, which indicates the name of the file containing the image to be displayed:

```
<COVER_IMAGE Source="Faun.gif" />
```

Adding an attribute provides an alternative way to include information in an element. Attributes offer several advantages. For example, if you write a valid document using a document type definition (DTD), you can constrain the types of data that can be assigned to an attribute and you can specify a default value that an attribute will be assigned if you omit the specification. (You'll learn these techniques in Chapter 5.) In contrast, in a DTD you can't specify a data type or a default value for the character data content of an element.

> **note**
>
> If you write a valid document using an XML schema, as described in Chapter 7, you can constrain the data type for either an attribute's value or an element's character data.

Typically, you place the bulk of the element's data that you intend to display within the element's content. And you use attributes to store various properties of the element, not necessarily intended to be displayed, such as a category or a display instruction. The XML specification, however, makes no rigid distinctions about the types of information that should be stored within attributes or content, and you can use them any way you want to organize your XML documents.

> **note**
>
> When you display an XML document using a CSS (the method covered in Chapters 8 and 9), the browser does not display attributes or their values. Displaying an XML document using data binding (Chapter 10), a script in an HTML page (Chapter 11), or an XSLT style sheet (Chapter 12), however, allows you to access attributes and their values and to display the values or perform other appropriate actions.

Rules for Creating Attributes

As you can see, an attribute specification consists of an attribute name followed by an equal sign (=) followed by an attribute value. You can choose any attribute name you want, provided that you follow these rules:

■ The name must begin with a letter or an underscore (_), followed by zero or more letters, digits, periods (.), hyphens (-), or underscores.

■ The XML specification states that names beginning with the prefix *xml* (in any combination of uppercase or lowercase letters) are "reserved for standardization." Although Internet Explorer doesn't enforce this restriction, it's better not to use this prefix to avoid future problems.

■ You can assign the attribute name to a namespace by placing a namespace prefix followed by a colon (:) in front of the attribute name, as explained in "Using Namespaces" on page 69. The attribute name itself must still conform to the first two rules, even if you place a namespace prefix and colon in front of it. That is, it must begin with a letter or underscore and it shouldn't start with *xml*.

■ A particular attribute name can appear only once in the same start-tag or empty-element tag. (You can, however, have identically named attributes in a tag if they are in different namespaces.)

note

You can assign an attribute a name that's already used by an element type. Doing so, however, might introduce an unnecessary source of confusion into your document.

For example, the attribute names in the following start-tags are legal:

```
<ANIMATION FileName="Waldo.ani">
<LIST _1stPlace="Sam">
<ENTRY Zip.Code="94941">
<STANZA xml:space="preserve"> <!-- 'xml:' is allowed because it
                                  designates a predefined
                                  namespace. -->
```

The following attribute names, however, are illegal:

```
<!-- Duplicated attribute name in same tag: -->
<ANIMATION FileName="Waldo1.ani" FileName="Waldo2.ani">
<LIST 1stPlace="Sam"> <!-- Digit not allowed as
                           first character. -->
```

Rules for Legal Attribute Values

The value you assign to an attribute is a series of characters delimited with quotes, known as a *quoted string* or *literal*. You can assign any literal value to an attribute, provided that you observe these rules:

- The string can be delimited using either single quotes (') or double quotes (").

- The string cannot contain the same quote character used to delimit it.

- The string can contain character references or references to general internal entities. (I'll explain character and entity references in Chapter 6.)

- The string cannot include the ampersand (&) character, except to begin a character or entity reference.

- The string cannot include the left angle bracket (<) character.

You've already seen examples of legal attribute specifications. The following attribute specifications are illegal:

```
<EMPLOYEE Status="""downsized""> <!-- Can't use delimiting quote
                                      within string. -->
<ALBUM Type="<CD>"> <!-- Can't use < within string. -->
<WEATHER Forecast="Cold & Windy"> <!-- Can't use & except to
                                      start a reference. -->
```

If you want to include double quotes (") within the attribute value, you can use single quotes (') to delimit the string, as in this example:

```
<EMPLOYEE Status='"downsized"'> <!-- Legal attribute value. -->
```

Likewise, to include a single quote within the value, delimit it using double quotes:

```
<CANDIDATE name="W.T. 'Bill' Bagley"> <!-- Legal attribute value. -->
```

tip

You can get around the character restrictions and enter *any* character into an attribute value (including a character not on your keyboard) by using a character reference or—if available—a predefined general entity reference. I'll explain character and predefined general entity references in Chapter 6.

If you create a well-formed document without a document type definition (DTD) or XML schema, as done in this chapter, you can assign an attribute any value that conforms to the rules described above. However, as you'll learn in Chapters 5 and 7, when you create a DTD or XML schema and define attributes within it, you can limit the types of values that can be assigned to a particular attribute. For example, you could define an attribute that can be assigned only the value *yes* or *no*.

> ## note
> Before the Internet Explorer XML processor passes the value of an attribute to the application, it replaces each tab character in an attribute's value with a single space character. Also, according to the XML specification, in all text it passes to the application, the processor must convert a carriage-return and line feed character pair, or a carriage-return without a following line feed, to a single line feed character. The XML specification calls for additional *normalization* (that is, editing) of white space in attribute values, but Internet Explorer doesn't conform to these requirements. (See the section "3.3.3 Attribute-Value Normalization" in the XML specification at *http://www.w3.org/TR/REC-xml.*)

Convert Content to Attributes

1   Open a new, empty text file in your text editor, and type in the XML document shown in Listing 3-3. (You'll find a copy of this listing on the companion CD under the filename Inventory04.xml.) If you want, you can use the Inventory.xml document you previously typed (given in Listing 2-1 and included on the companion CD) as a starting point.

2   Use your text editor's Save command to save the document on your hard disk with the filename Inventory04.xml.

Inventory04.xml

```
<?xml version="1.0"?>

<!-- File Name: Inventory04.xml -->

<?xml-stylesheet type="text/css" href="Inventory02.css"?>
```

```
<INVENTORY>
   <BOOK Binding="mass market paperback">
      <TITLE>The Adventures of Huckleberry Finn</TITLE>
      <AUTHOR Born="1835">Mark Twain</AUTHOR>
      <PAGES>298</PAGES>
      <PRICE>$5.49</PRICE>
   </BOOK>
   <BOOK Binding="hardcover">
      <TITLE>Leaves of Grass</TITLE>
      <AUTHOR Born="1819">Walt Whitman</AUTHOR>
      <PAGES>462</PAGES>
      <PRICE>$7.75</PRICE>
   </BOOK>
   <BOOK Binding="trade paperback">
      <TITLE>The Marble Faun</TITLE>
      <AUTHOR Born="1804">Nathaniel Hawthorne</AUTHOR>
      <PAGES>473</PAGES>
      <PRICE>$10.95</PRICE>
   </BOOK>
   <BOOK Binding="hardcover">
      <TITLE>Moby-Dick</TITLE>
      <AUTHOR Born="1819">Herman Melville</AUTHOR>
      <PAGES>724</PAGES>
      <PRICE>$9.95</PRICE>
   </BOOK>
</INVENTORY>
```

Listing 3-3.

note

The document you typed uses the CSS named Inventory02.css that you cre-ated in a previous exercise. (It's given in Listing 2-4 and on the companion CD.) Make sure that this style sheet file is in the same folder as Inventory04.xml.

3   In Windows Explorer or in a folder window, double-click the name of the file that you saved, Inventory04.xml: Inventory04.xml

Internet Explorer will now display the document as shown here:

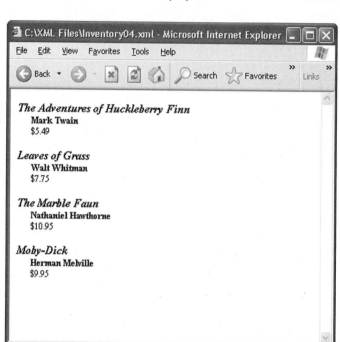

The document you typed is based on Inventory.xml, which you created in a previous exercise. In addition to having fewer elements than Inventory.xml, the new document has two modifications that illustrate the use of attributes:

- In each BOOK element, the book's binding information was converted from content (in the form of the BINDING nested element) to an attribute named *Binding*. You might make this conversion if, for example, you wanted to store the binding type but didn't want to show it along with the other book information when displaying the document using a CSS. (In the figure above, notice that Internet Explorer doesn't display the attribute values.) Also, if you included a DTD in the document, storing *Binding* as an attribute would allow you to restrict its permissible values to a set of choices (perhaps *hardcover* or *paperback*), as detailed in Chapter 5.

- An attribute named *Born* was added to each AUTHOR element to store the author's birth date. This is an example of less important information that you might want to store but not necessarily display.

One way to hide such information—and indicate its lesser importance—is to assign it to an attribute rather than placing it in the content of an element.

These are only a few of the many possible uses for attributes. You'll see more in
Chapter 5.

Using Namespaces

Combining XML data from several sources can result in conflicts in the names
of elements and attributes. Suppose, for example, that you keep track of your
books in one XML document:

```
<?xml version="1.0"?>
<COLLECTION>
    <ITEM Status="in">
        <TITLE>The Adventures of Huckleberry Finn</TITLE>
        <AUTHOR>Mark Twain</AUTHOR>
        <PRICE>$5.49</PRICE>
    </ITEM>
    <ITEM Status="out">
        <TITLE>Leaves of Grass</TITLE>
        <AUTHOR>Walt Whitman</AUTHOR>
        <PRICE>$7.75</PRICE>
    </ITEM>
    <ITEM Status="out">
        <TITLE>The Legend of Sleepy Hollow</TITLE>
        <AUTHOR>Washington Irving</AUTHOR>
        <PRICE>$2.95</PRICE>
    </ITEM>
    <ITEM Status="in">
        <TITLE>The Marble Faun</TITLE>
        <AUTHOR>Nathaniel Hawthorne</AUTHOR>
        <PRICE>$10.95</PRICE>
    </ITEM>
</COLLECTION>
```

and that you keep track of your CDs in another XML document:

```
<?xml version="1.0"?>
<COLLECTION>
    <ITEM>
        <TITLE>Violin Concerto in D</TITLE>
```

```
      <COMPOSER>Beethoven</COMPOSER>
      <PRICE>$14.95</PRICE>
   </ITEM>
   <ITEM>
      <TITLE>Violin Concertos Numbers 1, 2, and 3</TITLE>
      <COMPOSER>Mozart</COMPOSER>
      <PRICE>$16.49</PRICE>
   </ITEM>
</COLLECTION>
```

Now suppose you want to combine these documents into a single XML document that tracks both your collections, and you want to combine the applications (perhaps Web page scripts) that manage these documents into a single application (maybe a combined Web page script). The problem is that in the pooled document the new application would not be able to differentiate book items from CD items (ITEM elements), book titles from CD titles (TITLE elements), and book prices from CD prices (PRICE elements). This would make it difficult, for instance, for the application to list all CD items, to display all book titles, or to find the average price of your CDs. Although you could probably devise a way to distinguish the different types of ITEM, TITLE, and PRICE elements, the solution would probably involve rewriting parts of either the XML document or the application.

The XML namespace mechanism provides an easier way. It allows you to easily differentiate two or more elements, or two or more attributes, that have the same name by assigning each to a separate namespace. Listing 3-4 shows a combined document created by merging the two documents shown above. (You'll find a copy of this listing on the companion CD under the filename Collection.xml.) In the combined document, each of the elements for a book (ITEM, TITLE, AUTHOR, and PRICE) is assigned to the *book* namespace and each of the elements for a CD (ITEM, TITLE, COMPOSER, and PRICE) is assigned to the *cd* namespace. In this document, an application—or a human reader—can easily distinguish a book item (*book:ITEM*) from a CD item (*cd:ITEM*), a book title (*book:TITLE*) from a CD title (*cd:TITLE*), or a book price (*book:PRICE*) from a CD price (*cd:PRICE*).

Collection.xml

```
<?xml version="1.0"?>

<!-- File Name: Collection.xml -->

<COLLECTION
   xmlns:book="http://www.mjyOnline.com/books"
   xmlns:cd="http://www.mjyOnline.com/cds">

   <book:ITEM Status="in">
      <book:TITLE>The Adventures of Huckleberry Finn</book:TITLE>
      <book:AUTHOR>Mark Twain</book:AUTHOR>
      <book:PRICE>$5.49</book:PRICE>
   </book:ITEM>
   <cd:ITEM>
      <cd:TITLE>Violin Concerto in D</cd:TITLE>
      <cd:COMPOSER>Beethoven</cd:COMPOSER>
      <cd:PRICE>$14.95</cd:PRICE>
   </cd:ITEM>
   <book:ITEM Status="out">
      <book:TITLE>Leaves of Grass</book:TITLE>
      <book:AUTHOR>Walt Whitman</book:AUTHOR>
      <book:PRICE>$7.75</book:PRICE>
   </book:ITEM>
   <cd:ITEM>
      <cd:TITLE>Violin Concertos Numbers 1, 2, and 3</cd:TITLE>
      <cd:COMPOSER>Mozart</cd:COMPOSER>
      <cd:PRICE>$16.49</cd:PRICE>
   </cd:ITEM>
   <book:ITEM Status="out">
      <book:TITLE>The Legend of Sleepy Hollow</book:TITLE>
      <book:AUTHOR>Washington Irving</book:AUTHOR>
      <book:PRICE>$2.95</book:PRICE>
   </book:ITEM>
   <book:ITEM Status="in">
      <book:TITLE>The Marble Faun</book:TITLE>
      <book:AUTHOR>Nathaniel Hawthorne</book:AUTHOR>
      <book:PRICE>$10.95</book:PRICE>
   </book:ITEM>
</COLLECTION>
```

Listing 3-4.

To use a namespace, you must declare it within an element start-tag by using a special-purpose attribute specification. In the Collection.xml document in Listing 3-4, both namespaces are declared in the start-tag of the COLLECTION root element:

```
<COLLECTION
    xmlns:book="http://www.mjyOnline.com/books"
    xmlns:cd="http://www.mjyOnline.com/cds">
```

Here's a close up of the *book* namespace declaration:

```
xmlns:book="www.mjyOnline.com/books"
```

Namespace name

> **note**
>
> For guidelines on creating a DTD for an XML document that uses namespaces, see "Using Namespaces in Valid Documents" on page 118.

In the declaration, the *namespace name* is the actual identifier of the namespace and should be a URI (see the sidebar "URIs, URLs, and URNs" on page 73). A namespace is identified using a URI, not because the XML processor or application needs to actually access any information at that URI, but rather simply because URIs are globally unique. As a result, in an XML document you can use and combine elements or attributes belonging to literally any namespace created by an individual or organization anywhere without danger of conflicting names. When you create a namespace yourself (rather than use a namespace provided by another party), you should choose a permanent URI that you control (as I did in creating the examples in this section), to avoid conflicting with someone else's namespace. This is especially important if you intend for your elements, attributes, or applications to be used by others.

URIs, URLs, and URNs

In their specifications, the W3C uses the newer and broader term URI (Uniform Resource Identifier) rather than the more familiar but narrower term URL (Uniform Resource Locator). The term URI is all-inclusive, referring to Internet resource-addressing strings that use any of the present or future addressing schemes. URIs currently include the following:

- URLs, which use traditional addressing schemes such as http (for example, *http://www.mjyOnline.com*), ftp (for example, *ftp://ftp.microsoft.com/*), and mailto (for example, *mailto:someone@microsoft.com*).

- URNs (Uniform Resource Names), which use the newer URN addressing scheme. This scheme is intended to address Internet resources in a way that is location-independent and is stable over time (unlike URLs, which often change). The following are several examples of URNs drawn from the W3C namespace specification: *urn:loc.gov:books*, *urn:ISBN:0-395-36341-6*, and *urn:w3-org-ns:HTML*. For complete information on URN syntax, see *http://www.ietf.org/rfc/rfc2141.txt*.

For much more information on URIs, see the following page on the W3C Web site: *http://www.w3.org/Addressing/*.

The *xmlns* in the namespace declaration is a predefined prefix (you don't have to declare it) that is used specifically for defining namespaces. And *book* is the *namespace prefix*, which is a shorthand notation for the full namespace name. You use the namespace prefix to qualify the names of specific elements or attributes, indicating that they belong to the namespace. A valid namespace prefix must begin with a letter or underscore (_), followed by zero or more letters, digits, periods (.), hyphens (-), or underscores. Beginning a prefix with the letters *xml* (in any case combination) is reserved for prefixes defined by XML-related specifications.

You can use the prefix anywhere within the element in which the namespace has been defined or within any of its nested elements; this set of elements is known as the *scope* of the namespace. In the example document, the *book* prefix can be used to qualify names anywhere within the COLLECTION element. For instance, here's the way the *book* prefix is used to indicate that a TITLE element belongs to the *book* (that is, the *http://www.mjyOnline.com/books*) namespace:

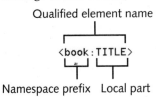

Qualified element name

`<book:TITLE>`

Namespace prefix   Local part

> **note**
>
> You can use a namespace prefix to qualify the name of the element in which the namespace is declared, even though the prefix is used before it's declared. In the example document, if you declared the *cd* namespace within a TITLE element (rather than within the COLLECTION element), you could still apply that prefix to the element name:
>
> ```
> <cd:TITLE xmlns:cd="http://www.mjyOnline.com/cds">
>     Violin Concerto in D
> </cd:TITLE>
> ```

As an alternative to creating a namespace prefix and using it to explicitly qualify individual names, you can declare a *default namespace* within an element, which will apply to the element in which it is declared (if that element has no namespace prefix), and to all elements with no prefix within the content of that element. Listing 3-5 shows the XML document from Listing 3-4 but with the *book* namespace (*http://www.mjyOnline.com/books*) declared as a default namespace, so that it doesn't have to be explicitly applied to each of the book-related elements. (You'll find a copy of this listing on the companion CD under the filename Collection Default.xml.)

Collection Default.xml

```
<?xml version="1.0"?>

<!-- File Name: Collection Default.xml -->

<COLLECTION
    xmlns="http://www.mjyOnline.com/books"
    xmlns:cd="http://www.mjyOnline.com/cds">

    <ITEM Status="in">
        <TITLE>The Adventures of Huckleberry Finn</TITLE>
        <AUTHOR>Mark Twain</AUTHOR>
        <PRICE>$5.49</PRICE>
    </ITEM>
    <cd:ITEM>
        <cd:TITLE>Violin Concerto in D</cd:TITLE>
        <cd:COMPOSER>Beethoven</cd:COMPOSER>
        <cd:PRICE>$14.95</cd:PRICE>
    </cd:ITEM>
    <ITEM Status="out">
```

```
        <TITLE>Leaves of Grass</TITLE>
        <AUTHOR>Walt Whitman</AUTHOR>
        <PRICE>$7.75</PRICE>
    </ITEM>
    <cd:ITEM>
        <cd:TITLE>Violin Concertos Numbers 1, 2, and 3</cd:TITLE>
        <cd:COMPOSER>Mozart</cd:COMPOSER>
        <cd:PRICE>$16.49</cd:PRICE>
    </cd:ITEM>
    <ITEM Status="out">
        <TITLE>The Legend of Sleepy Hollow</TITLE>
        <AUTHOR>Washington Irving</AUTHOR>
        <PRICE>$2.95</PRICE>
    </ITEM>
    <ITEM Status="in">
        <TITLE>The Marble Faun</TITLE>
        <AUTHOR>Nathaniel Hawthorne</AUTHOR>
        <PRICE>$10.95</PRICE>
    </ITEM>
</COLLECTION>
```

Listing 3-5.

You declare a default namespace by assigning the namespace name to the reserved *xmlns* attribute. In the example document in Listing 3-5, this is done in the COLLECTION element start-tag:

```
<COLLECTION
    xmlns="http://www.mjyOnline.com/books"
    xmlns:cd="http://www.mjyOnline.com/cds">
```

As a result, the COLLECTION element and all nested elements within it that don't have prefixes (namely, the book-related elements) belong to the namespace named *http://www.mjyOnline.com/books*. The CD-related elements all have the *cd* prefix, which explicitly assigns them to the *cd* namespace rather than the default namespace.

You can override the default namespace within a nested element by assigning a different value to *xmlns* within that element. For instance, in the example document in Listing 3-5, if you defined an ITEM element for a CD as follows, the ITEM element and all elements within it would *not* belong to a namespace. (If you assign an empty string to *xmlns*, all nonprefixed elements within the scope of the assignment are considered not to belong to a namespace.)

```
<ITEM xmlns="">
   <TITLE>Violin Concerto in D</TITLE>
   <COMPOSER>Beethoven</COMPOSER>
   <PRICE>$14.95</PRICE>
</ITEM>
```

Note that the default namespace does not apply to attributes within its scope. Rather, you always need to designate the namespace of an attribute by explicitly adding a namespace prefix, as in the following example:

```
<ITEM xmlns:inv="http://www.mjyOnline.com/Inventory Control"
     inv:Status="3" Status="in">
   <TITLE>The Marble Faun</TITLE>
   <AUTHOR>Nathaniel Hawthorne</AUTHOR>
   <PRICE>$10.95</PRICE>
</ITEM>
```

As shown here, you can have two attributes with the same name in a start-tag if you assign a unique namespace to one of them.

As you can see, the namespace mechanism makes XML more modular. It allows you to join together XML documents, as well as the applications that process them, without danger of conflicting element and attribute names. Also, XML standards for enhancing documents often require you to use specific elements and attributes so that the applications that handle the documents can recognize them. The names of these elements and attributes belong to unique namespaces to avoid colliding with names you've chosen to use in your documents. The following are examples of such standards covered in the book:

- The XML specification itself includes the reserved *xml:space* and *xml:lang* attributes described in this chapter. Because they belong to a unique namespace, which is referenced using the predefined *xml* namespace prefix, you are free to use the *space* and *lang* names for other attributes in your documents. Because the *xml* namespace prefix is defined by the XML specification itself, you don't have to declare it.

- As you'll learn in Chapter 7, you create an XML schema by using a standard set of elements that belong to the namespace named *http://www.w3.org/2001/XMLSchema*.

- As explained in Chapter 8, if you display a document using a CSS, you can insert HTML elements into your document by using XML elements that represent the HTML elements and that are prefaced with the *html* namespace prefix, which you need to declare.

■ When you create an XSLT style sheet, as described in Chapter 12, you use a standard set of elements that belong to the namespace named *http://www.w3.org/1999/XSL/Transform*.

note

For more information on using namespaces in XML, see the topic "Using Namespaces in Documents" in the Microsoft XML SDK 4.0 help file, or the same topic in the XML SDK documentation provided by the MSDN (Microsoft Developer Network) Library on the Web at *http://msdn.microsoft.com/library*. You'll find the official W3C XML namespace specification on the Web at *http://www.w3.org/TR/REC-xml-names/*.

Well-Formed Documents
3

Characters, Encoding, and Languages

The characters you can enter into an XML document are tab, carriage-return, line feed, and any of the legal characters belonging to the Unicode character set (or the equivalent ISO/IEC 10646 character set), which includes characters for all the world's written languages. (For more information on these character sets and the specific characters you can use in XML, see the section "2.2 Characters" in the XML specification at *http://www.w3.org/TR/REC-xml*.)

An XML file can represent, or *encode*, the Unicode characters in different ways. For example, if the file uses the encoding scheme known as UTF-8, it represents a capital *A* as the number 65 stored in 8 bits (41 in hexadecimal). However, if it uses the encoding scheme known as UTF-16, it represents a capital *A* as the number 65 stored in 16 bits (0041 in hexadecimal).

If you save your XML document in a plain text format using Notepad or another text or programming editor, and if you use only the standard ASCII characters (characters numbered 1 through 127 in the Unicode character set, which are the common characters you can directly enter using an English language keyboard), it's unlikely that you'll have to worry about encoding. That's because an XML processor will assume that the file uses the UTF-8 encoding scheme, and in a plain text file ASCII characters (and only ASCII characters) are normally encoded in conformance with the UTF-8 scheme.

continued

continued

Suppose, however, that you want to be able to type characters that aren't in the ASCII set directly into your element character data or your attribute values, such as the á and ñ in the following element:

```
<AUTHOR>Vicente Blasco Ibáñez</AUTHOR>
```

In this case, you must do two things:

1   Make sure that the XML file is encoded using a scheme that the XML processor can understand. All conforming XML processors must be able to handle UTF-8 and UTF-16 encoded files, so try to use one of these schemes. Some XML processors, however, support additional encoding schemes you can use.

To create your XML document, you must use a word processor or other program that can create text files in which all characters are uniformly encoded in a supported scheme. For example, you can create a UTF-8 encoded XML document by opening or creating it in Microsoft Word 2002, and then saving the file by choosing the Save As command from the File menu, selecting Plain Text (*.txt) in the Save As Type drop-down list in the Save As dialog box, clicking the Save button, and then in the File Conversion dialog box selecting the Unicode (UTF-8) encoding scheme. (In Word 2000, you need to select Encoded Text (*.txt) in the Save As Type drop-down list rather than Plain Text (*.txt).)

The Microsoft Notepad editor supplied with some versions of Windows also lets you select the encoding scheme when you save a file.

2   If your XML document is encoded in a scheme other than UTF-8 or UTF-16, you must specify the name of the scheme by including an *encoding declaration* in the XML declaration, immediately following the version information. For example, the following encoding declaration indicates that the file is encoded using the ISO-8859-1 scheme:

```
<?xml version="1.0" encoding="ISO-8859-1" ?>
```

(If you also include a *standalone* document declaration, as described in the sidebar "The *standalone* Document Declaration" on page 159, it must go *after* the encoding declaration.) If the XML processor can't handle the specified encoding scheme, it will generate a fatal error.

Also, if your XML document references an external DTD subset (described in Chapter 5) or an external parsed entity (described in Chapter

6), and if the file containing the subset or entity uses an encoding scheme other than UTF-8 or UTF-16, you must include a *text declaration* at the very beginning of the file. A text declaration is similar to an XML declaration, except that the version information is optional, the encoding declaration is mandatory, and it can't include a *standalone* document declaration. Here's an example:

```
<?xml version="1.0" encoding="ISO-8859-1" ?>
```

(In an external parsed entity, the text declaration *is not* part of the entity's replacement text that gets inserted by an entity reference.)

You can also insert non-ASCII characters into any XML document, regardless of its encoding, by using character references as discussed in "Inserting Character References" on page 153.

The XML specification's support for the Unicode character set allows you to freely include characters belonging to any written language. It might also be important to tell the application that handles your document the specific language used for the text in a particular element. For example, the application might need to know the language of the text in order to display it properly on the screen or to check its spelling. XML reserves an attribute named *xml:lang* for this purpose. (The *xml:* indicates that this attribute belongs to the *xml* namespace. Because this namespace is predefined, you don't have to declare it. See "Using Namespaces" on page 69.) To specify the language of the text in a particular element (the text in the element's character data as well as its attribute values) include an *xml:lang* attribute specification in the element's start-tag, assigning it an identifier for the language, as in the following example elements:

```
<!-- This element contains U.S. English text: -->
<TITLE xml:lang="en-US">The Color Purple</TITLE>

<!-- This element contains British English text: -->
<TITLE xml:lang="en-GB">Colours I Have Known</TITLE>

<!-- This element contains generic English text: -->
<TITLE xml:lang="en">The XML Story</TITLE>

<!-- This element contains German text: -->
<TITLE xml:lang="de">Der Richter und Sein Henker</TITLE>
```

Well-Formed Documents

3

continued

continued

For a description of the official language identifiers you can assign to *xml:lang*, see the section "2.12 Language Identification" in the XML specification at *http://www.w3.org/TR/REC-xml*. The *xml:lang* attribute specification applies to the element in which it occurs and to any nested elements, unless it is overridden by another *xml:lang* attribute specification in a nested element. To indicate the language of the text throughout your entire document, just include *xml:lang* in the document element.

The *xml:lang* attribute doesn't affect the behavior of the XML processor. The processor merely passes the attribute specification on to the application, which can use the value as appropriate. The XML specification doesn't say how the *xml:lang* setting must be used.

When you get to Chapters 5 and 7 on creating valid documents, keep in mind that in a valid document the *xml:lang* attribute must be defined just like any other attribute. (This will make sense when you read those chapters.) For instance, in a DTD you could define this attribute as in the following example attribute-list declaration:

```
<!ATTLIST TITLE   xml:lang NMTOKEN #REQUIRED>
```

4

Adding Comments, Processing Instructions, and CDATA Sections

In this chapter, you'll learn how to add three types of XML markup to your documents: comments, processing instructions, and CDATA sections. While these items aren't required in a well-formed (or valid) XML document, they can be useful. You can use comments to make your document more understandable when read by humans. You can use processing instructions to modify the way an application handles or displays your document. And you can use CDATA sections to include almost any combination of characters within an element's character data.

Inserting Comments

As you learned in Chapter 1, the sixth goal in the XML specification is that "XML documents should be human-legible and reasonably clear." Well-placed and meaningful comments can greatly enhance the human readability and clarity of an XML document, just as comments can make program source code such as C or BASIC much more understandable. The XML processor ignores comment text, although it may pass the text on to the application.

> **note**
>
> In Microsoft Internet Explorer, the XML processor makes the text of a comment available to a script written within an HTML Web page and to an XSLT style sheet. In Chapter 11, you'll learn how to use scripts to access comment text as well as other components of an XML document, and in Chapter 12 you'll discover how to create XSLT style sheets that can access and display comments and other XML document components. Internet Explorer also displays all comments contained in an XML document if you open the document directly in the browser and if the document doesn't have an attached style sheet.

The Form of a Comment

A comment begins with the <!-- characters and ends with the --> characters. Between these two delimiters, you can type any characters you want—except a double hyphen (--), or a hyphen at the end (in others words, you can't end a comment with --->). You can even type the often forbidden left angle bracket (<) and ampersand (&) characters. Here's an example of a legal comment:

```
<!-- Here you can type any text except a double hyphen.
     The < and & characters are OK! -->
```

Where You Can Place Comments

You can insert a comment anywhere in an XML document outside of other markup. In other words, you can put them in the document prolog:

```
<?xml version="1.0"?>
<!-- Here is a comment in the prolog. -->

<DOCELEMENT>
This is a very simple XML document.
</DOCELEMENT>
```

You can insert them following the document element:

```
<?xml version="1.0"?>

<DOCELEMENT>
This is a very simple XML document.
</DOCELEMENT>
<!-- This comment follows the document element. -->
```

And you can place them within an element's content:

```
<?xml version="1.0"?>

<DOCELEMENT>
<!-- This comment is part of the content of the root element. -->
This is a very simple XML document.
</DOCELEMENT>
```

Here's an example of a comment that's illegal because it's placed within markup:

```
<?xml version="1.0"?>

<DOCELEMENT <!-- This is an ILLEGAL comment! --> >
This is a very simple XML document.
</DOCELEMENT>
```

You can, however, place a comment within a document type definition (DTD)—even though a DTD is part of markup—provided that it's not within a markup declaration in the DTD. You'll learn all about DTDs and how to place comments within them in Chapter 5.

Using Processing Instructions

For the most part an XML document doesn't include information on how the data is to be formatted or processed. However, the XML specification does provide a form of markup known as a *processing instruction* that lets you pass information to the application that isn't part of the document's data. The XML processor itself doesn't act on processing instructions, but merely hands the text to the application, which can use the information as appropriate.

note

Recall from Chapter 2 that the XML processor is the software module that reads and stores the contents of an XML document. The application is a separate software module that obtains the document's contents from the processor and then manipulates and displays these contents. When you display XML in Internet Explorer, the browser provides both the XML processor and at least the front end of the application. (If you write a script to manipulate and display an XML document, you are supplying part of the application yourself.)

The Form of a Processing Instruction

A processing instruction has the following general form:

```
<?target instruction ?>
```

Here, *target* is the name of the application to which the instruction is directed. Note that you can't insert white space—that is, space, tab, carriage-return, or line feed characters—between the first question mark (?) in the processing instruction and *target*. Any name is allowable, provided it follows these rules:

- The name must begin with a letter or underscore (_), followed by zero or more letters, digits, periods (.), hyphens (-), or underscores.

- The target name *xml*, in any combination of uppercase or lowercase letters, is reserved. (As you've seen, you use *xml* in lowercase letters for the document's XML declaration, which is a special type of processing instruction.) To avert possible conflicts with current or future reserved target names, you should also avoid beginning a target name with *xml* (in any combination of cases), although the Internet Explorer parser doesn't prohibit the use of such names.

And *instruction* is the information passed to the application. It can consist of any sequence of characters, except the character pair ?> (which is reserved for terminating the processing instruction).

How You Can Use Processing Instructions

The particular processing instructions that will be recognized depend upon the application that will be handling your XML document. If you're using Internet Explorer to display and work with your XML documents (as described throughout this book), you'll find two main uses for processing instructions:

- You can use standard, reserved processing instructions to tell Internet Explorer how to handle or display the document. An example you'll see in this book is the processing instruction that tells Internet Explorer to display the document using a particular style sheet. For instance, the following processing instruction tells Internet Explorer to use the cascading style sheet (CSS) located in the file Inventory01.css:

```
<?xml-stylesheet type="text/css" href="Inventory01.css"?>
```

◼ If you write a Web page script to handle and display an XML document, you can insert any nonreserved processing instructions into the document, and your script can read these instructions and take appropriate action. For example, you might insert the following processing instruction into a document to tell your script the level of detail to show:

```
<?MyScript detail="2" ?>
```

In Chapter 11, you'll learn how to use a script to access the components of an XML document, including any processing instructions. You can also access processing instructions from XSLT style sheets, which are covered in Chapter 12.

Where You Can Place Processing Instructions

You can insert a processing instruction anywhere in an XML document outside other markup—that is, you can insert it in the same places you can insert comments: in the document prolog, following the document element, or within an element's content. Here's an XML document with a processing instruction in each of these legal places:

```
<?xml version="1.0"?>

<!-- The following is a processing instruction in the prolog: -->
<?xml-stylesheet type="text/css" href="Inventory01.css"?>

<INVENTORY>
   <BOOK>
      <!-- Here's a processing instruction within an
           element's content: -->
      <?ScriptA emphasize="yes" ?>

      <TITLE>The Adventures of Huckleberry Finn</TITLE>
      <AUTHOR>Mark Twain</AUTHOR>
      <BINDING>mass market paperback</BINDING>
      <PAGES>298</PAGES>
      <PRICE>$5.49</PRICE>
   </BOOK>
   <BOOK>
      <TITLE>Leaves of Grass</TITLE>
      <AUTHOR>Walt Whitman</AUTHOR>
      <BINDING>hardcover</BINDING>
      <PAGES>462</PAGES>
      <PRICE>$7.75</PRICE>
```

```
   </BOOK>
</INVENTORY>

<!-- And here's one following the document element: -->
<?ScriptA Category="books" Style="formal" ?>
```

Here's an example of a processing instruction illegally placed within markup:

```
<!-- The following element contains an ILLEGAL
     processing instruction: -->
<BOOK <?ScriptA emphasize="yes" ?> >
   <TITLE>Leaves of Grass</TITLE>
   <AUTHOR>Walt Whitman</AUTHOR>
   <BINDING>hardcover</BINDING>
   <PAGES>462</PAGES>
   <PRICE>$7.75</PRICE>
</BOOK>
```

You can, however, place a processing instruction within a document type definition (DTD)—even though a DTD is part of markup—provided that it's not within a markup declaration in the DTD. You'll learn all about DTDs and how to place processing instructions within them in Chapter 5.

Including CDATA Sections

As you learned in Chapter 3, you can't directly insert a left angle bracket (<) or an ampersand (&) as part of an element's character data, because the XML parser would interpret either of these characters as the start of markup. One way to get around this restriction is to use a character reference (< representing < or & representing &) or a predefined general entity reference (< representing < or & representing &). You'll learn about character and predefined general entity references in Chapter 6. However, if you need to insert many < or & characters, using these references is awkward and makes the data difficult for humans to read. In this case, it's easier to place the text containing the restricted characters inside a CDATA section.

The Form of a CDATA Section

A CDATA section begins with the characters <![CDATA[and ends with the characters]]>. Between these two delimiting character groups, you can type any characters except]]>. You can freely include the often forbidden < and & characters. You can't include]]> because these characters would be interpreted as ending the CDATA section. All characters within the CDATA section are treated as a literal part of the element's character data, not as XML markup. (Since all characters you type are interpreted as character data, you couldn't create actual nested elements, comments, or other types of markup within a CDATA section even if you wanted to.)

note
Only the CDATA section delimiters <![CDATA[and]]> are classified as markup. The text between the delimiters is character data.

Here's an example of a legal CDATA section:

```
<![CDATA[
Here you can type any characters except two right brackets followed
by a greater-than symbol.
]]>
```

note
The keyword CDATA, like other XML keywords you'll see later, must be written in all uppercase letters.

If you want to include a block of source code or markup as part of an element's actual character data that will be displayed in the browser, you can use a CDATA section to prevent the XML parser from interpreting the < or & character as XML markup. Here's an example:

```
<A-SECTION>
The following is an example of a very simple HTML page:
<![CDATA[
<HTML>
<HEAD>
<TITLE>R. Jones & Sons</TITLE>
</HEAD>

<BODY>
<P>Welcome to our home page!</P>
</BODY>
```

```
</HTML>
]]>
</A-SECTION>
```

Without the CDATA section, the processor would assume that <HTML>, for example, is the start of a nested element rather than being a part of the A-SEC-TION element's character data.

> **note**
>
> Since you can directly insert < and & characters within a CDATA section, you don't need to use character references (< and &) or predefined general entity references (< and &) to add these characters. (I'll explain these references in Chapter 6.) In fact, if you used such a reference within a CDATA section, the parser would interpret each of the characters in the reference literally and wouldn't replace the reference with the < or & character.

Where You Can Place CDATA Sections

You can insert a CDATA section anywhere that character data can occur—that is, within an element's content but not within XML markup. Here's a legally placed CDATA section:

```
<?xml version="1.0"?>

<MUSICAL>
   <TITLE_PAGE>
      <![CDATA[
         <Oklahoma!>
              By
      Rogers & Hammerstein
      ]]>
   </TITLE_PAGE>

   <!-- Other elements here... -->

</MUSICAL>
```

The malformed XML document shown below contains two illegal CDATA sections. The first one is not within the content of an element. The second one is within the content of the document element but is also within a start-tag markup.

```
<?xml version="1.0"?>

<![CDATA[ ILLEGAL: not within an element's content! ]]>

<DOC_ELEMENT>
   <SUB_ELEMENT <![CDATA[ ILLEGAL: inside of markup! ]]> >
      sub-element content...
   </SUB_ELEMENT>
 </DOC_ELEMENT>
```

note

CDATA sections do not nest. That is, you cannot insert one CDATA section within another.

5

Creating Valid XML Documents Using Document Type Definitions

Valid XML documents meet a stricter set of criteria than do the merely well-formed documents that you've learned about in the previous chapters. In the first two sections of this chapter, you'll learn the basic requirements for a valid XML document and explore the advantages of making a document valid. In the remaining sections, you'll learn how to define the content and structure of a valid XML document by writing a document type definition (DTD), either in the document itself or in a separate file. This is the original method for creating valid XML documents and the techniques are an integral part of the XML specification. Chapter 6 continues the discussion on DTDs by showing you how to use entities. Defined in a DTD, entities allow you to store frequently used blocks of XML text, to incorporate different types of data in an XML document, and to modularize your XML documents.

In Chapter 7, you'll learn how to define the content and structure of a valid XML document by creating an XML schema in a separate file, rather than writing a DTD. This is a newer method for creating valid XML documents and is described in a separate specification.

I recommend you start by learning how to create DTDs, because they embody the most basic concepts and are so ubiquitous in the XML world. You can then go on to learn XML schemas, which are potentially more complex than DTDs, but provide many more features (for example, the ability to define a data type for an element's character data). XML schemas also offer the advantage of being written using the familiar syntax of standard XML elements and attributes. (As you'll soon learn, DTDs employ a syntax of their own.)

tip

If you decide to skip DTDs and learn only XML schemas, you should still read the first two sections of this chapter because they apply to both methods for defining valid documents.

The Basic Criteria for a Valid XML Document

Every XML document must be well-formed, meaning that it must meet the minimal requirements for an XML document that are given in the XML specification. If a document isn't well-formed, it can't be considered an XML document.

A well-formed XML document can also be valid. A valid XML document is a well-formed document that meets either of the following two additional requirements:

- The prolog of the document includes a proper *document type declaration,* which contains or references a *document type definition* (DTD) that defines the content and structure of the XML document, and the rest of the document conforms to the content and structure defined in the DTD.

- The document conforms to the document content and structure defined in an XML schema, which is contained in a separate file. (In Chapter 7 you'll learn how to create a schema, and in Chapter 11 you'll learn how to check whether a particular document conforms to a schema.)

The Advantages of Making an XML Document Valid

Creating a valid XML document might seem to be a lot of unnecessary bother: You must first fully define the document's content and structure in a DTD or XML schema and then create the document itself, following all the DTD or schema specifications. It might seem much easier to just immediately add whatever elements and attributes you need, as you did in the examples of well-formed documents in previous chapters.

If, however, you want to make sure that your document conforms to a specific structure or set of standards, providing a DTD or XML schema that describes the structure or standards allows an XML processor to check whether your document is in conformance. In other words, a DTD or XML schema provides a standard blueprint to the processor so that in checking the validity of the document, it can enforce the desired structure and guarantee that your document meets the required standards. If any part of the document doesn't conform to the DTD or XML schema specification, the processor can display an error message so that you can edit the document and make it conform.

Making an XML document valid also fosters consistency within that document. For example, a DTD or XML schema can force you to always use the same element type for describing a given piece of information (for instance, to always enter a book title using a TITLE element rather than a NAME element); it can ensure that you always assign a designated value to an attribute (for instance, *hardcover* rather than *hardback*); and it can catch misspellings or typos in element or attribute names (for instance, typing PHILUM rather than PHYLUM for an element name).

Making XML documents valid is especially useful for ensuring uniformity among a group of similar documents. In fact, the XML standard defines a DTD as "a grammar for a class of documents." Consider, for example, a Web publishing company that needs all its editors to create XML documents that conform to a common structure. Creating a single DTD or XML schema and using it for all documents can ensure that these documents uniformly comply with the required structure, and that editors don't add arbitrary new elements, place information in the wrong order, assign the wrong data types to attributes, and so on. Of course, the document must be run through a processor that checks its validity.

Including a DTD or XML schema and checking validity is especially important if the documents are going to be processed by custom software (such as a Web page script) that expects a particular document content and structure. If all users of the software use a common appropriate DTD or XML schema for their XML documents, and if the documents are checked for validity, the users can be sure that their documents will be recognized by the processing software. For example, if a group of mathematicians are creating mathematical documents that will be displayed using a particular program, they could all include in their documents a common DTD that defines the required structure, elements, attributes, and other features.

In fact, most of the "real-world" XML applications listed at the end of Chapter 1, such as MathML, consist of a standard DTD or XML schema that all users of the application use with their XML documents, so that checking the documents for validity ensures that they conform to the application's structure and will be recognized by any software designed for that application.

note

The Microsoft Internet Explorer processor will check a document for validity only if the document contains a document type declaration and you open the document through an HTML Web page (using the techniques you'll learn in Chapters 10 and 11), or if you use an XML schema as explained in Chapter 11.

If you open an XML document—one with or without a style sheet—directly in Internet Explorer (as you have done so far in this book and will do in Chapters 8, 9, and 12), the processor will check the entire document—including any document type declaration it contains—for well-formedness and will display a fatal error message for any infraction it encounters. However, the Internet Explorer processor will *not* check the document for validity, even if it contains a document type declaration.

To test a document with a DTD or XML schema for validity and to see messages for any well-formedness or validity errors the document contains, you can use one of the validity checking scripts (contained in HTML Web pages) that are given in "Checking an XML Document for Validity" on page 396. (These scripts are also provided on the companion CD.) You might want to read the instructions in that section now so that you can begin checking the validity of the XML documents you create.

Adding the Document Type Declaration

A document type declaration is a block of XML markup that you add to the prolog of a valid XML document. It can go anywhere within the prolog—outside of other markup—following the XML declaration. (Recall that if you include the XML declaration, it must be at the very beginning of the document.)

Document type declaration can go here...

```
                                   <?xml version="1.0"?>                          ┐
                                                                                   ├── Prolog
                                   <!-- File Name: Inventory.xml -->               ┘
...or here ──────
                   <INVENTORY>
                      <BOOK>
                          <TITLE>The Adventures of Huckleberry Finn</TITLE>
                          <AUTHOR>Mark Twain</AUTHOR>
                          <BINDING>mass market paperback</BINDING>
                          <PAGES>298</PAGES>
                          <PRICE>$5.49</PRICE>
                      </BOOK>
                          .
Document ────         .
element               .
                      <BOOK>
                          <TITLE>The Turn of the Screw</TITLE>
                          <AUTHOR>Henry James</AUTHOR>
                          <BINDING>trade paperback</BINDING>
                          <PAGES>384</PAGES>
                          <PRICE>$3.35</PRICE>
                      </BOOK>
                   </INVENTORY>
```

A document type declaration defines the content and structure of the document. If you open a document without a document type declaration (or XML schema) in Internet Explorer, the Internet Explorer processor will merely check that the document is well-formed. If, however, you open a document with a document type declaration in Internet Explorer, the processor will, under certain circumstances, check the document for validity as well as for well-formedness, and your document must therefore conform to all declarations within the document type declaration. (See the note at the end of the previous section for a description of the circumstances under which Internet Explorer checks for validity.) You won't, for example, be able to include any elements or attributes in the document that you haven't declared in the document type declaration. And every element and attribute that you do include must match the specifications (such as the allowable content of an element or the permissible type of an attribute value) expressed in the corresponding declaration.

Document Type Definitions

The Form of the Document Type Declaration

A document type declaration has the following general form:

```
<!DOCTYPE Name DTD>
```

Here, *Name* specifies the name of the document element. The name of the actual document element in the document must exactly match the name you enter here. (For a description of the rules that govern element names, review "The Anatomy of an Element" on page 53.) For instance, if you were creating a document type declaration for the Inventory.xml example document shown in Chapter 2 (Listing 2-1), you would use the name INVENTORY:

```
<!DOCTYPE INVENTORY DTD>
```

(This isn't a complete document type declaration yet. *DTD* still has to be replaced with the actual content.)

DTD is the document type definition, which contains the declarations that define the document's elements, attributes, and other features. In the next section, you'll see its form.

note

DOCTYPE must be in all uppercase letters.

Creating the Document Type Definition

The document type definition (DTD) consists of a left square bracket character ([), followed by a series of markup declarations, followed by a right square bracket character (]). *Markup declarations* describe the logical content and structure of the document; that is, they define the document's elements, attributes, and other features. Here's a complete valid XML document containing a DTD with a single markup declaration that defines the document's one element type, SIMPLE:

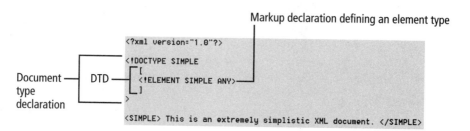

Markup declaration defining an element type

```
<?xml version="1.0"?>
<!DOCTYPE SIMPLE
  [
    <!ELEMENT SIMPLE ANY>
  ]
>
<SIMPLE> This is an extremely simplistic XML document. </SIMPLE>
```

Document type declaration — DTD

The DTD in this example document specifies that the document can contain only elements of type SIMPLE (that's the only element type defined), and that a SIMPLE element can have any possible type of content (the ANY keyword).

A DTD can contain the following types of markup declarations:

- **Element type declarations.** These define the types of elements the document can contain, as well as the content and order of the elements. Element type declarations are described in the next section.

- **Attribute-list declarations.** Each attribute-list declaration defines the names of the attributes that can be used with a particular element type, as well as the data types and default values of these attributes. I'll cover these declarations later in the chapter.

- **Entity declarations.** You can use entities to store frequently used blocks of text, to incorporate non-XML data in your document, and to modularize your XML documents. I'll explain them in Chapter 6.

- **Notation declarations.** A notation describes a data format, or identifies the program used to process a particular format. I'll discuss notations in Chapter 6.

- **Processing instructions.** I explained these in the section "Using Processing Instructions" in Chapter 4.

- **Comments.** I discussed these in the section "Inserting Comments" in Chapter 4.

- **Parameter entity references.** Any of the above items in this list can be contained within a parameter entity and inserted by means of a parameter entity reference. This statement won't really make sense until you read Chapter 6, but I've included it here for completeness.

note

The type of DTD discussed in this section (and shown in the examples in the following sections) is known as an *internal DTD subset* because it's included entirely within the document type declaration in the document. Near the end of the chapter, you'll learn how to use a DTD located in a separate file, which is known as an *external DTD subset*.

Well-Formedness and Validity Constraints

Well-formedness constraints are a set of rules given in the XML specification that you must follow—in addition to the rules specified in the formal XML grammar—to create a well-formed document. Because an XML document must be well-formed, any violation of a well-formedness constraint or any other failure to achieve well-formedness is considered a *fatal error*. When the XML processor encounters a fatal error, it must stop normal processing of the document and not attempt to recover.

Validity constraints are a further set of rules in the XML specification that you must follow if you've chosen to create a valid document by defining a DTD. (They don't apply if you've chosen to create a valid document using an XML schema.) Because validity is optional for an XML document, a violation of a validity constraint is considered only an *error*, as opposed to a fatal error. When a *validating XML processor* (that is, one that checks documents for validity) encounters an error, it can simply report the problem and attempt to recover from it. Validity constraints consist of specific rules for creating a proper document type declaration with its DTD, and for creating a document that conforms to the specifications within your DTD.

Declaring Element Types

In a valid XML document created using a DTD, you must explicitly declare the type of every element that you use in the document in an *element type declaration* within the DTD. An element type declaration indicates the name of the element type and the allowable content of the element (often specifying the order in which child elements can occur). Taken together, the element type declarations in the DTD map out the entire content and logical structure of the document. That is, the element type declarations indicate the element types that the document contains, the order of the elements, and the contents of these elements.

The Form of an Element Type Declaration

An element type declaration has the following general form:

```
<!ELEMENT Name contentspec>
```

Here, *Name* is the name of the element type being declared. (To review the rules for legal element names, see "The Anatomy of an Element" on page 53.) And *contentspec* is the *content specification*, which defines what the element can contain. The next section describes the different types of content specifications you can use.

The following is a declaration of an element type named TITLE, which is permitted to contain only character data (no child elements would be allowed):

```
<!ELEMENT TITLE (#PCDATA)>
```

And here's a declaration for an element type named GENERAL, which can contain any type of content:

```
<!ELEMENT GENERAL ANY>
```

As a final example, here's a complete XML document with two element types. The declaration of the COLLECTION element type indicates that it can contain one or more CD elements, and the declaration of the CD element type specifies that it can contain only character data. Notice that the document conforms to these declarations and is therefore valid:

```
<?xml version="1.0"?>

<!DOCTYPE COLLECTION
    [
    <!ELEMENT COLLECTION (CD)+>
    <!ELEMENT CD (#PCDATA)>
    <!-- You can also insert a comment in a DTD. -->
    ]
>

<COLLECTION>
    <CD>Mozart Violin Concertos 1, 2, and 3</CD>
    <CD>Telemann Trumpet Concertos</CD>
    <CD>Handel Concerti Grossi Op. 3</CD>
</COLLECTION>
```

note

You can declare a particular element type only once in a given document. For general information on redeclaring items in the DTD, see the sidebar "Redeclarations in a DTD" on page 148.

The Element's Content Specification

You can specify the content of an element—that is, fill in the *contentspec* part of the element type declaration—in four different ways:

- **EMPTY content.** You use the EMPTY keyword to indicate that the element must be empty—that is, that it cannot have content. Here's an example:

  ```
  <!ELEMENT IMAGE EMPTY>
  ```

  The following would be valid IMAGE elements you could enter into your document:

  ```
  <IMAGE></IMAGE>
  <IMAGE />
  ```

- **ANY content.** You use the ANY keyword to indicate that the element can have any legal content. That is, an element of this type can contain zero or more child elements of any declared type, in any order or number of repetitions, with or without interspersed character data. This is the most lax content specification, and creates an element type without content constraints. Here's an example of a declaration:

  ```
  <!ELEMENT MISC ANY>
  ```

- **Element content (also known as *children* content).** With this type of content specification, the element can contain child elements of the indicated types, but can't directly contain character data. I'll describe this option in the next section.

- **Mixed content.** With this type of content specification, the element can contain any quantity of character data. Also, if one or more child element types are specified in the declaration, the character data can be interspersed with any number of these child elements, in any order. I'll describe this option later in this chapter.

Specifying Element Content

If an element has element content, it can directly contain only the specified child elements. The element cannot contain character data, except for white space characters used to separate the child elements and enhance readability (for example, you can display each child element on a separate line and indent them using space or tab characters). As always, the processor must pass the white space characters on to the application, but the application will typically ignore them. (For more details, and to learn about an exception, see the sidebar "White Space in Elements" on page 56.)

Consider the following example XML document, which describes a single book:

```
<?xml version="1.0"?>

<!DOCTYPE BOOK
   [
   <!ELEMENT BOOK (TITLE, AUTHOR)>
   <!ELEMENT TITLE (#PCDATA)>
   <!ELEMENT AUTHOR (#PCDATA)>
   ]
>

<BOOK>
   <TITLE>The Scarlet Letter</TITLE>
   <AUTHOR>Nathaniel Hawthorne</AUTHOR>
</BOOK>
```

In this document, the BOOK element type is declared to have element content. The (TITLE, AUTHOR) following the element name in the declaration is known as the *content model*. A content model indicates the allowed types of child elements and their order. In this example, the content model indicates that a BOOK element must have exactly one TITLE child element followed by exactly one AUTHOR child element.

A content model can have either of the following two basic forms:

▪ **Sequence.** The sequence form of content model indicates that the element must contain a specific sequence of child element types. You separate the names of the child element types with commas. For example, the following DTD indicates that a MOUNTAIN document element must have one NAME child element, followed by one HEIGHT child element, followed by one STATE child element:

```
<!DOCTYPE MOUNTAIN
   [
   <!ELEMENT MOUNTAIN (NAME, HEIGHT, STATE)>
   <!ELEMENT NAME (#PCDATA)>
   <!ELEMENT HEIGHT (#PCDATA)>
   <!ELEMENT STATE (#PCDATA)>
   ]
>
```

Hence, the following document element would be valid:

```
<MOUNTAIN>
    <NAME>Wheeler</NAME>
    <HEIGHT>13161</HEIGHT>
    <STATE>New Mexico</STATE>
</MOUNTAIN>
```

The following document element, however, would be invalid because the order of the child element types isn't as declared:

```
<MOUNTAIN> <!-- Invalid element! -->
    <STATE>New Mexico</STATE>
    <NAME>Wheeler</NAME>
    <HEIGHT>13161</HEIGHT>
</MOUNTAIN>
```

Omitting a child element type or including the same child element type more than once would also be invalid. As you can see, this is a very rigid form of declaration.

■ **Choice.** The choice form of content model indicates that the element can have any one of a series of possible child element types, which are separated using | characters. For example, the following DTD specifies that a FILM element can contain one STAR child element, *or* one NARRATOR child element, *or* one INSTRUCTOR child element:

```
<!DOCTYPE FILM
    [
    <!ELEMENT FILM (STAR | NARRATOR | INSTRUCTOR)>
    <!ELEMENT STAR (#PCDATA)>
    <!ELEMENT NARRATOR (#PCDATA)>
    <!ELEMENT INSTRUCTOR (#PCDATA)>
    ]
>
```

Hence, the following document element would be valid:

```
<FILM>
    <STAR>Robert Redford</STAR>
</FILM>
```

as would this element:

```
<FILM>
    <NARRATOR>Sir Gregory Parsloe</NARRATOR>
</FILM>
```

as well as this one:

```
<FILM>
    <INSTRUCTOR>Galahad Threepwood</INSTRUCTOR>
</FILM>
```

The following document element, however, would be invalid because you can include only *one* of the child element types:

```
<FILM> <!-- Invalid element! -->
    <NARRATOR>Sir Gregory Parsloe</NARRATOR>
    <INSTRUCTOR>Galahad Threepwood</INSTRUCTOR>
</FILM>
```

You can modify either of these forms of content model by using the question mark (?), plus sign (+), and asterisk (*) characters, which have the meanings described in the following table:

Character	Meaning
?	Zero or one of the preceding item
+	One or more of the preceding item
*	Zero or more of the preceding item

For example, the following declarations mean that you can include one or more NAME child elements, and that the HEIGHT child element is optional:

```
<!ELEMENT MOUNTAIN (NAME+, HEIGHT?, STATE)>
<!ELEMENT NAME (#PCDATA)>
<!ELEMENT HEIGHT (#PCDATA)>
<!ELEMENT STATE (#PCDATA)>
```

Thus, the following element would be valid:

```
<MOUNTAIN>
    <NAME>Pueblo Peak</NAME>
    <NAME>Taos Mountain</NAME>
    <STATE>New Mexico</STATE>
</MOUNTAIN>
```

Document Type Definitions

As another example, the following declarations mean that you can include zero or more STAR child elements, *or* one NARRATOR child element, *or* one IN-STRUCTOR child element:

```
<!ELEMENT FILM (STAR* | NARRATOR | INSTRUCTOR)>
<!ELEMENT STAR (#PCDATA)>
<!ELEMENT NARRATOR (#PCDATA)>
<!ELEMENT INSTRUCTOR (#PCDATA)>
```

Accordingly, each of the following three elements would be valid:

```
<FILM>
    <STAR>Tom Hanks</STAR>
    <STAR>Meg Ryan</STAR>
</FILM>

<FILM>
    <NARRATOR>Sir Gregory Parsloe</NARRATOR>
</FILM>

<FILM/>
```

(The final element represents the STAR* choice, which allows FILM to contain zero elements.)

You can also use the question mark (?), plus sign (+), or asterisk (*) character to modify the entire content model by placing the character immediately following the closing parenthesis. For instance, the following declarations let you include one or more child elements of any of the three types, in any order:

```
<!ELEMENT FILM (STAR | NARRATOR | INSTRUCTOR)+>
<!ELEMENT STAR (#PCDATA)>
<!ELEMENT NARRATOR (#PCDATA)>
<!ELEMENT INSTRUCTOR (#PCDATA)>
```

This declaration makes the following elements valid:

```
<FILM>
    <NARRATOR>Bertram Wooster</NARRATOR>
    <STAR>Sean Connery</STAR>
    <NARRATOR>Plug Basham</NARRATOR>
</FILM>

<FILM>
    <STAR>Sean Connery</STAR>
```

```
    <STAR>Meg Ryan</STAR>
</FILM>

<FILM>
    <INSTRUCTOR>Stinker Pike</INSTRUCTOR>
</FILM>
```

Finally, you can form more complex content models by nesting a choice content model within a sequence model, or a sequence model within a choice model. For example, the following declarations specify that the FILM element must have one TITLE child element; followed by one CLASS child element; followed by one STAR, NARRATOR, or INSTRUCTOR child element:

```
<!ELEMENT FILM (TITLE, CLASS, (STAR | NARRATOR | INSTRUCTOR))>
<!ELEMENT TITLE (#PCDATA)>
<!ELEMENT CLASS (#PCDATA)>
<!ELEMENT STAR (#PCDATA)>
<!ELEMENT NARRATOR (#PCDATA)>
<!ELEMENT INSTRUCTOR (#PCDATA)>
```

According to these declarations, the following element is valid:

```
<FILM>
    <TITLE>The Net</TITLE>
    <CLASS>fictional</CLASS>
    <STAR>Sandra Bullock</STAR>
</FILM>
```

as is this one:

```
<FILM>
    <TITLE>How to Use XML</TITLE>
    <CLASS>instructional</CLASS>
    <INSTRUCTOR>Penny Donaldson</INSTRUCTOR>
</FILM>
```

Specifying Mixed Content

If an element has mixed content, it can always contain character data—that is, zero or more characters. And if you specify one or more child element types in the declaration, it can also contain child elements of any of those types in any position and with any number of repetitions (zero or more), interspersed with the character data. Thus, with mixed content you can constrain the types of the child elements, but you can't constrain the order or number of occurrences of a child element type, nor can you make a particular child element type mandatory.

To declare an element type of mixed content, you can use either of the following two forms of content model:

- **Character data only.** To declare an element type that can contain character data only—that is, zero or more characters—use the content model (#PCDATA). The following declaration, for example, allows a SUBTITLE element to contain only character data:

  ```
  <!ELEMENT SUBTITLE (#PCDATA)>
  ```

  The following two elements are valid according to this declaration:

  ```
  <SUBTITLE>A New Approach</SUBTITLE>
  <SUBTITLE></SUBTITLE>
  ```

  Notice in the second example that an element declared to contain character data can contain zero characters—that is, you can leave it empty.

  (With the character data only form of content model, the term *mixed content* is actually a misnomer.)

note

The keyword PCDATA stands for *parsed character data*. You learned in Chapter 3 that the XML processor *parses* character data within an element—that is, it scans the element looking for XML markup. You therefore cannot insert a left angle bracket (<), an ampersand (&), or the string]]> as a part of the character data because the parser would interpret each of these characters or strings as markup or the start of markup. You can, however, insert any character using a character reference or, if available, a predefined general entity reference (discussed in Chapter 6), and you can insert any characters except the string]]> using a CDATA section (covered in Chapter 4).

- **Character data plus optional child elements.** To declare an element type that can contain character data (zero or more characters) plus zero or more child elements, list each permissible child element type following the #PCDATA in the content model, separating the items with | characters and inserting an asterisk (*) at the end of the content model. Each element name can appear only once in the content model. For example, the following declarations allow a TITLE element to contain character data plus zero or more SUBTITLE child elements anywhere within the element:

```
<!ELEMENT TITLE (#PCDATA | SUBTITLE)*>
<!ELEMENT SUBTITLE (#PCDATA)>
```

The following are valid TITLE elements, conforming to this declaration:

```
<TITLE>Moby-Dick <SUBTITLE>Or, The Whale</SUBTITLE></TITLE>
```

```
<TITLE><SUBTITLE>Or, The Whale</SUBTITLE> Moby-Dick</TITLE>
```

```
<TITLE>Moby-Dick</TITLE>
```

```
<TITLE>
    <SUBTITLE>Or, The Whale</SUBTITLE>
    <SUBTITLE>Another Subtitle</SUBTITLE>
</TITLE>
```

```
<TITLE></TITLE>
```

Declaring Attributes

In a valid XML document, you must also explicitly declare all attributes that you intend to use with the document's elements. You define all the attributes associated with a particular element by using a type of DTD markup declaration known as an *attribute-list declaration*. This declaration does the following:

- It defines the names of the attributes associated with the element. In a valid document, you can include in an element start-tag only those attributes defined for that element.

- It specifies the data type of each attribute.

- It specifies for each attribute whether that attribute is required. If the attribute isn't required, the attribute-list declaration also indicates what the processor should do if the attribute is omitted. (The declaration might, for example, provide a default attribute value that the processor will pass to the application.)

note

You can declare elements and attributes in any order in a DTD. For example, you can declare the attribute-list specification for a particular element before you declare that element.

Document Type Definitions

The Form of an Attribute-List Declaration

An attribute-list declaration has the following general form:

```
<!ATTLIST Name AttDefs>
```

Here, *Name* is the type name of the element associated with the attribute or attributes. *AttDefs* is a series of one or more *attribute definitions,* each of which defines one attribute. (The order of the attribute definitions in the attribute-list declaration isn't significant. You can always include the attribute specifications in an element start-tag in any order.)

An attribute definition has the following form:

```
Name AttType DefaultDecl
```

Here, *Name* is the name of the attribute. (To review the rules for legal attribute names, see "Rules for Creating Attributes" on page 63.) *AttType* is the *attribute type,* which is the kind of value that can be assigned to the attribute. (I'll describe the attribute type in the next section.) And *DefaultDecl* is the *default declaration,* which indicates whether the attribute is required and provides other information. (I'll describe the default declaration later in this chapter.)

Say, for example, that you've declared an element type named FILM like this:

```
<!ELEMENT FILM (TITLE, (STAR | NARRATOR | INSTRUCTOR))>
```

Here's an example of an attribute-list declaration that declares two attributes—named *Class* and *Year*—for FILM elements:

```
<!ATTLIST FILM   Class CDATA "fictional"   Year CDATA #REQUIRED>
```

Here are the different parts of this declaration:

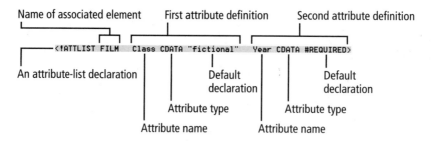

You can assign to the *Class* attribute any legal quoted string (the CDATA keyword); if you omit the attribute from a particular element, it will automatically be assigned the default value *fictional.* You can assign to the *Year* attribute any legal quoted string; this attribute, however, must be assigned a value in every FILM element (the #REQUIRED keyword), and it therefore doesn't have a default value.

The following complete XML document includes this attribute-list declaration as well as a FILM element:

```
<?xml version="1.0"?>

<!DOCTYPE FILM
   [
   <!ELEMENT FILM (TITLE, (STAR | NARRATOR | INSTRUCTOR))>
   <!ATTLIST FILM   Class CDATA "fictional"   Year CDATA #REQUIRED>
   <!ELEMENT TITLE (#PCDATA)>
   <!ELEMENT STAR (#PCDATA)>
   <!ELEMENT NARRATOR (#PCDATA)>
   <!ELEMENT INSTRUCTOR (#PCDATA)>
   ]
>


<FILM Year="1948">
   <TITLE>The Morning After</TITLE>
   <STAR>Morgan Attenbury</STAR>
</FILM>
```

In the FILM element, the *Year* attribute is assigned the value *1948*. The *Class* attribute is omitted; however, because this attribute has a default value (*fictional*), it is assigned that default value just as if you had included the attribute and typed the value.

> ## note
> If you include more than one attribute-list declaration for a given element type, the contents of the two declarations are merged. If an attribute with a given name is declared more than once for the same element, the first declaration is used and the second is ignored. (Multiple attribute-list declarations are more common when a document has both an internal and an external DTD subset, as I'll discuss later in the chapter.) For general information on redeclaring items in a DTD, see the sidebar "Redeclarations in a DTD" on page 148.

The Attribute Type

The attribute type is the second required component of an attribute definition. It specifies the kind of value that you can assign to the attribute within the document.

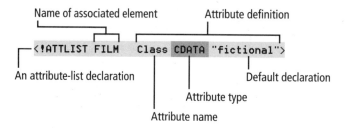

You can specify the attribute type in three different ways:

■ **String type.** A string type attribute can be assigned any *quoted string* (also known as a *literal*) that conforms to the general rules described in "Rules for Legal Attribute Values" on page 65. You declare a string type attribute using the keyword CDATA, as in the attribute definition of *Class* in the following example:

```
<!ATTLIST FILM    Class CDATA "fictional">
```

■ **Tokenized type.** The values that you can assign to a tokenized type attribute are constrained in various ways, as I'll describe in the next section.

■ **Enumerated type.** You can assign to an enumerated type attribute one of a list of specified values. I'll describe this type a little later in the chapter.

Specifying a Tokenized Type

Like any attribute value, the value you assign to a tokenized type must be a quoted string that conforms to the general rules described in "Rules for Legal Attribute Values" on page 65.

In addition, the value must conform to the particular constraint that you specify in the attribute definition by using an appropriate keyword. For example, in the following XML document, the *StockCode* attribute is defined as a tokenized type using the ID keyword. (ID is only one of the keywords you can use to declare a tokenized type.) This keyword means that for each element the attribute must be assigned a unique value. (For example, assigning the stock code "S021" to two ITEM elements would be invalid.)

```
<?xml version="1.0"?>

<!DOCTYPE INVENTORY
    [
    <!ELEMENT INVENTORY (ITEM*)>
```

```
    <!ELEMENT ITEM (#PCDATA)>
    <!ATTLIST ITEM   StockCode ID #REQUIRED>
    ]
>

<INVENTORY>
    <!-- Each ITEM must have a different StockCode value. -->
    <ITEM StockCode="S021">Peach Tea Pot</ITEM>
    <ITEM StockCode="S034">Electric Coffee Grinder</ITEM>
    <ITEM StockCode="S086">Candy Thermometer</ITEM>
</INVENTORY>
```

Here's a complete list of the keywords you can use to define tokenized type at-tributes and the constraints they impose on the attribute values:

- **ID.** In each element the attribute must have a unique value. The value must begin with a letter or underscore (_) followed by zero or more letters, digits, periods (.), hyphens (-), or underscores. How-ever, the XML specification states that ID attribute values beginning with the letters *xml* (in any combination of uppercase or lowercase letters) are "reserved for standardization." Although Internet Ex-plorer doesn't enforce this restriction, it's better not to begin names with *xml* to avoid future problems. In addition, a particular element type can have only one ID type attribute, and the attribute's default declaration must be either #REQUIRED or #IMPLIED (described later in the chapter). You can see an example of this type of attribute in the INVENTORY document given above.

> **note**
>
> #REQUIRED and #IMPLIED are the two forms of default declaration in which you don't specify a default value for the attribute. It doesn't make sense to give a default value to an ID type attribute, since the attribute must have a unique value in each attribute specification.

- **IDREF.** The attribute value must match the value of some ID type attribute in an element within the document. In other words, this type of attribute refers to the unique identifier of another attribute.

For example, you might add an IDREF attribute named *GoesWith* to the ITEM element:

```
<!ELEMENT ITEM (#PCDATA)>
<!ATTLIST ITEM
   StockCode ID #REQUIRED   GoesWith IDREF #IMPLIED>
```

You could then use this attribute to refer to another ITEM element, as shown here:

```
<ITEM StockCode="S034">Electric Coffee Grinder</ITEM>
<ITEM StockCode="S047" GoesWith="S034">
 Coffee Grinder Brush
</ITEM>
```

■ **IDREFS.** This type of attribute is just like an IDREF type, except that the value can include references to several identifiers—separated with white space characters—all within the quoted string. For example, if you assigned to the *GoesWith* attribute the IDREFS type like this:

```
<!ELEMENT ITEM (#PCDATA)>
<!ATTLIST ITEM
   StockCode ID #REQUIRED
   GoesWith IDREFS #IMPLIED>
```

you could use it to refer to several other elements:

```
<ITEM StockCode="S034">Electric Coffee Grinder</ITEM>
<ITEM StockCode="S039">
   1 pound Breakfast Blend Coffee Beans
</ITEM>
<ITEM StockCode="S047" GoesWith="S034 S039">
   Coffee Grinder Brush
</ITEM>
```

■ **ENTITY.** The attribute value must match the name of an unparsed entity declared in the DTD. An unparsed entity refers to an external file, typically one storing non-XML data. I'll discuss these entities in Chapter 6.

For example, in the DTD you might declare an element named IMAGE to represent a graphic image and an ENTITY type attribute named *Source* to indicate the source of the graphic data, like this:

```
<!ELEMENT IMAGE EMPTY>
<!ATTLIST IMAGE   Source ENTITY #REQUIRED>
```

If you've declared an unparsed entity named *Logo* (using techniques you'll learn in Chapter 6) that contains the graphic data for an image, you could assign that entity to the *Source* attribute of an IMAGE element in the document, like this:

```
<IMAGE Source="Logo" />
```

■ **ENTITIES.** This type of attribute is just like an ENTITY type, except that the value can include the names of several unparsed entities—separated with white space characters—all within the quoted string. For example, if you defined the *Source* attribute to have the ENTITIES type, like this:

```
<!ELEMENT IMAGE EMPTY>
<!ATTLIST IMAGE    Source ENTITIES #REQUIRED>
```

you could use it to refer to several unparsed entities (perhaps entities storing the graphics data in alternative formats), like this:

```
<IMAGE Source="LogoGif LogoBmp" />
```

(This example assumes that *LogoGif* and *LogoBmp* are the names of unparsed entities that have been declared in the DTD using techniques you'll learn in Chapter 6.)

■ **NMTOKEN.** The attribute value must be a *name token*, which consists of one or more letters, digits, periods (.), hyphens (-), or underscores (_). A name token can also contain a single colon (:) except in the first character position. (As you can see, the rules for a name token are less stringent than those for an ID attribute value or the name of an item such as an element, attribute, or entity.) For example, if you assigned to the ISBN attribute the NMTOKEN type, like this:

```
<!ELEMENT BOOK (#PCDATA)>
<!ATTLIST BOOK    ISBN NMTOKEN #REQUIRED>
```

you could assign it a value beginning with a number (a leading digit character is allowed for the NMTOKEN and NMTOKENS types, but not for any of the other tokenized types):

```
<BOOK ISBN="9-99999-999-9">The Portrait of a Lady</BOOK>
```

■ **NMTOKENS.** This type of attribute is just like an NMTOKEN type except that the value can include several name tokens—separated with white space characters—all within the quoted string. For example, if you assigned to the *Codes* attribute the NMTOKENS type, like this:

Document Type Definitions

5

```
<!ELEMENT SHIRT (#PCDATA)>
<!ATTLIST SHIRT    Codes NMTOKENS #REQUIRED>
```

you could assign it several name token values:

```
<SHIRT Codes="38 21 97">long sleeve Henley</SHIRT>
```

Specifying an Enumerated Type

Like any attribute value, the value you assign to an enumerated type must be a quoted string that conforms to the general rules described in "Rules for Legal Attribute Values" on page 65. In addition, the value must match one of the names that you list in the attribute-type specification, which can have either of the following two forms:

▪ An open parenthesis, followed by a list of name tokens separated with | characters, followed by a close parenthesis. Recall that a *name token* is a name that consists of one or more letters, digits, periods (.), hyphens (-), or underscores (_), and that can also contain a single colon (:) except in the first character position. For example, if you wanted to restrict the values of the *Class* attribute to *fictional, documentary,* or *instructional,* you could define this attribute as an enumerated type, like this:

```
<!ATTLIST FILM
    Class (fictional | documentary | instructional)
    "fictional">
```

Here's a complete XML document that shows the use of the *Class* attribute:

```
<?xml version="1.0"?>

<!DOCTYPE FILM
    [
    <!ELEMENT FILM (TITLE, (STAR | NARRATOR | INSTRUCTOR))>
    <!ATTLIST FILM
        Class (fictional | documentary | instructional)
        "fictional">
    <!ELEMENT TITLE (#PCDATA)>
    <!ELEMENT STAR (#PCDATA)>
    <!ELEMENT NARRATOR (#PCDATA)>
    <!ELEMENT INSTRUCTOR (#PCDATA)>
    ]
>
```

```
<FILM Class="instructional">
    <TITLE>The Use and Care of XML</TITLE>
    <INSTRUCTOR>Michael J. Young</INSTRUCTOR>
</FILM>
```

If you omitted the *Class* attribute, it would be assigned the default value *fictional*. Assigning to *Class* a value other than *fictional, documentary,* or *instructional* would be a validity error.

■ The keyword NOTATION, followed by space, followed by an open parenthesis, followed by a list of notation names separated with | characters, followed by a close parenthesis. Each of these names must exactly match the name of a notation declared in the DTD. A notation describes a data format or identifies the program used to process a particular format. I'll discuss notations in Chapter 6.

note

You cannot declare more than one NOTATION type attribute for a given element. Also, you cannot declare a NOTATION type attribute for an element that is declared as EMPTY.

For example, assuming that the notations HTML, SGML, and RTF are declared in your DTD, you could restrict the values of the *Format* attribute to one of these notation names by declaring it like this:

```
<!ELEMENT EXAMPLE_DOCUMENT (#PCDATA)>
<!ATTLIST EXAMPLE_DOCUMENT
    Format NOTATION (HTML|SGML|RTF) #REQUIRED>
```

You could then use the *Format* element to indicate the format of a particular EXAMPLE_DOCUMENT element, as in this example:

```
<EXAMPLE_DOCUMENT Format="HTML">
    <![CDATA[
        <HTML>
        <HEAD>
        <TITLE>Mike's Home Page</TITLE>
        </HEAD>

        <BODY>
        <P>Welcome!</P>
        </BODY>
```

Document Type Definitions 5

```
      </HTML>
   ]]>
</EXAMPLE_DOCUMENT>
```

Assigning *Format* a value other than HTML, SGML, or RTF would be a validity error. (Notice the use of the CDATA section here, which allows you to use the left angle bracket (<) character freely within the element's character data.)

The Default Declaration

The default declaration is the third and final required component of an attribute definition. It specifies whether the attribute is required, and, if the attribute isn't required, it indicates what the processor should do if the attribute is omitted. The declaration might, for example, provide a default attribute value that the processor should use if the attribute is absent.

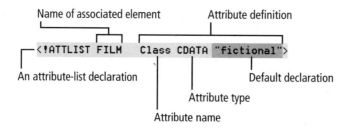

The default declaration has four possible forms:

- **#REQUIRED.** With this form, you must specify an attribute value for every element of the associated type. For example, the following declaration indicates that you must assign a value to the *Class* attribute within the start-tag of every FILM element in the document:

  ```
  <!ATTLIST FILM    Class CDATA #REQUIRED>
  ```

- **#IMPLIED.** This form indicates that you can either include or omit the attribute from an element of the associated type, and that if you omit the attribute, no default value is supplied to the processor. (This form "implies" rather than "states" a value, causing the application to use its own default value—hence the name.) For example, the following declaration indicates that assigning a value to the *Class* attribute within a FILM element is optional, and that the DTD doesn't supply a default *Class* value:

  ```
  <!ATTLIST FILM    Class CDATA #IMPLIED>
  ```

■ *AttValue,* where *AttValue* is a default attribute value. With this form, you can either include or omit the attribute from an element of the associated type. If you omit it, the processor will use the default value just as if you had included the attribute and typed that value. The default value you specify must, of course, conform to the stated attribute type. For example, the following declaration assigns the default value *fictional* to the *Class* attribute:

```
<!ATTLIST FILM    Class CDATA "fictional">
```

With this declaration, the following two elements are equivalent:

```
<FILM>The Graduate</FILM>
<FILM Class="fictional">The Graduate</FILM>
```

■ **#FIXED** *AttValue,* where *AttValue* is a default attribute value. With this form, you can either include or omit the attribute from an element of the associated type. If you omit the attribute, the processor will use the specified default value; if you include it, you must specify the default value. (Because you can specify only the default value, there's no compelling reason to include an attribute specification in an element, except perhaps to make the document clearer for human readers.) For example, the following declaration assigns a fixed default value to the *Class* attribute:

```
<!ATTLIST FILM    Class CDATA #FIXED "documentary">
```

With this declaration, the following two equivalent elements are valid:

```
<FILM>The Making of XML</FILM>
<FILM Class="documentary">The Making of XML</FILM>
```

while the following element is invalid:

```
<!-- Invalid element! -->
<FILM Class="instructional">The Making of XML</FILM>
```

Using Namespaces in Valid Documents

The section "Using Namespaces" on page 69 explained the general procedures for using namespaces in well-formed XML documents. The following are some guidelines for creating a DTD for an XML document that uses namespaces. These guidelines are illustrated in Listing 5-1, which gives a valid version of the Collection Default.xml document that was provided in Listing 3-5. The document includes both explicit and default namespace assignments. (You'll find a copy of Listing 5-1 on the companion CD under the filename Collection Default Valid.xml.)

Collection Default Valid.xml

```
<?xml version="1.0"?>

<!-- File Name: Collection Default Valid.xml -->

<!DOCTYPE COLLECTION
    [
    <!ELEMENT COLLECTION (ITEM | cd:ITEM)*>
    <!ATTLIST COLLECTION
        xmlns CDATA #REQUIRED
        xmlns:cd CDATA #REQUIRED>

    <!ELEMENT ITEM (TITLE, AUTHOR, PRICE)>
    <!ATTLIST ITEM   Status (in|out) #REQUIRED>
    <!ELEMENT TITLE (#PCDATA)>
    <!ELEMENT AUTHOR (#PCDATA)>
    <!ELEMENT PRICE (#PCDATA)>

    <!ELEMENT cd:ITEM (cd:TITLE, cd:COMPOSER, cd:PRICE)>
    <!ELEMENT cd:TITLE (#PCDATA)>
    <!ELEMENT cd:COMPOSER (#PCDATA)>
    <!ELEMENT cd:PRICE (#PCDATA)>
    ]
>


<COLLECTION
    xmlns="http://www.mjyOnline.com/books"
    xmlns:cd="http://www.mjyOnline.com/cds">

    <ITEM Status="in">
        <TITLE>The Adventures of Huckleberry Finn</TITLE>
        <AUTHOR>Mark Twain</AUTHOR>
        <PRICE>$5.49</PRICE>
    </ITEM>
    <cd:ITEM>
        <cd:TITLE>Violin Concerto in D</cd:TITLE>
        <cd:COMPOSER>Beethoven</cd:COMPOSER>
        <cd:PRICE>$14.95</cd:PRICE>
    </cd:ITEM>
    <ITEM Status="out">
        <TITLE>Leaves of Grass</TITLE>
```

```
      <AUTHOR>Walt Whitman</AUTHOR>
      <PRICE>$7.75</PRICE>
   </ITEM>
   <cd:ITEM>
      <cd:TITLE>Violin Concertos Numbers 1, 2, and 3</cd:TITLE>
      <cd:COMPOSER>Mozart</cd:COMPOSER>
      <cd:PRICE>$16.49</cd:PRICE>
   </cd:ITEM>
   <ITEM Status="out">
      <TITLE>The Legend of Sleepy Hollow</TITLE>
      <AUTHOR>Washington Irving</AUTHOR>
      <PRICE>$2.95</PRICE>
   </ITEM>
   <ITEM Status="in">
      <TITLE>The Marble Faun</TITLE>
      <AUTHOR>Nathaniel Hawthorne</AUTHOR>
      <PRICE>$10.95</PRICE>
   </ITEM>
</COLLECTION>
```

Listing 5-1.

- If an element or attribute name in the document is explicitly qualified using a namespace prefix, you must include that prefix when
  you declare the element or attribute in the DTD. Hence, the example
  document in Listing 5-1 declares the *cd:ITEM* element and its
  subelements as follows:

  ```
  <!ELEMENT cd:ITEM (cd:TITLE, cd:COMPOSER, cd:PRICE)>
  <!ELEMENT cd:TITLE (#PCDATA)>
  <!ELEMENT cd:COMPOSER (#PCDATA)>
  <!ELEMENT cd:PRICE (#PCDATA)>
  ```

- If an element is assigned to a namespace using a default namespace
  assignment in the document, you declare it using its unqualified
  name. Accordingly, the example document declares the COLLEC-
  TION element using its unqualified name, even though it belongs by
  default to the *http://www.mjyOnline.com/books* namespace:

  ```
  <!ELEMENT COLLECTION (ITEM | cd:ITEM)*>
  ```

- If a particular element name or attribute name belongs to several different namespaces—or to no namespace—you must declare each use

of the name separately. Hence, the example document declares both ITEM and *cd:ITEM*.

■ As with any attributes in a document, you must declare the attributes that appear in the special-purpose attribute specifications that are used to declare namespaces. In the example document, these attributes belong to the COLLECTION element and are declared as follows:

```
<!ATTLIST COLLECTION
    xmlns CDATA #REQUIRED
    xmlns:cd CDATA #REQUIRED>
```

Internet Explorer doesn't support default values for these attributes. In other words, you *can't* declare these attributes with default values and then omit the attribute specifications from the start-tag of the element that they belong to (COLLECTION in the example document). You must always explicitly assign attribute values.

Using an External DTD Subset

The document type definitions you've seen so far in this chapter are contained completely within the document type declaration in the document. This type of DTD is known as an *internal DTD subset*.

Alternatively, you can place all or part of the document's DTD in a separate file, and then refer to that file from the document type declaration. A DTD— or a portion of a DTD—contained in a separate file is known as an *external DTD subset*.

note

Using an external DTD subset is advantageous primarily for a common DTD employed by an entire group of documents. Each document can refer to a single DTD file (or copy of that file) as an external DTD subset. This saves having to copy the DTD contents into each document that uses it, and also makes it easier to maintain the DTD. (You need to modify only the single DTD file—and any copies of that file—rather than edit all the documents that use it.) Recall from Chapter 1 that many of the standard XML applications are based on a common DTD included in all XML documents that conform to the application. To review, take a look at "Standard XML Applications" and "Real-World Uses for XML," both in Chapter 1.

Using an External DTD Subset Only

To use only an external DTD subset, omit the block of markup declarations and the square bracket ([]) characters that contain them, and instead include the keyword SYSTEM followed by a quoted description of the location of the separate file that contains the DTD. Consider, for instance, the SIMPLE document you saw earlier in the chapter, which has an internal DTD subset:

```
<?xml version="1.0"?>

<!DOCTYPE SIMPLE
    [
    <!ELEMENT SIMPLE ANY>
    ]
>

<SIMPLE>This is an extremely simplistic XML document.</SIMPLE>
```

If this document used an external DTD subset, it would appear like this:

```
<?xml version="1.0"?>

<!DOCTYPE SIMPLE SYSTEM "Simple.dtd">

<SIMPLE>This is an extremely simplistic XML document.</SIMPLE>
```

And the file Simple.dtd would have the following contents:

```
<!ELEMENT SIMPLE ANY>
```

The file containing the external DTD subset can include any of the markup declarations that can be included in an internal DTD subset. I listed these in "Creating the Document Type Definition" on page 96.

note

For information on including a text declaration at the beginning of a file containing an external DTD subset, see the sidebar "Characters, Encoding, and Languages" on page 77.

The description of the file location (*Simple.dtd* in the example) is known as the *system identifier*. It can be delimited using either single quotes (') or double quotes ("). It can include any characters except the quotation character used to delimit it, and it must specify a valid URI (Uniform Resource Indicator) for the file containing the external DTD subset. Currently, the most common form of URI is a traditional URL (Uniform Resource Locator). (See the sidebar "URIs, URLs, and URNs" on page 73.) You can use a fully qualified URL, such as:

```
<!DOCTYPE SIMPLE SYSTEM "http://www.mjyOnline.com/dtds/Simple.dtd">
```

Or, you can use a partial URL that specifies a location relative to the location of the XML document containing the URL, such as:

```
<!DOCTYPE SIMPLE SYSTEM "Simple.dtd">
```

Relative URLs in XML documents work just like relative URLs in HTML pages. In the second example, if the full URL of the XML document were *http://www.mjyOnline.com/documents/Simple.xml*, *Simple.dtd* would refer to *http://www.mjyOnline.com/documents/Simple.dtd*. Likewise, if the XML document were located at *file:///C:\XML Step by Step\Example Source\Simple.xml*, *Simple.dtd* would refer to *file:///C:\XML Step by Step\Example Source\Simple.dtd*.

Using Both an External DTD Subset and an Internal DTD Subset

To use both an external DTD subset and an internal DTD subset, include the SYSTEM keyword together with the system identifier giving the location of the external DTD subset file, followed by the internal DTD subset markup declarations within square bracket ([]) characters.

Here's an example of a simple XML document with both an internal and an external DTD subset:

```
<?xml version="1.0"?>

<!DOCTYPE BOOK SYSTEM "Book.dtd"
   [
   <!ATTLIST BOOK    ISBN CDATA #IMPLIED    Year CDATA "2000">
   <!ELEMENT TITLE (#PCDATA)>
   ]
>

<BOOK Year="1998">
   <TITLE>The Scarlet Letter</TITLE>
</BOOK>
```

Here are the contents of the file containing the external DTD subset, Book.dtd:

```
<!ELEMENT BOOK ANY>
<!ATTLIST BOOK    ISBN NMTOKEN #REQUIRED>
```

When you include both an external and an internal DTD subset, here's how the XML processor combines their contents:

- It merges the contents of the two subsets to form the complete DTD. In the example document, the resultant merged DTD defines two elements, TITLE and BOOK, and two attributes for the BOOK element, ISBN and Year.

- It processes the internal DTD subset *before* the external DTD subset (even though the external subset reference appears first in the document type declaration). Thus, if a particular item (element, attribute, entity, or notation) is declared with the same name in both the internal and external subsets, the declaration in the internal subset takes precedence and the declaration in the external subset is considered a redeclaration.

  For instance, if an attribute with the same name and element type is declared in both subsets, the processor uses the declaration in the internal subset and ignores the one in the external subset. (As explained earlier in this chapter, the processor uses the first declaration for a particular attribute and ignores any subsequent ones.) In the example document, the XML processor considers the ISBN attribute to have the CDATA type and the #IMPLIED default declaration, and therefore the following element (which leaves out ISBN) is valid:

```
<BOOK Year="1850">
    <TITLE>The Scarlet Letter</TITLE>
</BOOK>
```

note

For more information on redeclaring elements, attributes, entities, and notations, see the sidebar "Redeclarations in a DTD" on page 148. I'll discuss entity and notation declarations in Chapter 6.

The way the XML processor combines an internal and an external DTD subset lets you use a common DTD (such as one provided for an XML application like MathML) as an external DTD subset, but then customize the DTD for the current document by including an internal subset. Your internal subset can add elements, attributes, entities, or notations—and it can change the definitions of attributes or entities.

Conditionally Ignoring Sections of an External DTD Subset

You can have the XML processor ignore a portion of an external DTD subset by using an IGNORE section. You might, for example, use an IGNORE section while you're developing a document to temporarily deactivate an alternative or optional block of markup declarations, so that you don't need to delete the lines and possibly reinsert them later. (If you happen to be a programmer, you'll recognize that this technique is similar to "commenting out" a block of code you want temporarily ignored.) An IGNORE section begins with the characters <![IGNORE[and ends with the characters]]>.

Here's an example of a complete external DTD subset that includes an IGNORE section:

```
                    <!ELEMENT BOOK ANY>
                    <!ATTLIST BOOK    ISBN NMTOKEN #REQUIRED>
Start of ———————— <![IGNORE[
IGNORE section      ┌ <!-- an optional block of markup declarations
                    │  that are temporarily deactivated -->
Ignored markup ———— │ <!ATTLIST BOOK    Category CDATA "fiction">     ── An
declarations        │ <!ELEMENT TITLE (#PCDATA)>                         IGNORE
                    └ <!ELEMENT AUTHOR (#PCDATA)>                        section
End of ———————————— ]]>
IGNORE section
```

If you want to temporarily reactivate a block of markup declarations in an IGNORE section, you can simply replace the keyword IGNORE with INCLUDE, without having to remove all the delimiting characters (<![, [, and]]>), as in this example:

```
<![INCLUDE[
    <!-- an optional block of markup declarations
         that are temporarily reactivated -->
    <!ATTLIST BOOK    Category CDATA "fiction">
    <!ELEMENT TITLE (#PCDATA)>
    <!ELEMENT AUTHOR (#PCDATA)>
]]>
```

You could then quickly deactivate the section again by simply putting back the IGNORE. Note that a nested INCLUDE section within an IGNORE section is still ignored.

> **note**
>
> You can use IGNORE and INCLUDE conditional sections only in an external DTD subset or in a parameter external entity, *not* in an internal DTD subset. (As you'll learn in Chapter 6, a parameter external entity is a separate file that—like an external DTD subset—contains markup declarations.)

Converting a Well-Formed Document to a Valid Document

In this section, you'll get some hands-on experience with the concepts presented in this chapter by converting a well-formed document to a valid document. You'll modify the Inventory.xml document you created in Chapter 2 to make the document valid. You'll also add a new element and two attributes to gain experience with additional techniques you learned in this chapter.

Make a Document Valid

1   In your text editor, open the Inventory.xml document you created in Chapter 2. (The document is provided in Listing 2-1 and on the companion CD.)

2   Just above the document element—named INVENTORY—type in the following document type declaration:

```
<!DOCTYPE INVENTORY
   [
   <!ELEMENT INVENTORY (BOOK)*>

   <!ELEMENT BOOK (TITLE, AUTHOR, BINDING, PAGES, PRICE)>
   <!ATTLIST BOOK   InStock (yes|no) #REQUIRED>

   <!ELEMENT TITLE (#PCDATA | SUBTITLE)*>

   <!ELEMENT SUBTITLE (#PCDATA)>

   <!ELEMENT AUTHOR (#PCDATA)>
   <!ATTLIST AUTHOR   Born CDATA #IMPLIED>

   <!ELEMENT BINDING (#PCDATA)>
```

```
<!ELEMENT PAGES (#PCDATA)>

<!ELEMENT PRICE (#PCDATA)>
  ]
>
```

tip

In performing the modifications given in this exercise, you can refer to the complete modified document contained in Listing 5-2 at the end of this chapter.

Notice that the name following the DOCTYPE keyword matches the name of the document element, INVENTORY, as required. The DTD consists of an internal subset only, which defines the document's elements and attributes as follows:

- The document element, INVENTORY, has element content. It can contain zero or more BOOK child elements.

- The BOOK element also has element content. It must contain exactly one of each of the following elements, in the order listed in the element declaration: TITLE, AUTHOR, BINDING, PAGES, and PRICE.

- The TITLE element has mixed content. It can contain character data interspersed with zero or more SUBTITLE elements.

- The SUBTITLE, AUTHOR, BINDING, PAGES, and PRICE elements also each have mixed content. These elements, however, can contain only character data and not child elements.

- The BOOK element has an enumerated type attribute named *InStock*, which is a required attribute that can be assigned either *yes* or *no*.

- The AUTHOR element has a string type attribute named *Born*, which is optional and has no default value.

3   Add the following SUBTITLE child element to the TITLE element for the *Moby-Dick* book:

```
<BOOK>
    <TITLE>Moby-Dick
      <SUBTITLE>Or, The Whale</SUBTITLE>
    </TITLE>
```

4   Add the required *InStock* attribute to each BOOK element, assigning it either *yes* or *no* as shown in this example:

```
<BOOK InStock="yes">
    <TITLE>The Adventures of Huckleberry Finn</TITLE>
    <AUTHOR>Mark Twain</AUTHOR>
    <BINDING>mass market paperback</BINDING>
    <PAGES>298</PAGES>
    <PRICE>$5.49</PRICE>
</BOOK>
```

5   Add the optional *Born* element to one or more elements. Although you can assign to this attribute any legal quoted string, its purpose is to store the author's birth date. Here's an example:

```
<AUTHOR Born="1835">Mark Twain</AUTHOR>
```

6   To reflect the new filename you're going to assign, change the comment at the beginning of the document from this:

```
<!-- File Name: Inventory.xml -->
```

to this:

```
<!-- File Name: Inventory Valid.xml -->
```

7   Use your text editor's Save As command to save a copy of the modified document under the file name Inventory Valid.xml.

The complete XML document is shown in Listing 5-2. (You'll find a copy of this listing on the companion CD under the filename Inventory Valid.xml.)

Inventory Valid.xml

```
<?xml version="1.0"?>

<!-- File Name: Inventory Valid.xml -->

<!DOCTYPE INVENTORY
    [
    <!ELEMENT INVENTORY (BOOK)*>
```

```
        <!ELEMENT BOOK (TITLE, AUTHOR, BINDING, PAGES, PRICE)>
        <!ATTLIST BOOK    InStock (yes|no) #REQUIRED>

        <!ELEMENT TITLE (#PCDATA | SUBTITLE)*>

        <!ELEMENT SUBTITLE (#PCDATA)>

        <!ELEMENT AUTHOR (#PCDATA)>
        <!ATTLIST AUTHOR    Born CDATA #IMPLIED>

        <!ELEMENT BINDING (#PCDATA)>

        <!ELEMENT PAGES (#PCDATA)>

        <!ELEMENT PRICE (#PCDATA)>
        ]
>


<INVENTORY>
    <BOOK InStock="yes">
        <TITLE>The Adventures of Huckleberry Finn</TITLE>
        <AUTHOR Born="1835">Mark Twain</AUTHOR>
        <BINDING>mass market paperback</BINDING>
        <PAGES>298</PAGES>
        <PRICE>$5.49</PRICE>
    </BOOK>
    <BOOK InStock="no">
        <TITLE>Leaves of Grass</TITLE>
        <AUTHOR Born="1819">Walt Whitman</AUTHOR>
        <BINDING>hardcover</BINDING>
        <PAGES>462</PAGES>
        <PRICE>$7.75</PRICE>
    </BOOK>
    <BOOK InStock="yes">
        <TITLE>The Legend of Sleepy Hollow</TITLE>
        <AUTHOR>Washington Irving</AUTHOR>
        <BINDING>mass market paperback</BINDING>
        <PAGES>98</PAGES>
        <PRICE>$2.95</PRICE>
    </BOOK>
    <BOOK InStock="yes">
```

```
            <TITLE>The Marble Faun</TITLE>
            <AUTHOR Born="1804">Nathaniel Hawthorne</AUTHOR>
            <BINDING>trade paperback</BINDING>
            <PAGES>473</PAGES>
            <PRICE>$10.95</PRICE>
        </BOOK>
        <BOOK InStock="no">
            <TITLE>Moby-Dick <SUBTITLE>Or, The Whale</SUBTITLE></TITLE>
            <AUTHOR Born="1819">Herman Melville</AUTHOR>
            <BINDING>hardcover</BINDING>
            <PAGES>724</PAGES>
            <PRICE>$9.95</PRICE>
        </BOOK>
        <BOOK InStock="yes">
            <TITLE>The Portrait of a Lady</TITLE>
            <AUTHOR>Henry James</AUTHOR>
            <BINDING>mass market paperback</BINDING>
            <PAGES>256</PAGES>
            <PRICE>$4.95</PRICE>
        </BOOK>
        <BOOK InStock="yes">
            <TITLE>The Scarlet Letter</TITLE>
            <AUTHOR>Nathaniel Hawthorne</AUTHOR>
            <BINDING>trade paperback</BINDING>
            <PAGES>253</PAGES>
            <PRICE>$4.25</PRICE>
        </BOOK>
        <BOOK InStock="no">
            <TITLE>The Turn of the Screw</TITLE>
            <AUTHOR>Henry James</AUTHOR>
            <BINDING>trade paperback</BINDING>
            <PAGES>384</PAGES>
            <PRICE>$3.35</PRICE>
        </BOOK>
    </INVENTORY>
```

Listing 5-2.

8   If you want to test the validity of your document, read the instructions for using the DTD validity-testing page that is presented in "Checking an XML Document for Validity Using a DTD" on page 396.

6

Defining and Using Entities

An important benefit of adding document type definitions (DTDs) to your XML documents is that they allow you to define entities. You can use entities to save time and reduce the size of your XML documents, to modularize your documents, and to incorporate diverse types of data into your documents. You define an entity in a DTD using a syntax similar to that used to declare an element or attribute in a valid XML document, as described in Chapter 5.

In this chapter, you'll first learn some of the basic terminology used with entities and the different ways entities are classified. You'll then discover how to declare each of the different entity types, and how to insert or identify the entities in your document where you need them. Next you'll learn how to use two XML features that let you insert any type of character in any context: character references and predefined entities. The chapter concludes with a hands-on exercise to give you some practice working with entities within a complete XML document.

Entity Definitions and Classifications

The XML specification uses the term *entity* in a broad, general sense to refer to any of the following types of storage units associated with XML documents:

- The entire XML document itself, which is known as the *document entity*

- An external DTD subset (discussed in "Using an External DTD Subset" in Chapter 5)

- An external file defined as an external entity in the DTD and used within the document

■ A quoted string defined as an internal entity in the DTD and used
within the document

I'll define the terms in the last two items shortly. Note that the first three types
of storage units in this list are files, while the last one is a quoted string.

This chapter, however, uses the term *entity* in a narrower sense—to refer to the
last two types of storage units, namely, external files or quoted strings defined as
entities in the document's DTD and used within the document. For example, the
following DTD for a document containing an article defines the external file
Topics.xml (a file containing a list of the topics covered in the article) as an external entity named *topics,* and it defines a quoted string ("*A Short History of
XML*") as an internal entity named *title*:

```
<!DOCTYPE ARTICLE
   [
   <!ELEMENT ARTICLE (TITLEPAGE, INTRODUCTION, SECTION*)>
   <!ELEMENT TITLEPAGE (#PCDATA)>
   <!ELEMENT INTRODUCTION (#PCDATA)>
   <!ELEMENT SECTION (#PCDATA)>

   <!ENTITY topics SYSTEM "Topics.xml">
   <!ENTITY title "A Short History of XML">
   ]
>
```

You could then insert the complete list of topics anywhere you needed it in the
article (for example, in the abstract, introduction, or conclusion) by simply including an *entity reference* (&*topics;*) as in the following element:

```
<INTRODUCTION>
   This article will cover the following topics:
   &topics; <!-- a reference to the 'topics' entity -->
</INTRODUCTION>
```

You could also insert the article title wherever you needed it by including an entity reference (&*title;*) as shown in this element:

```
<TITLEPAGE>
   Title: &title;  <!-- a reference to the 'title' entity -->
   Author: Michael J. Young
</TITLEPAGE>
```

The entity mechanism is especially useful for storing frequently used blocks of
XML text. For example, if an article title appeared in many locations through-

out the article, using an entity (as in the previous example) would reduce typing, help ensure consistency, reduce the size of the XML document (and the bandwidth required to transmit it), and make it easy to modify the title. You could change the title throughout the whole article by simply editing the entity declaration in the DTD, perhaps to the following:

```
<!ENTITY title "A Long History of XML"> <!-- modified entity
                                              declaration -->
```

If you happen to be a programmer, you'll recognize the similarity between the XML entity mechanism and defined constants in a programming language (such as those declared using the *#define* preprocessor directive in C).

As you'll see later, the entity mechanism is also useful for modularizing your XML documents: You can store blocks of markup declarations or content for elements in separate files and combine them in XML documents in various ways by declaring the files as external entities. And entities are indispensable for identifying non-XML data in an XML document, such as the graphics data for an image.

Types of Entities

Entities can be a bit confusing at first because they come in so many different varieties. Although the material in this section might seem a little abstract at this point (before you've seen the details and examples), having this information to refer back to should make your study of entities considerably easier.

Entities can be classified in three different ways:

- **General vs. parameter.** A *general entity* contains XML text or other text or nontext data that you can use within the document element. Both examples of entities shown in the previous section (*title* and *topics*) are general entities. A *parameter entity* contains XML text that you can use within the DTD. In the XML specification, the unqualified term *entity* refers to a general entity.

- **Internal vs. external.** An *internal entity* consists of a quoted string in the entity declaration in the DTD (such as the *title* entity in the previous section). An *external entity* is a separate file that has been declared as an entity in the DTD (such as the *topics* entity in the previous section).

- **Parsed vs. unparsed.** A *parsed entity* contains XML text (character data, markup, markup declarations, or a combination of these).

When you insert a reference to a parsed entity into the document, the reference is replaced with the entity's contents (also known as its *replacement text*), which become an integral part of the document. The XML parser scans the entity's contents in the same way it scans text you have typed directly into the document. Both example entities shown in the previous section (*title* and *topics*) are parsed entities.

An *unparsed entity* can contain any type of data: XML text or, more commonly, non-XML data. Non-XML data can be either text data (such as a title) or nontext data (such as graphics data for an image). Because an unparsed entity typically does not contain XML, you can't insert its contents into the document using an entity reference and the XML parser doesn't scan its contents. However, you can identify the entity by assigning the entity name to an ENTITY or ENTITIES type attribute, so that the application can access the entity's name and description and do what it wants with the data.

Because entities are classified in these three ways, and each classification has two categories, theoretically there are eight potential types of entities, as diagrammed here:

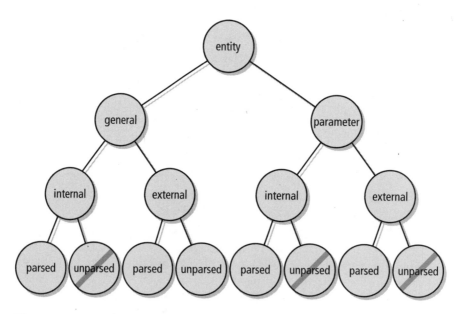

However, XML does not provide the three entity types that are barred out in the figure, and thus XML actually has only five entity types, which you'll learn how to define and use in this chapter:

- General internal parsed

- General external parsed

- General external unparsed

- Parameter internal parsed

- Parameter external parsed

Declaring General Entities

You create an entity by declaring it in the document's DTD, using a type of markup declaration similar to that used to declare elements and attributes. In the following sections, you'll learn how to declare each type of general entity.

Declaring a General Internal Parsed Entity

A declaration for a general internal parsed entity has the following form:

```
<!ENTITY EntityName EntityValue>
```

Here, *EntityName* is the name of the entity. You can select any name provided that you follow these rules:

- The name must begin with a letter or underscore (_), followed by zero or more letters, digits, periods (.), hyphens (-), or underscores.

- The XML specification states that names beginning with the letters *xml* (in any combination of uppercase or lowercase letters) are "reserved for standardization." Although Microsoft Internet Explorer doesn't enforce this restriction, it's better not to begin names with *xml* to avoid future problems.

- Remember that case is significant in all text within markup, including entity names. Thus, an entity named *Bowser* is a different entity than one named *bowser*.

EntityValue is the value of the entity. The value you assign a general internal entity is a series of characters delimited with quotes, known as a *quoted string* or *literal*. You can assign any literal value to a general internal entity provided that you observe these rules:

- The string can be delimited using either single quotes (') or double quotes (").

- The string cannot contain the same quotation character used to delimit it. For example, you can't insert a double quote within the string if you use double quotes to delimit the string.

- The string cannot include an ampersand (&) except to begin a character or general entity reference. Nor can it include a percent sign (%) (for an exception, see the sidebar "An Additional Location for Parameter Entity References" on page 151).

- The contents of the string must, of course, be legal for the location where you intend to insert the entity. For example, if you insert the entity within an element, it must contain one or more of the items that can legally be inserted into elements (nested elements, character data, and so on, as described in "Types of Content in an Element" on page 54). Or, if you insert the entity within an attribute value, it must contain characters that are legal for attribute values (as described in "Rules for Legal Attribute Values" on page 65). I'll describe the places where you can insert a reference to a general internal entity later in this chapter.

For example, the following DTD defines a general internal entity named *title*:

```
<!DOCTYPE ARTICLE
   [
   <!ELEMENT ARTICLE (TITLEPAGE, INTRODUCTION, SECTION*)>
   <!ELEMENT TITLEPAGE (#PCDATA|SUBTITLE)*>
   <!ELEMENT SUBTITLE (#PCDATA)>
   <!ELEMENT INTRODUCTION ANY>
   <!ELEMENT SECTION ANY>

   <!ENTITY title
      "The Story of XML
      <SUBTITLE>The Future Language of the Internet</SUBTITLE>">
   ]
>
```

The *title* entity contains character data plus an element (SUBTITLE). According to the declarations in the DTD, this content can be validly inserted within a TITLEPAGE, INTRODUCTION, or SECTION element, as shown here:

```
<TITLEPAGE>
   Title:  &title;
   Author: Michael J. Young
</TITLEPAGE>
```

The XML processor will replace the entity reference (*&title;*) with the entity contents, and process the contents just as if you had typed them into the document at the position of the reference, like this:

```
<TITLEPAGE>
   Title:  The Story of XML
      <SUBTITLE>The Future Language of the Internet</SUBTITLE>
   Author: Michael J. Young
</TITLEPAGE>
```

Declaring a General External Parsed Entity

A declaration for a general external parsed entity has the following form:

```
<!ENTITY EntityName SYSTEM SystemLiteral>
```

Here, *EntityName* is the name of the entity. You can select any name as long as you follow the general entity naming rules provided in the previous section.

SystemLiteral is a system identifier that describes the location of the file containing the entity data. The system identifier can be delimited using either single quotes (') or double quotes ("), and it can contain any characters except the quote character used to delimit it.

The system identifier specifies the URI (Uniform Resource Indicator) of the file containing the entity data. Currently, the most common form of URI is a traditional URL (Uniform Resource Locator). (See the sidebar "URIs, URLs, and URNs" on page 73.) You can use a fully qualified URL, such as:

```
<!ENTITY abstract
  SYSTEM "http://www.mjyOnline.com/documents/Abstract.xml">
```

Or, you can use a partial URL that specifies a location relative to the location of the XML document containing the URL, such as:

```
<!ENTITY abstract SYSTEM "Abstract.xml">
```

Relative URLs in XML documents work just like relative URLs in HTML pages. For more details on exactly how they work, see "Using an External DTD Subset Only" on page 121.

The entity file contains the entity's replacement text, which can include only items that can legally be inserted into an element (character data, nested elements, and so on, as described in "Types of Content in an Element" on page 54). As you'll learn later in this chapter, you can ultimately insert a general external parsed entity only within an element's content, and *not* within an attribute's value.

> **note**
>
> In a general external parsed entity file, you can optionally include a text declaration in addition to the entity's replacement text. The text declaration must come at the very beginning of the file. For information, see the sidebar "Characters, Encoding, and Languages" on page 77.

As an example, the following DTD defines the external file Topics.xml as a general external parsed entity:

```
<!DOCTYPE ARTICLE
    [
    <!ELEMENT ARTICLE (TITLEPAGE, INTRODUCTION, SECTION*)>
    <!ELEMENT TITLEPAGE (#PCDATA)>
    <!ELEMENT INTRODUCTION ANY>
    <!ELEMENT SECTION (#PCDATA)>
    <!ELEMENT HEADING (#PCDATA)>
    <!ENTITY topics SYSTEM "Topics.xml">
    ]
>
```

Here are the contents of the Topics.xml file:

```
<HEADING>Topics</HEADING>
    The Need for XML
    The Official Goals of XML
    Standard XML Applications
    Real-World Uses for XML
```

This particular external entity file contains two of the items that you can include in an XML element: a nested element and a block of character data. Its contents can be validly inserted within an INTRODUCTION element (which can have any type of content), as shown in this example:

```
<INTRODUCTION>
   Here's what this article covers:
   &topics;
</INTRODUCTION>
```

The XML processor will replace the entity reference (*&topics;*) with the replacement text from the external entity file, and process the text just as if you had typed it into the document at the position of the reference, like this:

```
<INTRODUCTION>
   Here's what this article covers:
   <HEADING>Topics</HEADING>
   The Need for XML
   The Official Goals of XML
   Standard XML Applications
   Real-World Uses for XML
</INTRODUCTION>
```

Declaring a General External Unparsed Entity

A declaration for a general external unparsed entity has this form:

```
<!ENTITY EntityName SYSTEM SystemLiteral NDATA NotationName>
```

Here, *EntityName* is the name of the entity. You can select any name, provided that you follow the general entity naming rules given in "Declaring a General Internal Parsed Entity" earlier in this chapter.

SystemLiteral is a system identifier that describes the location of the file containing the entity data. It works the same way as the system identifier for describing the location of a general external parsed entity, which I explained in the previous section.

> **note**
>
> The keyword NDATA indicates that the entity file contains unparsed data. This keyword derives from SGML, where it stands for notation data.

Defining Entities

6

NotationName is the name of a notation declared in the DTD. The notation describes the format of the data contained in the entity file or gives the location of a program that can process that data. I'll explain notation declarations in the next section.

The general external unparsed entity file can contain any type of text or nontext data. It should, of course, conform to the format description provided by the specified notation.

For example, the DTD in the following XML document defines the file Faun.gif (which contains an image of a book cover) as a general external unparsed entity named *faun*. The name of this entity's notation is GIF, which is defined to point to the location of a program that can display a graphics file in the GIF format (ShowGif.exe). The DTD also defines an empty element named COVERIMAGE, and an ENTITY type attribute for that element named *Source*:

```
<?xml version="1.0"?>

<!DOCTYPE BOOK
    [
    <!ELEMENT BOOK (TITLE, AUTHOR, COVERIMAGE)>
    <!ELEMENT TITLE (#PCDATA)>
    <!ELEMENT AUTHOR (#PCDATA)>
    <!ELEMENT COVERIMAGE EMPTY>
    <!ATTLIST COVERIMAGE   Source ENTITY #REQUIRED>

    <!NOTATION GIF SYSTEM "ShowGif.exe">
    <!ENTITY faun SYSTEM "Faun.gif" NDATA GIF>
    ]
>

<BOOK>
    <TITLE>The Marble Faun</TITLE>
    <AUTHOR>Nathaniel Hawthorne</AUTHOR>
    <COVERIMAGE Source="faun" />
</BOOK>
```

In the document element, the *Source* attribute of the COVERIMAGE element is assigned the name of the external entity that contains the graphics data for the cover image to be displayed. Because *Source* has the ENTITY type, you can assign it the name of a general external unparsed entity. In fact, the only way you can use this type of entity is to assign its name to an ENTITY or ENTITIES type attribute.

note

Unlike an external parsed entity file, a general external unparsed entity file is not accessed directly by the XML processor. Rather, the processor merely provides the entity name, system identifier, and notation name to the application. Likewise, the processor doesn't access a location or program indicated by a notation, but only passes the notation name and system identifier to the application. In fact, the Internet Explorer XML processor doesn't even check whether a general external unparsed entity file, or the target of a notation, exists. The application can do what it wants with the entity and notation information. For example, it might run the program associated with the notation and have it display the data in the entity file. In Chapter 11, you'll learn how to write Web page scripts that access entities and notations.

Declaring a Notation

A notation describes a particular data format. It does this by providing the address of a description of the format, the address of a program that can handle data in that format, or a simple format description. You can use a notation to describe the format of a general external unparsed entity (as you saw in the previous section), or you can assign a notation to an attribute that has the NOTATION enumerated type (as described in "Specifying an Enumerated Type" in Chapter 5).

A notation has the following general form:

```
<!NOTATION NotationName SYSTEM SystemLiteral>
```

Here, *NotationName* is the notation name. You can choose any name you want, provided that it begins with a letter or underscore (_), followed by zero or more letters, digits, periods (.), hyphens (-), or underscores. You should normally choose a meaningful name that indicates the format. For example, if you define a notation to describe the bitmap format, you might name it BMP. (However, the XML specification states that names beginning with the letters *xml,* in any combination of uppercase or lowercase letters, are "reserved for standardization." Although Internet Explorer doesn't enforce this restriction, it's better not to begin names with *xml* to avoid future problems.)

SystemLiteral is a system identifier that can be delimited using either single quotes (') or double quotes ("), and can contain any characters except the quotation character used to delimit it. You can include in the system identifier any format description that would be meaningful to the application that is going to display or handle the XML document. (Remember that the XML processor

Defining Entities — 6

doesn't use the notation information itself, but merely passes it on to the application, which might be a script in a Web page.) For example, you might include one of the following in the system identifier:

- The URI of a program that can process or display the data format, as in the following examples:

```
<!NOTATION BMP SYSTEM "Pbrush.exe">
<!NOTATION GIF
  SYSTEM "http://www.mjyOnline.com/ShowGif.exe">
```

- The URI of an online document that describes the format, such as:

```
<!NOTATION STRANGEFORMAT
  SYSTEM "http://www.mjyOnline.com/StrangeFormat.htm">
```

- A simple description of the format, such as:

```
<!NOTATION GIF SYSTEM "Graphic Interchange Format">
```

For information on URIs, see the sidebar "URIs, URLs, and URNs" on page 73.

Duplicate Names in Markup Declarations

The names of elements, attributes, general entities, parameter entities, and notations don't conflict with each other. In other words, in an XML document you can assign the same name to an element, an attribute, a general entity, a parameter entity, and a notation. For example, it would be valid (although fairly ludicrous) to have all of the following markup declarations in a single DTD:

```
<!ELEMENT AUTHOR (#PCDATA)>
<!ATTLIST AUTHOR   AUTHOR CDATA "lack of imagination">
<!ENTITY AUTHOR "more lack of imagination">
<!ENTITY % AUTHOR "<!-- yet more lack of imagination -->">
<!NOTATION AUTHOR SYSTEM "the ultimate in lack of
imagination">
```

Unless you have some reason for assigning the same name to different types of items, however, you will avoid unnecessary confusion by choosing unique names.

Declaring Parameter Entities

You declare a parameter entity using a form of markup declaration similar to that used for general entities. In the following sections, you'll learn how to declare both types of parameter entities.

Declaring a Parameter Internal Parsed Entity

A declaration for a parameter internal parsed entity has the following general form:

```
<!ENTITY % EntityName EntityValue>
```

Here, *EntityName* is the name of the entity. You can select any name, provided that you follow these rules:

- The name must begin with a letter or underscore (_), followed by zero or more letters, digits, periods (.), hyphens (-), or underscores.

- The XML specification states that names beginning with the letters *xml* (in any combination of uppercase or lowercase letters) are "reserved for standardization." Although Internet Explorer doesn't enforce this restriction, it's better not to begin names with *xml* to avoid future problems.

- Remember that case is significant in all text within markup, including entity names. Thus, an entity named *Spot* is a different entity than one named *spot*.

EntityValue is the value of the entity. The value you assign a parameter internal entity is a series of characters delimited with quotes, known as a *quoted string* or *literal*. You can assign any literal value to a parameter internal entity, provided that you observe these rules:

- The string can be delimited using either single quotes (') or double quotes (").

- The string cannot contain the same quotation character used to delimit it.

- The string cannot include an ampersand (&) except to begin a character or general entity reference. Nor can it include the percent sign (%) (for an exception, see the sidebar "An Additional Location for Parameter Entity References" on page 151).

Defining Entities   6

▨ You can insert a parameter internal entity only where a markup declaration can occur in the DTD, not *within* a markup declaration. Therefore, the *EntityValue* string must contain one or more complete markup declarations of the types allowed in a DTD. Specifically, a parameter entity can contain element type declarations, attribute-list declarations, general entity declarations, notation declarations, processing instructions, or comments. I described these types of markup declarations in "Creating the Document Type Definition" in Chapter 5. Parameter entity declarations and references are not allowed. (For exceptions to the guidelines given in this paragraph, see the sidebar "An Additional Location for Parameter Entity References" on page 151.)

As an example, the following DTD declares a parameter internal entity named *author* that contains three markup declarations: a comment, an element type declaration, and an attribute-list declaration. The contents of the entity are inserted at the end of the DTD by means of a parameter entity reference (*%author;*):

```
<!DOCTYPE BOOK
   [
   <!ENTITY % author
      "<!-- author information -->
      <!ELEMENT AUTHOR (#PCDATA)>
      <!ATTLIST AUTHOR   Nationality CDATA 'American'>"
   >

   <!ELEMENT BOOK (TITLE, AUTHOR)>
   <!ELEMENT TITLE (#PCDATA)>
   %author;
   ]
>
```

Notice that the default attribute value contained in the entity declaration (*American*) is delimited with single quotes to avoid using the same quotation character used to delimit the entire entity value. The above DTD is equivalent to the following one:

```
<!DOCTYPE BOOK
   [
   <!ELEMENT BOOK (TITLE, AUTHOR)>
   <!ELEMENT TITLE (#PCDATA)>
```

```
<!-- author information -->
<!ELEMENT AUTHOR (#PCDATA)>
<!ATTLIST AUTHOR   Nationality CDATA 'American'>
]
>
```

> **note**
>
> For a brief description of a more useful way to employ parameter internal parsed entities (available only within an external file), see the sidebar "An Additional Location for Parameter Entity References" on page 73.

Declaring a Parameter External Parsed Entity

A declaration for a parameter external parsed entity has the following general form:

```
<!ENTITY % EntityName SYSTEM SystemLiteral>
```

Here, *EntityName* is the name of the entity. You can select any name provided that you follow the parameter entity naming rules given in the previous section.

SystemLiteral is a system identifier that describes the location of the file containing the entity data. The system identifier can be delimited using either single quotes (') or double quotes ("), and it can contain any characters except the quotation character used to delimit it.

The system identifier specifies the URI (Uniform Resource Indicator) of the file containing the parameter entity data. Currently, the most common form of URI is a traditional URL (Uniform Resource Locator). (See the sidebar "URIs, URLs, and URNs" on page 121.) You can use a fully qualified URL, such as:

```
<!ENTITY % declarations
    SYSTEM "http://www.mjyOnline.com/documents/Declarations.dtd">
```

Or, you can use a partial URL that specifies a location that is relative to the location of the XML document containing the URL, such as:

```
<!ENTITY % declarations SYSTEM "Declarations.dtd">
```

As I mentioned earlier, relative URLs in XML documents work just like relative URLs in HTML pages. For more details on exactly how they work, see "Using an External DTD Subset Only" on page 151.

The entity file contains the entity's replacement text, which must consist of complete markup declarations of the types allowed in a DTD—specifically, element type declarations, attribute-list declarations, entity declarations, notation declarations, processing instructions, or comments. (I described these types of markup declarations in "Creating the Document Type Definition" in Chapter 5.) You can also include parameter entity references between markup declarations, and you can include IGNORE and INCLUDE sections. I described IGNORE and INCLUDE sections in "Conditionally Ignoring Sections of an External DTD Subset" in Chapter 5. (For exceptions to the guidelines given in this paragraph, see the sidebar "An Additional Location for Parameter Entity References" on page 151.)

> **note**
>
> In a parameter external entity file, you can optionally include a text declaration in addition to the entity's replacement text. The text declaration must come at the very beginning of the file. For information, see the sidebar "Characters, Encoding, and Languages" on page 77.

You can use parameter external entities to store groups of related declarations. Say, for example, that your business sells books, CDs, posters, and other items. You could place the declarations for each type of item in a separate file. This would allow you to combine these groups of declarations in various ways. For instance, you might want to create an XML document that describes only your inventory of books and CDs. To do this, you could include your book and CD declarations in the document's DTD by using parameter external entities, as shown in this example XML document:

```
<?xml version="1.0"?>

<!DOCTYPE INVENTORY
   [
   <!ELEMENT INVENTORY (BOOK | CD)*>

   <!ENTITY % book_decls SYSTEM "Book.dtd">
   <!ENTITY % cd_decls SYSTEM "CD.dtd">

   %book_decls;
   %cd_decls;
   ]
>
```

```
<INVENTORY>
  <BOOK>
     <BOOKTITLE>The Marble Faun</BOOKTITLE>
     <AUTHOR>Nathaniel Hawthorne</AUTHOR>
     <PAGES>473</PAGES>
  </BOOK>
  <CD>
     <CDTITLE>Concerti Grossi Opus 3</CDTITLE>
     <COMPOSER>Handel</COMPOSER>
     <LENGTH>72 minutes</LENGTH>
  </CD>
  <BOOK>
     <BOOKTITLE>Leaves of Grass</BOOKTITLE>
     <AUTHOR>Walt Whitman</AUTHOR>
     <PAGES>462</PAGES>
  </BOOK>

  <!-- additional items... -->

</INVENTORY>
```

Here are the contents of the Book.dtd entity file:

```
<!ELEMENT BOOK (BOOKTITLE, AUTHOR, PAGES)>
<!ELEMENT BOOKTITLE (#PCDATA)>
<!ELEMENT AUTHOR (#PCDATA)>
<!ELEMENT PAGES (#PCDATA)>
```

And here are the contents of the CD.dtd entity file:

```
<!ELEMENT CD (CDTITLE, COMPOSER, LENGTH)>
<!ELEMENT CDTITLE (#PCDATA)>
<!ELEMENT COMPOSER (#PCDATA)>
<!ELEMENT LENGTH (#PCDATA)>
```

Notice that a parameter external entity works much like an external DTD subset. Parameter external entities, however, are more flexible—they allow you to include several external declaration files and to include them in any order. (Recall that an external DTD subset is always processed after the entire internal DTD subset has been processed.)

Defining Entities

Inserting Entity References

As you've learned, you insert the contents (that is, the replacement text) of an entity into a document by using an entity reference. You've already seen quite a few examples of entity references. To review and summarize, general entities are referenced as:

`&EntityName;`

and parameter entities are referenced as:

`%EntityName;`

where *EntityName* is the name assigned to the entity in the declaration. The one exception is a general external unparsed entity, which you cannot insert by using a reference. The only way to use this type of entity is to assign its name to an attribute that has the ENTITY or ENTITIES type. (See "Specifying a Tokenized Type" in Chapter 5.)

The declaration of an entity must precede any reference to that entity. (An exception is that you can include a reference to a general entity in the literal value of a general internal entity declaration *before* the referenced entity is declared.)

Redeclarations in a DTD

Although it's fairly easy to spot the redeclaration of an item if all your markup declarations are in an internal DTD subset, it might not be so easy to spot a redeclaration if markup declarations are contained in an external DTD subset or in one or more parameter external entities. An XML processor handles a redeclaration in one of two ways:

- Redeclaring an attribute with the same name and same element type, or an entity with the same name and same type (general or parameter), is valid. The processor uses the first declaration it encounters and simply ignores any redeclarations. Because the processor handles the internal DTD subset (including the contents of any parameter external entities that the subset references) *before* it handles an external DTD subset, you can use the internal subset to override the declaration of an attribute or entity declared in the external subset. This can be a way of customizing or fine-tuning an external DTD subset for a particular XML document.

- Redeclaring an element type with the same name, or a notation with the same name, is a validity error.

Also, a parsed entity must not contain a direct or indirect reference to itself, which is known as a *recursive reference* and would result in an infinite reference loop if a processor attempted to expand the entity reference. The following entity contains an illegal direct recursive reference:

```
<!ENTITY RecursionDemo "ILLEGAL direct recursive reference:
&RecursionDemo;">
```

And the following entities demonstrate an illegal indirect recursive reference:

```
<!ENTITY OtherEntity "&RecursionDemo;">
<!ENTITY RecursionDemo "ILLEGAL indirect recursive reference:
&OtherEntity;">
```

For each type of entity, the following table gives the form of the entity reference and lists the places where you can insert references to the entity. At the end of the description of each insertion place, the table cites the section in this chapter where you'll find an example. I'll discuss character references later in the chapter, but I've included them in the table for completeness.

Entity type	Form of entity reference, where *EntityName* is the name of the entity	Places where you can insert an entity reference (example)
General internal parsed	*&EntityName;*	■ In an element's content (see "Declaring a General Internal Parsed Entity") ■ In an attribute value (the default value in an attribute definition, or the assigned value in an element start-tag) (see "Entity Reference Example 1") ■ In the literal value of an internal entity declaration (see "Entity Reference Example 2")
General external parsed	*&EntityName;*	■ In an element's content (see "Declaring a General External Parsed Entity") ■ In the literal value of a general internal entity declaration, although in this case the general internal entity can't be inserted into an attribute value (see "Entity Reference Example 2")

continued

continued

Entity type	Form of entity reference, where *EntityName* is the name of the entity	Places where you can insert an entity reference (example)
General external unparsed	*EntAttr*='*EntityName*' where *EntAttr* is an ENTITY or ENTITIES type attribute	■ You can't insert a reference to this type of entity, but you can identify the entity by assigning its name to an attribute that has the ENTITY or ENTITIES type (see "Declaring a General External Unparsed Entity")
Parameter internal parsed	%*EntityName*;	■ In a DTD where markup declarations can occur, not *within* markup declarations (for an exception, see the sidebar "An Additional Location for Parameter Entity References" following this table) (see "Declaring a Parameter Internal Parsed Entity")
Parameter external parsed	%*EntityName*;	■ In a DTD where markup declarations can occur, not *within* markup declarations (for an exception, see the sidebar "An Additional Location for Parameter Entity References" following this table) (see "Declaring a Parameter External Parsed Entity")
Character reference		 or &#x*h*; where 9 is the numeric code for the character in decimal, and *h* is the numeric code in hexadecimal	■ In an element's content (see "Inserting Character References") ■ In an attribute value (the default value in an attribute definition, or the assigned value in an element start-tag) (see "Inserting Character References") ■ In the literal value of an internal entity declaration (see "Inserting Character References")

An Additional Location for Parameter Entity References

In this chapter, I've stated that you can insert a parameter entity reference only where markup declarations can occur in a DTD—not within markup declarations—and therefore a parameter entity must contain one or more complete markup declarations of the types allowed in a DTD. This is a safe rule that you can use in any situation and that will let you work with parameter entities without undue complexity.

The XML specification, however, does allow you to insert a reference to an internal or external parameter entity within markup declarations, as well as between markup declarations, *provided* that the markup declarations occur in an external DTD subset or in a parameter external parsed entity file and *not* in an internal DTD subset. The permissible content of an entity depends upon where you are going to insert it. If you insert an entity reference within a markup declaration, the entity can of course contain a legal *fragment* of a markup declaration rather than a complete markup declaration. You can insert a parameter entity reference in most places within markup (including within the literal value of an internal entity declaration).

The ability to insert parameter entity references within markup declarations makes parameter internal entities much more useful than implied by the example I gave earlier in the chapter in "Declaring a Parameter Internal Parsed Entity." You could, for example, store a complex attribute definition in a parameter internal entity and then assign that attribute to an entire group of elements by simply inserting the entity reference into each element's attribute-list declaration. (This would save typing, reduce the size of the document, and make it easier to modify the attribute definition.)

However, the guidelines for including references to parameter entities within markup declarations are complex. The XML specification includes more than a dozen distinct rules describing where parameter entities can be inserted in markup declarations, what they can contain, and how they must nest with the surrounding markup declaration content (hence my decision to omit the details from this chapter). But if you want to explore this territory, you'll find complete information in sections 2, 3, and 4 of the XML specification at *http://www.w3.org/TR/REC-xml*.

Entity Reference Example 1

The following XML document declares two general internal parsed entities, *am* and *en*. The document uses a reference to *am* to assign a default value to the *Nationality* attribute, and it uses a reference to *en* to assign a value to the *Nationality* attribute in the AUTHOR element. An advantage of using an entity here is that you could change the value throughout the entire document (assuming it had many elements) by simply editing the entity declaration (for example, changing the value of *en* from "English" to "British").

```
<?xml version="1.0"?>

<!DOCTYPE INVENTORY
   [
   <!ENTITY am "American">
   <!ENTITY en "English">

   <!ELEMENT INVENTORY (BOOK*)>
   <!ELEMENT BOOK (TITLE, AUTHOR)>
   <!ELEMENT TITLE (#PCDATA)>
   <!ELEMENT AUTHOR (#PCDATA)>
   <!ATTLIST AUTHOR   Nationality CDATA "&am;">
   ]
>
<INVENTORY>
   <BOOK>
      <TITLE>David Copperfield</TITLE>
      <AUTHOR Nationality="&en;">Charles Dickens</AUTHOR>
   </BOOK>

   <!-- other elements... -->

</INVENTORY>
```

Entity Reference Example 2

The following DTD defines a general internal parsed entity (*int_entity*) and a general external parsed entity (*ext_entity*). It then defines another general internal parsed entity (*combo_entity*) and inserts both previous entities into the *combo_entity* value.

```
<!DOCTYPE INVENTORY
   [
   <!ENTITY int_entity "internal entity value">
```

```
<!ENTITY ext_entity SYSTEM "Entity.xml">

<!ENTITY combo_entity
    "value composed of &ext_entity; plus &int_entity;">

<!-- other markup declarations... -->

]
>
```

Because *combo_entity* contains a reference to an external entity, you could *not* insert a reference to *combo_entity* in an attribute's value. The XML specification states that an attribute value cannot contain a direct or indirect reference to an external entity. A reference to *combo_entity* constitutes an indirect reference to an external entity.

Inserting Character References

You can use a character reference to insert a character that isn't on your keyboard (for example, ß), or to insert a character that would be illegal to insert literally in the current context (for example, a left angle bracket (<) or ampersand (&) as part of an element's character data). You don't need to define anything to be able to use a character reference—you can simply insert it where you need it.

> **note**
> You can directly insert a character that doesn't appear on your keyboard by using the Windows Character Map program, or the Alt key in conjunction with the numeric keypad (for example, pressing Alt+0223 to enter a ß character). However, the non-keyboard characters for an English-language keyboard are outside of the ASCII character set. As explained in the sidebar "Characters, Encoding, and Languages" on page 77, non-ASCII characters are illegal in an XML document unless the document is properly encoded. You can avoid this problem by using character references to insert an occasional non-ASCII character. To insert many non-ASCII characters (for example, to write a document in a language other than English), read the information on encoding in the "Characters, Encoding, and Languages" sidebar.

A character reference has two different forms. The first form is:

	

where 9 is one or more decimal digits (0 through 9), representing the numeric code for the character in the Unicode character set (or the equivalent ISO/IEC 10646 character set).

The second form of character reference is:

&#xh;

where *h* is one or more hexadecimal digits (0 through f or F), also representing the numeric code for the character in the Unicode character set.

For example, both *A* and *A* insert the capital letter *A*. (The numeric code for *A* is 65 in decimal and 41 in hexadecimal.)

You can use a character reference to insert only a character that is legal in an XML document. The following table gives the numeric codes for the Unicode characters you can legally use in XML documents. Inserting a character reference for a character outside of this legal set will cause a fatal (well-formedness) error.

Decimal codes for legal XML characters	Equivalent hexadecimal codes
9, 10, 13 (tab, line feed, and carriage-return)	9, A, D
32 through 127 (standard ASCII characters)	20 through 7F
128 through 55295	80 through D7FF
57344 through 65533	E000 through FFFD
65536 through 1114111	10000 through 10FFFF

The Unicode characters with numeric codes less than 128 (decimal) belong to the well-known ASCII character set and have the same codes as they do in the ASCII standard. The following figure shows all the Unicode characters that are legal in XML and that have numeric codes less than 256 (decimal). In each item in the figure, the initial number (1:, 2:, 3:, and so on) is the decimal code for the character, and the character following the colon is the actual character—if any—that Internet Explorer displays.

9:	62: >	95: _	128: □	161: ¡	194: Â	227: ã
10:	63: ?	96: `	129: □	162: ¢	195: Ã	228: ä
13:	64: @	97: a	130: □	163: £	196: Ä	229: å
32:	65: A	98: b	131: □	164: ¤	197: Å	230: æ
33: !	66: B	99: c	132: □	165: ¥	198: Æ	231: ç
34: "	67: C	100: d	133: □	166: ¦	199: Ç	232: è
35: #	68: D	101: e	134: □	167: §	200: È	233: é
36: $	69: E	102: f	135: □	168: ¨	201: É	234: ê
37: %	70: F	103: g	136: □	169: ©	202: Ê	235: ë
38: &	71: G	104: h	137: □	170: ª	203: Ë	236: ì
39: '	72: H	105: i	138: □	171: «	204: Ì	237: í
40: (	73: I	106: j	139: □	172: ¬	205: Í	238: î
41:)	74: J	107: k	140: □	173:	206: Î	239: ï
42: *	75: K	108: l	141: □	174: ®	207: Ï	240: ð
43: +	76: L	109: m	142: □	175: ¯	208: Ð	241: ñ
44: ,	77: M	110: n	143: □	176: °	209: Ñ	242: ò
45: -	78: N	111: o	144: □	177: ±	210: Ò	243: ó
46: .	79: O	112: p	145: □	178: ²	211: Ó	244: ô
47: /	80: P	113: q	146: □	179: ³	212: Ô	245: õ
48: 0	81: Q	114: r	147: □	180: ´	213: Õ	246: ö
49: 1	82: R	115: s	148: □	181: µ	214: Ö	247: ÷
50: 2	83: S	116: t	149: □	182: ¶	215: ×	248: ø
51: 3	84: T	117: u	150: □	183: ·	216: Ø	249: ù
52: 4	85: U	118: v	151: □	184: ¸	217: Ù	250: ú
53: 5	86: V	119: w	152: □	185: ¹	218: Ú	251: û
54: 6	87: W	120: x	153: □	186: º	219: Û	252: ü
55: 7	88: X	121: y	154: □	187: »	220: Ü	253: ý
56: 8	89: Y	122: z	155: □	188: ¼	221: Ý	254: þ
57: 9	90: Z	123: {	156: □	189: ½	222: Þ	255: ÿ
58: :	91: [	124:		157: □	190: ¾	223: ß	
59: ;	92: \	125: }	158: □	191: ¿	224: à	
60: <	93:]	126: ~	159: □	192: À	225: á	
61: =	94: ^	127: □	160:	193: Á	226: â	

For example, you can see in the table that the decimal character code for ß is 223. You could therefore insert this character in your document by entering the following character reference:

```
&#223;
```

> **note**
>
> See the table on page 149 for a concise list of the document locations where you can insert a character reference. An example of each location follows.

In the following element, the left angle bracket (<) is inserted into the element's character data by using the character reference < (60 is the decimal code for <). Recall that it's illegal to insert < literally into character data.

```
<TITLE>&#60;The Legend of Sleepy Hollow></TITLE>
```

In the following element, the ä character reference is used to insert ä into an attribute's value. This character doesn't appear on an English-language keyboard. Also, if you inserted it directly into a text file created with a typical text editor, it would probably not be encoded properly for XML.

Defining Entities
6

```
<RESIDENT Address="Seilerst&#228;tte 30, Wien">Mike Young
</RESIDENT>
```

Finally, in the following general internal parsed entity declaration in a DTD, the % character reference is used to insert the percent sign (%) (37 is the decimal code for %), which can't be entered literally into an internal entity value:

```
<!ENTITY heading1 "&#37; Complete">
```

> ## tip
>
> If you frequently insert a particular non-keyboard character, such as an em dash (—), into your XML documents, declare a general internal parsed entity containing the character reference. For example, if you declared the following entity for an em dash,
>
> ```
> <!ENTITY em-dash "&#8212;">
> ```
>
> you could insert the character using the entity reference &em-dash;, which is simpler to remember than the character reference and would make your documents easier for humans to read.

Using Predefined Entities

In an XML document, you can use a reference to a predefined entity to insert any of the five characters listed in the following table in a location where inserting the literal character would be illegal.

Predefined entity reference	Character inserted	Equivalent character reference
&amp;	&	&#38;
&lt;	<	&#60;
&gt;	>	&#62;
&apos;	'	&#39;
&quot;	"	&#34;

Inserting one of these predefined entity references is equivalent to inserting the corresponding character reference. The predefined entity references are just easier to remember and to understand when you see them in a document.

The predefined entities work like other general internal entities, except that you can use references to them without declaring the entities. You can insert predefined entities in the same places as general internal entities, namely:

- In an element's content

- In an attribute's value (the default value in an attribute declaration or the assigned attribute value in an element's start-tag)

- In the literal value of an internal entity declaration

In the following three examples, predefined entity references are used to insert characters that would be illegal to insert literally.

In the first example, *<* is used to insert a left angle bracket (<) into an element's content:

```
<TITLE>&lt;The Legend of Sleepy Hollow></TITLE>
```

In the second example, *&* is used to insert an ampersand (&) into an attribute value:

```
<PRODUCT Company="Ongaro &amp; Sons">3/4" T fitting</PRODUCT>
```

In the third example, *"* is used to insert a double quote (") into an entity value (which would be illegal to enter literally because it's the same character used to delimit the string):

```
<!ENTITY heading "Christopher &quot;Kit&quot; Carson">
```

Adding Entities to a Document

In the following exercise, you'll get some hands-on experience with entities by adding several general entities to the Inventory Valid.xml example document that you created in Chapter 5.

Add Entities to the Example Document

1　In your text editor, open the Inventory Valid.xml document you created in "Converting a Well-Formed Document to a Valid Document" in Chapter 5. (The document is given in Listing 5-2 and on the companion CD.)

2　At the beginning of the document's DTD (the block of text delimited with [] characters near the top of the document), add the following entity and notation declarations:

```
<!-- entities for assigning to the BINDING element: -->
<!ENTITY mass "mass market paperback">
<!ENTITY trade "trade paperback">
<!ENTITY hard "hardcover">
```

```
<!-- external entities containing reviews -->
<!-- to be assigned to Review attribute of BOOK elements -->
<!NOTATION DOC SYSTEM "Microsoft Word document">
<!NOTATION TXT SYSTEM "plain text file">
<!ENTITY rev_leaves SYSTEM "Review of Leaves of Grass.doc"
    NDATA DOC>
<!ENTITY rev_faun1 SYSTEM "Review 01 of The Marble Faun.doc"
    NDATA DOC>
<!ENTITY rev_faun2 SYSTEM "Review 02 of The Marble Faun.txt"
    NDATA TXT>
<!ENTITY rev_screw
    SYSTEM "Review of The Turn of the Screw.txt"
    NDATA TXT>
```

The first three entities are general internal parsed entities that you can insert in BINDING elements rather than typing the actual binding description into each element. Using entities can help ensure that your descriptions of a given binding type are consistent from book to book. Also, entities make it easier to modify a description. (For example, you could change *hardcover* to *hardback* in every BINDING element where it occurs by simply editing the *hard* entity.)

The next (and final) four entities are general external unparsed entities that allow you to attach external files containing book reviews to BOOK elements.

3   Add the *Reviews* attribute to the attribute-list declaration for the BOOK element, later in the DTD, so that it reads like this:

```
<!ATTLIST BOOK    InStock (yes|no) #REQUIRED
                  Reviews ENTITIES #IMPLIED>
```

Reviews is an optional attribute (#IMPLIED) to which you can assign the names of one or more general external unparsed entities (*Reviews* has the ENTITIES type).

4   In each BINDING element, replace the binding description with the corresponding entity reference. For example, you would change the BINDING element for *The Adventures of Huckleberry Finn* from:

```
<BINDING>mass market paperback</BINDING>
```
to:
```
<BINDING>&mass;</BINDING>
```

5   Add *Reviews* attributes to BOOK elements as follows:
   ▪ For Leaves of Grass:

```
<BOOK InStock="no" Reviews="rev_leaves">
```

The *standalone* Document Declaration

As you learned near the beginning of Chapter 3, you can optionally include a *standalone* document declaration in the XML declaration at the start of an XML document. The *standalone* document declaration tells the processor whether the document contains any external markup declarations that affect the document content passed to the application. An *external markup declaration* is one that is contained in an external DTD subset, in an external parameter entity, or even in an internal parameter entity. (An internal parameter entity is included because a non-validating XML processor isn't required to read its contents, just as it isn't required to read an external DTD subset or external parameter entity.) Examples of external markup declarations that can affect the document's content include an entity declaration, or an attribute-list declaration that supplies a default attribute value.

If an XML document has external markup declarations, but none of these declarations affects the document content, you should set *standalone* to *yes*, as in this XML declaration:

```
<?xml version="1.0" standalone="yes"?>
```

(As with the version number—1.0 in this example—you can enclose the *standalone* value in either double or single quotes. If you also include an encoding declaration in the XML declaration, as explained in the sidebar "Characters, Encoding, and Languages" on page 77, it must go after the version specification but before the *standalone* document declaration.)

If, however, the document contains external markup declarations that affect the document's content, you should set *standalone* to *no* or omit the *standalone* declaration. (If you omit the *standalone* declaration, the processor will assume the value *no*.)

Correctly setting the *standalone* declaration can help the processor process the XML document appropriately. For example, if you correctly set *standalone* to *yes*, the processor will, appropriately, generate a fatal well-formedness error if it encounters a reference to an entity but doesn't find a declaration for that entity among the internal markup declarations. The *standalone* setting might also help an application correctly interpret the document content it receives from a non-validating processor.

For more information on the *standalone* document declaration, including a list of all cases where external markup declarations affect a document's content (and thereby prohibit setting *standalone* to *yes*), see the section "2.9 Standalone Document Declaration" in the XML specification at *http://www.w3.org/TR/REC-xml*.

Defining Entities

6

- For The Marble Faun:

  ```
  <BOOK InStock="yes" Reviews="rev_faun1 rev_faun2">
  ```

- For The Turn of the Screw:

  ```
  <BOOK InStock="no" Reviews="rev_screw">
  ```

6   To reflect the new filename you're going to assign, change the comment at the beginning of the document from:

```
<!-- File Name: Inventory Valid.xml -->
```
to:
```
<!-- File Name: Inventory Valid Entity.xml -->
```

7   Use your text editor's Save As command to save a copy of the modified document under the filename Inventory Valid Entity.xml.

Listing 6-1 shows the complete XML document. (You'll find a copy of this listing on the companion CD under the filename Inventory Valid Entity.xml.)

Inventory Valid Entity.xml

```
<?xml version="1.0"?>

<!-- File Name: Inventory Valid Entity.xml -->

<!DOCTYPE INVENTORY
   [
   <!-- entities for assigning to the BINDING element: -->
   <!ENTITY mass "mass market paperback">
   <!ENTITY trade "trade paperback">
   <!ENTITY hard "hardcover">

   <!-- external entities containing reviews -->
   <!-- to be assigned to Review attribute of BOOK elements -->
   <!NOTATION DOC SYSTEM "Microsoft Word document">
   <!NOTATION TXT SYSTEM "plain text file">
   <!ENTITY rev_leaves SYSTEM "Review of Leaves of Grass.doc"
      NDATA DOC>
   <!ENTITY rev_faun1 SYSTEM "Review 01 of The Marble Faun.doc"
      NDATA DOC>
   <!ENTITY rev_faun2 SYSTEM "Review 02 of The Marble Faun.txt"
      NDATA TXT>
   <!ENTITY rev_screw
      SYSTEM "Review of The Turn of the Screw.txt"
      NDATA TXT>
```

```
<!ELEMENT INVENTORY (BOOK)*>

<!ELEMENT BOOK (TITLE, AUTHOR, BINDING, PAGES, PRICE)>
<!ATTLIST BOOK    InStock (yes|no) #REQUIRED
                  Reviews ENTITIES #IMPLIED>

<!ELEMENT TITLE (#PCDATA | SUBTITLE)*>

<!ELEMENT SUBTITLE (#PCDATA)>

<!ELEMENT AUTHOR (#PCDATA)>
<!ATTLIST AUTHOR    Born CDATA #IMPLIED>

<!ELEMENT BINDING (#PCDATA)>

<!ELEMENT PAGES (#PCDATA)>

<!ELEMENT PRICE (#PCDATA)>
    ]
>

<INVENTORY>
    <BOOK InStock="yes">
        <TITLE>The Adventures of Huckleberry Finn</TITLE>
        <AUTHOR Born="1835">Mark Twain</AUTHOR>
        <BINDING>&mass;</BINDING>
        <PAGES>298</PAGES>
        <PRICE>$5.49</PRICE>
    </BOOK>
    <BOOK InStock="no" Reviews="rev_leaves">
        <TITLE>Leaves of Grass</TITLE>
        <AUTHOR Born="1819">Walt Whitman</AUTHOR>
        <BINDING>&hard;</BINDING>
        <PAGES>462</PAGES>
        <PRICE>$7.75</PRICE>
    </BOOK>
    <BOOK InStock="yes">
        <TITLE>The Legend of Sleepy Hollow</TITLE>
        <AUTHOR>Washington Irving</AUTHOR>
        <BINDING>&mass;</BINDING>
        <PAGES>98</PAGES>
```

```
        <PRICE>$2.95</PRICE>
     </BOOK>
     <BOOK InStock="yes" Reviews="rev_faun1 rev_faun2">
        <TITLE>The Marble Faun</TITLE>
        <AUTHOR Born="1804">Nathaniel Hawthorne</AUTHOR>
        <BINDING>&trade;</BINDING>
        <PAGES>473</PAGES>
        <PRICE>$10.95</PRICE>
     </BOOK>
     <BOOK InStock="no">
        <TITLE>Moby-Dick <SUBTITLE>Or, The Whale</SUBTITLE></TITLE>
        <AUTHOR Born="1819">Herman Melville</AUTHOR>
        <BINDING>&hard;</BINDING>
        <PAGES>724</PAGES>
        <PRICE>$9.95</PRICE>
     </BOOK>
     <BOOK InStock="yes">
        <TITLE>The Portrait of a Lady</TITLE>
        <AUTHOR>Henry James</AUTHOR>
        <BINDING>&mass;</BINDING>
        <PAGES>256</PAGES>
        <PRICE>$4.95</PRICE>
     </BOOK>
     <BOOK InStock="yes">
        <TITLE>The Scarlet Letter</TITLE>
        <AUTHOR>Nathaniel Hawthorne</AUTHOR>
        <BINDING>&trade;</BINDING>
        <PAGES>253</PAGES>
        <PRICE>$4.25</PRICE>
     </BOOK>
     <BOOK InStock="no" Reviews="rev_screw">
        <TITLE>The Turn of the Screw</TITLE>
        <AUTHOR>Henry James</AUTHOR>
        <BINDING>&trade;</BINDING>
        <PAGES>384</PAGES>
        <PRICE>$3.35</PRICE>
     </BOOK>
</INVENTORY>
```

Listing 6-1.

8   If you want to test the validity of your document, read the instructions for using the DTD validity-testing page in "Checking an XML Document for Validity Using a DTD" on page 396.

CHAPTER

7

Creating Valid XML Documents Using XML Schemas

An *XML schema* is a document that defines the content and structure of a class of XML documents. For example, an XML schema might define the content and structure of XML documents that are suitable for keeping track of book inventories. Specifically, an XML schema describes the elements and attributes that may be contained in a conforming document and the ways the elements may be arranged within in the hierarchical document structure. (In the remainder of the chapter, I usually refer to an XML schema as simply a *schema*.)

In Chapter 5, you learned how to create a valid XML document by adding a document type definition (DTD) to that document and making the document conform to the DTD's declarations. Writing a schema, or using an existing one, and then writing an XML document that conforms to the schema is an *alternative* way to create a valid XML document.

note

If you haven't already done so, be sure to read the general introduction to valid XML documents in Chapter 5. This information covers both DTDs and schemas and is contained in the opening paragraphs of that chapter and in the first two sections: "The Basic Criteria for a Valid XML Document" and "The Advantages of Making an XML Document Valid."

Schemas offer two primary advantages over DTDs. First, they are considerably more sophisticated, providing a much finer level of constraint over the content and structure of a class of documents. Secondly, schemas are written using the standard familiar XML syntax that's used to define the content of an XML document element. (As you saw in Chapters 5 and 6, DTDs use a unique syntax.)

Mastering the art of writing schemas, however, can be challenging simply because of the large number of features that schemas provide compared to DTDs. This chapter provides only a brief introduction to schemas, which could easily form the topic for an entire book. The chapter should, however, provide you with a solid grounding in the basics and help you decide if you want to study schemas in greater detail.

In this chapter, you'll learn how to use schemas to define the same kinds of document constraints that you can specify using a DTD, and you'll learn a sampling of the schema features that go beyond DTDs. The chapter concludes with an exercise in which you'll create both a schema and a conforming XML document, using most of the techniques discussed in this chapter. The schema you'll create is similar to the DTD you wrote at the end of Chapter 5, but offers much more control over the document's content and structure, clearly showing the added power of XML schemas.

This chapter covers XML schemas as defined by the World Wide Web Consortium (W3C) XML Schema specification, which achieved the status of recommendation in May 2001. You'll find the complete text of the specification in the following three pages on the Web: "XML Schema Part 0: Primer" at *http://www.w3.org/TR/xmlschema-0/*, "XML Schema Part 1: Structures" at *http://www.w3.org/TR/xmlschema-1/*, and "XML Schema Part 2: Datatypes" at *http://www.w3.org/TR/xmlschema-2/*.

caution

To check the validity of an XML document using an XML schema that has been created as described in this chapter, MSXML 4.0 *must* be installed on the computer. For information on MSXML 4.0, see "*XML Step by Step*, Internet Explorer, and MSXML" in the Introduction.

note

For more information on XML schemas as supported by Microsoft Internet Explorer and MSXML 4.0, see the topic "XML Schemas" in the Microsoft XML SDK 4.0 help file, or the same topic in the XML SDK documentation provided by the MSDN (Microsoft Developer Network) Library on the Web at *http://msdn.microsoft.com/library/*.

XML Schema Basics

A schema and an XML document described by the schema are stored in separate files. (In this respect, a schema is similar to an external DTD subset, which is stored separately from the document it constrains.) The schema itself is actually a special kind of XML document—specifically, it's an XML document that is written according to the rules given in the W3C XML Schema specification. These rules constitute a language, known as the *XML Schema definition language*, which is a specific application of XML (hence the letters *xsd* used by convention for both the XML Schema namespace prefix and the schema file extension).

A particular XML document that conforms to the strictures of a schema is known as an *instance document* of that schema. An instance document is considered to be valid with respect to the schema, just as a document that contains a DTD and conforms to the DTD's strictures is considered valid with respect to its DTD.

Listing 7-1 presents a simple schema, and Listing 7-2 contains a valid XML document that conforms to this schema. (You'll find copies of these listings on the companion CD under the filenames Book Schema.xsd and Book Instance.xml.)

Book Schema.xsd

```
<?xml version="1.0"?>

<!-- File Name: Book Schema.xsd -->

<xsd:schema xmlns:xsd="http://www.w3.org/2001/XMLSchema">
   <xsd:element name="BOOK">
      <xsd:complexType>
         <xsd:sequence>
            <xsd:element name="TITLE" type="xsd:string"/>
            <xsd:element name="AUTHOR" type="xsd:string"/>
            <xsd:element name="BINDING" type="xsd:string"/>
            <xsd:element name="PAGES" type="xsd:positiveInteger"/>
            <xsd:element name="PRICE" type="xsd:decimal"/>
         </xsd:sequence>
         <xsd:attribute name="InStock" type="xsd:boolean"
            use="required"/>
      </xsd:complexType>
   </xsd:element>
</xsd:schema>
```

Listing 7-1.

XML Schemas

Book Instance.xml

```
<?xml version="1.0"?>

<!-- File Name: Book Instance.xml -->

<BOOK InStock="true">
   <TITLE>The Marble Faun</TITLE>
   <AUTHOR>Nathaniel Hawthorne</AUTHOR>
   <BINDING>trade paperback</BINDING>
   <PAGES>473</PAGES>
   <PRICE>10.95</PRICE>
</BOOK>
```

Listing 7-2.

As a well-formed XML document, the schema file in Listing 7-1 starts with an XML declaration and has a single document element, *xsd:schema*. In a schema, the document element must be named *schema* and it must belong to the *http://www.w3.org/2001/XMLSchema* namespace. The document element contains a collection of special-purpose schema elements that define the content and structure of conforming XML documents.

> # note
> All of the special-purpose elements of the XML Schema definition language, such as *schema*, *element*, and *complexType*, belong to the namespace named *http://www.w3.org/2001/XMLSchema*. Some of the values you assign to attributes in schema elements, such as *string* and *decimal*, also belong to this namespace. (For an attribute that can be assigned either a built-in value or a user-defined value, the namespace is used to clearly identify a built-in value— that is, a value that is part of the schema language—and to avoid conflicts with user-defined values.) The examples in this chapter use the conventional namespace prefix *xsd*. However, you can use a different prefix if you want. For information on namespaces, see "Using Namespaces" on page 69.

Notice that the conforming XML document in Listing 7-2 contains no link to the schema file (in contrast to an XML document with an external DTD subset or a style sheet, which contains an explicit link to the external file). You might therefore wonder how the processor knows that you want it to check the document's validity against a schema file and where that file is located. You provide this information by opening the XML document using a script in an HTML page, as explained in "Checking an XML Document for Validity Using an XML Schema" on page 400. Briefly, the script tells the Internet Explorer processor to load a particular XML document and, when doing so, to check its validity against the XML schema contained in a specified file.

The section "Checking an XML Document for Validity Using an XML Schema" presents a ready-to-run HTML page that you can use to check the validity of an XML document against a specified schema. The page displays any well-formedness or validity error found in the XML document, and also causes the browser to display any error found in the schema itself—either a well-formedness error or a violation of one of the rules of the XML Schema definition language. You might want to read the instructions in that section for using the testing page now, so that you can begin checking the validity of your XML documents using schemas.

note

The techniques for writing a schema to validate an XML instance document that uses namespaces is beyond the scope of this chapter. For information, see the section "3. Advanced Concepts I: Namespaces, Schemas & Qualification" in the "XML Schema Part 0: Primer" page at *http://www.w3.org/TR/xmlschema-0/*.

Declaring Elements

In a schema, to *declare* an element or attribute means to allow an element or attribute with a specified name, type, and other features to appear in a particular context within a conforming XML document. (For an explanation of the *type* of an element or attribute, see the following Note.) You declare an XML element by using the *xsd:element* schema element. To declare the document element (that is, the root element of a conforming XML document), you place the *xsd:element* element immediately within the *xsd:schema* element, at the top level of the schema. You declare all other elements when you define the type of the document element or the type of one of the child elements nested within the document element.

XML Schemas

> **note**
>
> In the core XML specification, the term *element type* refers to a class of elements that have the same name, and that you have possibly declared using an element type declaration in a DTD. The XML Schema specification, however, uses the term *element type* or *attribute type* in a somewhat narrower sense to refer specifically to the *data* type of the element or attribute—that is, to the permissible content and attributes of an element or the allowable values of an attribute. The type specification is only part of an element or attribute declaration.

For example, the schema given in Listing 7-1 declares BOOK as the document element by including an *xsd:element* element immediately within *xsd:schema*:

```
<xsd:schema xmlns:xsd="http://www.w3.org/2001/XMLSchema">
   <xsd:element name="BOOK"> <!-- declare the document element-->
      <!-- nested elements that define the BOOK element's
           type... -->
   </xsd:element>
</xsd:schema>
```

The nested elements contained within the *xsd:element* element serve to define the type of the BOOK element—that is, they specify the allowable content of a BOOK element (five child elements: TITLE, AUTHOR, BINDING, PAGES, and PRICE) as well as the BOOK element's one attribute (*InStock*).

An element declaration can specify either a *simple type* or a *complex type*. A simple type can permit the element to contain only character data. The TITLE, AUTHOR, BINDING, PAGES, and PRICE elements are all declared with simple types. A complex type can allow the element to contain one or more child elements or attributes in addition to character data. The BOOK element is declared with a complex type.

> **note**
>
> An attribute always has a simple type. You'll learn how to declare attributes and specify their types later in the chapter.

Declaring an Element with a Simple Type

To declare an element (or attribute) with a simple type, you can use a *built-in* simple type—that is, one defined as part of the XML Schema definition language. Or, you can use a new simple type that you define by deriving it from an existing simple type.

Declaring an Element Using a Built-In Simple Type

To declare an element with a built-in simple type, assign the name of that type to the *type* attribute in the *xsd:element* start-tag. For instance, in the example schema of Listing 7-1, the TITLE element is assigned the *xsd:string* built-in simple type, which allows the element to contain any sequence of legal XML characters:

```
<xsd:element name="TITLE" type="xsd:string"/>
```

Of the built-in types, *xsd:string* is the least restrictive. Table 7-1 describes a sampling of other useful built-in simple types that you can assign to the elements you declare. For a complete list of these types, some of which are fairly intricate, see the section "2.3 Simple Types" in the "XML Schema Part 0: Primer" page at *http://www.w3.org/TR/xmlschema-0/*.

Built-in simple type	Description	Example(s)
xsd:string	A sequence of any of the legal XML characters	This is a string.
xsd:boolean	The value *true* or *false*, or *1* or *0* (indicating true or false, respectively)	true false 1 0
xsd:decimal	A number that may contain a decimal component	-5.2 -3.0 1 2.5
xsd:integer	A whole number	-389 -7 0 5 229
xsd:positiveInteger	A positive whole number (not including 0)	5 229
xsd:negativeInteger	A negative whole number (not including 0)	-389 -7
xsd:date	A calendar date, represented as CCYY-MM-DD	1948-05-21 2001-10-15

continued

XML Schemas

continued

Built-in simple type	Description	Example(s)
xsd:time	A time of day, represented as hh:mm:ss.ss	11:30:00.00 (11:30 A.M.) 14:29:03 (2:29 P.M. and 3 seconds) 05:16:00.0 (5:16 A.M.)
xsd:dateTime	A date and time of day, represented as CCYY-MM-DD Thh:mm:ss.ss	1948-05-21T17:28:00.00
xsd:gMonth	A Gregorian calendar month, represented as --MM--	--05-- (May) --12-- (December)
xsd:gYear	A Gregorian calendar year, represented as CCYY	1948 2001
xsd:gDay	A day of a Gregorian calendar month, represented as ---DD	---05 ---31
xsd:gYearMonth	A Gregorian calendar year and month, represented as CCYY-MM	1948-05 (May, 1948)
xsd:anyURI	A URI (Uniform Resource Identifier; see the sidebar "URIs, URLs, and URNs" on page 73)	http://www.mjyOnline.com

Table 7-1. *Useful built-in simple types you can use for declaring elements or attributes.*

You can control the number of occurrences of the element within the context where it is declared by including the *minOccurs* attribute (the minimum number of occurrences), the *maxOccurs* attribute (the maximum number of occurrences), or both attributes. The default value of each of these attributes is 1, so if you omit them, the element must appear exactly once in the context where it's declared.

note

It's an error for the *minOccurs* value to be greater than the *maxOccurs* value.

For instance, in the example schema of Listing 7-1, each of the elements TITLE, AUTHOR, BINDING, PAGES, and PRICE must occur exactly once as a child of the BOOK element (and as you'll learn later in the chapter, these elements must occur in the order in which they are declared). You can assign either attribute an integer greater than or equal to zero. You can also assign *maxOccurs* the value *unbounded*, which means the element can occur an unlimited number of times. For example, the following element is declared as optional—that is, it can appear once or not at all:

```
<xsd:element name="PUBLISH_DATE" type="xsd:gYearMonth"
   minOccurs="0"/>
```

And, the following element can be included any number of times, or it can be omitted:

```
<xsd:element name="AUTHOR" type="xsd:string" minOccurs="0"
   maxOccurs="unbounded"/>
```

note

You can't use the *minOccurs* or *maxOccurs* attribute with the declaration of the document element, which must occur exactly once.

note

For a description of additional *xsd:element* attributes you can use when declaring an element, see the section "3.3.2 XML Representation of Element Declaration Schema Components" in the "XML Schema Part 1: Structures" page at *http://www.w3.org/TR/xmlschema-1/*.

Declaring an Element Using a Defined Simple Type

When you declare an element (or attribute), as an alternative to using a built-in simple type, you can use a new simple type that you define by deriving it from one of the built-in simple types (or from another derived simple type already defined in the schema).

Consider, for instance, the Book Schema.xsd schema shown in Listing 7-1, in which the PRICE element is declared to have the *xsd:decimal* built-in simple type:

```
<xsd:element name="PRICE" type="xsd:decimal">
```

Because the *xsd:decimal* type would allow the element to contain values such as -10.50 and 5000, you might want to define a new type for the BOOK element that restricts the values to a reasonable range. You could do this with the following declaration:

```
<xsd:element name="PRICE">
   <xsd:simpleType>
      <xsd:restriction base="xsd:decimal">
         <xsd:minExclusive value="0"/>
         <xsd:maxExclusive value="100"/>
      </xsd:restriction>
   </xsd:simpleType>
</xsd:element>
```

This declaration assigns the PRICE element a new defined type that is derived from the built-in type *xsd:decimal*. The new type has all the features of *xsd:decimal* except that the value entered into the element must be greater than 0 and less than 100.

You always define a new simple type using the *xsd:simpleType* schema element. You can simultaneously define the type and assign it to the element you're declaring by including the *xsd:simpleType* element inside the *xsd:element* element and omitting the *type* attribute from *xsd:element*, as done in the example PRICE declaration given above. (For an alternative way to define a type, see the sidebar "Anonymous vs. Named Types," later in this section.)

The most common way to define a simple type is to start with a built-in type and restrict its possible values in various ways. You do this by including the *xsd:restriction* element within the *xsd:simpleType* element, as in the example PRICE declaration shown above. The *xsd:restriction* element specifies the base type (that is, the starting type) and includes special schema elements known as *facets*, which indicate the precise way the base type is to be restricted. (For alternatives to the *xsd:restriction* element, see the Tip at the end of this section.)

The example PRICE element declaration uses the *xsd:minExclusive* and *xsd:maxExclusive* facets to indicate a permissible range of values that *doesn't* include the specified end values (0 and 100). To indicate a range that does include the specified end values, you can use the similar *xsd:minInclusive* and *xsd:maxInclusive* facet elements.

You can use a series of *xsd:enumeration* facets to limit the element's content (or attribute's value) to one of a set of specific values. For instance, in the Book Schema.xsd schema, the BINDING element is declared to have the *xsd:string* type, which allows the element to contain any sequence of legal characters:

```
<xsd:element name="BINDING" type="xsd:string"/>
```

Anonymous vs. Named Types

The example type definitions given so far in this chapter are known as *anonymous* type definitions. Another way to define a simple or complex type is to place the definition—that is, the *xsd:simpleType* or *xsd:complexType* element—directly within the *xsd:schema* element (along with the declaration of the document element) and assign the definition a name. You can then apply the type to one or more elements or attributes by assigning the type's name to the *type* attribute in the declaration, in the same way you assign *type* the name of a built-in type.

For instance, you could define a named type for a PRICE element by including the *xsd:simpleType* element directly within *xsd:schema* as follows:

```
<xsd:schema xmlns:xsd="http://www.w3.org/2001/XMLSchema">


    <xsd:simpleType name="PriceType">
        <xsd:restriction base="xsd:decimal">
            <xsd:minExclusive value="0"/>
            <xsd:maxExclusive value="100"/>
        </xsd:restriction>
    </xsd:simpleType>


    <!-- other schema elements... -->

</xsd:schema>
```

You could then declare the PRICE element as follows:

```
<xsd:element name="PRICE" type="PriceType"/>
```

An advantage of using a named type is that you can define the type once but assign it to several elements or attributes in your schema, which reduces typing, decreases the document's size, and makes it easier to maintain the type definition. Also, using a named type can make your schema easier to read and work with, especially if you are declaring an element with many nested elements and attributes, where including anonymous types could make the declaration deeply indented and unwieldy.

XML Schemas

7

You could limit the permissible content to a set of specific strings by deriving the element's type from *xsd:string* using *xsd:enumeration* facets, as shown here:

```
<xsd:element name="BINDING">
   <xsd:simpleType>
      <xsd:restriction base="xsd:string">
         <xsd:enumeration value="hardcover"/>
         <xsd:enumeration value="mass market paperback"/>
         <xsd:enumeration value="trade paperback"/>
      </xsd:restriction>
   </xsd:simpleType>
</xsd:element>
```

A BINDING element containing anything other than one of the three strings specified by the *value* attributes of the *xsd:enumeration* elements would be invalid.

As a final example, you can require that an element's content (or an attribute's value) match a particular pattern of characters by restricting the *xsd:string* type using the *xsd:pattern* facet, as shown in this declaration:

```
<xsd:element name="ISBN">
   <xsd:simpleType>
      <xsd:restriction base="xsd:string">
         <xsd:pattern value="\d{1}-\d{4}-\d{4}-\d{1}"/>
      </xsd:restriction>
   </xsd:simpleType>
</xsd:element>
```

You assign the *value* attribute of the *xsd:pattern* facet a description of the required pattern, which is known as a *regular expression*. The regular expression in the preceding example requires the content to consist of one digit followed by a hyphen, four digits, another hyphen, four digits, another hyphen, and a single digit. Hence, the following would be a valid ISBN element:

```
<ISBN>0-7356-1020-7</ISBN>
```

For a description of the regular expressions you can use with the *xsd:pattern* element, see Appendix D "Regular Expressions" in the "XML Schema Part 0: Primer" page at *http://www.w3.org/TR/xmlschema-0/*.

The specific facets you can use depend on the particular type you are restricting. For a complete list of all the different facets you can use to restrict each of the built-in simple types, see the appendix "B Simple Types & their Facets" in the "XML Schema Part 0: Primer" page at *http://www.w3.org/TR/xmlschema-0/*.

> ## tip
>
> As an alternative to using an *xsd:restriction* element inside *xsd:simpleType* to derive a new simple type, you can use the *xsd:list* or *xsd:union* element. The *xsd:list* element creates a new simple type that allows the element (or attribute) to contain a sequence of values of the base type, which are separated with white space characters (spaces, tabs, or line breaks). The *xsd:union* element creates a new simple type that allows the element (or attribute) to contain a value that conforms to any one of a group of specified base types. For details, see the sections "2.3.1 List Types" and "2.3.2 Union Types" in the "XML Schema Part 0: Primer" page at *http://www.w3.org/TR/xmlschema-0/*.

> ## note
>
> Keep in mind that an *xsd:element* element with a defined type can use the *minOccurs* and *maxOccurs* attributes described in the previous section, as well as any of the other available *xsd:element* attributes.

Declaring an Element with a Complex Type

A complex type can allow an element to contain one or more child elements or attributes, in addition to character data.

The only built-in complex type you can use for declaring an element is *xsd:anyType*. This is the default element type that is assigned if you omit the *type* attribute specification from the *xsd:element* start-tag and don't include an anonymous type definition. Here's an example of an element explicitly declared with this type:

```
<xsd:element name="NOTE" type="xsd:anyType"/>
```

An element with the *xsd:anyType* type can include any type of character data. It can also include any element or attribute that is declared directly within the schema's *xsd:schema* element.

XML Schemas

note

As explained earlier in the chapter, declaring an element as a direct child of *xsd:schema* allows that element to appear as the document element of a conforming XML document. You can actually include several element declarations, as well as attribute declarations or named type definitions, as direct children of *xsd:schema*. Such declarations or type definitions are classified as *global*. A global element declaration cannot include the *minOccurs* or *maxOccurs* attribute, nor can a global attribute declaration include the *use* attribute (discussed later in the chapter). Note that declaring several global elements introduces some ambiguity into the schema, because any of these elements can appear as the document element of a conforming XML document.

For most elements with a complex type, you'll want to explicitly define the type so you can specify the elements, attributes, or type of character data that the element can contain.

You define a complex type using the *xsd:complexType* schema element, which is analogous to the *xsd:simpleType* element for defining a simple type. In the following three sections, you'll learn how to use *xsd:complexType* to declare an element with element content (child elements only), with mixed content (child elements plus character data), or with empty content (neither child elements nor character data). Later in the chapter, you'll learn how to add attributes to elements with any of these three types of content.

Declaring an Element with Element Content

An element declared with element content can contain one or more child elements of the specified type or types, as well as attributes (if declared, as discussed later). To declare an element with element content, you define the element's type using *xsd:complexType* and include within it a *content model* that describes the permissible child elements, the allowed arrangement of these elements, and the rules for their occurrences. You create the content model by using the *xsd:sequence*, *xsd:choice*, or *xsd:all* schema element, or a combination of these elements. Each of these schema elements adds a group of element declarations to the content model. The meaning of the group depends upon which schema element you use.

A group of child elements declared in an *xsd:sequence* element must appear in the exact order listed. For example, the following declaration of the MOUNTAIN element uses *xsd:sequence* to stipulate that a MOUNTAIN element must contain exactly one NAME, one HEIGHT, and one STATE child element, in that order:

```
<xsd:element name="MOUNTAIN">
   <xsd:complexType>
      <xsd:sequence>
         <xsd:element name="NAME" type="xsd:string"/>
         <xsd:element name="HEIGHT" type="xsd:positiveInteger"/>
         <xsd:element name="STATE" type="xsd:string"/>
      </xsd:sequence>
   </xsd:complexType>
</xsd:element>
```

Here's an example of a valid MOUNTAIN element in an XML instance document:

```
<MOUNTAIN>
   <NAME>Wheeler</NAME>
   <HEIGHT>13161</HEIGHT>
   <STATE>New Mexico</STATE>
</MOUNTAIN>
```

You can regulate the number of occurrences of a child element by adding a *minOccurs* or *maxOccurs* attribute specification, or both specifications, to that element's declaration. An individual element can be omitted if *minOccurs* is set to 0, and it can be repeated if *maxOccurs* is assigned a value greater than 1. (Recall that the default value of each of these attributes is 1.) But because the elements are declared in an *xsd:sequence* group, they can't appear out of order.

If a group of child elements is declared within an *xsd:choice* schema element, *any one* of the child elements can appear within the parent element. For example, the following declaration indicates that a FILM element can contain a STAR element, *or* a NARRATOR element, *or* an INSTRUCTOR element:

```
<xsd:element name="FILM">
   <xsd:complexType>
      <xsd:choice>
         <xsd:element name="STAR" type="xsd:string"/>
         <xsd:element name="NARRATOR" type="xsd:string"/>
         <xsd:element name="INSTRUCTOR" type="xsd:string"/>
      </xsd:choice>
   </xsd:complexType>
</xsd:element>
```

XML Schemas 7

Here's an example a valid FILM element:

```
<FILM>
   <STAR>Sandra Bullock</STAR>
</FILM>
```

Again, you can regulate the number of occurrences of a particular child element by adding a *minOccurs* or a *maxOccurs* attribute specification, or both specifications, to that element's declaration.

Finally, if you declare a group of child elements within an *xsd:all* schema element, the child elements can occur in any order. By default, each child element must occur exactly once. However, you can make a particular child element optional by including the attribute specification *minOccurs=* "*0*" in the *xsd:element* start-tag. For an element in an *xsd:all* group, you can assign the *minOccurs* or *maxOccurs* attribute only the value 0 or 1.

For example, the following declaration indicates that the child elements of a MOUNTAIN element can occur in any order. The NAME element must appear exactly once. The HEIGHT and STATE elements can each appear one time or not at all.

```
<xsd:element name="MOUNTAIN">
   <xsd:complexType>
      <xsd:all>
         <xsd:element name="NAME" type="xsd:string"/>
         <xsd:element name="HEIGHT" type="xsd:positiveInteger"
            minOccurs="0"/>
         <xsd:element name="STATE" type="xsd:string"
            minOccurs="0"/>
      </xsd:all>
   </xsd:complexType>
</xsd:element>
```

Given this declaration, the following MOUNTAIN element is valid:

```
<MOUNTAIN>
   <STATE>New Mexico</STATE>
   <HEIGHT>13161</HEIGHT>
   <NAME>Wheeler</NAME>
</MOUNTAIN>
```

as is this one:

```
<MOUNTAIN>
   <NAME>Wheeler</NAME>
</MOUNTAIN>
```

To create a more complex content model, you can nest an *xsd:sequence* element within an *xsd:choice* element, or an *xsd:choice* element within an *xsd:sequence* element. (You can't nest an *xsd:all* element within an *xsd:sequence* or *xsd:choice* element. Nor can you nest an *xsd:sequence* or *xsd:choice* element within an *xsd:all* element.) For example, in the following FILM element declaration an *xsd:choice* element is nested within an *xsd:sequence* element. The content model stipulates that a FILM element must contain one TITLE element, followed by one CLASS element, followed by one STAR, NARRATOR, or INSTRUCTOR element.

```
<xsd:element name="FILM">
   <xsd:complexType>
      <xsd:sequence>
         <xsd:element name="TITLE" type="xsd:string"/>
         <xsd:element name="CLASS">
            <xsd:simpleType>
               <xsd:restriction base="xsd:string">
                  <xsd:enumeration value="fictional"/>
                  <xsd:enumeration value="documentary"/>
                  <xsd:enumeration value="instructional"/>
               </xsd:restriction>
            </xsd:simpleType>
         </xsd:element>
         <xsd:choice>
            <xsd:element name="STAR" type="xsd:string"/>
            <xsd:element name="NARRATOR" type="xsd:string"/>
            <xsd:element name="INSTRUCTOR" type="xsd:string"/>
         </xsd:choice>
      </xsd:sequence>
   </xsd:complexType>
</xsd:element>
```

Here's an example of a valid FILM element:

```
<FILM>
   <TITLE>The Net</TITLE>
   <CLASS>fictional</CLASS>
   <STAR>Sandra Bullock</STAR>
</FILM>
```

XML Schemas

As you've seen, you can control the occurrences of individual elements within an *xsd:sequence*, *xsd:choice*, or *xsd:all* group by assigning values—other than the default value of 1—to the *minOccurs* and *maxOccurs* attributes of the individual elements within the group. You can also include a *minOccurs* or *maxOccurs* attribute specification within the *xsd:sequence*, *xsd:choice*, or *xsd:all* element itself to control the number of occurrences of the entire group. (As with *xsd:element* elements, the default value of both attributes is 1.) You'll see an example of this practice in the declaration of the PARA element given in the next section.

Declaring an Element with Mixed Content

An element declared with mixed content can contain any type of character data, interspersed with any child elements that are declared in the type definition. To specify a mixed content element, declare the element with element content exactly as described in the previous section, but add the *mixed="true"* attribute specification to the *xsd:complexType* element's start-tag. For example, according to the following declaration, a TITLE element can contain any type of character data before or after its one child element, SUBTITLE:

```
<xsd:element name="TITLE">
   <xsd:complexType mixed="true">
      <xsd:sequence>
         <xsd:element name="SUBTITLE"/>
      </xsd:sequence>
   </xsd:complexType>
</xsd:element>
```

Here's an example of a valid element:

```
<TITLE>Moby-Dick <SUBTITLE>Or, The Whale</SUBTITLE></TITLE>
```

Recall from Chapter 5 that if you declare an element with "mixed content" using a DTD, the specified child elements can occur in any order and with any number of repetitions (zero or more), interspersed with any amount of character data. The following schema declaration emulates a mixed content declaration in a DTD. Specifically, it stipulates that a PARA element can contain BOLD, ITALIC, or UNDERLINE child elements in any order and with any number of repetitions (zero or more), interspersed with character data.

```
<xsd:element name="PARA">
   <xsd:complexType mixed="true">
      <xsd:choice minOccurs="0" maxOccurs="unbounded">
         <xsd:element name="BOLD" type="xsd:string"/>
```

```
        <xsd:element name="ITALIC" type="xsd:string"/>
        <xsd:element name="UNDERLINE" type="xsd:string"/>
      </xsd:choice>
    </xsd:complexType>
  </xsd:element>
```

The following is an example of a valid PARA element:

```
<PARA>A PARA element may contain character data plus any number of
nested elements for marking <ITALIC>italic</ITALIC> text,
<BOLD>boldface</BOLD> text, or <UNDERLINE>underlined</UNDERLINE>
text. These nested elements can be used in any order.</PARA>
```

Declaring an Element with Empty Content

An element declared with empty content cannot contain either child elements or character data. (It can have attributes if they are declared as explained later in the chapter.) To specify this type of element, define the element's type using the *xsd:complexType* element, but omit the content model, as shown in the following example:

```
<xsd:element name="BR">
   <xsd:complexType>
   </xsd:complexType>
</xsd:element>
```

The following is a conforming element:

```
<BR></BR>
```

as is this one:

```
<BR/>
```

> **note**
>
> To declare an element with empty content, be sure to include the empty *xsd:complexType* element in the declaration. If you omit it, the element you're declaring will have the *xsd:anyType* type rather than empty content.

XML Schemas

7

Declaring Attributes

You declare an attribute by using the *xsd:attribute* schema element. An attribute always has a simple type. As when you declare a simple-type element, you can declare an attribute either by using a built-in simple type or by defining a new simple type. You use a built-in simple type by assigning the type's name to the *type* attribute of the *xsd:attribute* element. You can define a new simple type by including the *xsd:simpleType* schema element within the *xsd:attribute* element.

Here's an example of an attribute declared using the built-in simple type *xsd:positiveInteger*:

```
<xsd:attribute name="IndexPages" type="xsd:positiveInteger"/>
```

And here's an attribute declared with a newly defined type that is derived from the built-in type *xsd:string*:

```
<xsd:attribute name="Class">
   <xsd:simpleType>
      <xsd:restriction base="xsd:string">
         <xsd:enumeration value="fictional"/>
         <xsd:enumeration value="documentary"/>
         <xsd:enumeration value="instructional"/>
      </xsd:restriction>
   </xsd:simpleType>
</xsd:attribute>
```

You can use the same built-in simple types for an attribute that you can use for an element. For a description of some useful built-in simple types, see Table 7-1 on page 169. For a complete list of these types, see the section "2.3 Simple Types" in the "XML Schema Part 0: Primer" page at *http://www.w3.org/TR/xmlschema-0/*. And for instructions on using the *xsd:simpleType* schema element to define a new simple type for an attribute, see "Declaring an Element Using a Defined Simple Type" on page 171.

In addition to the *name* and *type* attributes of the *xsd:attribute* element, which supply the attribute's name and simple type, you can include the *use* attribute to control the attribute's occurrence in the element for which it is declared. If you assign *use* the value *optional* (the default value), or omit the *use* attribute, the attribute can be included or left out. If you assign the value *required*, the attribute must be included. And if you assign the value *prohibited*, the attribute can't be included. For example, the following declaration requires that an *InStock* attribute specification always be included in the start-tag of the element for which the attribute is declared:

```
<xsd:attribute name="InStock" type="xsd:boolean" use="required"/>
```

You can use the *default* attribute to specify a default value for an attribute, as in this example declaration:

```
<xsd:attribute name="PartNum" type="xsd:string" default="0-00-0"/>
```

If the *PartNum* attribute specification is omitted from the start-tag of the element for which it is declared, the XML processor will pass the value *0-00-0* to the application. If the *PartNum* attribute specification is included, the processor will pass the specified value. Note that to include a *default* attribute specification in the *xsd:attribute* element, the *use* attribute must be set to *optional* or omitted.

The *fixed* attribute provides an alternative to the *default* attribute, as shown in this attribute declaration:

```
<xsd:attribute name="Priority" type="xsd:string" fixed="high"/>
```

If the *Priority* attribute specification is omitted from the element's start-tag, the XML processor will pass the value *high* to the application (as with the *default* attribute). If the *Priority* attribute specification is included, it must have the value *high* (and of course, the processor will pass this value to the application). Note that you can't have both a *fixed* and a *default* attribute specification in the same *xsd:attribute* element.

caution

Keep in mind that a default attribute value, specified using the *default* or *fixed* attribute, won't be passed to the application (such as a script in an HTML page) unless the XML document is validated against the schema when the document is loaded, as demonstrated in the validity-testing page given in "Checking an XML Document for Validity Using an XML Schema" on page 400.

note

For a description of all *xsd:attribute* attributes, see the section "3.2.2 XML Representation of Attribute Declaration Schema Components" in the "XML Schema Part 1: Structures" page at *http://www.w3.org/TR/xmlschema-1/*.

To add an attribute to an element declaration, so that the attribute can (or must) be used with that element, you must place the *xsd:attribute* schema element within the element's content model. How you do this depends upon the type of the element, as discussed in the following two sections.

Adding Attributes to an Element with Element, Mixed, or Empty Content

To add an attribute to an element with element content, mixed content, or empty content, you simply include the attribute declaration within the element's content model inside the *xsd:complexType* schema element. You must, however, include the attribute declaration *after* any *xsd:sequence*, *xsd:choice*, or *xsd:all* element.

The following is an example of a declaration for an element (FILM) with element content that includes a declaration for an attribute (*Class*) at the end of its content model:

```
<xsd:element name="FILM">
   <xsd:complexType>
      <xsd:sequence>
         <xsd:element name="TITLE" type="xsd:string"/>
         <xsd:choice>
            <xsd:element name="STAR" type="xsd:string"/>
            <xsd:element name="NARRATOR" type="xsd:string"/>
            <xsd:element name="INSTRUCTOR" type="xsd:string"/>
         </xsd:choice>
      </xsd:sequence>
      <xsd:attribute name="Class">
         <xsd:simpleType>
            <xsd:restriction base="xsd:string">
               <xsd:enumeration value="fictional"/>
               <xsd:enumeration value="documentary"/>
               <xsd:enumeration value="instructional"/>
            </xsd:restriction>
         </xsd:simpleType>
      </xsd:attribute>
   </xsd:complexType>
</xsd:element>
```

Here is a valid FILM element according to this declaration:

```
<FILM Class="fictional">
   <TITLE>The Net</TITLE>
   <STAR>Sandra Bullock</STAR>
</FILM>
```

The following is an example of a declaration for an element with empty content (IMAGE) that includes a declaration for an attribute (*Source*) as the only declaration within its content model:

```
<xsd:element name="IMAGE">
   <xsd:complexType>
      <xsd:attribute name="Source" type="xsd:string"
         use="required"/>
   </xsd:complexType>
</xsd:element>
```

Here's an example of a valid element conforming to this declaration:

```
<IMAGE Source="Logo.gif"/>
```

Adding Attributes to an Element Containing Character Data Only

Recall that an element with one or more attributes has a complex type, even if the element contains only character data. A simple way to assign an attribute to an element whose content includes only *xsd:string* type character data is to define the element's type using *xsd:complexType*, include the *xsd:mixed="true"* attribute specification in *xsd:complexType* to allow the character data, and insert the attribute declaration inside *xsd:complexType* to allow the attribute. Here's an example of a declaration:

```
<xsd:element name="AUTHOR">
   <xsd:complexType mixed="true">
      <xsd:attribute name="Born" type="xsd:gYear"/>
   </xsd:complexType>
</xsd:element>
```

And here's a conforming AUTHOR element:

```
<AUTHOR Born="1819">Walt Whitman</AUTHOR>
```

The *xsd:mixed="true"* attribute specification allows the element to contain character data of an unconstrained type, just like the *xsd:string* built-in simple type.

You can't use this method, however, if you want to constrain the character data—that is, to assign the character data a type other than *xsd:string*. The method you must use to add an attribute to an element that contains only constrained character data is fairly logical and consistent with the overall schema model, but is also quite indirect and cumbersome. Briefly stated, you must start with a simple type that describes the character data (for example, *xsd:positiveInteger* or *xsd:date*), and then derive from it a new complex type

XML Schemas

that allows the element to include the desired attribute along with the character data. The following declaration is an example. It specifies that a PAGES element must contain only character data that consists of a positive integer, and that PAGES has an optional attribute named *IndexPages*, the value of which must also be a positive integer:

```
<xsd:element name="PAGES">
   <xsd:complexType>
      <xsd:simpleContent>
         <xsd:extension base="xsd:positiveInteger">
            <xsd:attribute name="IndexPages"
               type="xsd:positiveInteger"/>
         </xsd:extension>
      </xsd:simpleContent>
   </xsd:complexType>
</xsd:element>
```

Here's a conforming PAGES element:

```
<PAGES IndexPages="23">473</PAGES>
```

The *xsd:simpleContent* element included as a child of *xsd:complexType* indicates that you are going to derive a new complex type from a simple type, rather than build up a content model as was done in the previous examples. The *xsd:extension* element within *xsd:simpleContent* does the actual deriving. Its *base* attribute specifies the simple type of the PAGES element's character data. The *xsd:attribute* element within *xsd:extension* declares the attribute that PAGES can include along with the character data (thereby "extending" the derived type beyond mere character data).

Creating an XML Schema and an Instance Document

In the following exercises you'll first create an XML schema and then an XML instance document that conforms to the schema. These files illustrate almost all the techniques covered in this chapter.

Create the Schema

1   Open a new, empty text file in your text editor, and type in the XML schema given in Listing 7-3. (You'll find a copy of this listing on the companion CD under the filename Inventory Schema.xsd.)

Inventory Schema.xsd

```xml
<?xml version="1.0"?>

<!-- File Name: Inventory Schema.xsd -->

<xsd:schema xmlns:xsd="http://www.w3.org/2001/XMLSchema">

    <xsd:element name="INVENTORY">
        <xsd:complexType>
            <xsd:sequence>
                <xsd:element name="BOOK" type="BookType"
                    minOccurs="0" maxOccurs="unbounded"/>
            </xsd:sequence>
        </xsd:complexType>
    </xsd:element>

    <xsd:complexType name="BookType">
        <xsd:sequence>

            <xsd:element name="TITLE">
                <xsd:complexType mixed="true">
                    <xsd:sequence>
                        <xsd:element name="SUBTITLE" type="xsd:string"
                            minOccurs="0" maxOccurs="1"/>
                    </xsd:sequence>
                </xsd:complexType>
            </xsd:element>

            <xsd:element name="AUTHOR">
                <xsd:complexType>
                    <xsd:sequence>
                        <xsd:element name="FIRSTNAME" type="xsd:string"/>
                        <xsd:element name="LASTNAME" type="xsd:string"/>
                    </xsd:sequence>
                    <xsd:attribute name="Born" type="xsd:gYear"/>
                </xsd:complexType>
            </xsd:element>

            <xsd:element name="BINDING">
                <xsd:simpleType>
                    <xsd:restriction base="xsd:string">
```

```
                <xsd:enumeration value="hardcover"/>
                <xsd:enumeration value="mass market paperback"/>
                <xsd:enumeration value="trade paperback"/>
            </xsd:restriction>
        </xsd:simpleType>
    </xsd:element>

    <xsd:element name="PAGES">
        <xsd:complexType>
            <xsd:simpleContent>
                <xsd:extension base="xsd:positiveInteger">
                    <xsd:attribute name="FrontMatter"
                        type="xsd:positiveInteger"/>
                </xsd:extension>
            </xsd:simpleContent>
        </xsd:complexType>
    </xsd:element>

    <xsd:element name="PRICE">
        <xsd:simpleType>
            <xsd:restriction base="xsd:decimal">
                <xsd:minExclusive value="0"/>
                <xsd:maxExclusive value="100"/>
            </xsd:restriction>
        </xsd:simpleType>
    </xsd:element>

    <xsd:element name="PUBLISH_DATE" type="xsd:gYearMonth"
        minOccurs="0"/>

    <xsd:element name="ISBN">
        <xsd:simpleType>
            <xsd:restriction base="xsd:string">
                <xsd:pattern value="\d{1}-\d{4}-\d{4}-\d{1}"/>
            </xsd:restriction>
        </xsd:simpleType>
    </xsd:element>

</xsd:sequence>
```

```
        <xsd:attribute name="InStock" type="xsd:boolean"
            use="required" />

    </xsd:complexType>

</xsd:schema>
```

Listing 7-3.

2   Save the document on your hard disk, assigning it the filename Inventory Schema.xsd.

The schema you created describes a conforming XML document as follows. (All of the techniques are explained in this chapter.)

- The document element is named INVENTORY and contains any number of BOOK elements (zero or more).

- A BOOK element contains the following child elements, in the order listed: TITLE, AUTHOR, BINDING, PAGES, PRICE, PUBLISH_DATE, and ISBN. The PUBLISH_DATE element occurs once or not at all; all other elements appear exactly once.

- The TITLE element contains unconstrained character data plus an optional child element named SUBTITLE. SUBTITLE contains unconstrained (*xsd:string*) character data, and appears once or not at all.

- The AUTHOR element contains two child elements, FIRSTNAME and LASTNAME, each of which contains unconstrained (*xsd:string*) character data and appears exactly once in the order listed. AUTHOR also has an optional attribute named *Born*, the value of which is a Gregorian calendar year represented as CCYY.

- The BINDING element contains one of the following three strings: *hardcover*, *mass market paperback*, or *trade paperback*.

- The PAGES element contains a positive integer and has an optional attribute named *FrontMatter*, the value of which is also a positive integer.

- The PRICE element contains a decimal value that is greater than 0 and less than 100.

- The optional PUBLISH_DATE element contains a Gregorian calendar year and month, represented as CCYY-MM.

- The ISBN element contains one digit, followed by a hyphen, four digits, another hyphen, four digits, another hyphen, and a single digit.

- A BOOK element has a mandatory attribute named *InStock*, which has the value *true*, *false*, *1*, or *0*.

Create the Instance Document

1   Open a new, empty text file in your text editor, and type in the XML in-
     stance document given in Listing 7-4. (You'll find a copy of this listing on
     the companion CD under the filename Inventory Instance.xml.) If you want,
     you can use the Inventory.xml document you created in Chapter 2 (given in
     Listing 2-1 and included on the companion CD) as a starting point.

Inventory Instance.xml

```
<?xml version="1.0"?>

<!-- File Name: Inventory Instance.xml -->

<?xml version="1.0"?>

<!-- File Name: Inventory Instance.xml -->

<INVENTORY>
   <BOOK InStock="true">
      <TITLE>The Adventures of Huckleberry Finn</TITLE>
      <AUTHOR Born="1835">
         <FIRSTNAME>Mark</FIRSTNAME>
         <LASTNAME>Twain</LASTNAME>
      </AUTHOR>
      <BINDING>mass market paperback</BINDING>
      <PAGES FrontMatter="8">298</PAGES>
      <PRICE>5.49</PRICE>
      <PUBLISH_DATE>2000-03</PUBLISH_DATE>
      <ISBN>9-9999-9999-9</ISBN>
   </BOOK>
   <BOOK InStock="false">
      <TITLE>Leaves of Grass</TITLE>
      <AUTHOR Born="1819">
         <FIRSTNAME>Walt</FIRSTNAME>
         <LASTNAME>Whitman</LASTNAME>
      </AUTHOR>
      <BINDING>hardcover</BINDING>
      <PAGES>462</PAGES>
      <PRICE>7.75</PRICE>
      <PUBLISH_DATE>1985-12</PUBLISH_DATE>
      <ISBN>9-9999-9999-9</ISBN>
   </BOOK>
   <BOOK InStock="true">
```

```
        <TITLE>The Legend of Sleepy Hollow</TITLE>
        <AUTHOR>
            <FIRSTNAME>Washington</FIRSTNAME>
            <LASTNAME>Irving</LASTNAME>
        </AUTHOR>
        <BINDING>mass market paperback</BINDING>
        <PAGES FrontMatter="6">98</PAGES>
        <PRICE>2.95</PRICE>
        <PUBLISH_DATE>1973-06</PUBLISH_DATE>
        <ISBN>9-9999-9999-9</ISBN>
    </BOOK>
    <BOOK InStock="true">
        <TITLE>The Marble Faun</TITLE>
        <AUTHOR Born="1804">
            <FIRSTNAME>Nathaniel</FIRSTNAME>
            <LASTNAME>Hawthorne</LASTNAME>
        </AUTHOR>
        <BINDING>trade paperback</BINDING>
        <PAGES>473</PAGES>
        <PRICE>10.95</PRICE>
        <ISBN>9-9999-9999-9</ISBN>
    </BOOK>
    <BOOK InStock="false">
        <TITLE>Moby-Dick <SUBTITLE>Or, the Whale</SUBTITLE></TITLE>
        <AUTHOR Born="1819">
            <FIRSTNAME>Herman</FIRSTNAME>
            <LASTNAME>Melville</LASTNAME>
        </AUTHOR>
        <BINDING>hardcover</BINDING>
        <PAGES FrontMatter="20">724</PAGES>
        <PRICE>9.95</PRICE>
        <PUBLISH_DATE>2001-06</PUBLISH_DATE>
        <ISBN>9-9999-9999-9</ISBN>
    </BOOK>
    <BOOK InStock="true">
        <TITLE>The Portrait of a Lady</TITLE>
        <AUTHOR>
            <FIRSTNAME>Henry</FIRSTNAME>
            <LASTNAME>James</LASTNAME>
        </AUTHOR>
        <BINDING>mass market paperback</BINDING>
        <PAGES FrontMatter="8">256</PAGES>
```

```
      <PRICE>4.95</PRICE>
      <ISBN>9-9999-9999-9</ISBN>
   </BOOK>
   <BOOK InStock="true">
      <TITLE>The Scarlet Letter</TITLE>
      <AUTHOR>
         <FIRSTNAME>Nathaniel</FIRSTNAME>
         <LASTNAME>Hawthorne</LASTNAME>
      </AUTHOR>
      <BINDING>trade paperback</BINDING>
      <PAGES>253</PAGES>
      <PRICE>4.25</PRICE>
      <PUBLISH_DATE>1987-01</PUBLISH_DATE>
      <ISBN>9-9999-9999-9</ISBN>
   </BOOK>
   <BOOK InStock="false">
      <TITLE>The Turn of the Screw</TITLE>
      <AUTHOR>
         <FIRSTNAME>Henry</FIRSTNAME>
         <LASTNAME>James</LASTNAME>
      </AUTHOR>
      <BINDING>trade paperback</BINDING>
      <PAGES FrontMatter="10">384</PAGES>
      <PRICE>3.35</PRICE>
      <PUBLISH_DATE>1974-07</PUBLISH_DATE>
      <ISBN>9-9999-9999-9</ISBN>
   </BOOK>
</INVENTORY>
```

Listing 7-4.

2   Save the document on your hard disk, assigning it the filename Inventory
     Instance.xsd.

3   If you want to test the validity of the instance document against the XML
     schema, read the instructions for using the XML schema validity-testing
     page presented in "Checking an XML Document for Validity Using an XML
     Schema" on page 400.

PART 3

Displaying XML Documents on the Web

8

Displaying XML Documents Using Basic Cascading Style Sheets

In this chapter and in Chapter 9, you'll learn how to display an XML document in the Microsoft Internet Explorer browser by linking a cascading style sheet (CSS) to the document and then opening the document directly in the browser. A cascading style sheet is a file that contains instructions for formatting the elements in the XML document. Linking a cascading style sheet is the first method covered in this book for displaying XML documents in the Internet Explorer browser.

Because you invent your own elements in XML, a browser has no built-in knowledge of how to properly display them. Creating and linking a cascading style sheet to your XML document is one way to tell the browser how to display each of the document's elements. Because an XML document with an attached cascading style sheet can be opened directly in Internet Explorer, you don't need to use an HTML page to access and display the data (as you do with the methods for displaying XML that I'll present in Chapters 10 and 11).

Keeping the display instructions in a style sheet separate from the actual XML document enhances the XML document's flexibility and makes it easier to maintain. You could, for example, quickly adapt a single XML document for a variety of different display situations (different browsers, applications, contexts, devices, and so on) by simply attaching an appropriate style sheet for each situation, without having to restructure or edit the document itself. Also, you could rapidly update the formatting of a group of similar XML documents by merely revising the common style sheet that is attached to these documents, without having to open and edit each document.

Creating and linking a cascading style sheet is probably the simplest method for displaying an XML document. The CSS language is already familiar to many Web page designers because of its established use with HTML pages, and most current Web browsers provide a high level of support for cascading style sheets.

However, compared to the XML display methods you'll learn in later chapters, linking a cascading style sheet to an XML document is a fairly limited means for controlling the display of the document. Although a cascading style sheet provides a high level of control over the way the browser formats the content of each of the elements in an XML document, it doesn't let you select, filter, rearrange, or add to the elements' data, or work with that information in other ways. Also, a CSS doesn't allow you to access XML attributes, unparsed entities, processing instructions, and other document components—or to process the information that these components contain. (But take a look at the Note at the end of this section for an explanation of the importance of CSS properties regardless of the method you use to display your XML documents.)

In this chapter, you'll learn the basic steps for using a cascading style sheet, how these style sheets work, and the meaning of the term "cascading." You'll also learn how to use the CSS properties that control the most basic formatting features of your XML documents, such as the text font, color, background, spacing, and alignment. In Chapter 9, you'll learn how to use CSS properties to achieve more sophisticated formatting effects; for example, you'll learn how to add margins and borders to an element's content, how to control the exact size and position of an element, and how to format just the first letter or line of an element.

note

Chapters 8 and 9 cover CSS as defined by the World Wide Web Consortium (W3C) and as implemented by Internet Explorer. These chapters cover most of the features defined by the W3C's original CSS specification (CSS Level 1), and present a sampling of the features defined by the W3C's more recent CSS specification (CSS Level 2), which is largely a superset of CSS Level 1. (Internet Explorer only partially implements CSS Level 2.) You can view the W3C specification for CSS Level 1 at *http://www.w3.org/TR/REC-CSS1* and the W3C specification for CSS Level 2 at *http://www.w3.org/TR/REC-CSS2*. To learn more about the CSS features supported by Internet Explorer, see the topic "Cascading Style Sheets" in the MSDN (Microsoft Developer Network) Library on the Web at *http://msdn.microsoft.com/library/*.

In Chapters 10 through 12, you'll learn somewhat more complex—but also more flexible—ways to display XML documents. In Chapter 10, you'll learn how to link an XML document to an HTML page and display the XML elements by binding standard HTML elements to them. In Chapter 11, you'll learn how to access and display individual elements, attributes, and other components of an XML document by writing script code in an HTML page. And in Chapter 12, you'll discover how to use a more powerful style sheet language—Extensible Stylesheet Language Transformations (XSLT)—which allows you to select and transform an XML document's data in highly flexible ways, to display its data using HTML elements, and to format the data using CSS properties.

note

Even if you choose to use the XML display methods given in Chapters 10 through 12 instead of linking cascading style sheets to your documents, the CSS properties and techniques you'll learn in Chapters 8 and 9 will still be the primary tools that you'll ultimately use to format the data from your XML documents. That's because the methods in Chapters 10 through 12 all use HTML elements to display XML data, and CSS properties are the most powerful means for formatting HTML elements.

In Chapters 10 through 12, you'll see many examples in which an individual HTML element is formatted by directly applying one or more CSS property settings using the STYLE attribute in the element's start-tag. Keep in mind that you can also embed an entire cascading style sheet within an HTML page by using the HTML STYLE element. You can also attach an external cascading style sheet by using the HTML LINK element. For an introduction to these techniques, see the topic "2.1 A brief CSS2 tutorial for HTML" in the W3C page "2 Introduction to CSS2" at *http://www.w3.org/TR/REC-CSS/intro.html*.

The Basic Steps for Using a Cascading Style Sheet

To use a cascading style sheet to format an XML document that you open directly in the Internet Explorer browser, you must complete the following two basic steps:

1   Create the style sheet file.

2   Link the style sheet to the XML document.

Basic Cascading Style Sheets   8

The First Step: Creating the Style Sheet File

A cascading style sheet is a plain text file, typically with the .css extension, that contains a set of rules telling the browser how to format and display the elements in a specific XML document. As with an XML document, you can create a style sheet using your favorite text editor.

Listing 8-1 contains an example of a simple cascading style sheet. (You'll find a copy of this listing on the companion CD under the filename Inventory01.css.)

Inventory01.css

```
/* File Name: Inventory01.css */

BOOK
    {display:block;
     margin-top:12pt;
     font-size:10pt}

TITLE
    {font-style:italic}

AUTHOR
    {font-weight:bold}
```

Listing 8-1.

This style sheet is designed to be attached to the XML document shown in Listing 8-2. (You'll find a copy of this listing on the companion CD under the filename Inventory01.xml.) You might want to put a sticky note on the page with Listing 8-2—it's used with other examples in this chapter, and you'll probably want to refer back to it.

Inventory01.xml

```
<?xml version="1.0"?>

<!-- File Name: Inventory01.xml -->

<?xml-stylesheet type="text/css" href="Inventory01.css"?>

<INVENTORY>
   <BOOK>
      <TITLE>The Adventures of Huckleberry Finn</TITLE>
      <AUTHOR>Mark Twain</AUTHOR>
      <BINDING>mass market paperback</BINDING>
```

```
      <PAGES>298</PAGES>
      <PRICE>$5.49</PRICE>
</BOOK>
<BOOK>
      <TITLE>Leaves of Grass</TITLE>
      <AUTHOR>Walt Whitman</AUTHOR>
      <BINDING>hardcover</BINDING>
      <PAGES>462</PAGES>
      <PRICE>$7.75</PRICE>
</BOOK>
<BOOK>
      <TITLE>The Legend of Sleepy Hollow</TITLE>
      <AUTHOR>Washington Irving</AUTHOR>
      <BINDING>mass market paperback</BINDING>
      <PAGES>98</PAGES>
      <PRICE>$2.95</PRICE>
</BOOK>
<BOOK>
      <TITLE>The Marble Faun</TITLE>
      <AUTHOR>Nathaniel Hawthorne</AUTHOR>
      <BINDING>trade paperback</BINDING>
      <PAGES>473</PAGES>
      <PRICE>$10.95</PRICE>
</BOOK>
<BOOK>
      <TITLE>Moby-Dick</TITLE>
      <AUTHOR>Herman Melville</AUTHOR>
      <BINDING>hardcover</BINDING>
      <PAGES>724</PAGES>
      <PRICE>$9.95</PRICE>
</BOOK>
<BOOK>
      <TITLE>The Portrait of a Lady</TITLE>
      <AUTHOR>Henry James</AUTHOR>
      <BINDING>mass market paperback</BINDING>
      <PAGES>256</PAGES>
      <PRICE>$4.95</PRICE>
</BOOK>
<BOOK>
      <TITLE>The Scarlet Letter</TITLE>
      <AUTHOR>Nathaniel Hawthorne</AUTHOR>
      <BINDING>trade paperback</BINDING>
```

```
        <PAGES>253</PAGES>
        <PRICE>$4.25</PRICE>
    </BOOK>
    <BOOK>
        <TITLE>The Turn of the Screw</TITLE>
        <AUTHOR>Henry James</AUTHOR>
        <BINDING>trade paperback</BINDING>
        <PAGES>384</PAGES>
        <PRICE>$3.35</PRICE>
    </BOOK>
</INVENTORY>
```

Listing 8-2.

> **note**
>
> The example style sheet in Listing 8-1 and the example XML document in Listing 8-2 are copies of files you created in the exercise given in "Display the XML Document Using a Cascading Style Sheet" in Chapter 2.

A style sheet consists of one or more *rules* (sometimes known as *rule sets*). A rule contains the display information for a particular element type in the XML document. The example style sheet contains three rules: one for BOOK elements, one for TITLE elements, and one for AUTHOR elements. Here's the rule for BOOK elements, with all of its parts labeled:

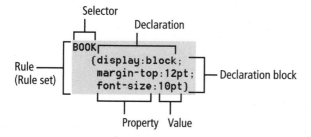

The *selector* is the name of the element type to which the display information applies.

Following the selector is a *declaration block,* which is delimited with brace characters ({}) and contains one or more *declarations* separated with semicolons (;).

Each declaration specifies the setting of a particular *property,* such as the size of the font to use for displaying the element. A declaration consists of a property, followed by a colon (:), followed by a *value* for that property. For example, the following declaration sets the *font-size* property to the value *10pt* (10 points):

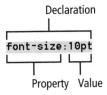

A style sheet can also contain *comments*. A style sheet comment begins with the slash and asterisk characters (/*) and ends with the asterisk and slash characters (*/). Between these two delimiting character pairs, you can type any text you want, and when the browser reads the style sheet to format the document, it will ignore that text. You can use comments to help document or explain the style sheet for the benefit of human readers. An example is the comment at the beginning of the example style sheet in Listing 8-1:

```
/* File Name: Inventory01.css */
```

You can also use comments as you develop a style sheet to temporarily deactivate a rule or a part of a rule. For example, if you wanted to see how BOOK elements would look without a top margin, you could temporarily add comment characters as in the following BOOK rule:

```
BOOK
    {display:block;
    /* margin-top:12pt; */
    font-size:10pt}
```

note

White space characters (spaces, tabs, and line breaks) are used to separate different CSS components, such as the individual declarations in the declaration block. The way I use white space in this book is only one possible style. You can use white space in whatever way helps you to organize and clarify your own style sheets. For example, you might put all declarations belonging to a rule on the same line, rather than on separate lines as you see in the examples.

The example style sheet in Listing 8-1 includes the following declarations:

- *display:block.* Inserts a line break before and after the element's text.

- *margin-top:12pt.* Adds a 12-point-wide margin above the element's text.

- *font-size:10pt.* Sets the size of the font used to display the element's text to 10 points.

- *font-style:italic.* Displays the element's text in italic characters.

- *font-weight:bold.* Displays the element's text in bold characters.

Here's how Internet Explorer displays the XML document that uses this style sheet, following the instructions provided by these declarations:

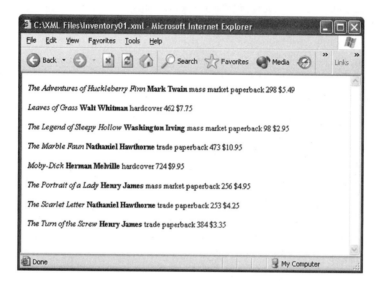

The properties available in cascading style sheets are similar to those you can apply to text in a word processor. Later in the chapter, you'll learn about the different properties you can use and the specific values you can assign to them.

Case Insensitivity in CSS

With Internet Explorer, cascading style sheets are case-insensitive. That is, when Internet Explorer processes a style sheet, it ignores the case of the letters. For example, you could type the following rule in any of these three ways:

```
TITLE
    {font-style:italic}
Title
    {FONT-STYLE:Italic}
title
    {Font-Style:ITALIC}
```

Case insensitivity in cascading style sheets has an important implication for XML. Because XML documents are case-*sensitive,* you can normally have two distinct element types whose names vary only in case, such as *Book* and BOOK. In a cascading style sheet, however, these two names would be regarded as the *same* element type, and you wouldn't be able to assign them different property settings. Therefore, if you intend to display your XML document using a cascading style sheet, you should not have element types whose names vary only in the case of one or more letters.

Inheritance of Property Settings

In general, a property setting that you assign to a particular element (such as BOOK) affects all child elements nested directly or indirectly within it, unless it's overridden by a different setting made for a specific child element.

The following properties, however, are exceptions and are *not* inherited by child elements:

- The *display* property, discussed in "Setting the *Display* Property" later in this chapter

- The background properties (*background-color, background-image, background-repeat*, and *background-position*), described in "Setting Background Properties" later in this chapter

- The *vertical-align* and *text-decoration* properties, explained in "Setting Text Spacing and Alignment Properties" later in this chapter

- The box properties, covered in "Setting Box Properties" in Chapter 9

For instance, the example style sheet in Listing 8-1 formats the BOOK elements (in the document in Listing 8-2) like this:

```
BOOK
    {display:block;
     margin-top:12pt;
     font-size:10pt}
```

Each BOOK element has five child elements. Because *font-size* is an inherited property, all of the child elements within a BOOK element are displayed in a 10-point font. Child elements do not, however, inherit the *display* and *margin-top* property settings (*margin-top* is one of the box properties).

With a noninherited property, if you don't specify a property value for a particular element, the browser will use that property's default value. For example, the default value for the *display* property is *inline*. This chapter gives the default values for all noninherited properties.

Since many property values are inherited, when you design a style sheet, you might want to start with the top-level elements, and then work down toward the more deeply nested elements, where you'll need only do some fine-tuning and add an occasional overriding setting. This approach helps minimize unnecessary property settings (namely, those that child elements inherit and that you therefore don't need to specify).

You'll learn more about inheritance and how it fits into the overall cascading mechanism in the section "Cascading in Cascading Style Sheets" later in the chapter.

Using Multiple Elements and Multiple Rules

You can apply a single rule to several element types by including all the element type names in the selector and separating the names with commas. For example, the following rule applies to the POEM, TITLE, AUTHOR, DATE, and STANZA element types:

```
POEM, TITLE, AUTHOR, DATE, STANZA
    {display:block;
     margin-bottom:12pt}
```

If a group of element types share a common set of property settings, you'll make your style sheet shorter and easier to understand and maintain by including all of these elements in a single rule rather than duplicating the settings in separate rules.

You can also include a given element type in more than one rule within the same style sheet. For example, the following rules both include the DATE element:

```
POEM, TITLE, AUTHOR, DATE, STANZA
    {display:block;
     margin-bottom:12pt}


DATE
    {font-style:italic}
```

The first rule contains the declarations that DATE shares with the other elements listed, while the second rule fine-tunes DATE—that is, it specifies a property setting that applies to DATE alone.

Using Contextual Selectors

In a selector, you can preface the element type name with the names of one or more ancestor elements (the parent, the parent plus the parent's parent, and so on), and the rule will apply only to elements with that name that are so nested. A selector that includes one or more ancestor element names is known as a *contextual* selector. A selector that does not include ancestor element names (such as those you've seen in the previous sections) is known as a *generic* selector.

If a particular property has one setting in a rule with a contextual selector, and has another setting in a rule with a generic selector for the same element, the setting in the contextual rule takes precedence because it's more specific.

Assume, for example, that the following is the root element of an XML document:

```
<MAPS>
   <CITY>
      <NAME>Santa Fe</NAME>
      <STATE>New Mexico</STATE>
   </CITY>
   <STATE>California</STATE>
</MAPS>
```

The following rules in an attached style sheet would cause the browser to format "New Mexico" in a normal font, but "California" in italic:

```
CITY STATE
   {font-style:normal}

STATE
   {font-style:italic}
```

Although the "New Mexico" STATE element matches both the contextual selector in the CITY STATE rule and the generic selector in the STATE rule, the selector in the CITY STATE rule is more specific and therefore has precedence. (You'll learn more about the precedence of conflicting rules in "Cascading in Cascading Style Sheets" later in the chapter.)

caution

Be sure that you don't insert commas between the element names in a contextual selector. Otherwise, the rule will apply to all of the elements (as described in the previous section) rather than to just the child element listed last.

Referencing Namespaces

If an element name in the XML document contains an explicit namespace prefix, you must include that prefix in the selector of a CSS rule used to format that element. Namespaces are covered in "Using Namespaces" on page 69. Consider, for instance, the example XML document given in Listing 3-5 (Collection Default.xml). This document includes elements that are prefaced with the *cd* namespace prefix, such as the following:

```
<cd:ITEM>
    <cd:TITLE>Violin Concerto in D</cd:TITLE>
    <cd:COMPOSER>Beethoven</cd:COMPOSER>
    <cd:PRICE>$14.95</cd:PRICE>
</cd:ITEM>
```

In a CSS selector, you would refer to the *cd:ITEM* element, for example, as shown in the following rule:

```
cd\:ITEM
    {display:block;
     margin-top:12pt;
     font-size:10pt}
```

You must insert the backslash (\) immediately before the colon (:) to distinguish a namespace prefix from a pseudo-element. (Pseudo-elements are discussed in "Using Pseudo-Elements" in Chapter 9.)

The following are two limitations on accessing namespaces from a CSS:

- The namespace prefix must be declared within the start-tag of the XML document's root element. A CSS won't recognize a namespace prefix that's declared within a descendent element of the root element.

- If an element is within the scope of a default namespace and its name doesn't include a prefix, you refer to that element in a CSS selector using the unqualified element name (such as ITEM or TITLE). Because a CSS doesn't provide a way to reference a default namespace, you can't apply different formatting to two elements that have the same name but are in different default namespaces (or to two elements, one of which is in a default namespace and the other in no namespace).

Using the STYLE Attribute

You can use the special STYLE attribute within your XML document—rather than within the style sheet—to assign one or more specific property settings to an individual element. If a property setting assigned through a STYLE attribute conflicts with a property setting made in the attached style sheet, the STYLE setting takes precedence. Thus, the STYLE attribute is a convenient way to override—for a particular element—the general property settings made for the element type in the attached style sheet. However, using STYLE does violate the CSS principle of keeping the formatting information separate from the definition of the document's content and structure in the XML file.

To specify one or more property settings, include the declarations in the quoted STYLE attribute value, separating the individual declarations with semicolons, just as you do in a CSS declaration block.

For instance, the example style sheet in Listing 8-1 formats TITLE elements in an italic, 10-point font. However, if you included the following STYLE attribute in the start-tag for a *specific* TITLE element in the document, that element alone would be displayed in a roman (nonitalic), 14-point font:

```
<TITLE STYLE='font-style:normal; font-size:14pt'>
The Adventures of Huckleberry Finn
</TITLE>
```

Here's how the document would look in Internet Explorer:

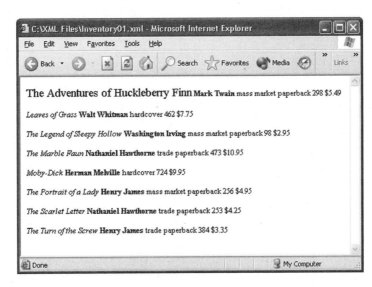

Importing Other Style Sheets

You can use the *@import* directive in your cascading style sheet to incorporate one or more other style sheets. The option of importing separate style sheets allows you to store related style rules in separate files, and then combine them as needed for particular types of documents.

Here's the general form of the *@import* directive, where *StyleSheetURL* is the fully qualified or relative URL of the file containing the cascading style sheet that you want to import:

```
@import url(StyleSheetURL);
```

For information on URL values, see the sidebar "Specifying URL Values" on page 209. For instance, the following directive (which uses a relative URL) placed at the beginning of the style sheet in Listing 8-1 would import the style sheet contained in the file Book.css (which must be within the same folder as the importing style sheet):

```
/* File Name: Inventory01.css */

@import url(Book.css);

BOOK
    {display:block;
     margin-top:12pt;
     font-size:10pt}

/* rest of style sheet... */
```

The *@import* directive must go at the beginning of the style sheet, before any rules. You can include several *@import* directives at the beginning of a style sheet.

When you import one or more style sheets, the browser merges the rules contained in the imported and the importing style sheets. However, if any rules conflict, the importing style sheet takes precedence over the imported style sheets. And if you import several style sheets, the rules in a style sheet imported later in the file take precedence over those in a style sheet imported previously. For more information on precedence, see "Cascading in Cascading Style Sheets" later in this chapter.

The Second Step: Linking the Style Sheet to the XML Document

To link a cascading style sheet to an XML document, you insert the reserved *xml-stylesheet* processing instruction into the document. This processing instruction has the following general form, where *CSSFilePath* is a quoted URL indicating the location of the style sheet file:

```
<?xml-stylesheet type="text/css" href=CSSFilePath?>
```

You can use a fully qualified URL, such as this:

```
<?xml-stylesheet type="text/css"
    href="http://www.mjyOnline.com/Inventory01.css"?>
```

Specifying URL Values

A URL (Uniform Resource Locator) is a standard Internet address, such as *http://www.microsoft.com/mspress/*. The *@import* directive and the *background-image* and *list-style-image* properties all require a URL value to indicate the location of the associated resource (the style sheet or the image file). You specify a URL using the following form, where *URL* is the URL. Note that you *can't* include space between the *url* and the opening parenthesis.

```
url(URL)
```

You can use a fully qualified URL, as in these examples:

```
@import url(http://www.mjyOnline.com/stylesheets/MyStyles.css);

INVENTORY
{background-image:url(file:///E:\ExampleCode\Background.gif)}
```

Or, you can use a partial URL that specifies a location relative to the location of the style sheet file containing the URL. Relative URLs in style sheets work just like relative URLs in HTML pages. For example, if the style sheet file were located in the Example Code folder, the following relative URL would be equivalent to the fully qualified URL in the previous example (namely, *file:///E:\Example Code\Background.gif*):

```
INVENTORY {background-image:url(Background.gif)}
```

More commonly, however, you would use a partial URL that specifies a location relative to the location of the XML document containing the *xml-stylesheet* processing instruction, such as this:

```
<?xml-stylesheet type="text/css" href="Inventory01.css"?>
```

(A relative URL is more common because you typically store a style sheet file in the same folder where you store the XML document, or in one of its subfolders.)

You normally add the *xml-stylesheet* processing instruction to the XML document's prolog, following the XML declaration, as you can see in the example XML document in Listing 8-2. (For more information on processing instructions, and for a description of all the places where you can legally insert them, see "Using Processing Instructions" in Chapter 4.)

The ability to attach an external style sheet to an XML document makes formatting the document very flexible. You can radically change the document's formatting by simply attaching a different style sheet. And to attach a different style sheet, you need only edit the URL in the *xml-stylesheet* processing instruction—without making any other changes in the XML document.

When you've linked a style sheet to an XML document, you can open that document directly in Internet Explorer. For example, you can enter the document's URL or file path into the Internet Explorer Address Bar and press Enter:

Or, assuming that Internet Explorer is your default browser, you can simply double-click the XML document's filename in Windows Explorer or in a folder window: ▣ Inventory01.xml

Internet Explorer will open the XML document and display it using the instructions in the linked style sheet.

> ## note
> If the browser can't find the style sheet file specified in the *xml-stylesheet* processing instruction, it will display the document text using its own property settings (for example, its current font and font-size settings). And, as you learned in Chapter 2, if the XML document isn't linked to a style sheet (that is, the document doesn't contain an *xml-stylesheet* processing instruction), Internet Explorer will display the XML source for the document rather than its content.

You can include more than one style sheet in an XML document by inserting an *xml-stylesheet* processing instruction for each one, as in this example of the beginning of an XML document:

```
<?xml version="1.0"?>

<?xml-stylesheet type="text/css" href="Book01.css"?>
<?xml-stylesheet type="text/css" href="Book02.css"?>

<INVENTORY>
   <!-- contents of document element... -->
</INVENTORY>
```

The option of linking several style sheets allows you to store groups of related rules in separate files, and then combine them as needed for particular types of XML documents.

When you link more than one style sheet, Internet Explorer merges the rules from the different sheets. If separate style sheets contain conflicting rules, the rules in a style sheet linked later in the document take precedence over those in a style sheet linked previously in the document. (In the preceding example, rules in Book02.css would have priority over conflicting rules in Book01.css.) You'll learn more about precedence among conflicting rules in the next section.

Cascading in Cascading Style Sheets

The "cascading" in Cascading Style Sheets means that you can assign values to properties at several different levels (just as a cascading stream spills through different levels). The following list describes the main levels at which you can assign a value to a property. The levels are listed in their order of precedence—from highest to lowest. When the browser goes to display an element, if a given property such as *font-size* is assigned conflicting values for that element at different levels, the browser will use the setting given at the highest precedence level.

1   If you assign a value to a property in the STYLE attribute of a specific element in the XML document, the browser will use that value for displaying the element. For example, it would display the following element in bold:

```
<TITLE STYLE="font-weight:bold">Leaves of Grass</TITLE>
```

2   If you don't set a property through a STYLE attribute, the browser will use a property value declared in a CSS rule with a contextual selector (that is, a selector that specifies an element together with one or more of its ancestor elements, as discussed earlier in "Using Contextual Selectors"). Assume, for example, that the following is the document element of an XML document:

```
<MAPS>
   <CITY>
      <NAME>Santa Fe</NAME>
      <STATE>New Mexico</STATE>
   </CITY>
   <STATE>California</STATE>
</MAPS>
```

Assume also that the attached style sheet contains the following rules:

```
CITY STATE
   {font-style:normal}


STATE
   {font-style:italic}
```

The browser would use the CITY STATE rule to format the "New Mexico" STATE element, because it has a contextual selector and therefore takes precedence over the STATE rule, which has only a generic selector. "New Mexico" would thus appear in a normal font.

3   If you don't declare the value of a particular property in a rule with a matching contextual selector, the browser will use the value declared in a rule with a generic selector (that is, a selector that includes only the element type name). For instance, in the example style sheet given in item 2, the browser wouldn't find a matching contextual rule for the "California" STATE element, so it would use the generic STATE rule, and would therefore display "California" in italics.

4   If you don't declare the value of a particular property in a generic rule for the element type, the browser will use the property's setting declared for the closest ancestor element (parent, parent of parent, and so on). For instance, in the style sheet in Listing 8-1, the rule for the TITLE element doesn't assign a value to the *font-size* property:

```
TITLE
    {font-style:italic}
```

Therefore, the browser will use the *font-size* setting from this element's parent element, BOOK (BOOK is the parent of TITLE in the XML document that uses the style sheet):

```
BOOK
    {display:block;
     margin-top:12pt;
     font-size:10pt}
```

It will therefore display the TITLE element's text using 10-point characters.

Note, however, that this process will occur only for an inherited property. For a noninherited property, the browser will use the property's default value (see "Inheritance of Property Settings" earlier in this chapter).

5   If the style sheet doesn't include a property setting for any ancestor element, the browser will use its own setting. This setting might be a default value built into the browser or one set by the browser's user. For instance, because the example style sheet in Listing 8-1 doesn't set the *font-family* property for any element, the browser will use its own *font-family* value to display all elements. (In Internet Explorer, this is Times New Roman unless the browser user chooses a different font family through the Internet Options command on the Tools menu.)

Again, this process applies only to inherited properties. For noninherited properties, the browser uses the property's default value.

As you can see from this list, the general principle is this: If you assign a property conflicting values at different levels, the browser gives preference to the *more specific* rule. For example, a property setting for the element itself is more specific than a setting for the element's parent and therefore takes precedence. You can use this principle to figure out more complex cases. (For example, if a child element's parent has both a contextual rule and a generic rule, which rule will the browser use for the child element? You're right: The browser will use the contextual rule!)

> **note**
>
> The order of precedence in the preceding list isn't cast in stone. It's possible for the browser's property settings to take precedence over the property settings in the style sheet that you attach to your XML document. This enables users with special needs to have control over formatting (for instance, a user with impaired vision could use an extra-large font). In Internet Explorer, for example, a user can give the browser's property settings precedence over your style sheet settings by choosing the Internet Options command from the Tools menu, clicking the Accessibility button in the General tab of the Internet Options dialog box, and choosing appropriate options.

What happens if a particular property is given conflicting settings *at the same level?* In this case, the browser uses the *last* setting that it processes. For instance, if two generic rules for the same element have conflicting settings for the *font-style* property, as in the following example, the browser would use the second one because it processes it last:

```
TITLE, AUTHOR, BINDING, PRICE
    {display:block;
     font-size:12pt;
     font-weight:bold;
     font-style:italic}

AUTHOR
    {font-style:normal}
```

Thus, in this example, it would format the AUTHOR elements using a normal rather than an italic font.

The following points describe the order in which the browser processes style sheet rules:

■ If you link several style sheets to the document using *xml-stylesheet* processing instructions, the browser processes the style sheets in the order that you list the processing instructions.

■ If you import one or more other style sheets into a style sheet using the *@import* directive (as explained in the earlier section "Importing Other Style Sheets"), the browser processes the imported style sheets before the importing style sheet, and it processes them in the order in which you imported them.

- In a particular style sheet, the rules are processed in the order in which they are listed.

> **note**
>
> The rule whereby the browser uses the last style property setting that it processes is the opposite of the rule an XML processor uses when it encounters multiple attribute or entity declarations. Recall from previous chapters that the XML processor uses the first attribute or entity declaration and ignores any subsequent ones.

Setting the *display* Property

The *display* property controls the basic way the browser displays an element's text. You can assign it one of the following four CSS keywords:

- *block.* The browser always inserts a line break before and after the element's text (which includes the text belonging to any child elements). As a result, the element's text is displayed in a separate "block" with the preceding document text above it and the following document text below it. A *block* element is thus similar to a paragraph in a word-processing program.

- *inline* (the default). The browser does not insert a line break between the text of two elements that have the *inline* setting of the *display* property (unless the first element's text has reached the right edge of the window and the browser must wrap the text down to the next line). It inserts line breaks within an *inline* element's text only as necessary to make the text fit within the window. An *inline* element is thus similar to a sequence of characters *within* a paragraph in a word-processing program.

> **note**
>
> The browser doesn't insert an extra line break between two adjoining *block* elements. It inserts a *single* line break between a *block* element and an adjoining *inline* element, as well as between two adjoining *block* elements.

tip

(Internet Explorer 5.5–6.0 only.) Normally, the browser inserts a line break within the text of a *block* or *inline* element when a line of text reaches the right edge of the window. This text wrapping allows the reader to view the entire text without scrolling back and forth. However, you can suppress the insertion of these automatic line breaks by assigning the CSS keyword *nowrap* to an element's *white-space* property, as in the following example:

```
VERSE {white-space:nowrap} /* text in VERSE elements won't
be wrapped */
```

The default value of this property is *normal*, which allows automatic line breaks.

- *list-item* (**Internet Explorer 6.0 only**). The browser treats the element as a *block* element and formats its content as a bulleted or numbered list item. For details, see the next section.

- *none*. The browser does not display the content of the element or any of its child elements (even if a child element has a different *display* setting). See the sidebar "Hiding the Content of an Element" later in this section.

note

The CSS specification indicates that the *display* property isn't inherited by child elements. This is clearly true if you assign the *block* or *list-item* setting to an element's *display* property. However, child elements effectively inherit the *none* setting, because when you assign this setting to the parent's *display* property, you hide all child elements as well. Also, the child elements of an *inline* element will likewise be *inline* if they don't have a *display* value, because *inline* is the default setting.

For more information on assigning CSS keywords to properties, see the sidebar "Specifying CSS Keyword Values" at the end of this section.

Assume, for instance, that you use the following style sheet to display the example XML document in Listing 8-2 (recall that to change the style sheet used to display an XML document, you need to edit the *xml-stylesheet* processing instruction within the document):

```
BOOK
   {display:block;
    margin-top:12pt;
    font-size:10pt}

TITLE
   {font-style:italic}

AUTHOR
   {font-weight:bold}

PAGES
   {display:none}
```

Hiding the Content of an Element

The CSS standard provides two ways to hide the content of an element: You can assign the element's *display* property the value *none*, or you can assign its *visibility* property the CSS keyword *hidden*. If you assign *none* to an element's *display* property, the element—plus any child elements—is hidden and doesn't take up space on the page. In contrast, if you assign *hidden* to an element's *visibility* property, the browser leaves a blank area in the page where the element would have been displayed. The size of the blank area is equal to the size of the hidden element, based on its content and its other property settings. Also, the *hidden* setting doesn't necessarily hide child elements.

The *visibility* property can be assigned one of the following three CSS keyword values:

- *inherit* (the default). The element inherits the visibility of its parent.
- *visible.* The element is made visible (even if its parent is *hidden*).
- *hidden.* The element is hidden.

For example, if the following rules were applied to the XML document in Listing 8-2, all the child elements of a BOOK element would be hidden except TITLE, resulting in a simple list of titles. (However, the other child elements would take up space on the page, possibly causing extra blank lines to appear between titles.)

```
BOOK {visibility:hidden}

TITLE {visibility:visible}
```

Basic Cascading Style Sheets

8

Because the BOOK element's *display* property is assigned the *block* value, the browser always inserts a line break before and after the element's text. (BOOK has element content. Its text consists of the text belonging to all of its child elements.)

Because the style sheet doesn't assign *display* property values for the TITLE, AUTHOR, BINDING, and PRICE elements (and these elements don't inherit the *display* value from their parent element), the browser treats them as *inline* elements, which is the default value. Therefore, the browser doesn't insert line breaks between these elements, and—provided the browser window is wide enough—it displays them all on the same line.

Because the PAGES element's *display* property is assigned the value *none*, the browser doesn't display that element.

Here's the overall result:

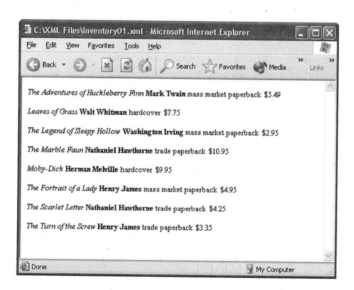

note

The CSS specification includes quite a few properties that are largely redundant—that is, it often provides two or more properties that allow you to set the same formatting feature in slightly different ways. For example, you can apply a text border to any combination of edges either by using the single *border-style* property or by using the separate *border-left, border-right, border-top,* and *border-bottom* properties. To provide room for covering more topics, I often omit redundant properties from the discussions in this chapter and in Chapter 9. In each case, I've attempted to select the most basic, convenient set of properties that you can use to apply any of the available formats, and to omit the properties that merely provide alternative ways to apply these same features. For instance, in the section on applying borders, I present the basic *border-style, border-width,* and *border-color* properties, but omit the other 17 border properties that offer some possible convenience but don't actually provide additional formatting features (for example, *border-left, border-left-style, border-left-width,* and *border-left-color*).

Specifying CSS Keyword Values

With many of the CSS properties, you can—or must—assign a value by using a predefined CSS keyword. The specific keywords that you can use depend upon the particular property. For example, you can assign the *display* property one of four keywords: *block, inline, list-item,* or *none*. You can assign the *color* property one of 16 keywords that describe the basic colors, such as *red, green, yellow,* or *fuchsia,* as in this example:

```
PARA {color:fuchsia}
```

And you can assign the *border-style* property one of nine possible keywords: *solid, dotted, dashed, double, groove, ridge, inset, outset,* or *none* as shown here:

```
SECTION {border-style:solid}
```

Creating Bulleted and Numbered Lists (Internet Explorer 6.0 only)

If an XML document is going to be displayed using Internet Explorer 6.0, you can create a bulleted or numbered list by setting the *display* property of one or more element types to the value *list-item*. This setting causes the browser to treat the element as a *block* element and to display a *list marker* to the left of the element's content. A list marker can be either a bullet or an automatically incremented number or letter. You control the formatting of the list marker by using the properties described in the following table. These properties are inherited by child elements.

List formatting property	Property effect and values
list-style-type	Controls the type of list marker that's displayed if the *list-style-image* property (described next) is set to *none* or is omitted. The following are the possible keyword values and the resulting marker types: ■ *disc* (default): a solid circle ■ *circle*: an open circle ■ *square*: a solid square ■ *decimal*: 1, 2, 3, ... ■ *lower-roman*: i, ii, iii, ... ■ *upper-roman*: I, II, III, ... ■ *lower-alpha*: a, b, c, ... ■ *upper-alpha*: A, B, C, ... ■ *none*: no list marker
list-style-image	Allows you to use a custom image as a list marker. The possible values are as follows: ■ *none* (default): A custom image isn't used. The list marker that's displayed is determined by the setting of the *list-style-type* property. ■ The URL of the graphics file containing the list marker image, as in this example: `list-style-image:url(MyBullet.bmp)` See the sidebar "Specifying URL Values" on page 209.
list-style-position	Controls the position of the list marker. The following are the possible values: ■ *outside* (default): The marker is outdented— that is, it's placed to the left of the block of text. You must assign the element a positive left margin to show the marker. (A left margin of at least 30 points is recommended; see "Setting the Margin Properties" on page 259.) ■ *inside*: The marker is not outdented—that is, it's displayed in the first character position within the block of text.

As an example, you could format the list of books in the XML document of Listing 8-2 as an automatically numbered list by replacing the BOOK rule given in the attached style sheet (Listing 8-1) with the following rule:

```
BOOK
    {display:list-item;
     list-style-type:decimal;
     list-style-position:outside;
     margin-left:30pt;
     margin-top:12pt;
     font-size:10pt}
```

The declaration *display:list-item* causes all BOOK elements to be displayed as list items. The declaration *list-style-type:decimal* sets the list item markers to automatically incremented decimal numbers, and the declaration *list-style-position:outside* places the markers to the left of the blocks of BOOK text. The declaration *margin-left:30pt* creates a 30-point left margin and is needed to reveal the markers, which would otherwise be hidden. Here's the result:

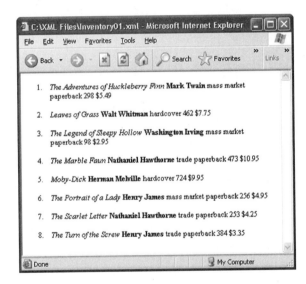

Setting Font Properties

The CSS standard provides the following properties that modify the font used to display an element's text:

■ *font-family*

■ *font-size*

■ *font-style*

- *font-weight*

- *font-variant*

All of these properties are inherited by child elements.

Setting the *font-family* Property

The *font-family* property specifies the name of the font used to display the element's text, as shown in this example:

```
BOOK {font-family:Arial}
```

You can enter any font name that you want. (They aren't predefined CSS keywords.) If the browser can't find the requested font, it will substitute an available font.

tip
If a font name contains spaces, surround the whole thing with single or double quotes, as in this example: *BOOK {font-family:"Times New Roman"}*.

You can increase your chances of getting the type of font you want by listing several alternative choices, separated with commas, in the order of your preference. Here's an example:

```
BOOK {font-family:Arial, Helvetica}
```

If a font named Arial isn't available, the browser will use Helvetica. If Helvetica isn't available, it will substitute some other available font.

You can further increase your chances of getting a desirable font by including a CSS keyword—normally at the end of the list—that indicates the general type of font you want, as in this example:

```
BOOK {font-family:Arial, Helvetica, sans-serif}
```

Here, if the browser can't find Arial or Helvetica, it will substitute some other sans serif font (that is, a font without serifs, also known as a *gothic* font).

The following table lists the CSS keywords you can use to indicate the general type of font that you want. The CSS specification calls these *generic family names*. For each generic family name, the table also gives the name of a specific font that belongs to that family, as well as a sample of the text that Internet Explorer displays when you request that family. (The particular fonts that Internet Explorer displays depend upon the set of fonts currently installed in Microsoft Windows, so the fonts you see might be different.)

font-family generic family name keyword	Example of a specific font	Text sample
serif	Times New Roman	The Adventures of Huckleberry Finn
sans-serif	Arial	The Adventures of Huckleberry Finn
cursive	ZapfChancery	*The Adventures of Huckleberry Finn*
fantasy	Western	THE ADVENTURES OF HUCKLEBERRY FINN
monospace	Courier New	The Adventures of Huckleberry Finn

For example, if you attached the following style sheet to the example XML document given in Listing 8-2, Internet Explorer would display the document as shown in the following figure:

```
BOOK
    {display:block;
     margin-top:12pt;
     font-family:Arial, sans-serif;
     font-size:12pt}


TITLE
    {font-style:italic}


AUTHOR
    {font-family:"Times New Roman", serif}
```

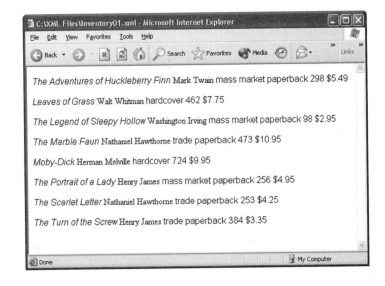

The Arial font assigned to the BOOK element's *font-family* property is inherited by all child elements except AUTHOR, which has its own overriding *font-family* value (*"Times New Roman"*, *serif*).

Setting the *font-size* Property

The *font-size* property sets the height of the font used to display the element's text. You can assign this property four different types of values:

- **A value relative to the size of the browser's font.** You can specify a font size that is relative to the size of the browser's current font by assigning the *font-size* property one of the keyword values in the following table. With Internet Explorer, the value *small* causes the browser to use its currently selected font size; the other values are scaled down or up from there.

font-size keyword:	*xx-small*
Example CSS rule:	`TITLE {font-size:xx-small}`
Description:	The smallest font size that can be set by keyword
Text sample:	The Adventures of Huckleberry Finn

font-size keyword:	*x-small*
Example CSS rule:	`TITLE {font-size:x-small}`
Description:	Approximately 1.5 times the size of *xx-small*
Text sample:	The Adventures of Huckleberry Finn

font-size keyword:	*small*
Example CSS rule:	`TITLE {font-size:small}`
Description:	Approximately 1.5 times the size of *x-small*. This value causes Internet Explorer to use its current font size.
Text sample:	The Adventures of Huckleberry Finn

font-size keyword:	*medium*
Example CSS rule:	`TITLE {font-size:medium}`
Description:	Approximately 1.5 times the size of *small*
Text sample:	The Adventures of Huckleberry Finn

font-size keyword:	*large*
Example CSS rule:	`TITLE {font-size:large}`
Description:	Approximately 1.5 times the size of *medium*
Text sample:	The Adventures of Huckleberry Finn

font-size keyword:	*x-large*
Example CSS rule:	`TITLE {font-size:x-large}`
Description:	Approximately 1.5 times the size of *large*
Text sample:	The Adventures of Huckleberry

font-size keyword:	*xx-large*
Example CSS rule:	`TITLE {font-size:xx-large}`
Description:	Approximately 1.5 times the size of *x-large*
Text sample:	The Adventures of Huckleb

note

The CSS Level 1 specification recommends the 1.5 scaling factor, and the CSS Level 2 specification recommends 1.2. However, in Internet Explorer, the actual ratio between the different sizes varies quite a bit. For example, *medium* is actually only about 1.15 times as large as *small*.

■ **A value relative to the size of the parent's font.** You can specify a font size that is relative to the size of the parent element's current font by assigning one of the following keyword values to the *font-size* property:

font-size keyword:	*smaller*
Example CSS rule:	`TITLE {font-size:smaller}`
Description:	A font approximately 33% smaller than the parent element's font (or, for the root element, 33% smaller than the browser's font)
Text sample:	The Adventures of Huckleberry Finn

font-size keyword:	*larger*
Example CSS rule:	`TITLE {font-size:larger}`
Description:	A font approximately 50% larger than the parent element's font (or, for the root element, 50% larger than the browser's font)
Text sample:	The Adventures of Huckleberry Finn

Basic Cascading Style Sheets

8

note

The 33% and 50% percentages given in the preceding table are based on the 1.5 scaling factor recommended in the CSS Level 1 specification. The actual results might vary.

- **A percentage of the size of the parent's font.** Rather than using the *smaller* or *larger* keyword, you can specify a font size that is relative to the size of the parent element's current font with greater precision by assigning a percentage value to the *font-size* property. For example, the following rule requests a font size that is one and one-half times the size of the parent's font:

  ```
  TITLE {font-size:150%}
  ```

  (If the browser used the recommended scaling ratio of 1.5, this rule would be equivalent to the rule *TITLE {font-size:larger}*.)

  The following rule requests a font size that is slightly larger than the one requested by the previous rule:

  ```
  TITLE {font-size:160%}
  ```

  Note that for the root element, the percentage is based on the browser's font size. (For more information on assigning percentage values to properties, see the sidebar "Specifying Percentage Values" on page 227.)

- **A specific size value.** You can also specify an element's font size by assigning *font-size* a *size value*. (I describe the different types of size values in the sidebar "Specifying Size Values" on page 227.) For example, the following rule specifies a 12-point font size:

  ```
  TITLE {font-size:12pt}
  ```

  And the next rule specifies a font that's twice as big as the parent element's font:

  ```
  TITLE {font-size:2em}
  ```

  (The second example is equivalent to *TITLE {font-size:200%}*.)

Specifying Percentage Values

You can assign certain properties a percentage value. Percentage values are useful when you're more concerned with the relative sizes of different components than with their actual sizes.

A percentage value specifies the size of some property as a percentage of some other value. What that other value is depends on the particular property you're setting. Usually, it's the font size of the element itself. For example, the following setting makes the line height two times the height of the element's current font, resulting in double-spaced lines:

```
SECTION {line-height:200%}
```

For the *font-size* property, however, a percentage value refers to the current font size of the element's parent. For example, the following rule sets the element's font height to three-quarters of the height of its parent element's current font:

```
PARAGRAPH {font-size:75%}
```

Note that if a child element inherits a percentage property value, it inherits the calculated *result* of the percentage, not the percentage itself. (Otherwise, if a series of descendent elements inherited a percentage value, the size would keep getting smaller or larger with each successive generation.)

Specifying Size Values

Many CSS properties can, or must, be assigned a size value (termed a *length* value in the CSS specifications). Size values are used to specify font sizes, positions of background images, text spacings, indentations, line heights, margin widths, border widths, widths and heights of elements, and other properties. You can assign either an absolute size value or a relative size value to any property that takes a size value.

An *absolute size value* is one that specifies an exact size using standard units of measurement, such as inches, points, or millimeters. The following table lists the different units you can specify. For each type of unit, it gives the abbreviation you must use to indicate the unit in a rule, and it shows the equivalent numbers of the other units.

continued

Basic Cascading Style Sheets

8

continued

Abbreviation*	Centimeters	Inches	Millimeters	Picas	Points
cm	1	0.3937	10.0	2.3622	28.3465
in	2.54	1	25.4	6	72
mm	0.1	0.03937	1	0.23622	2.83465
pc	0.42333	0.16667	4.23333	1	12
pt	0.03528	0.01389	0.35278	0.08333	1

* *cm* = centimeters; *in* = inches; *mm* = millimeters; *pc* = picas; *pt* = points

For example, the following two rules employ absolute size values:

```
STANZA {font-size:12pt}
PARAGRAPH {margin-top:.25in}
```

A *relative size value* is one that specifies a size relative to the height of the element's current font, or relative to the size of a pixel on the monitor used to display the document. (A *pixel* is a picture element—one of the individual dots that make up the image on a computer monitor.) The following table lists the different relative size units that you can use:

Unit	Size of unit
em	The height of the element's current font
ex	The height of a lowercase *x* in the element's current font
px	The size of a pixel on the monitor

One exception is that when you assign *em* or *ex* units to the *font-size* property, the value refers to the size of the *parent* element's font.

For example, the following rule adds a top margin to an element. The height of the margin would equal the height of the element's font:

```
BOOK {margin-top:1em}
```

The following rule creates a top margin that is 15 pixels high:

```
SECTION {margin-top:15px}
```

And the following rule sets the element's font height to three-quarters of the height of its parent element's font:

continued

```
PARAGRAPH {font-size:.75em}
```
(This final rule is equivalent to the *PARAGRAPH {font-size:75%}* example rule you saw in the previous sidebar.)

Note that if a child element inherits a relative value, it inherits the calculated *result* of the value, not the relative value itself.

Setting the *font-style* Property

The *font-style* property controls whether an element's text is displayed in italic or in normal upright (roman) characters. You can assign this property one of the following three CSS keyword values:

font-style keyword:	*italic*
Example CSS rule:	`TITLE {font-style:italic}`
Effect:	Assigns an italic font if available. If one is not available, it assigns an oblique font.
Text sample:	*The Adventures of Huckleberry Finn*

font-style keyword:	*oblique*
Example CSS rule:	`TITLE {font-style:oblique}`
Effect:	Assigns an oblique font if available. (A font generated by slanting the letters of a normal font.)
Text sample:	*The Adventures of Huckleberry Finn*

font-style keyword:	*normal*
Example CSS rule:	`TITLE {font-style:normal}`
Effect:	Assigns a roman font
Text sample:	The Adventures of Huckleberry Finn

Setting the *font-weight* Property

The *font-weight* property determines how bold (that is, how dark and thick) an element's characters appear. You can assign this property one of the following 13 CSS keyword values:

font-weight keyword:	*normal*
Example CSS rule:	`TITLE {font-weight:normal}`
Effect:	Displays the text in the normal level of boldness
Text sample:	The Adventures of Huckleberry Finn

8

Basic Cascading Style Sheets

font-weight keyword: *bold*

Example CSS rule:	TITLE {font-weight:bold}
Effect:	Displays the text in typical bold characters
Text sample:	**The Adventures of Huckleberry Finn**

font-weight keyword: *bolder*

Example CSS rule:	TITLE {font-weight:bolder}
Effect:	Displays the text in a bolder font than the parent element's font (or, for the root element, than the browser's font)
Text sample:	**The Adventures of Huckleberry Finn**

font-weight keyword: *lighter*

Example CSS rule:	TITLE {font-weight:lighter}
Effect:	Displays the text in a lighter font than the parent element's font (or, for the root element, than the browser's font)
Text sample:	The Adventures of Huckleberry Finn

font-weight keyword: *100*

Example CSS rule:	TITLE {font-weight:100}
Effect:	Displays the text in the lightest available font weight. The following values in this table (200-900) display the text with increasing degrees of boldness.
Text sample:	The Adventures of Huckleberry Finn

font-weight keyword: *200*

Example CSS rule:	TITLE {font-weight:200}
Text sample:	The Adventures of Huckleberry Finn

font-weight keyword: *300*

Example CSS rule:	TITLE {font-weight:300}
Text sample:	The Adventures of Huckleberry Finn

font-weight keyword: *400*

Example CSS rule:	TITLE {font-weight:400}
Effect:	Equivalent to assigning the *normal* keyword value
Text sample:	The Adventures of Huckleberry Finn

font-weight keyword: *500*

Example CSS rule:	TITLE {font-weight:500}
Text sample:	The Adventures of Huckleberry Finn

font-weight keyword: *600*

Example CSS rule:	`TITLE {font-weight:600}`
Text sample:	**The Adventures of Huckleberry Finn**

font-weight keyword: *700*

Example CSS rule:	`TITLE {font-weight:700}`
Effect:	Equivalent to assigning the *bold* keyword value
Text sample:	**The Adventures of Huckleberry Finn**

font-weight keyword: *800*

Example CSS rule:	`TITLE {font-weight:800}`
Text sample:	**The Adventures of Huckleberry Finn**

font-weight keyword: *900*

Example CSS rule:	`TITLE {font-weight:900}`
Effect:	The boldest available font weight
Text sample:	**The Adventures of Huckleberry Finn**

A browser might not be able to display all of these different degrees of boldness. The samples in the table show the actual text that Internet Explorer displays in response to each of the *font-weight* values.

Setting the *font-variant* Property

You can use the *font-variant* property to convert an element's text to all capital letters. You can assign this property one of the following two keyword values:

font-variant keyword: *small-caps*

Example CSS rule:	`TITLE {font-variant:small-caps}`
Effect:	Converts the text to all capital letters. Internet Explorer 6.0 makes the letters that were lowercase in the original text smaller than those that were originally uppercase (as shown in the text sample).
Text sample:	THE ADVENTURES OF HUCKLEBERRY FINN

font-variant keyword: *normal*

Example CSS rule:	`TITLE {font-variant:normal}`
Effect:	Leaves the text in its original mix of uppercase and lowercase letters (that is, the text is *not* converted)
Text sample:	The Adventures of Huckleberry Finn

Setting the *color* Property

The *color* property sets the color of an element's text. You can assign this property a color value by using any of the formats discussed in the sidebar "Specifying Color Values" on page 233. For example, the following rule sets the color of the AUTHOR element's text to light blue:

```
AUTHOR {color:blue}
```

And the following rule sets the AUTHOR element's text to light red:

```
AUTHOR {color:rgb(255,0,0)}
```

The *color* property is inherited by child elements. Thus, if you attached the following style sheet to the example XML document in Listing 8-2, all text would be light blue except the PRICE text, which would be light red because the style sheet includes an overriding color setting for this element:

```
BOOK
    {display:block;
     margin-top:12pt;
     font-size:10pt;
     color:blue}

TITLE
    {font-style:italic}

AUTHOR
    {font-weight:bold}

PRICE
    {color:red}
```

tip
The *color* property sets the color of the individual letters in the text (sometimes called the text *foreground color*). To set the text background color, use the *background-color* property discussed in "Setting the *background-color* Property" later in the chapter.

Specifying Color Values

Properties to which you can assign color values include *color, background-color,* and *border-color.* You can assign a color value by using one of four different formats, which the following example rules illustrate. These rules are equivalent—each of them assigns the color light red to the *color* property.

```
PARA {color:red}
PARA {color:rgb(255,0,0)}
PARA {color:#FF0000}
PARA {color:rgb(100%,0%,0%)}
```

The first format uses a CSS keyword (*red*), while each of the other three formats assigns a color by specifying the relative intensities of the red, green, and blue components of the color, in that order. In the second format, each color intensity is specified by a decimal value ranging from 0 to 255. In the third format, the color is specified by using a six-digit hexadecimal number ranging from 000000 to FFFFFF, where the first two digits specify the red intensity, the second two the green intensity, and the last two the blue intensity. In the final format, each color intensity is specified by using a percentage value ranging from 0% to 100%.

The following table lists the basic color values that you can assign using a CSS keyword, and for each color it shows the equivalent color specifications in all four formats. (The CSS keywords use picturesque names for the colors, while the first column in this table uses the standard color names that are employed in photography and optics.)

Color	CSS keyword	Decimal RGB format	Hexadecimal RGB format	Percentage RGB format
light red	*red*	rgb(255,0,0)	#FF0000	rgb(100%,0%,0%)
dark red	*maroon*	rgb(128,0,0)	#800000	rgb(50%,0%,0%)
light green	*lime*	rgb(0,255,0)	#00FF00	rgb(0%,100%,0%)
dark green	*green*	rgb(0,128,0)	#008000	rgb(0%,50%,0%)
light blue	*blue*	rgb(0,0,255)	#0000FF	rgb(0%,0%,100%)
dark blue	*navy*	rgb(0,0,128)	#000080	rgb(0%,0%,50%)
light yellow	*yellow*	rgb(255,255,0)	#FFFF00	rgb(100%,100%,0%)
dark yellow	*olive*	rgb(128,128,0)	#808000	rgb(50%,50%,0%)
light cyan	*aqua*	rgb(0,255,255)	#00FFFF	rgb(0%,100%,100%)
dark cyan	*teal*	rgb(0,128,128)	#008080	rgb(0%,50%,50%)

Basic Cascading Style Sheets

8

continued

continued

Color	CSS keyword	Decimal RGB format	Hexadecimal RGB format	Percentage RGB format
light magenta	*fuchsia*	rgb(255,0,255)	#FF00FF	rgb(100%,0%,100%)
dark magenta	*purple*	rgb(128,0,128)	#800080	rgb(50%,0%,50%)
white	*white*	rgb(255,255,255)	#FFFFFF	rgb(100%,100%,100%)
black	*black*	rgb(0,0,0)	#000000	rgb(0%,0%,0%)
light gray	*silver*	rgb(192,192,192)	#C0C0C0	rgb(75%,75%,75%)
dark gray	*gray*	rgb(128,128,128)	#808080	rgb(50%,50%,50%)

If you use one of the RGB formats, you can of course create many more custom colors than shown in the table. In fact, because you can assign each of the three color components 256 different values, you can specify a total of 16,777,216 different custom colors (256 * 256 * 256). And, if you display the document on a system with a 24-bit or greater color depth, the monitor can actually display each of these different colors.

note

The color names listed in the table in the preceding sidebar are the basic ones suggested in the CSS specifications. Internet Explorer supports a large set of additional color names, many of which are even more picturesque than the specification names, such as *aliceblue, bisque, cornsilk,* and *peachpuff.*

Internet Explorer also provides a separate group of color names for selecting system colors that are currently set through the Display icon of the Windows Control Panel. For example, the color name *appworkspace* specifies the "Application Background" color that is set in the Control Panel. And the color name *background* specifies the "Desktop" color set in the Control Panel.

You'll find a list of all the Internet Explorer color names under the topic "Color Table" in the MSDN Library on the Web at *http://msdn.microsoft.com/library/.*

Setting Background Properties

The CSS standard provides the following properties that allow you to modify an element's background:

- *background-color*

- *background-image*

- *background-repeat*

- *background-position*

The background is the area surrounding the individual characters of the element's text. You can assign either a solid color or an image to an element's background.

Technically, child elements inherit none of these properties. However, by default, an element's background is *transparent*. This means that if you omit all background properties from a child element, the parent element's (or browser's) background color or image shows through, effectively giving the child element the same background as the parent (or browser).

Setting the *background-color* Property

You can apply a solid background color to an element by assigning a color value to its *background-color* property. The different types of color values you can assign are described in the sidebar "Specifying Color Values" on page 233. For example, the following rule sets the background color of the TITLE element to light yellow:

```
TITLE {background-color:yellow}
```

Recall that the *color* property sets an element's foreground color—that is, the color of the characters themselves. Thus, the following rule creates blue letters on a yellow background:

```
TITLE
    {color:blue;
     background-color:yellow}
```

If you don't want to specify a solid background color for an element, you can assign the *background-color* property the *transparent* value, as shown here:

```
TITLE {background-color:transparent}
```

Or, because *transparent* is the default value, you can simply omit the *background-color* property from that element. Unless you assign a background image to the element, the *transparent* setting causes the parent element's (or browser's) background to show through.

Setting the *background-image* Property

You can add a background image to an element by assigning the URL of an image file to the *background-image* property. For information on specifying URLs, see the sidebar "Specifying URL Values" on page 209. For example, the following rule assigns the background image contained in the file Leaf.bmp to the STANZA element:

```
STANZA {background-image:url(Leaf.bmp)}
```

To illustrate further, consider the style sheet shown in Listing 8-3, which is attached to the XML document shown in Listing 8-4. (You'll find a copy of both listings on the companion CD under the filenames Leaves.css and Leaves.xml.)

Leaves.css

```
/* File Name: Leaves.css */

POEM
    {font-size:140%}

POEM, TITLE, SUBTITLE, AUTHOR, SECTION, NUMBER, STANZA, VERSE
    {display:block}

SECTION, STANZA
    {margin-top:1em}

STANZA
    {background-image:url(Leaf.bmp)}
```

Listing 8-3.

Leaves.xml

```
<?xml version="1.0"?>

<!-- File Name: Leaves.xml -->

<?xml-stylesheet type="text/css" href="Leaves.css"?>

<POEM>
```

```
<TITLE>Leaves of Grass
    <SUBTITLE>I Sing the Body Electric</SUBTITLE>
</TITLE>
<AUTHOR>by Walt Whitman</AUTHOR>

<SECTION>
<NUMBER>1.</NUMBER>
<STANZA>
    <VERSE>I SING the Body electric;</VERSE>
    <VERSE>The armies of those I love engirth me,
            and I engirth them;</VERSE>
    <VERSE>They will not let me off till I go with them,
            respond to them,</VERSE>
    <VERSE>And discorrupt them, and charge them full with
            the charge of the Soul.</VERSE>
</STANZA>
<STANZA>
    <VERSE>Was it doubted that those who corrupt their own
            bodies conceal themselves;</VERSE>
    <VERSE>And if those who defile the living are as
            bad as they who defile the dead?</VERSE>
    <VERSE>And if the body does not do as much as
            the Soul?</VERSE>
    <VERSE>And if the body were not the Soul, what is
            the Soul?</VERSE>
</STANZA>
</SECTION>

</POEM>
```

Listing 8-4.

Here are the contents of the bitmap graphic file Leaf.bmp:

Internet Explorer would display Leaves.xml as shown here:

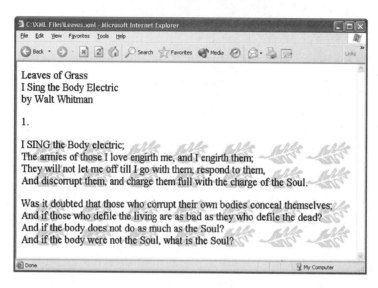

Notice that the image is repeated (that is, tiled) as needed to fill the entire area occupied by the element's content, extending almost to the right edge of the browser window. (The next section describes how to control tiling.) Notice also that any portion of an image that extends above or below the element's text is cropped (that is, eliminated). In the example, only a very small portion of the images on the bottom row of each STANZA element is cropped.

If you don't want to specify a background image for an element, you can assign the *background-image* property the value *none*, like this:

```
STANZA {background-image:none}
```

Or, because *none* is the default value, you can simply omit the *background-image* property from that element. Unless you assign a solid background color to the element, the *none* setting causes the parent's (or browser's) background to show through.

> ## note
>
> If you assign both a background image and a solid background color (using the *background-color* property), the image will cover the solid color.

Setting the *background-repeat* Property

If you've assigned an image file to the *background-image* property, you can control the way the image repeats by assigning the *background-repeat* property one of the following CSS keyword values:

- *repeat* (**the default**). Repeats the image both horizontally and vertically. Because this is the default value, adding *background-repeat:repeat* to the STANZA rule in the style sheet of Listing 8-3, as shown here, would have no effect on the way the document is displayed, as shown in the following figure:

```
STANZA
    {background-image:url(Leaf.bmp);
    background-repeat:repeat}
```

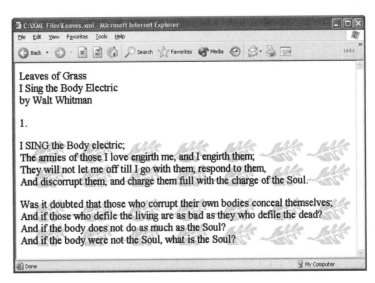

- *repeat-x*. Repeats the image in the horizontal direction only. For example, this STANZA rule would display the document as shown in the following figure:

```
STANZA
    {background-image:url(Leaf.bmp);
    background-repeat:repeat-x}
```

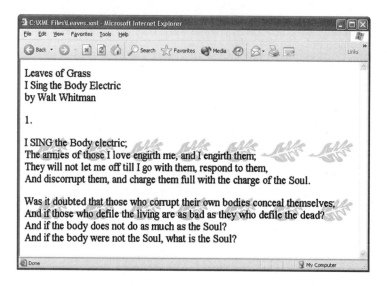

- *repeat-y.* Repeats the image in the vertical direction only. For example, the STANZA rule given here would display the document as shown in the following figure:

```
STANZA
    {background-image:url(Leaf.bmp);
     background-repeat:repeat-y}
```

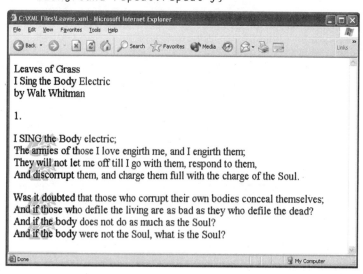

- *no-repeat.* Causes the image to be displayed only once. For example, this STANZA rule would display the document as shown in the following figure:

```
STANZA
    {background-image:url(Leaf.bmp);
     background-repeat:no-repeat}
```

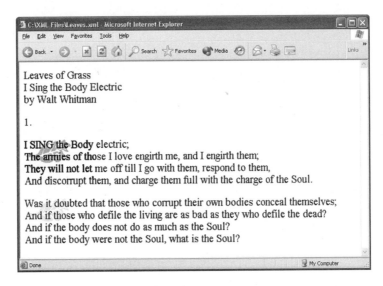

Setting the *background-position* Property

By default, the upper left corner of the background image (or the upper left corner of the upper left copy of the image if it repeats) aligns with the upper left corner of the element. You can change this alignment by assigning a value to the *background-position* property. You can assign this property three different types of values:

- **Horizontal and vertical size values.** You can assign the *background-position* property two size values. The first value indicates the horizontal position of the left edge of the image within the element, and the second value indicates the vertical position of the top edge of the image within the element. You can assign any of the types of size values described in the sidebar "Specifying Size Values" on page 227. For example, the following rule places the upper left corner of the image .5 inches to the right and .25 inches down from the upper left corner of a STANZA element:

```
STANZA
    {background-image:url(Leaf.bmp);
     background-repeat:no-repeat;
     background-position:.5in .25in}
```

Basic Cascading Style Sheets

Here's the result of this rule:

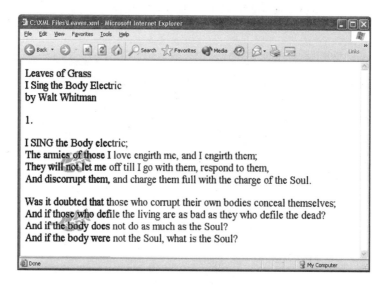

If the image repeats as specified in the following rule, the entire pattern of repeated images shifts by the amount indicated, as shown in the figure:

```
STANZA
    {background-image:url(Leaf.bmp);
     background-repeat:repeat;
     background-position:.5in .25in}
```

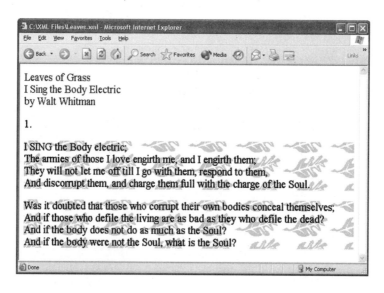

- **Horizontal and vertical percentage values.** You can assign the *background-position* property two percentage values. The first percentage indicates the horizontal position of the image within the element, where 0% places the left edge of the image at the left edge of the element (in its default horizontal position), 50% places the center of the image at the horizontal center of the element, and 100% places the right edge of the image at the right edge of the element. The second percentage indicates the vertical position of the image, where 0% places the top edge of the image at the top edge of the element (in its default vertical position), 50% places the center of the image at the vertical center of the element, and 100% places the bottom edge of the image at the bottom edge of the element.

For example, the following rule would put the image in the middle of the element:

```
STANZA
    {background-image:url(Leaf.bmp);
     background-repeat:no-repeat;
     background-position:50% 50%}
```

Here's the result of this rule:

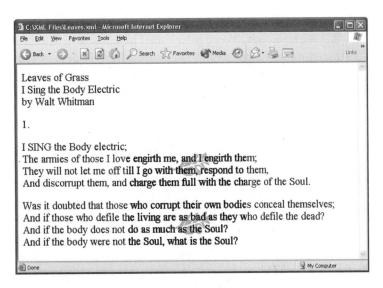

If the image is repeated, the browser displays one copy of the image as indicated by the percentage values and repeats the image in all directions from that copy. For example, the following rule places a copy of the leaf image in the center of the element, with the image repeating in all directions from that copy, as shown in the figure:

```
STANZA
    {background-image:url(Leaf.bmp);
     background-repeat:repeat;
     background-position:50% 50%}
```

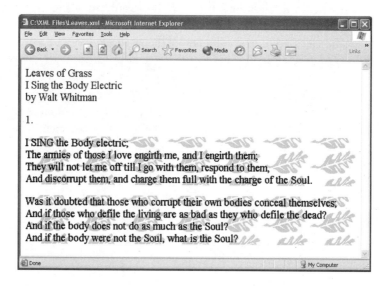

▨ **Keyword values.** You can specify the background image position by assigning the *background-position* property one or two CSS keywords. For example, entering the *right* and *bottom* keywords, as in the following rule, places the image at the bottom right of the element, as shown in the figure:

```
STANZA
    {background-image:url(Leaf.bmp);
     background-repeat:no-repeat;
     background-position:right bottom}
```

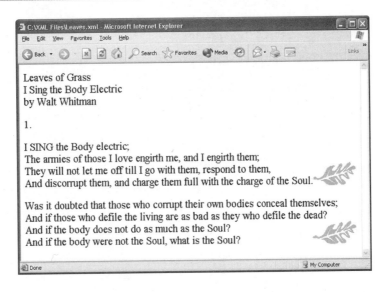

The following figure shows the image position resulting from each combination of keywords.

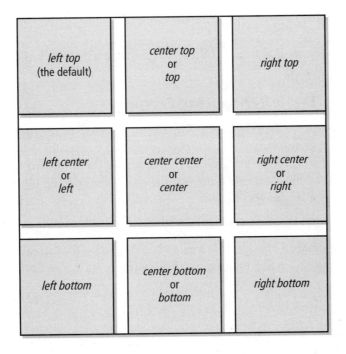

The order of the keywords is unimportant. For example, *background-position:bottom right* is equivalent to *background-position:right bottom*.

Setting Text Spacing and Alignment Properties

The CSS standard provides the following properties that modify the spacing, alignment, and other features of the text:

- *letter-spacing*

- *word-spacing* (Internet Explorer 6.0 only)

- *vertical-align*

- *text-align*

- *text-indent*

- *line-height*

- *text-transform*

- *text-decoration*

Child elements inherit all of these properties except *vertical-align* and *text-decoration*.

Setting the *letter-spacing* Property

You can use the *letter-spacing* property to increase or decrease the spacing between the characters of an element's text. You can assign *letter-spacing* a positive size value to increase the character spacing by the indicated amount. For example, the following rule increases the character spacing by an amount equal to one-quarter of the text height:

```
TITLE {letter-spacing:.25em}
```

You can assign *letter-spacing* a negative size value to decrease the character spacing by the indicated amount. For example, this rule decreases the character spacing by one-half point:

```
TITLE {letter-spacing:-.5pt}
```

For information on the different kind of size values you can assign, see the sidebar "Specifying Size Values" on page 227.

Or, you can select normal character spacing by assigning *letter-spacing* the CSS keyword value *normal*. For example, the following style sheet, attached to the XML document in Listing 8-4, assigns an expanded character spacing to the

TITLE element, and it assigns a normal character spacing to the SUBTITLE element (the second assignment is necessary to override the expanded character spacing that SUBTITLE would otherwise inherit from its parent element, TITLE):

```
POEM
    {font-size:140%}

POEM, TITLE, SUBTITLE, AUTHOR, SECTION, NUMBER, STANZA, VERSE
    {display:block}

SECTION, STANZA
    {margin-top:1em}

TITLE
    {letter-spacing:.5em}

SUBTITLE
    {letter-spacing:normal}
```

With the rules in this style sheet, here's how Internet Explorer displays the XML document that it's attached to:

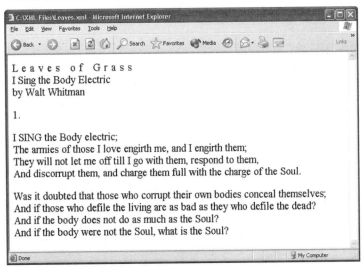

Setting the *word-spacing* Property (Internet Explorer 6.0 only)

The *word-spacing* property works just like the *letter-spacing* property except that it increases or decreases the spacing between entire words. As with *word-spacing*, you can assign *letter-spacing* a positive or negative size value to change the default word spacing, or you can assign it the CSS keyword *normal* to use the default word spacing.

If, for example, you attached the following style sheet to the XML document in Listing 8-4, Internet Explorer 6.0 would add 1.5em of additional word spacing to both the TITLE element and to its child element SUBTITLE (which would inherit the *word-spacing* setting from TITLE).

```
POEM
    {font-size:140%}

POEM, TITLE, SUBTITLE, AUTHOR, SECTION, NUMBER, STANZA, VERSE
    {display:block}

SECTION, STANZA
    {margin-top:1em}

TITLE
    {word-spacing:1.5em}
```

Here's how the XML document would appear:

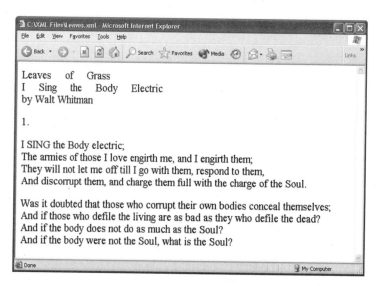

Setting the *vertical-align* Property

You can use the *vertical-align* property to create superscript or subscript text. This property affects only *inline* elements. (An *inline* element is one whose *display* property is set to *inline*, as discussed in the section "Setting the *display* Property" earlier in the chapter.)

You can assign *vertical-align* one of the CSS keywords in the following table. To create each text sample, I assigned the setting to the *vertical-align* property of *only* the CHILD element, which is an *inline* element that appears in the document like this:

```
<PARENT>PARENT ELEMENT<CHILD>CHILD ELEMENT</CHILD></PARENT>
```

I also reduced the size of the CHILD element's font to 75% of the size of the PARENT element's font, as shown in the example CSS rules.

vertical-align keyword: *baseline* (default)

Example CSS rule:
```
CHILD
    {font-size:75%; vertical-align:baseline}
```

Effect: Aligns the baseline of the element with the baseline of the parent element

Text sample: PARENT ELEMENT CHILD ELEMENT

vertical-align keyword: *sub*

Example CSS rule:
```
CHILD
    {font-size:75%; vertical-align:sub}
```

Effect: Displays the element's text as subscript

Text sample: PARENT ELEMENT CHILD ELEMENT

vertical-align keyword: *super*

Example CSS rule:
```
CHILD
    {font-size:75%; vertical-align:super}
```

Effect: Displays the element's text as superscript

Text sample: PARENT ELEMENT CHILD ELEMENT

vertical-align keyword: *text-top* (Internet Explorer 5.5–6.0 only)

Example CSS rule:
```
CHILD
    {font-size:75%; vertical-align:text-top}
```

Effect: Aligns the top of the element with the top of the parent element's font

Text sample: PARENT ELEMENTCHILD ELEMENT

vertical-align keyword: *text-bottom* (Internet Explorer 5.5–6.0 only)

Example CSS rule:
```
CHILD
    {font-size:75%; vertical-align:text-bottom}
```

Effect: Aligns the bottom of the element with the bottom of the parent element's font

Text sample: PARENT ELEMENTCHILD ELEMENT

vertical-align keyword:	*top* (Internet Explorer 5.5–6.0 only)
Example CSS rule:	CHILD
	{font-size:75%; vertical-align:top}
Effect:	Aligns the top of the element with the tallest element on the current line
Text sample:	PARENT ELEMENTCHILD ELEMENT

vertical-align keyword:	*bottom* (Internet Explorer 5.5–6.0 only)
Example CSS rule:	CHILD
	{font-size:75%; vertical-align:bottom}
Effect:	Aligns the bottom of the element with the lowest element on the current line
Text sample:	PARENT ELEMENTCHILD ELEMENT

vertical-align keyword:	*middle* (Internet Explorer 5.5–6.0 only)
Example CSS rule:	CHILD
	{font-size:75%; vertical-align:middle}
Effect:	Aligns the vertical midpoint of the element with the vertical midpoint of the parent element
Text sample:	PARENT ELEMENTCHILD ELEMENT

tip

With Internet Explorer 6.0, you can also assign the *vertical-align* property a positive or negative size value to specify the absolute distance by which the element is to be raised or lowered; or you can assign it a positive or negative percentage value to indicate the amount by which the element is to be raised or lowered as a percentage of the line height of the current element. (An element's line height is determined by the *line-height* property, discussed later.)

Also, with any of the Internet Explorer versions covered in this book (5.0 through 6.0), you can use relative positioning to raise or lower text from its normal position by any amount, as explained in "Setting the Relative and Absolute Positioning Properties" in Chapter 9.

Setting the *text-align* Property

You can use the *text-align* property to control the horizontal alignment of an element's text. This property works only if you explicitly assign it to a *block* element. It will then affect the element itself, plus any child elements it contains, whether the child elements are *block* or *inline* (*block* and *inline* elements are described in the earlier section "Setting the *display* Property.")

The *text-align* property affects the alignment of the text *within the text content area*. By default, the text content area extends across almost the entire width of the browser window. However, as you'll learn in the next chapter (in "Setting Box Properties"), you can modify both the width and the position of an element's text content area.

You can assign *text-align* one of the following three keyword values:

- **left.** Aligns each line at the left. Assume, for example, that you apply the following rule to the XML document of Listing 8-4 (in addition to the other rules shown in the style sheet in Listing 8-3, except the *background-image* setting, which I removed for clarity):

```
POEM {text-align:left}
```

The poem would be aligned like this:

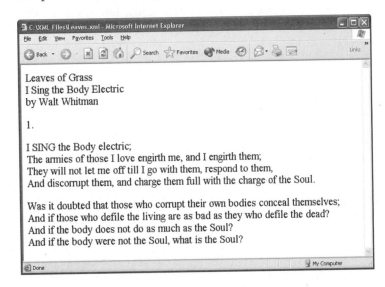

- **right.** Aligns each line at the right. For example, the following rule aligns the poem to the right, as shown in the figure:

```
POEM {text-align:right}
```

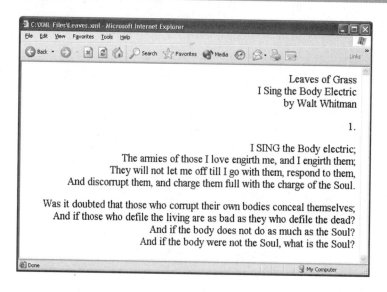

■ **center.** Centers each line horizontally. For example, the following rule centers the entire poem, as you can see in the figure:

```
POEM {text-align:center}
```

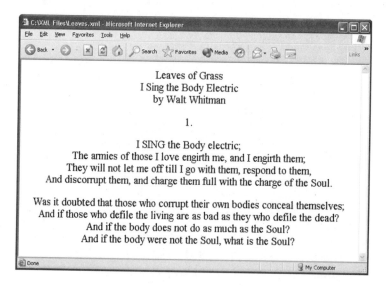

Setting the *text-indent* Property

You can use the *text-indent* property to indent the first line of an element's text. You can assign *text-indent* any of the kinds of size values described in the sidebar "Specifying Size Values" on page 227. For example, the following rule indents the first line of a VERSE element by three times the height of its font:

```
VERSE {text-indent:3em}
```

Here's how a VERSE element would look:

    It is in his walk, the carriage of his
neck, the flex of his waist and knees—dress
does not hide him;

Alternatively, you can specify the indentation as a percentage of the total width of the element's text. For example, this rule indents the first line of a VERSE element an amount equal to half of the width of the element:

```
VERSE {text-indent:50%}
```

Here's a VERSE element showing how this would look:

    It is in his walk, the
carriage of his neck, the flex of his waist
and knees—dress does not hide him;

> **tip**
>
> To indent all lines of an element (instead of just the first line), use the *margin-left* property, described in "Setting the Margin Properties" in Chapter 9.

You can assign a negative value—either a size value or percentage—to move the first line out to the left of the other lines. However, if you simply assign a negative value to the *text-indent* property, the first part of the line will be hidden, as shown here:

in his walk, the carriage of his neck, the flex
  of his waist and knees—dress does not hide
  him;

To avoid hiding text, you can apply a left margin to the element. For example, the following rule applies a 4em left margin (*margin-left:4em*) and then moves the first line out by 2em (*text-indent:-2em*), creating a hanging indent, as shown in the figure:

```
VERSE
    {margin-left:4em;
     text-indent:-2em}
```

> It is in his walk, the carriage of his
> neck, the flex of his waist and
> knees—dress does not hide him;

Setting the *line-height* Property

The *line-height* property controls the distance between the baselines of successive lines of an element's text. You can use it to adjust the text's vertical line spacing.

You can assign *line-height* any of the kinds of size values described in the sidebar "Specifying Size Values" on page 227. Assume, for example, that you apply the following rule to the XML document in Listing 8-4 (in addition to the rules in the style sheet in Listing 8-3, except the *background-image* setting, which I removed for clarity):

```
STANZA {line-height:2em}
```

STANZA text would be displayed in double-spaced lines, as shown here:

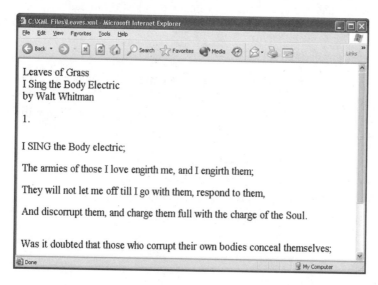

Alternatively, you can specify the line-height as a percentage of the height of the element's text. The following rule, for instance, would be equivalent to the rule given above and would generate double line spacing:

```
STANZA {line-height:200%}
```

Setting the *text-transform* Property

You can use the *text-transform* property to control the capitalization style of an element's text as the browser displays it. You can assign *text-transform* one of the following CSS keyword values:

text-transform keyword: *capitalize*
Example CSS rule: STANZA {text-transform:capitalize}
Effect: Capitalizes the first letter of every word
Text sample: And If The Body Were Not The Soul, What Is The Soul?

text-transform keyword: *uppercase*
Example CSS rule: STANZA {text-transform:uppercase}
Effect: Capitalizes every letter
Text sample: AND IF THE BODY WERE NOT THE SOUL, WHAT IS THE SOUL?

text-transform keyword: *lowercase*
Example CSS rule: STANZA {text-transform:lowercase}
Effect: Displays every letter in lowercase
Text sample: and if the body were not the soul, what is the soul?

text-transform keyword: *none*
Example CSS rule: STANZA {text-transform:none}
Effect: Displays the text without changing its capitalization style
Text sample: And if the body were not the Soul, what is the Soul?

Setting the *text-decoration* Property

You can use the *text-decoration* property to draw various types of lines through an element's text. Here are the keyword values you can assign to this property:

text-decoration keyword: *underline*
Example CSS rule: TITLE {text-decoration:underline}
Effect: Draws a line under the text
Text sample: Leaves of Grass

text-decoration keyword:	*overline*
Example CSS rule:	`TITLE {text-decoration:overline}`
Effect:	Draws a line above the text
Text sample:	<u>Leaves of Grass</u>

text-decoration keyword:	*line-through*
Example CSS rule:	`TITLE {text-decoration:line-through}`
Effect:	Draws a line through the text
Text sample:	~~Leaves of Grass~~

text-decoration keyword:	*none*
Example CSS rule:	`TITLE {text-decoration:none}`
Effect:	Displays the text without a line
Text sample:	Leaves of Grass

You can apply more than one type of line by assigning *text-decoration* several values. (Including the keyword *none*, however, cancels the effect of all previously listed keywords.) For example, the following rule causes the browser to draw a line above and below the text:

```
TITLE {text-decoration:underline overline}
```

CHAPTER

9

Displaying XML Documents Using Advanced Cascading Style Sheets

This chapter continues the discussion started in Chapter 8 on using cascading style sheets to display XML documents. As explained in Chapter 8, if you link a cascading style sheet (CSS) to an XML document, you can open that document directly in the Microsoft Internet Explorer browser and the browser will display and format the document's elements according to the property settings in the CSS.

In this chapter, you'll learn how to use some slightly more advanced CSS properties. First, you'll learn how to use the powerful *box properties*, which allow you to display borders, margins (space outside borders), and padding (space inside borders) around an element's content; to control the displayed size of an element; and to place an element at a precise position on the page outside the normal flow of text. You'll then learn how to use *pseudo-elements* to apply formatting to just the first letter or the first line of an element. Next you'll learn how to have the browser render and display specific HTML elements when it displays your XML document. The chapter concludes with an exercise in which you'll create and apply a full-featured style sheet that uses most of the techniques and properties covered in Chapters 8 and 9.

Advanced CSS

Setting Box Properties

The CSS specification provides a set of properties known as *box properties* that you can use to format the block of text belonging to an element. The different types of box properties are as follows:

- **Margin** properties add a transparent margin around the element, outside of any visible border.

- **Border** properties display a visible border—in a variety of styles—around the element.

- **Padding** properties add space immediately outside of the element's content, inside of any visible border.

- **Size** properties, *height* and *width,* control the dimensions of the element's content area plus any padding or border that's included (as shown in the following figure).

- **Relative and absolute positioning** properties allow you to place the element at a specific position on the page, outside of the normal flow of text.

- **Float positioning** properties, *float* and *clear,* control whether the element is *floating*. A floating element is displayed to the left or right of the following document content rather than in its normal position within the flow of text.

The following figure illustrates the first four groups of box properties applied to a *block* element:

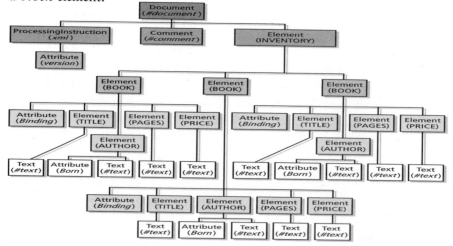

Recall from the section "Setting the *display* Property" in Chapter 8 that a *block* element is one whose *display* property is set to the value *block,* while an *inline* element is one whose *display* property is set to *inline.* With Internet Explorer 5.0 and 5.01, the first three groups of properties (margin, border, and padding) have an effect only on *block* elements. With Internet Explorer 5.5 through 6.0, however, you can use these properties with either *block* or *inline* elements. With any of the Internet Explorer versions covered in this book (5.0 through 6.0), you can apply the size or positioning properties (relative, absolute, or float) to either *block* or *inline* elements.

Child elements do not inherit the box properties.

Setting the Margin Properties

By default, the width of the margins around an element is zero. To add a margin to one or more sides of an element, you can assign a nonzero value to one or more of the following properties:

- *margin-top*

- *margin-right*

- *margin-bottom*

- *margin-left*

You can assign these properties any of the kinds of size values described in the sidebar "Specifying Size Values" on page 227. For example, the following rule adds a margin to the left and right of a STANZA element. The width of the margin is two times the height of the element's text:

```
STANZA
    {margin-left:2em;
     margin-right:2em}
```

You can also specify the size of a margin as a percentage of the width of the element's parent (or, if the parent isn't a *block* element, of the closest ancestor that is a *block* element). For example, the following rule creates a left margin equal to one-quarter of the width of the element's parent:

```
STANZA {margin-left:25%}
```

As a shortcut, you can add equal-sized margins to all four sides of an element by assigning a single value—a size value or a percentage—to the *margin* property. To illustrate, first consider the style sheet given in Listing 9-1, which is linked to the XML document given in Listing 9-2, and displays the text without margins.

(Because this style sheet doesn't set the margins, they default to zero.) You'll find copies of these two listings on the companion CD under the filenames Raven.css and Raven.xml.

Raven.css

```
/* File Name: Raven.css */

POEM
    {font-size:small}

POEM, TITLE, AUTHOR, DATE, STANZA, VERSE
    {display:block}
```

Listing 9-1.

Raven.xml

```
<?xml version="1.0"?>

<!-- File Name: Raven.xml -->

<?xml-stylesheet type="text/css" href="Raven.css"?>

<POEM>

<TITLE>The Raven</TITLE>
<AUTHOR>Edgar Allan Poe</AUTHOR>
<DATE>1845</DATE>

<STANZA>
    <VERSE>Once upon a midnight dreary, while I pondered,
            weak and weary,</VERSE>
    <VERSE>Over many a quaint and curious volume of
            forgotten lore&#8212;</VERSE>
    <VERSE>While I nodded, nearly napping,
            suddenly there came a tapping,</VERSE>
    <VERSE>As of some one gently rapping,
            rapping at my chamber door.</VERSE>
    <VERSE>"'Tis some visitor," I muttered,
            "tapping at my chamber door&#8212;</VERSE>
    <VERSE>Only this, and nothing more."</VERSE>
</STANZA>
<STANZA>
```

```
<VERSE>Ah, distinctly I remember it was in the
        bleak December,</VERSE>
<VERSE>And each separate dying ember wrought its
        ghost upon the floor.</VERSE>
<VERSE>Eagerly I wished the morrow;&#8212;vainly I had
        sought to borrow</VERSE>
<VERSE>From my books surcease of sorrow&#8212;sorrow
        for the lost Lenore&#8212;</VERSE>
<VERSE>For the rare and radiant maiden whom the angels
        name Lenore&#8212;</VERSE>
<VERSE>Nameless here for evermore.</VERSE>
</STANZA>

</POEM>
```

Listing 9-2.

> **note**
>
> — is a character reference for the em dash (—).

Here's how the elements look without margins:

Adding the following rule to the style sheet inserts a 2.5em margin around all four sides of both STANZA elements, as shown in the figure:

```
STANZA {margin:2.5em}
```

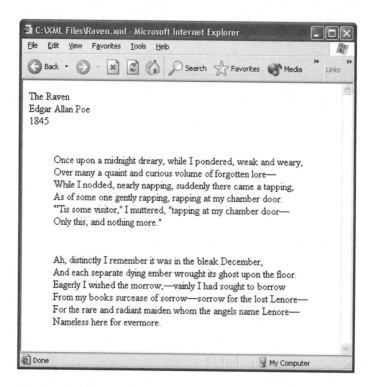

Notice that the total vertical margin height between the two STANZA elements is the same as the width of the left or right margin (2.5em), and is *not* the sum of the bottom margin of the first STANZA element plus the top margin of the second STANZA element (which would be a total margin height of 5em). That's because the browser always *collapses* adjoining vertical (top or bottom) margins to use the maximum of the individual margin values. In the example, both vertical margins are 2.5em, so the browser collapses the two margins into a single 2.5em margin. The rationale for collapsing margins is that the result is usually more visually pleasing and closer to what the style sheet author expects.

note

The margin area is always transparent, meaning that the parent element's (or browser's) background color or image shows through it.

Setting the Border Properties

You can use the following properties to draw visible borders around an element:

- *border-style*
- *border-width*
- *border-color*

Setting the *border-style* Property

You can use the *border-style* property to add a visible border to one or more sides of an element, and to set the border's style. You can assign *border-style* any of the CSS keyword values shown in the following table:

***border-style* keyword:**	*solid*
Example CSS rule:	`TITLE {border-style:solid}`
Text sample:	The Raven

***border-style* keyword:**	*dotted* (Internet Explorer 5.5–6.0 only)
Example CSS rule:	`TITLE {border-style:dotted}`
Text sample:	The Raven

***border-style* keyword:**	*dashed* (Internet Explorer 5.5–6.0 only)
Example CSS rule:	`TITLE {border-style:dashed}`
Text sample:	The Raven

***border-style* keyword:**	*double*
Example CSS rule:	`TITLE {border-style:double}`
Text sample:	The Raven

***border-style* keyword:**	*groove*
Example CSS rule:	`TITLE {border-style:groove}`
Text sample:	The Raven

***border-style* keyword:**	*ridge*
Example CSS rule:	`TITLE {border-style:ridge}`
Text sample:	The Raven

border-style keyword:	*inset*
Example CSS rule:	`TITLE {border-style:inset}`
Text sample:	The Raven

border-style keyword:	*outset*
Example CSS rule:	`TITLE {border-style:outset}`
Text sample:	The Raven

border-style keyword:	*none* (default)
Example CSS rule:	`TITLE {border-style:none}`
Text sample:	The Raven

note

To create some of the text samples in the preceding table, I altered the background color to make the border style more effective.

You can vary the style of the border on each side of an element by assigning four different keyword values to the *border-style* property. The values refer to the top, right, bottom, and left borders, in that order. For example, the following rule displays a solid border on the top and bottom sides of a TITLE element, but no border on the left or right sides:

```
TITLE {border-style:solid none solid none}
```

As another example, adding the following rule to the style sheet shown in Listing 9-1 displays a border on all sides of each STANZA element in the XML document of Listing 9-2, with a margin outside of the borders:

```
STANZA
    {margin:2.5em;
     border-style:double solid double solid}
```

The top and bottom borders are double, while the left and right borders are solid, as shown here:

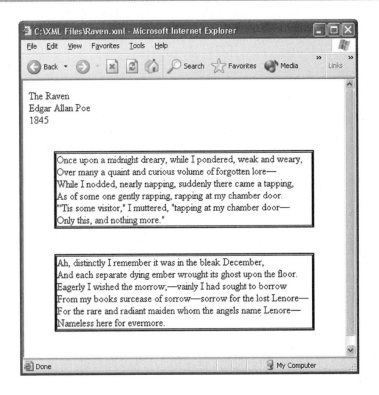

Setting the *border-width* Property

If you've applied a visible border to one or more sides of an element using the *border-style* property, you can adjust the width of the borders by assigning one of the CSS keyword values shown in the following table to the *border-width* property:

> *border-width* keyword: *thin*
>
> Example CSS rule: TITLE
>   {border-style:solid;
>   border-width:thin}
>
> Text sample: The Raven
>
> *border-width* keyword: *medium* (default)
>
> Example CSS rule: TITLE
>   {border-style:solid;
>   border-width:medium}
>
> Text sample: The Raven

Advanced CSS

border-width **keyword:**   *thick*

Example CSS rule: TITLE
                          {border-style:solid;
                          border-width:thick}

Text sample: The Raven

Alternatively, you can give a border a specific thickness by assigning *border-width* any of the types of size values described in the sidebar "Specifying Size Values" on page 227. For example, the following rule assigns the TITLE element a border that's 1 pixel wide (the thinnest border that a monitor can display) on all sides:

```
TITLE
    {border-style:solid;
     border-width:1px}
```

You can vary the thickness of the border on each side of an element by assigning four different values—CSS keywords or size values—to the *border-width* property. The values refer to the top, right, bottom, and left borders, in that order. For instance, adding the following rule to the example style sheet shown in Listing 9-1 creates a solid border on all sides of a STANZA element:

```
STANZA
    {margin:2.5em;
     border-style:solid;
     border-width:1px thick 1px thick}
```

The top and bottom borders have the minimum thickness, while the left and right borders are thick, as shown here:

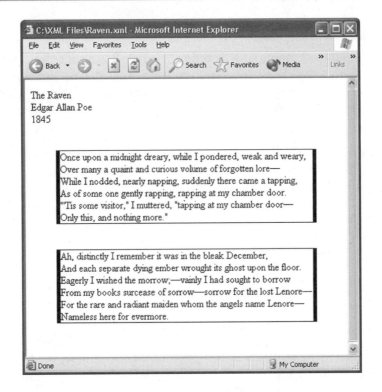

Setting the *border-color* Property

By default, the borders you create using the *border-style* property have the same color as the element's current *color* property setting. You can alter the color of all four borders by assigning the *border-color* property any of the kinds of color values described in the sidebar "Specifying Color Values" on page 233. For example, the following rule adds solid red borders to all sides of a TITLE element:

```
TITLE
    {border-style:solid;
    border-color:red}
```

You can vary the color of the individual borders around an element by assigning *border-color* four different color values. The values refer to the top, right, bottom, and left borders, in that order. For example, the following rule assigns solid red borders to the top and bottom of a TITLE element, and solid green borders to the left and right of the element:

```
TITLE
    {border-style:solid;
    border-color:red green red green}
```

Advanced CSS

9

Setting the Padding Properties

Recall from the beginning of the section "Setting Box Properties," earlier in this chapter, that the padding properties add space immediately surrounding an element's content, inside of any visible border the element has. Without padding, borders appear quite close to the element's text. You can improve the appearance of a border by adding padding.

By default, the width of the padding area around an element is zero. To add padding to one or more sides of an element, you can assign a nonzero value to one or more of the following properties:

- *padding-top*

- *padding-right*

- *padding-bottom*

- *padding-left*

You can assign these properties any of the kinds of size values described in the sidebar "Specifying Size Values" on page 227. For example, the following rule adds padding to the top and bottom of the STANZA element. The width of the padding area is two times the height of the element's text:

```
STANZA
   {padding-top:2em;
    padding-bottom:2em}
```

You can also specify the width of the padding area as a percentage of the width of the element's parent (or, if the parent isn't a *block* element, of the closest ancestor that is a *block* element). For example, the following rule adds padding to the left of a STANZA element. The thickness of the padding is equal to one-quarter of the width of the element's parent:

```
STANZA {padding-left:25%}
```

As a shortcut, you can add padding of equal thickness to all four sides of an element by assigning a single value—a size value or a percentage—to the *padding* property. Assume, for example, that you add the following rule to the example style sheet shown in Listing 9-1:

```
STANZA
    {margin:2.5em;
     border-style:solid;
     padding:2em}
```

This rule would display the following formatting features around each STANZA element:

- Padding, 2em thick, immediately surrounding the element

- A solid border outside of the padding

- A 2.5em margin outside of the border

Here's how the document looks in Internet Explorer:

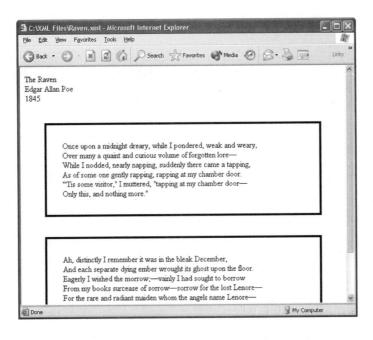

> **note**
>
> Like the element's content area, the padding area shows any background color or image that you've assigned to the element. (Recall that, in contrast, the margin area is transparent—that is, it shows the background of the parent element or browser.)

Setting the Size Properties

The size properties, *width* and *height,* control the dimensions of the element's content area, plus any included padding or border. (See the first figure in the section "Setting Box Properties," on page 258).

You can assign the *width* and *height* properties the following types of values:

- **Any of the kinds of size values described in the sidebar "Specifying Size Values" on page 227.** For example, the following rule sets the STANZA element's *width* property to 3 inches, and its *height* property to 2 inches:

  ```
  STANZA
      {width:3in;
       height:2in}
  ```

- **A percentage of the width or height of the parent element.** For example, the following rule sets the STANZA element's *width* and *height* properties to one-half the width and height of its parent element:

  ```
  STANZA
      {width:50%;
       height:50%}
  ```

- **The CSS keyword value *auto,* which is the default.** This value causes the browser to adjust the *width* and *height* properties to accommodate the actual size of the text. For example, the following rule sets both the *width* and *height* properties to *auto* (which has the same effect as simply omitting the *width* and *height* property settings):

  ```
  STANZA
      {width:auto;
       height:auto}
  ```

If you make the *width* property so narrow that the lines of text don't fit within the resulting content area, the browser will wrap the text to make it fit. If, however, the text doesn't fit vertically in the content area resulting from your *height* setting, the browser will increase the *height* setting to accommodate the text, just as if you'd set *height* to *auto*.

As an example, if you added the following rule to the style sheet shown in Listing 9-1, the browser would display the XML document in Listing 9-2 (to which the style sheet is linked), as shown in the following figure:

```
STANZA
   {border-style:solid;
    width:2.5in;
    height:1in}
```

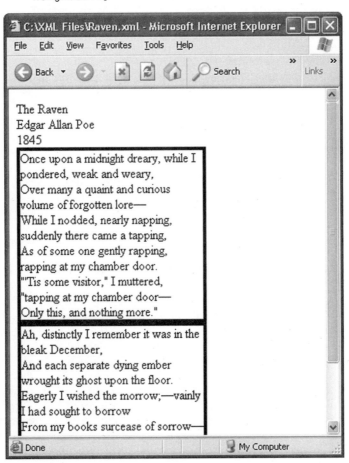

Notice that the text wraps to fit within the requested 2.5-inch width, but that the height expands far beyond the requested 1 inch to accommodate the full content of the text.

> **note**
>
> The *width* and *height* properties as implemented by Internet Explorer do *not* conform to the CSS specifications, which state that these properties should specify the dimensions of just the element's content area, *not* including any padding, border, or margins.

Setting the Relative and Absolute Positioning Properties

You can use the relative and absolute positioning properties to place an element's content at a specific position on the page, outside of the normal flow of text and graphics on the page and possibly overlapping the content of other elements. The following table summarizes the most important of these properties and their possible values:

Property	Purpose	Possible values
position	Specifies the type of positioning to be used for the element's content.	■ *static* (default). The content is placed in its normal position within the flow of text and graphics on the page. ■ *relative*. The content is displaced from its normal position within the flow of text and graphics by the amount specified by the *left* and *top* properties. Surrounding content does *not* fill in the gap left by the displaced content. ■ *absolute*. The content is placed at the position on the page specified by the *left* and *top* properties. Surrounding content fills in the gap left by the positioned content.
left	If *position* is set to *relative*, specifies the horizontal offset of the displaced element. If *position* is set to *absolute*, specifies the horizontal position of the left edge of the content within the page.	■ A size value specifying an exact offset or page position (see the sidebar "Specifying Size Values" on page 227). ■ *auto* (default). For a relatively positioned element, the same as the size value 0. For an absolutely positioned element, causes the browser to assign the content a default horizontal position.

continued

continued

Property	Purpose	Possible values
top	If *position* is set to *relative*, specifies the vertical offset of the displaced element. If *position* is set to *absolute*, specifies the vertical position of the top edge of the content within the page.	▨ A size value specifying an exact offset or page position. ▨ *auto* (default). For a relatively positioned element, the same as the size value *0*. For an absolutely positioned element, causes the browser to assign the content a default vertical position.
z-index	Specifies the order in which overlapping content of an element is drawn.	▨ An integer. To display the content of a relatively or absolutely positioned element *behind* non-positioned text, assign a negative value. To display the content *in front of* non-positioned text, assign a value greater than or equal to *0* (or assign *auto* or omit the property). ▨ *auto* (default). Displays the content of a positioned element in front of non-positioned text.

note

If an absolutely positioned element has an ancestor element that is itself relatively or absolutely positioned (that is, its position property is set to *relative* or *absolute*), then the *left* and *top* properties give the position of the element's content within the area occupied by the ancestor element, rather than giving the position of the content within the page.

You can use the relative and absolute positioning properties to create a watermark effect. To illustrate, consider the Raven.css and Raven.xml files given in Listings 9-1 and 9-2 earlier in the chapter. To display the content of the AUTHOR element (*Edgar Allen Poe*) as a watermark, you might start by including the following rule in Raven.css in addition to the rules already in this file:

```
AUTHOR
   {font-size:45pt;
    color:rgb(200,200,200)}
```

9

Advanced CSS

This rule displays the contents of the AUTHOR element in a large, light-gray font, as shown in here:

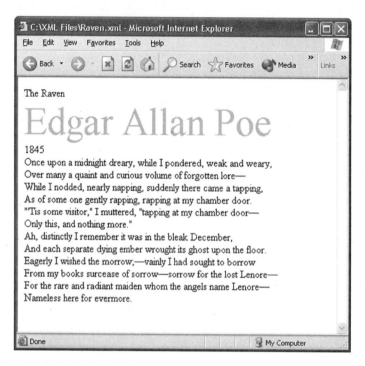

You could display the AUTHOR element behind the text of the first STANZA element by positioning it relatively, as follows:

```
AUTHOR
    {font-size:45pt;
     color:rgb(200,200,200);
     position:relative;
     top:95px;
     z-index:-1}
```

The three added declarations make AUTHOR a relatively positioned element, shift it 95 pixels down from its normal position, and cause it to be displayed behind the overlapping text of the non-positioned STANZA element. The following is the result:

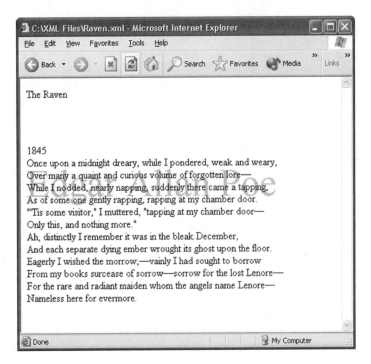

Notice, however, that the document text that comes before and after the AUTHOR element is still positioned as if AUTHOR had its original location, leaving an empty gap in the page. To close this gap, you could position AUTHOR absolutely rather than relatively using the following rule:

```
AUTHOR
    {font-size:45pt;
     color:rgb(200,200,200);
     position:absolute;
     top:65px;
     z-index:-1}
```

The last three declarations in this rule assign the AUTHOR element absolute positioning, place it 65 pixels down from the top of the page, and cause it to be displayed behind the overlapping text of the first STANZA element. Here's the final result:

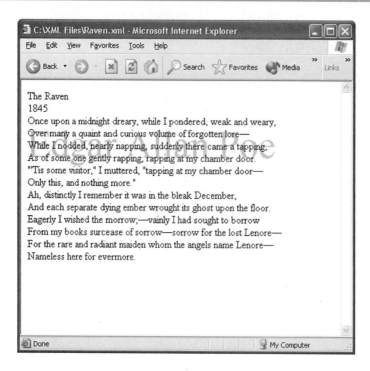

Setting the Float Positioning Properties

The float positioning properties are *float* and *clear*. You can use the *float* property to create a *floating* element. The content of a floating element is usually displayed to the left or right of the following document content, rather than in its normal position within the flow of text and graphics on the page. You can use the *clear* property to selectively prevent an element from floating.

Setting the *float* Property

You can assign the *float* property one of the following three CSS keyword values:

float keyword	Effect
left	Displays the element's content to the left of the following document content. The element becomes a floating element.
right	Displays the element's content to the right of the following document content. The element becomes a floating element.
none (default)	Displays the element's content in its normal position within the flow of text and graphics on the page. The element is not a floating element.

In the exercises in the following two sections, you'll learn how to use the *float* property to create a margin note, and to display a floating image next to an element's text.

Create a Margin Note

1   In your text editor, open the Raven.css style sheet file given in Listing 9-1 and provided on the companion CD.

2   Modify the style sheet so that it appears as shown in Listing 9-3.

These are the main new features you added to the original style sheet:

- You gave the STANZA elements a one-inch left margin.
- You formatted the NOTE element (which you'll add to the document later) as a margin note displayed in the left margin area of the first STANZA element. Specifically:
  - You gave it a 1-pixel-wide border.
  - You centered its text.
  - You assigned both its *width* and *height* properties a value of one inch.
  - You made it float to the left of the following element's text.

3   Use your text editor's Save As command to save a copy of the modified document under the filename Raven01.css.

Raven01.css

```
/* File Name: Raven01.css */

POEM
    {font-size:12pt}

POEM, TITLE, AUTHOR, DATE, NOTE, STANZA, VERSE
    {display:block}

DATE
    {margin-bottom:.25in}

STANZA
    {margin-left:1in;
     margin-bottom:.25in}

NOTE
    {border-style:solid;
     border-width:1px;
     text-align:center;
     width:1in;
     height:1in;
     float:left}
```

Listing 9-3.

4   In your text editor, open the Raven.xml document given in Listing 9-2 and provided on the companion CD.

5   In Raven.xml, edit the *xml-stylesheet* processing instruction at the beginning of the file so that it points to the new style sheet you just created—Raven01.css—like this:

```
<?xml-stylesheet type="text/css" href="Raven01.css"?>
```

6   In Raven.xml, add the following new element just above the first STANZA element:

```
<NOTE>This is a floating margin note.</NOTE>
```

Because you assigned NOTE the *float:left* property setting in the style sheet, it will float to the left of the following document text—that is, to the left of the first STANZA element.

7   Use your text editor's Save As command to save a copy of the modified document under the filename Raven01.xml.

You can see the complete document in Listing 9-4. It's also provided on the companion CD under the filename Raven01.xml.

Raven01.xml

```
<?xml version="1.0"?>

<!-- File Name: Raven01.xml -->

<?xml-stylesheet type="text/css" href="Raven01.css"?>

<POEM>

<TITLE>The Raven</TITLE>
<AUTHOR>Edgar Allan Poe</AUTHOR>
<DATE>1845</DATE>

<NOTE>This is a floating margin note.</NOTE>

<STANZA>
    <VERSE>Once upon a midnight dreary, while I pondered,
        weak and weary,</VERSE>
    <VERSE>Over many a quaint and curious volume of
        forgotten lore&#8212;</VERSE>
```

```
<VERSE>While I nodded, nearly napping,
        suddenly there came a tapping,</VERSE>
<VERSE>As of some one gently rapping,
        rapping at my chamber door.</VERSE>
<VERSE>"'Tis some visitor," I muttered,
        "tapping at my chamber door&#8212;</VERSE>
<VERSE>Only this, and nothing more."</VERSE>
</STANZA>
<STANZA>
<VERSE>Ah, distinctly I remember it was in the
        bleak December,</VERSE>
<VERSE>And each separate dying ember wrought its
        ghost upon the floor.</VERSE>
<VERSE>Eagerly I wished the morrow;&#8212;vainly I had
        sought to borrow</VERSE>
<VERSE>From my books surcease of sorrow&#8212;sorrow
        for the lost Lenore&#8212;</VERSE>
<VERSE>For the rare and radiant maiden whom the angels
        name Lenore&#8212;</VERSE>
<VERSE>Nameless here for evermore.</VERSE>
</STANZA>

</POEM>
```

Listing 9-4.

8   Open Raven01.xml in Internet Explorer, which will display it like this:

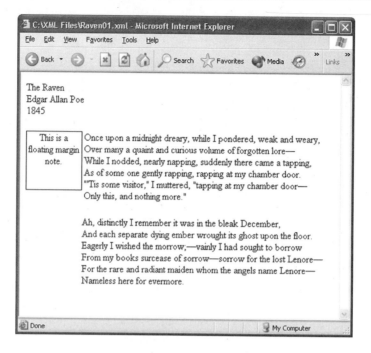

Display a Floating Image

1   In your text editor, open the Raven.css style sheet file given in Listing 9-1 and provided on the companion CD.

2   Modify the style sheet so that it appears as shown in Listing 9-5.

The main addition to the original style sheet is the rule for the IMAGE elements:

```
IMAGE
    {background-image:url(Raven.bmp);
     background-repeat:no-repeat;
     background-position:center;
     width:89px;
     height:58px;
     float:left}
```

IMAGE is an empty element (which you'll add to the XML document later) designed for displaying a floating image. The element contains no text, but is assigned a background image to display instead (through the first three property settings in the rule).

You assigned the element's *width* and *height* properties the exact width and height of the image. Because the image file is bitmapped, it's important to assign the size in pixels so that the whole image will be displayed on any monitor and in any graphics mode. Note that if you didn't assign *width* and *height* values to the element, its size would become zero because it contains no text, and it would thus be hidden.

Finally, you assigned the *float* property the value *left* so that the image floats to the left of the document text that follows it.

3 Use your text editor's Save As command to save a copy of the modified style sheet under the filename Raven02.css.

Raven02.css

```
/* File Name: Raven02.css */

POEM
    {font-size:12pt}

POEM, TITLE, AUTHOR, DATE, IMAGE, STANZA, VERSE
    {display:block}

DATE, STANZA
    {margin-bottom:.25in}

IMAGE
    {background-image:url(Raven.bmp);
     background-repeat:no-repeat;
     background-position:center;
     width:89px;
     height:58px;
     float:left}
```

Listing 9-5.

4 In your text editor, open the Raven.xml document given in Listing 9-2 and provided on the companion CD.

5 In Raven.xml, edit the *xml-stylesheet* processing instruction at the beginning of the file so that it points to the new style sheet you just created—Raven02.css—like this:

```
<?xml-stylesheet type="text/css" href="Raven02.css"?>
```

6 In Raven.xml, add the following empty IMAGE element immediately above each STANZA element:

```
<IMAGE />
```

Because you assigned the IMAGE elements the *float:left* property setting in the style sheet, they will float to the left of each STANZA element (which contain the following document text).

7   Use your text editor's Save As command to save a copy of the modified document under the filename Raven02.xml.

You can see the complete document in Listing 9-6. A copy is also provided on the companion CD under the filename Raven02.xml.

Raven02.xml

```
<?xml version="1.0"?>

<!-- File Name: Raven02.xml -->

<?xml-stylesheet type="text/css" href="Raven02.css"?>

<POEM>

<TITLE>The Raven</TITLE>
<AUTHOR>Edgar Allan Poe</AUTHOR>
<DATE>1845</DATE>

<IMAGE />
<STANZA>
    <VERSE>Once upon a midnight dreary, while I pondered,
            weak and weary,</VERSE>
    <VERSE>Over many a quaint and curious volume of
            forgotten lore&#8212;</VERSE>
    <VERSE>While I nodded, nearly napping,
            suddenly there came a tapping,</VERSE>
    <VERSE>As of some one gently rapping,
            rapping at my chamber door.</VERSE>
    <VERSE>"'Tis some visitor," I muttered,
            "tapping at my chamber door&#8212;</VERSE>
    <VERSE>Only this, and nothing more."</VERSE>
</STANZA>

<IMAGE />
<STANZA>
    <VERSE>Ah, distinctly I remember it was in the
            bleak December,</VERSE>
    <VERSE>And each separate dying ember wrought its
```

```
                    ghost upon the floor.</VERSE>
        <VERSE>Eagerly I wished the morrow;&#8212;vainly I had
            sought to borrow</VERSE>
        <VERSE>From my books surcease of sorrow&#8212;sorrow
            for the lost Lenore&#8212;</VERSE>
        <VERSE>For the rare and radiant maiden whom the angels
            name Lenore&#8212;</VERSE>
        <VERSE>Nameless here for evermore.</VERSE>
    </STANZA>

    </POEM>
```

Listing 9-6

8   Open Raven02.xml in Internet Explorer, which will display it like this:

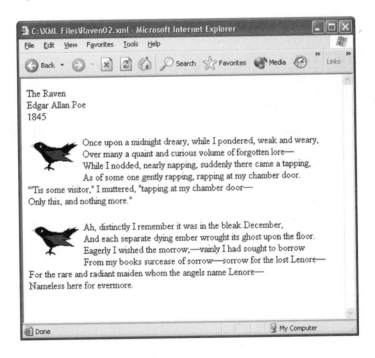

Setting the *clear* Property

By default, a floating element (that is, an element whose *float* property has been assigned *left* or *right*) will be displayed on the left or right side of the following document content. You can, however, use the *clear* property with a particular element to prevent a previous floating element from being displayed alongside it.

You can assign an element's *clear* property one of the following four CSS keyword values:

clear keyword	Effect
left	The element will be displayed below—rather than alongside—a preceding floating element with the *float:left* property setting.
right	The element will be displayed below—rather than alongside—a preceding floating element with the *float:right* property setting.
both	The element will be displayed below—rather than alongside—a preceding floating element with the *float:left* or *float:right* property setting.
none (default)	The element will be displayed alongside a preceding floating element.

note

The *clear* property does not affect the floating behavior of a descendent element. For instance, if you assign *left, right,* or *both* to the *clear* property of an element PARENT, and PARENT contains a floating child element CHILD, CHILD will still be floated to the left or right of PARENT. The *clear* property will turn off floating only of a floating element that comes *before* PARENT in the XML document.

For example, if you added the following rule to the style sheet of Listing 9-5, each STANZA element would be displayed *below* rather than alongside the preceding (floating) IMAGE element, as shown in the figure below:

```
STANZA
    {clear:left}
```

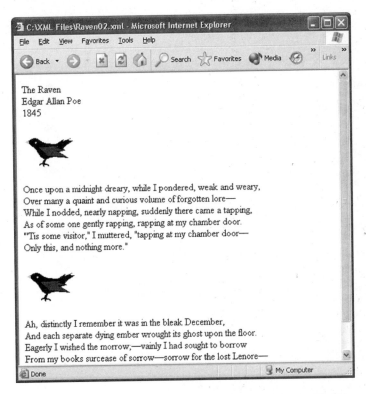

In this example, you could have achieved the same basic result by simply removing the *float* setting from the IMAGE element, rather than using both a *float* setting and a counteracting *clear* setting. In a more complex document, however, the IMAGE element might appear before several different element types. By using the *clear* property with a particular element type, you could selectively turn off floating for just that element type, while allowing floating with all the other element types.

Using Pseudo-Elements (Internet Explorer 5.5 through 6.0 Only)

If you're going to display an XML document in Internet Explorer 5.5 through 6.0, you can create a rule that applies to only the first letter of a *block* element by appending *:first-letter* to the element's name in the selector. Likewise, you can create a rule that applies only to the first line of a *block* element by appending *:first-line* to the element's name in the selector. Using either of these expressions creates what is known as a *pseudo-element*—"pseudo" in the sense that the rule applies to a block of text that isn't a complete element.

Advanced CSS

9

For example, if an XML document contained a series of PARAGRAPH elements, the following rules would display the first letter of each element in a larger font, and would convert the first line to all capital letters:

```
PARAGRAPH
    {display:block;
     font-size:small}

PARAGRAPH:first-letter
    {font-size:large}

PARAGRAPH:first-line
    {text-transform:uppercase}
```

Here's how Internet Explorer would display a PARAGRAPH element:

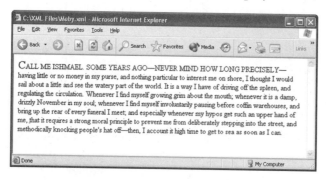

(The quotation is from the first paragraph of *Moby-Dick* by Herman Melville.)

Inserting HTML Elements into XML Documents

Although you can use a cascading style sheet to add basic formatting features to the XML elements in your document, it would be nice to be able to add standard HTML elements—such as hyperlinks, images, and horizontal rules—so that your document could benefit from their built-in features. Fortunately, when you display your document by means of an attached cascading style sheet, you can insert a standard HTML element into your document and have the browser display that element. To do this, you simply include an XML element that has the same name as the desired HTML element but with the *html* namespace prefix. As always, you must declare the namespace prefix according to the guidelines described in "Using Namespaces" on page 69. Customarily, you assign *http://www.w3c.org/TR/REC-html40/* or *http://www.w3.org/Profiles/XHTML-transitional* as the namespace name.

For example, if the following element is contained in an XML document with an attached CSS and you open that document directly in Internet Explorer, the browser will render it as an HTML IMG (image) element and will display the associated graphics file (Raven.bmp):

```
<html:IMG xmlns:html="http://www.w3c.org/TR/REC-html40/"
   SRC="Raven.bmp" />
```

If an XML element has the same name as an HTML element (for example, IMG or BR) but doesn't include the *html* namespace prefix, Internet Explorer treats it as a normal XML element. (Thus, you can freely use an element in your XML document that has the same name as an HTML element, but doesn't have the *html* prefix, without danger that it will be misinterpreted as HTML.)

Keep in mind that when you insert an HTML element using this technique, the element must be well-formed according to the rules of XML. For instance, to include an HTML IMG or BR element, you must use an empty-element tag (one ending with a / as in the example above) or include the end-tag. You can't include just a regular start-tag without an end-tag as you can in an actual HTML page.

note

According to the W3C namespace specification, if an XML application requires you to use a particular namespace, you should be able to use *any* unique namespace prefix in your document, as long as the namespace name (*http://www.w3c.org/TR/REC-html40/* in the example above) has the expected value. This is the way namespaces work with XML schemas (described in Chapter 7) and with XSLT style sheets (described in Chapter 12). However, the requirements for the *html* namespace used with a CSS are non-conforming and are in fact just the opposite of the specification. Namely, you can assign any namespace name as long as you use the *html* namespace prefix. For instance, you could actually declare *html* as follows:

```
<html:IMG xmlns:html="anything" SRC="Raven.bmp" />
```

But you *couldn't* use the following declaration:

```
<myHTM:IMG xmlns:myHTM="http://www.w3c.org/TR/REC-html40/"
      SRC="Raven.bmp" /> <!-- this WON'T be rendered as HTML -->
```

Advanced CSS

9

An Example

The version of the RAVEN document shown in Listing 9-7 (and also provided on the companion CD under the filename Raven03.xml) illustrates the techniques for including HTML in an XML document. Notice that this document links the original version of the style sheet, Raven.css, which you'll find in Listing 9-1 and on the companion CD.

The document includes three standard HTML elements:

- It includes an image through the following XML element:

  ```
  <html:IMG xmlns:html="http://www.w3c.org/TR/REC-html40/"
      SRC="Raven.bmp" ALIGN="LEFT" />
  ```

  This element inserts a standard HTML IMG (image) element. The HTML attribute ALIGN="LEFT" makes the image float to the left of the following document text. This is an alternative to the method for displaying an image that you learned in the earlier section "Display a Floating Image."

- It makes the author name (formerly stored in the AUTHOR element) a hyperlink by including the following XML element (in place of AUTHOR):

  ```
  <html:A xmlns:html="http://www.w3c.org/TR/REC-html40/"
      HREF="http://www.mjyOnline.com/Edgar">
      Edgar Allan Poe
  </html:A>
  ```

  This element inserts a standard HTML A (anchor) element.

- It inserts two horizontal dividing lines using the following XML element in both places:

  ```
  <html:HR xmlns:html="http://www.w3c.org/TR/REC-html40/" />
  ```

  This element inserts a standard HTML HR (horizontal rule) element.

Here's how Internet Explorer displays the document:

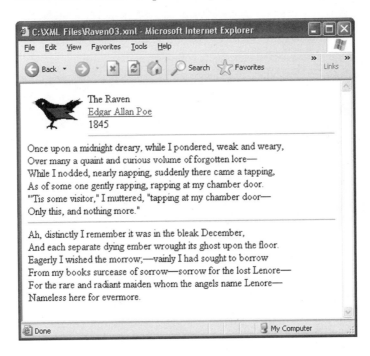

Raven03.xml

```
<?xml version="1.0"?>

<!-- File Name: Raven03.XML -->

<?xml-stylesheet type="text/css" href="Raven.css"?>

<POEM>

<html:IMG xmlns:html="http://www.w3c.org/TR/REC-html40/"
    SRC="Raven.bmp" ALIGN="LEFT" />

<TITLE>The Raven</TITLE>

<html:A xmlns:html="http://www.w3c.org/TR/REC-html40/"
    HREF="http://www.mjyOnline.com/Edgar">
    Edgar Allan Poe
</html:A>
```

```
<DATE>1845</DATE>

<html:HR xmlns:html="http://www.w3c.org/TR/REC-html40/" />

<STANZA>
    <VERSE>Once upon a midnight dreary, while I pondered,
            weak and weary,</VERSE>
    <VERSE>Over many a quaint and curious volume of
            forgotten lore&#8212;</VERSE>
    <VERSE>While I nodded, nearly napping,
            suddenly there came a tapping,</VERSE>
    <VERSE>As of some one gently rapping,
            rapping at my chamber door.</VERSE>
    <VERSE>"'Tis some visitor," I muttered,
            "tapping at my chamber door&#8212;</VERSE>
    <VERSE>Only this, and nothing more."</VERSE>
</STANZA>

<html:HR xmlns:html="http://www.w3c.org/TR/REC-html40/" />

<STANZA>
    <VERSE>Ah, distinctly I remember it was in the
            bleak December,</VERSE>
    <VERSE>And each separate dying ember wrought its
            ghost upon the floor.</VERSE>
    <VERSE>Eagerly I wished the morrow;&#8212;vainly I had
            sought to borrow</VERSE>
    <VERSE>From my books surcease of sorrow&#8212;sorrow
            for the lost Lenore&#8212;</VERSE>
    <VERSE>For the rare and radiant maiden whom the angels
            name Lenore&#8212;</VERSE>
    <VERSE>Nameless here for evermore.</VERSE>
</STANZA>

</POEM>
```

Listing 9-7.

Creating and Using a Full-Featured Cascading Style Sheet

In the following exercises, you'll create an XML document containing the first four stanzas of "The Raven." You'll then create a cascading style sheet that extensively formats this document, and in the process uses almost every property discussed in Chapters 8 and 9. The following figure shows how the poem will look in Internet Explorer:

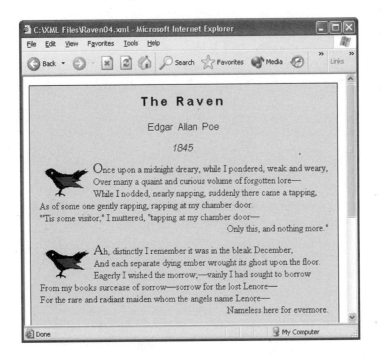

Create the Document

1   Open a new, empty text file in your text editor, and type in the XML document shown in Listing 9-8. (You'll find a copy of this listing on the companion CD under the filename Raven04.xml.)

Note the following important features of Raven04.xml:

- It links the cascading style sheet Raven04.css, which you'll create in the next exercise.

- It has an empty IMAGE element immediately before each STANZA element. You'll use the IMAGE elements to display floating images of a raven at the start of each stanza.

■ The first and last verses in each stanza are placed in special elements named FIRSTVERSE and LASTVERSE. This allows you to format these verses differently than the other verses. (The first verse will have a larger first letter and the last verse will be right justified rather than left.)

2 Use your text editor's Save command to save the document on your hard disk, assigning it the filename Raven04.xml.

Raven04.xml

```
<?xml version="1.0"?>

<!-- File Name: Raven04.xml -->

<?xml-stylesheet type="text/css" href="Raven04.css"?>

<POEM>
<TITLE>The Raven</TITLE>
<AUTHOR>
    Edgar Allan Poe
    <AUTHOR-BIO>
       Edgar Allan Poe was an American writer who lived
       from 1809 to 1849.
    </AUTHOR-BIO>
</AUTHOR>
<DATE>1845</DATE>
<IMAGE/>
<STANZA>
    <FIRSTVERSE>Once upon a midnight dreary, while I
                pondered, weak and weary,</FIRSTVERSE>
    <VERSE>Over many a quaint and curious volume of
           forgotten lore&#8212;</VERSE>
    <VERSE>While I nodded, nearly napping,
           suddenly there came a tapping,</VERSE>
    <VERSE>As of some one gently rapping,
           rapping at my chamber door.</VERSE>
    <VERSE>"'Tis some visitor," I muttered,
           "tapping at my chamber door&#8212;</VERSE>
    <LASTVERSE>Only this, and nothing more."</LASTVERSE>
</STANZA>
<IMAGE/>
<STANZA>
    <FIRSTVERSE>Ah, distinctly I remember it was in the
```

```
                              bleak December,</FIRSTVERSE>
         <VERSE>And each separate dying ember wrought its
                ghost upon the floor.</VERSE>
         <VERSE>Eagerly I wished the morrow;&#8212;vainly I had
                sought to borrow</VERSE>
         <VERSE>From my books surcease of sorrow&#8212;sorrow
                for the lost Lenore&#8212;</VERSE>
         <VERSE>For the rare and radiant maiden whom the angels
                name Lenore&#8212;</VERSE>
         <LASTVERSE>Nameless here for evermore.</LASTVERSE>
    </STANZA>
    <IMAGE/>
    <STANZA>
         <FIRSTVERSE>And the silken sad uncertain rustling
                     of each purple curtain</FIRSTVERSE>
         <VERSE>Thrilled me&#8212;filled me with fantastic
                terrors never felt before;</VERSE>
         <VERSE>So that now, to still the beating of my heart,
                I stood repeating:</VERSE>
         <VERSE>"'Tis some visitor entreating entrance at
                my chamber door&#8212;</VERSE>
         <VERSE>Some late visitor entreating entrance
                at my chamber door;</VERSE>
         <LASTVERSE>This it is, and nothing more."</LASTVERSE>
    </STANZA>
    <IMAGE/>
    <STANZA>
         <FIRSTVERSE>Presently my soul grew stronger;
                     hesitating then no longer,</FIRSTVERSE>
         <VERSE>"Sir," said I, "or Madam, truly your
                forgiveness I implore;</VERSE>
         <VERSE>But the fact is I was napping, and so
                gently you came rapping,</VERSE>
         <VERSE>And so faintly you came tapping,
                tapping at my chamber door,</VERSE>
         <VERSE>That I scarce was sure I heard you"&#8212;here
                I opened wide the door;&#8212;</VERSE>
         <LASTVERSE>Darkness there, and nothing more.</LASTVERSE>
    </STANZA>
    </POEM>
```

Listing 9-8

Create the Style Sheet

1   Open a new, empty text file in your text editor, and type in the cascading style sheet shown in Listing 9-9. (You'll find a copy of this listing on the companion CD under the filename Raven04.css.)

Here are a few things to keep in mind about this style sheet:

- The style sheet demonstrates almost all of the CSS properties given in Chapters 8 and 9, which provide explanations for all of the techniques used.

- The image file (RavShade.bmp) displayed using the IMAGE elements is the same as the image displayed by the previous versions of the Raven.xml document, except that it has a shaded background that matches the background color of the POEM element.

- The style sheet hides the contents of the AUTHOR-BIO element by assigning *none* to its *display* property.

2   Use your text editor's Save command to save the document on your hard disk, assigning it the filename Raven04.css.

Raven04.css

```
/* File Name: Raven04.css */

POEM
    {display:block;
     font-size:12pt;
     width:5.5in;
     padding:1em;
     border-style:solid;
     border-width:1px;
     background-color:rgb(225,225,225)}

TITLE, AUTHOR, DATE
    {display:block;
     margin-bottom:1em;
     font-family:Arial,sans-serif;
     text-align:center}

TITLE
    {font-size:16pt;
     font-weight:bold;
     letter-spacing:.25em}
```

```
AUTHOR
    {word-spacing:.25em}

AUTHOR-BIO
    {display:none}

DATE
    {font-style:italic}

IMAGE
    {background-image:url(RavShade.bmp);
     background-repeat:no-repeat;
     background-position:center;
     width:89px;
     height:58px;
     float:left}

STANZA
    {display:block;
     margin-bottom:1em;
     color:navy;
     line-height:1.25em}

VERSE, FIRSTVERSE, LASTVERSE
    {display:block}

FIRSTVERSE:first-letter
    {font-size:large}

LASTVERSE
    {text-align:right}
```

Listing 9-9

3   Display the document by opening the Raven04.xml file directly in Internet Explorer: Raven04.xml

Displaying XML Documents Using Data Binding

Data binding is the first technique that you'll learn for displaying an XML document from within a conventional HTML page. Displaying XML from within HTML pages gives you the best of both worlds: the ability to store data using XML, with its capacity for describing and structuring virtually any type of information, plus the ability to display and work with that information using HTML, with its feature-rich elements (such as tables, hyperlinks, images, frames, forms, buttons, and other controls) and its dynamic programmability.

In data binding, you link an XML document to an HTML page, and then bind standard HTML elements, such as SPANs or TABLEs, to individual XML elements or attributes. The HTML elements then automatically display the contents of the XML elements or attributes to which they're bound.

Data binding and the related techniques you'll learn in this chapter work best with an XML document that is structured symmetrically, like a typical database—namely, a document whose elements can be interpreted as a set of records and fields. In its simplest form, such a document consists of a root element containing a series of elements of the same type (the records), each of which has the same set of child elements that all contain character data (the fields). An example is the Inventory.xml document you'll see in Listing 10-1, in which the BOOK elements can be interpreted as records, and the elements nested within each BOOK element (TITLE, AUTHOR, and so on) can be interpreted as fields. Later in the chapter, you'll learn more about the specific document structures that are suitable for data binding. For documents that aren't suitable, you can use the scripting techniques you'll explore in Chapter 11.

In this chapter, you'll first gain an overview of the two main steps for data binding. You'll then learn in detail how to link the XML document to the HTML page (the first main step), and how to bind HTML elements to XML elements and attributes (the second main step). Finally, you'll learn how to program a Web page using scripts that employ the same underlying programming object as data binding (namely, the Data Source Object, or DSO). You can use these scripts in conjunction with data binding—or independently of it.

In Chapter 11, you'll learn an entirely different way to access, manage, and display an XML document from within an HTML page. The techniques given there will let you traverse the entire logical structure of an XML document, and you can use them with any type of XML document.

tip

For more information on using data binding and the DSO with Microsoft Internet Explorer, see the topics "Binding the XML Data Source Object to Data," "Using the C++ XML Data Source Object," and "Using the Master/Detail Feature with the C++ XML Data Source Object" in the Microsoft XML SDK 4.0 help file, or the same topics in the XML SDK documentation provided by the MSDN (Microsoft Developer Network) Library on the Web at *http://msdn.microsoft.com/library/*.

The Main Steps

There are two main steps for using data binding:

1   **Linking the XML document to the HTML page in which you want to display the XML data.** This step is normally done by including an HTML element named XML within the HTML page. For example, the following element in an HTML page links the XML document Inventory.xml to the page:

    ```
    <XML ID="dsoInventory" SRC="Inventory.xml"></XML>
    ```

2   **Binding HTML elements to XML elements or attributes.** When you bind an HTML element to an XML element or attribute, the HTML element automatically displays the content of the XML element or the value of the XML attribute. For instance, the following SPAN element in an HTML page is bound to the AUTHOR element in the linked XML document:

    ```
    <SPAN DATASRC="#dsoInventory" DATAFLD="AUTHOR"></SPAN>
    ```

    As a result, the SPAN HTML element displays the contents of the AUTHOR XML element.

The basic technique of data binding really is as simple as this, although you'll learn many variations in the way you can use it. The following sections cover these two steps in detail.

The First Step: Linking the XML Document to the HTML Page

To display an XML document in an HTML page, you must link the document to the page. The easiest way to do this with Microsoft Internet Explorer is to include in the page an HTML element named XML, which is also known as a *data island*. You can use one of two different forms for a data island.

The first form of data island includes the entire text of the XML document between the XML start-tag and end-tag. The data island in the following HTML page is an example:

```
<HTML>
<HEAD>
    <TITLE>Book Inventory</TITLE>
</HEAD>

<BODY>
    <XML ID="dsoInventory">
        <?xml version="1.0"?>

        <INVENTORY>
          <BOOK>
              <TITLE>The Adventures of Huckleberry Finn</TITLE>
              <AUTHOR>Mark Twain</AUTHOR>
              <BINDING>mass market paperback</BINDING>
              <PAGES>298</PAGES>
              <PRICE>$5.49</PRICE>
          </BOOK>
          <BOOK>
              <TITLE>Leaves of Grass</TITLE>
              <AUTHOR>Walt Whitman</AUTHOR>
              <BINDING>hardcover</BINDING>
              <PAGES>462</PAGES>
              <PRICE>$7.75</PRICE>
          </BOOK>
          <BOOK>
              <TITLE>The Legend of Sleepy Hollow</TITLE>
              <AUTHOR>Washington Irving</AUTHOR>
```

Data Binding

10

```
            <BINDING>mass market paperback</BINDING>
            <PAGES>98</PAGES>
            <PRICE>$2.95</PRICE>
         </BOOK>

         <!-- other BOOK elements -->

      </INVENTORY>
      </XML>

      <!-- other HTML elements ... -->

</BODY>
</HTML>
```

> **note**
>
> In the first form of data island, the XML document must not contain an element named XML, in any combination of uppercase and lowercase letters. (As mentioned in Chapter 3, in an XML document it's actually never a good practice to name an element XML, nor even to begin an element name with the letters XML in any combination of uppercase or lowercase.)

In the second form of data island, the XML HTML element stays empty, and includes only the URL of the XML document. An example is the data island in the following HTML page:

```
<HTML>
<HEAD>
   <TITLE>Book Inventory</TITLE>
</HEAD>

<BODY>

   <XML ID="dsoInventory" SRC="Inventory.xml"></XML>

   <!-- other HTML elements... -->

</BODY>
</HTML>
```

In this example, the text of the XML document would be contained in the separate Inventory.xml file:

```xml
<?xml version="1.0"?>

<!-- File Name: Inventory.xml -->

<INVENTORY>
   <BOOK>
      <TITLE>The Adventures of Huckleberry Finn</TITLE>
      <AUTHOR>Mark Twain</AUTHOR>
      <BINDING>mass market paperback</BINDING>
      <PAGES>298</PAGES>
      <PRICE>$5.49</PRICE>
   </BOOK>
   <BOOK>
      <TITLE>Leaves of Grass</TITLE>
      <AUTHOR>Walt Whitman</AUTHOR>
      <BINDING>hardcover</BINDING>
      <PAGES>462</PAGES>
      <PRICE>$7.75</PRICE>
   </BOOK>
   <BOOK>
      <TITLE>The Legend of Sleepy Hollow</TITLE>
      <AUTHOR>Washington Irving</AUTHOR>
      <BINDING>mass market paperback</BINDING>
      <PAGES>98</PAGES>
      <PRICE>$2.95</PRICE>
   </BOOK>

   <!-- other BOOK elements -->

</INVENTORY>
```

The second form of data island conforms more closely to the basic XML tenet of keeping the data itself (the XML document) separate from the formatting and processing information (the style sheet, or in this chapter, the HTML page). In particular, the second form makes it easier to maintain the XML document, especially when a single document is displayed in several different HTML pages. Therefore, you'll see only the second form of data island in the examples in this book.

You should assign to the data island's ID attribute a unique identifier, which you'll use to access the XML document from within the HTML page. (In the previous example, I assigned ID the value *dsoInventory.*)

In the second form of data island, you assign to the SRC attribute the URL of the file containing the XML data. You can use a fully qualified URL, as in this example:

```
<XML
    ID="dsoInventory"
    SRC="http://www.mjyOnline.com/documents/Inventory.xml">
</XML>
```

More commonly, however, you use a partial URL that specifies a location relative to the location of the HTML page containing the data island. For example, the SRC attribute in the following data island indicates that Inventory.xml is in the same folder as the HTML page:

```
<XML ID="dsoInventory" SRC="Inventory.xml"></XML>
```

Relative URLs are more common because the XML document is typically contained in the same folder as the HTML page, or perhaps in one of its subfolders.

How the XML Data Is Stored

When Internet Explorer opens the HTML page, its XML processor reads and parses the XML document. Internet Explorer also creates a programming object known as a Data Source Object (DSO), which stores, or *caches,* the XML data and provides access to this data. The DSO stores the XML data as a record set—that is, as a collection of records and their fields. For example, if you were to include the Inventory.xml document (shown in Listing 10-1) in a page as a data island, the DSO would store each BOOK element as a record, and each of the child elements within BOOK (TITLE, AUTHOR, and so on) as a field.

When you bind an HTML element to an XML element, the DSO automatically supplies the value of the XML element and handles all the details. The DSO also lets you directly access and manipulate the stored record set through a collection of methods, properties, and events. *Methods* are functions that you can call from the page to access or modify the record set. (For example, you can use methods to move through the records.) *Properties* are current feature settings that you can read and sometimes modify from the page. (For example, you can read a property that tells you if you've reached the last record.) And *events* are occurrences (such as a record value changing) that you can handle from a script function that you include in the page.

In the page, the identifier that you assigned to the ID attribute in the data island represents the DSO. (In the example in the previous section, this identifier is *dsoInventory.*)

Checking for XML Errors

As you've seen in previous chapters, if you open an XML document (with or without a style sheet) directly in Internet Explorer, the browser checks whether the document is well-formed. If it encounters any well-formedness errors, it stops displaying the document and displays a fatal error message that can help you fix the problem.

When you open an XML document through a data island in an HTML page, Internet Explorer checks the document for well-formedness and also—if the document includes a document type declaration—for validity. However, if the document contains an error, Internet Explorer just quietly fails to display the XML data in the bound HTML elements, without showing an error message.

To see a helpful description of any well-formedness or validity error in the linked XML document, you can test that document using one of the validity testing pages presented in "Checking an XML Document for Validity" on page 396.

The Second Step: Binding HTML Elements to XML Elements

You can bind HTML elements to XML elements in two basic ways:

- **Table data binding,** which means binding an HTML TABLE element to XML data so that the table automatically displays the entire set of records belonging to the XML document.

- **Single-record data binding,** which means binding non-table HTML elements (SPAN elements, for example) to XML elements so that only one record at a time is displayed.

The following sections discuss these two techniques in detail.

Using Table Data Binding

The easiest way to display an XML document that consists of a series of records (such as Inventory.xml, shown in Listing 10-1) is to bind an HTML TABLE element to the XML data so that the table automatically displays all records at once (or one page of records at a time if you enable paging). With this approach, Internet Explorer handles all the details for you; you don't need to write scripts or call methods. (One exception is that if you choose paging, you'll need to include a few simple method calls, as described later in the chapter.)

You can use a single HTML table to display an XML document structured as a simple record set, or you can use nested HTML tables to display an XML docu-

10

Data Binding

ment that contains a hierarchical record set (a more complex record structure that I'll describe later in the chapter). The following sections explain both approaches to displaying record sets.

Using a Single HTML Table to Display a Simple Record Set

You can use a single HTML TABLE element to display an XML document in which the data is organized as a simple record set—that is, an XML document organized as follows:

- The root element contains a series of *record* elements, all of the same type. (In this chapter, I sometimes call record elements simply *records*.)

- Each record element contains the same set of *field* elements, and in this set a given element type occurs only once. (In this chapter, I sometimes call field elements simply *fields*.)

- Each field element contains character data only.

> ### note
> If a record element contains more than one child element of the same type, or if a child element contains nested elements, the DSO interprets the child element as a nested record or record set, not as a field. You'll learn how to display nested records in "Using a Nested Table to Display a Hierarchical Record Set" later in the chapter.

An example of this type of XML document is Inventory.xml, which you've seen in previous chapters. It is given again in Listing 10-1 for convenient reference. (You'll find a copy of this file on the companion CD.) In this document, the root element (INVENTORY) contains a set of eight record elements (BOOK elements), and each record element has the same set of field elements, which contain only character data (TITLE, AUTHOR, BINDING, PAGES, and PRICE).

Inventory.xml

```
<?xml version="1.0"?>

<!-- File Name: Inventory.xml -->

<INVENTORY>
   <BOOK>
```

```
    <TITLE>The Adventures of Huckleberry Finn</TITLE>
    <AUTHOR>Mark Twain</AUTHOR>
    <BINDING>mass market paperback</BINDING>
    <PAGES>298</PAGES>
    <PRICE>$5.49</PRICE>
</BOOK>
<BOOK>
    <TITLE>Leaves of Grass</TITLE>
    <AUTHOR>Walt Whitman</AUTHOR>
    <BINDING>hardcover</BINDING>
    <PAGES>462</PAGES>
    <PRICE>$7.75</PRICE>
</BOOK>
<BOOK>
    <TITLE>The Legend of Sleepy Hollow</TITLE>
    <AUTHOR>Washington Irving</AUTHOR>
    <BINDING>mass market paperback</BINDING>
    <PAGES>98</PAGES>
    <PRICE>$2.95</PRICE>
</BOOK>
<BOOK>
    <TITLE>The Marble Faun</TITLE>
    <AUTHOR>Nathaniel Hawthorne</AUTHOR>
    <BINDING>trade paperback</BINDING>
    <PAGES>473</PAGES>
    <PRICE>$10.95</PRICE>
</BOOK>
<BOOK>
    <TITLE>Moby-Dick</TITLE>
    <AUTHOR>Herman Melville</AUTHOR>
    <BINDING>hardcover</BINDING>
    <PAGES>724</PAGES>
    <PRICE>$9.95</PRICE>
</BOOK>
<BOOK>
    <TITLE>The Portrait of a Lady</TITLE>
    <AUTHOR>Henry James</AUTHOR>
    <BINDING>mass market paperback</BINDING>
    <PAGES>256</PAGES>
    <PRICE>$4.95</PRICE>
</BOOK>
<BOOK>
```

```
        <TITLE>The Scarlet Letter</TITLE>
        <AUTHOR>Nathaniel Hawthorne</AUTHOR>
        <BINDING>trade paperback</BINDING>
        <PAGES>253</PAGES>
        <PRICE>$4.25</PRICE>
    </BOOK>
    <BOOK>
        <TITLE>The Turn of the Screw</TITLE>
        <AUTHOR>Henry James</AUTHOR>
        <BINDING>trade paperback</BINDING>
        <PAGES>384</PAGES>
        <PRICE>$3.35</PRICE>
    </BOOK>
</INVENTORY>
```

Listing 10-1.

When you bind the table to the XML document, the data belonging to each record element is displayed in a separate table row, with each of its child field elements displayed in a separate cell within that row.

As an example, the HTML page in Listing 10-2 contains a table bound to the data in the Inventory.xml document of Listing 10-1. (You'll find a copy of Listing 10-2 on the companion CD under the filename Inventory Table.htm.)

Inventory Table.htm

```
<!-- File Name: Inventory Table.htm -->

<HTML>

<HEAD>
    <TITLE>Book Inventory</TITLE>
</HEAD>

<BODY>

    <XML ID="dsoInventory" SRC="Inventory.xml"></XML>

    <H2>Book Inventory</H2>

    <TABLE DATASRC="#dsoInventory" BORDER="1" CELLPADDING="5">
        <THEAD>
            <TH>Title</TH>
```

```
            <TH>Author</TH>
            <TH>Binding</TH>
            <TH>Pages</TH>
            <TH>Price</TH>
        </THEAD>
        <TR ALIGN="center">
            <TD><SPAN DATAFLD="TITLE"
                STYLE="font-style:italic"></SPAN></TD>
            <TD><SPAN DATAFLD="AUTHOR"></SPAN></TD>
            <TD><SPAN DATAFLD="BINDING"></SPAN></TD>
            <TD><SPAN DATAFLD="PAGES"></SPAN></TD>
            <TD><SPAN DATAFLD="PRICE"></SPAN></TD>
        </TR>
    </TABLE>

</BODY>

</HTML>
```

Listing 10-2.

The XML document of Listing 10-1 is linked to the HTML page of Listing 10-2
through a data island in the page that has the ID *dsoInventory*:

```
<XML ID="dsoInventory" SRC="Inventory.xml"></XML>
```

The page's TABLE element is bound to the entire XML document by assigning
to the element's DATASRC attribute the ID of the data island, prefaced with a
pound sign (#):

```
<TABLE DATASRC="#dsoInventory" BORDER="1" CELLPADDING="5">
```

The table is defined with a standard heading (the THEAD element), and one
row (the TR element). Each cell in that row (that is, each TD element) contains
a SPAN element that is bound to one of the fields in the XML document so that
it will display the contents of that field. For example, the first cell contains a
SPAN bound to the TITLE field:

```
<TD><SPAN DATAFLD="TITLE"
    STYLE="font-style:italic"></SPAN></TD>
```

The SPAN element is bound to the XML field by assigning the field's name
(TITLE, in this example) to the element's DATAFLD attribute. Notice the use of
the STYLE attribute for formatting the content of the SPAN element using a cascading style sheet (CSS) property setting (*font-style:italic*). For information on
CSS properties, see Chapters 8 and 9.

10

Data Binding

Here's how the data binding works: Even though the TABLE element defines only a single row, when the browser displays the table, it repeats the row element for each record in the XML document. That is, the first row following the heading displays the fields (TITLE, AUTHOR, and so on) belonging to the first record (the BOOK element for *The Adventures of Huckleberry Finn*). The next row displays the fields for the second record (the BOOK element for *Leaves of Grass*), and so on. Here's how the document looks in Internet Explorer:

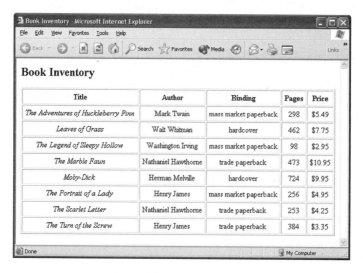

You might wonder why the cell (TD) elements aren't bound directly to the XML fields. The reason is that the TD element is not one of the bindable HTML elements. (Table 10-1, later in this chapter, lists the bindable elements.) Therefore, you need to include a bindable element, typically a SPAN, within each TD element.

tip

For information on working with HTML and Dynamic HTML (DHTML) as implemented in Internet Explorer, see the topic "HTML and Dynamic HTML" in the MSDN Library on the Web at *http://msdn.microsoft.com/library/*. To read the official specification for the latest version of HTML 4, see the following Web site, provided by the World Wide Web Consortium (W3C): *http://www.w3.org/TR/html4/*.

Using Paging

If the XML document contains many records, you can use *paging* to display the records one group at one time, rather than showing them all at once in a huge table. To activate paging for a particular bound table, perform the following steps:

1   Set the DATAPAGESIZE attribute of the bound TABLE element to the maximum number of records that you want to display at one time. Each *page* of records will contain, at most, the number of records you specify. For example, the following start-tag for a TABLE element assigns 5 to DATAPAGESIZE, causing the table to display five records at a time:

```
<TABLE DATASRC="#dsoInventory" DATAPAGESIZE="5">
```

2   Assign a unique identifier to the ID attribute of the TABLE element, as in the following start-tag:

```
<TABLE ID="InventoryTable" DATASRC="#dsoInventory"

    DATAPAGESIZE="5">
```

3   To navigate through the records, call the TABLE element methods listed in the following table. Note that the example calls in the last column assume that the table has the *InventoryTable* ID.

TABLE element method	Effect	Example call
firstPage	Displays the first page of records	`InventoryTable.firstPage()`
previousPage	Displays the previous page of records	`InventoryTable.previousPage()`
nextPage	Displays the next page of records	`InventoryTable.nextPage()`
lastPage	Displays the last page of records	`InventoryTable.lastPage()`

If the first page is currently displayed, a call to the *previousPage* method is ignored, and if the last page is displayed, a call to *nextPage* is ignored.

You can call any of these methods from a script that you write (as discussed later in the chapter). The easiest way to call one of them, however, is by assigning the method to the ONCLICK attribute of an HTML BUTTON element, as shown here:

```
<BUTTON ONCLICK="InventoryTable.nextPage()">Next Page</BUTTON>
```

10

Data Binding

This element displays a push button. When the user clicks the button, the method assigned to the ONCLICK attribute, *InventoryTable.nextPage*, gets called.

Listings 10-3 and 10-4 demonstrate the techniques for paging. Listing 10-3 is an expanded version of the Inventory.xml document shown in Listing 10-1. Listing 10-4 is an HTML page that displays this XML document in a table whose DATAPAGESIZE attribute is assigned the value 5. (You'll find copies of Listings 10-3 and 10-4 on the companion CD under the filenames Inventory Big.xml and Inventory Big Table.htm.)

At the top of the page are four BUTTON elements, each of which executes one of the table's paging methods. When you first open the page, the table shows the first five records. Clicking the Next Page button displays the next five records (or, at the end, however many records are left), and clicking the Previous button displays the previous five records (or, at the beginning, the first five records). Clicking the First Page or Last Page button displays the first five records or the last five records. Here's how Listing 10-4 looks when you open it in Internet Explorer:

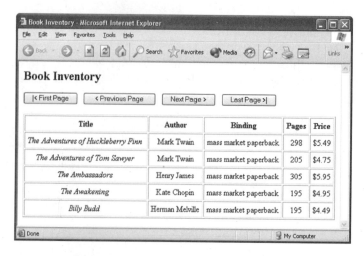

Inventory Big.xml

```xml
<?xml version="1.0"?>

<!-- File Name: Inventory Big.xml -->

<INVENTORY>
   <BOOK>
      <TITLE>The Adventures of Huckleberry Finn</TITLE>
      <AUTHOR>Mark Twain</AUTHOR>
      <BINDING>mass market paperback</BINDING>
```

```
      <PAGES>298</PAGES>
      <PRICE>$5.49</PRICE>
   </BOOK>
   <BOOK>
      <TITLE>The Adventures of Tom Sawyer</TITLE>
      <AUTHOR>Mark Twain</AUTHOR>
      <BINDING>mass market paperback</BINDING>
      <PAGES>205</PAGES>
      <PRICE>$4.75</PRICE>
   </BOOK>
   <BOOK>
      <TITLE>The Ambassadors</TITLE>
      <AUTHOR>Henry James</AUTHOR>
      <BINDING>mass market paperback</BINDING>
      <PAGES>305</PAGES>
      <PRICE>$5.95</PRICE>
   </BOOK>
   <BOOK>
      <TITLE>The Awakening</TITLE>
      <AUTHOR>Kate Chopin</AUTHOR>
      <BINDING>mass market paperback</BINDING>
      <PAGES>195</PAGES>
      <PRICE>$4.95</PRICE>
   </BOOK>
   <BOOK>
      <TITLE>Billy Budd</TITLE>
      <AUTHOR>Herman Melville</AUTHOR>
      <BINDING>mass market paperback</BINDING>
      <PAGES>195</PAGES>
      <PRICE>$4.49</PRICE>
   </BOOK>
   <BOOK>
      <TITLE>A Connecticut Yankee in King Arthur's Court</TITLE>
      <AUTHOR>Mark Twain</AUTHOR>
      <BINDING>mass market paperback</BINDING>
      <PAGES>385</PAGES>
      <PRICE>$5.49</PRICE>
   </BOOK>
   <BOOK>
      <TITLE>Joan of Arc</TITLE>
      <AUTHOR>Mark Twain</AUTHOR>
      <BINDING>trade paperback</BINDING>
```

```
      <PAGES>465</PAGES>
      <PRICE>$6.95</PRICE>
   </BOOK>
   <BOOK>
      <TITLE>Leaves of Grass</TITLE>
      <AUTHOR>Walt Whitman</AUTHOR>
      <BINDING>hardcover</BINDING>
      <PAGES>462</PAGES>
      <PRICE>$7.75</PRICE>
   </BOOK>
   <BOOK>
      <TITLE>The Legend of Sleepy Hollow</TITLE>
      <AUTHOR>Washington Irving</AUTHOR>
      <BINDING>mass market paperback</BINDING>
      <PAGES>98</PAGES>
      <PRICE>$2.95</PRICE>
   </BOOK>
   <BOOK>
      <TITLE>The Marble Faun</TITLE>
      <AUTHOR>Nathaniel Hawthorne</AUTHOR>
      <BINDING>trade paperback</BINDING>
      <PAGES>473</PAGES>
      <PRICE>$10.95</PRICE>
   </BOOK>
   <BOOK>
      <TITLE>Moby-Dick</TITLE>
      <AUTHOR>Herman Melville</AUTHOR>
      <BINDING>hardcover</BINDING>
      <PAGES>724</PAGES>
      <PRICE>$9.95</PRICE>
   </BOOK>
   <BOOK>
      <TITLE>Passing</TITLE>
      <AUTHOR>Nella Larsen</AUTHOR>
      <BINDING>trade paperback</BINDING>
      <PAGES>165</PAGES>
      <PRICE>$5.95</PRICE>
   </BOOK>
   <BOOK>
      <TITLE>The Portrait of a Lady</TITLE>
      <AUTHOR>Henry James</AUTHOR>
      <BINDING>mass market paperback</BINDING>
```

```
            <PAGES>256</PAGES>
            <PRICE>$4.95</PRICE>
        </BOOK>
        <BOOK>
            <TITLE>Roughing It</TITLE>
            <AUTHOR>Mark Twain</AUTHOR>
            <BINDING>mass market paperback</BINDING>
            <PAGES>324</PAGES>
            <PRICE>$5.25</PRICE>
        </BOOK>
        <BOOK>
            <TITLE>The Scarlet Letter</TITLE>
            <AUTHOR>Nathaniel Hawthorne</AUTHOR>
            <BINDING>trade paperback</BINDING>
            <PAGES>253</PAGES>
            <PRICE>$4.25</PRICE>
        </BOOK>
        <BOOK>
            <TITLE>The Turn of the Screw</TITLE>
            <AUTHOR>Henry James</AUTHOR>
            <BINDING>trade paperback</BINDING>
            <PAGES>384</PAGES>
            <PRICE>$3.35</PRICE>
        </BOOK>
</INVENTORY>
```

Listing 10-3.

Inventory Big Table.htm

```
<!-- File Name: Inventory Big Table.htm -->

<HTML>

<HEAD>
    <TITLE>Book Inventory</TITLE>
</HEAD>

<BODY>

    <XML ID="dsoInventory" SRC="Inventory Big.xml"></XML>

    <H2>Book Inventory</H2>
```

Data Binding

10

```
<BUTTON ONCLICK="InventoryTable.firstPage()">
    |&lt; First Page
</BUTTON>
  
<BUTTON ONCLICK="InventoryTable.previousPage()">
    &lt; Previous Page
</BUTTON>
  
<BUTTON ONCLICK="InventoryTable.nextPage()">
    Next Page &gt;
</BUTTON>
  
<BUTTON ONCLICK="InventoryTable.lastPage()">
    Last Page &gt;|
</BUTTON>
<P>

<TABLE ID="InventoryTable" DATASRC="#dsoInventory"
    DATAPAGESIZE="5" BORDER="1" CELLPADDING="5" WIDTH="100%">
    <THEAD>
        <TH>Title</TH>
        <TH>Author</TH>
        <TH>Binding</TH>
        <TH>Pages</TH>
        <TH>Price</TH>
    </THEAD>
    <TR ALIGN="center">
        <TD><SPAN DATAFLD="TITLE"
            STYLE="font-style:italic"></SPAN></TD>
        <TD><SPAN DATAFLD="AUTHOR"></SPAN></TD>
        <TD><SPAN DATAFLD="BINDING"></SPAN></TD>
        <TD><SPAN DATAFLD="PAGES"></SPAN></TD>
        <TD><SPAN DATAFLD="PRICE"></SPAN></TD>
    </TR>
</TABLE>

</BODY>

</HTML>
```

Listing 10-4.

Using a Nested Table to Display a Hierarchical Record Set

In the previous sections, you learned how to use a single table to display an XML document structured as a simple record set. (A simple record set is described at the beginning of the earlier section "Using a Single HTML Table to Display a Simple Record Set.") You'll now learn how to use nested tables to display an XML document whose elements are structured in a hierarchical record set.

In a hierarchical record set, each record can contain, in addition to an optional fixed set of fields, zero or more nested records (see the following Note). Listing 10-5 shows an example of an XML document structured as a hierarchical record set. (You'll find a copy of this listing on the companion CD under the filename Inventory Hierarchy.xml.) In this document, the root element (INVENTORY) contains a series of CATEGORY records. Each CATEGORY record begins with a single CATNAME field, which contains character data only, and then has two or more nested BOOK records. Each nested BOOK record has exactly five fields (TITLE, AUTHOR, BINDING, PAGES, and PRICE).

note

As a general rule, if an element contains one or more children (or attributes, as explained later), *or* if the same element type occurs more than once within a given parent, the DSO interprets the element or elements as a record (or set of records), rather than as a field (or set of fields). In Inventory Hierarchy.xml, the CATEGORY and BOOK elements meet both of these criteria, so they are clearly considered to be records. (The CATNAME, TITLE, AUTHOR, BINDING, PAGES, and PRICE elements meet neither criteria, so they are considered to be fields.) A TABLE element is the only type of HTML element that you can bind to an XML record.

Inventory Hierarchy.xml

```xml
<?xml version="1.0"?>

<!-- File Name: Inventory Hierarchy.xml -->

<INVENTORY>
   <CATEGORY>
      <CATNAME>Middle Ages</CATNAME>
      <BOOK>
         <TITLE>The Canterbury Tales</TITLE>
         <AUTHOR>Geoffrey Chaucer</AUTHOR>
         <BINDING>hardcover</BINDING>
         <PAGES>692</PAGES>
```

```
                <PRICE>$18.95</PRICE>
            </BOOK>
            <BOOK>
                <TITLE>Piers Plowman</TITLE>
                <AUTHOR>William Langland</AUTHOR>
                <BINDING>trade paperback</BINDING>
                <PAGES>385</PAGES>
                <PRICE>$10.95</PRICE>
            </BOOK>
        </CATEGORY>
        <CATEGORY>
            <CATNAME>Renaissance</CATNAME>
            <BOOK>
                <TITLE>The Blazing World</TITLE>
                <AUTHOR>Margaret Cavendish</AUTHOR>
                <BINDING>trade paperback</BINDING>
                <PAGES>225</PAGES>
                <PRICE>$8.79</PRICE>
            </BOOK>
            <BOOK>
                <TITLE>Oroonoko</TITLE>
                <AUTHOR>Aphra Behn</AUTHOR>
                <BINDING>mass market paperback</BINDING>
                <PAGES>295</PAGES>
                <PRICE>$4.95</PRICE>
            </BOOK>
            <BOOK>
                <TITLE>Doctor Faustus</TITLE>
                <AUTHOR>Christopher Marlowe</AUTHOR>
                <BINDING>hardcover</BINDING>
                <PAGES>472</PAGES>
                <PRICE>$15.95</PRICE>
            </BOOK>
        </CATEGORY>
        <CATEGORY>
            <CATNAME>18th Century</CATNAME>
            <BOOK>
                <TITLE>Gulliver's Travels</TITLE>
                <AUTHOR>Jonathan Swift</AUTHOR>
                <BINDING>hardcover</BINDING>
                <PAGES>324</PAGES>
                <PRICE>$11.89</PRICE>
```

```
        </BOOK>
        <BOOK>
            <TITLE>The History of Tom Jones: A Foundling</TITLE>
            <AUTHOR>Henry Fielding</AUTHOR>
            <BINDING>hardcover</BINDING>
            <PAGES>438</PAGES>
            <PRICE>$16.95</PRICE>
        </BOOK>
        <BOOK>
            <TITLE>Love in Excess</TITLE>
            <AUTHOR>Eliza Haywood</AUTHOR>
            <BINDING>trade paperback</BINDING>
            <PAGES>429</PAGES>
            <PRICE>$12.95</PRICE>
        </BOOK>
        <BOOK>
            <TITLE>Tristram Shandy</TITLE>
            <AUTHOR>Laurence Sterne</AUTHOR>
            <BINDING>hardcover</BINDING>
            <PAGES>322</PAGES>
            <PRICE>$9.49</PRICE>
        </BOOK>
    </CATEGORY>
    <CATEGORY>
        <CATNAME>19th Century</CATNAME>
        <BOOK>
            <TITLE>Dracula</TITLE>
            <AUTHOR>Bram Stoker</AUTHOR>
            <BINDING>hardcover</BINDING>
            <PAGES>395</PAGES>
            <PRICE>$17.95</PRICE>
        </BOOK>
        <BOOK>
            <TITLE>Great Expectations</TITLE>
            <AUTHOR>Charles Dickens</AUTHOR>
            <BINDING>mass market paperback</BINDING>
            <PAGES>639</PAGES>
            <PRICE>$6.95</PRICE>
        </BOOK>
        <BOOK>
            <TITLE>Percival Keene</TITLE>
            <AUTHOR>Frederick Marryat</AUTHOR>
```

```
      <BINDING>trade paperback</BINDING>
      <PAGES>425</PAGES>
      <PRICE>$12.89</PRICE>
   </BOOK>
   <BOOK>
      <TITLE>Treasure Island</TITLE>
      <AUTHOR>Robert Louis Stevenson</AUTHOR>
      <BINDING>trade paperback</BINDING>
      <PAGES>283</PAGES>
      <PRICE>$11.85</PRICE>
   </BOOK>
   <BOOK>
      <TITLE>Wuthering Heights</TITLE>
      <AUTHOR>Emily Bronte</AUTHOR>
      <BINDING>hardcover</BINDING>
      <PAGES>424</PAGES>
      <PRICE>$12.95</PRICE>
   </BOOK>
   </CATEGORY>
</INVENTORY>
```

Listing 10-5.

Listing 10-6 contains an HTML page that uses a nested table to display the hierarchical record structure of the XML document in Listing 10-5. (You'll find a copy of Listing 10-6 on the companion CD under the filename Inventory Hierarchy.htm.)

Inventory Hierarchy.htm

```
<!-- File Name: Inventory Hierarchy.htm -->

<HTML>

<HEAD>
   <TITLE>Inventory of Classic English Literature</TITLE>
</HEAD>

<BODY>

   <XML ID="dsoInventory" SRC="Inventory Hierarchy.xml"></XML>

   <TABLE DATASRC="#dsoInventory" BORDER="1">
      <THEAD>
         <TH>Classic English Literature</TH>
```

```
        </THEAD>
        <TR>
          <TD><SPAN DATAFLD="CATNAME"></SPAN></TD>
        </TR>
        <TR>
          <TD>
            <TABLE DATASRC="#dsoInventory" DATAFLD="BOOK"
                BORDER="0" CELLSPACING="10">
              <THEAD>
                <TH WIDTH="25%">Title</TH>
                <TH WIDTH="25%">Author</TH>
                <TH WIDTH="25%">Binding</TH>
                <TH WIDTH="10%">Pages</TH>
                <TH WIDTH="15%">Price</TH>
              </THEAD>
              <TR ALIGN="CENTER">
                <TD WIDTH="25%">
                  <SPAN DATAFLD="TITLE"
                      STYLE="font-style:italic"></SPAN>
                </TD>
                <TD WIDTH="25%">
                  <SPAN DATAFLD="AUTHOR"></SPAN>
                </TD>
                <TD WIDTH="25%">
                  <SPAN DATAFLD="BINDING"></SPAN>
                </TD>
                <TD WIDTH="10%">
                  <SPAN DATAFLD="PAGES"></SPAN>
                </TD>
                <TD WIDTH="15%">
                  <SPAN DATAFLD="PRICE"></SPAN>
                </TD>
              </TR>
            </TABLE>
          </TD>
        </TR>
    </TABLE>

</BODY>

</HTML>
```

Listing 10-6.

In Listing 10-6, the outer table is bound to the XML document, as you can see in its start-tag:

```
<TABLE DATASRC="#dsoInventory" BORDER="1">
```

The outer table includes a heading (a THEAD element displaying "Classic English Literature"), plus two table rows (two TR elements). The browser repeats the two rows for each top-level record (that is, for each CATEGORY record). The first row displays the CATNAME field. So far, everything works just like the example table that displays a simple record set, given previously in Listing 10-2. However, the second row, rather than displaying fields, contains a nested table that displays the contents of each nested BOOK record within the current category. Here's the markup for only the nested table:

```
<TABLE DATASRC="#dsoInventory" DATAFLD="BOOK"
   BORDER="0" CELLSPACING="10">
   <THEAD>
      <TH WIDTH="25%">Title</TH>
      <TH WIDTH="25%">Author</TH>
      <TH WIDTH="25%">Binding</TH>
      <TH WIDTH="10%">Pages</TH>
      <TH WIDTH="15%">Price</TH>
   </THEAD>
   <TR ALIGN="CENTER">
      <TD WIDTH="25%">
         <SPAN DATAFLD="TITLE"
            STYLE="font-style:italic"></SPAN>
      </TD>
      <TD WIDTH="25%">
         <SPAN DATAFLD="AUTHOR"></SPAN>
      </TD>
      <TD WIDTH="25%">
         <SPAN DATAFLD="BINDING"></SPAN>
      </TD>
      <TD WIDTH="10%">
         <SPAN DATAFLD="PAGES"></SPAN>
      </TD>
      <TD WIDTH="15%">
         <SPAN DATAFLD="PRICE"></SPAN>
      </TD>
   </TR>
</TABLE>
```

Notice that you must bind the nested table not only to the XML document (*DATASRC="#dsoInventory"*) but also to the nested BOOK records (*DATAFLD="BOOK"*) so that the table will display the contents of each BOOK record nested within the current CATEGORY record. In other words, the row element (TR) in this table will be repeated for each of these BOOK elements. (Note that the outer table is bound by default to the top-level records—the CATEGORY records in this example—so that it displays each of them in turn.)

Here's how Listing 10-6 looks when you open it in Internet Explorer:

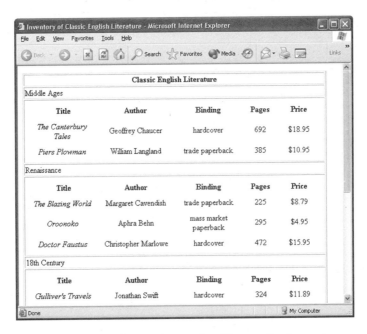

You could use additional nested tables to display a document that contains additional layers of nested records. Consider, for instance, the example document of Listing 10-5. Assume that you replace each AUTHOR field:

```
<AUTHOR>Geoffrey Chaucer</AUTHOR>
```

with one or more nested AUTHOR records, each of which has the following form:

```
<AUTHOR>
    <FIRSTNAME>Geoffrey</FIRSTNAME>
    <LASTNAME>Chaucer</LASTNAME>
</AUTHOR>
```

In this case, you could use an additional nested table to display all the authors for each BOOK element, employing the same basic techniques shown for a singly nested table. (Although in the example XML document each book has only a single author, an additional nested table would display multiple authors, if present. For the additional nested table, you would set DATAFLD equal to "AUTHOR".)

Using Single-Record Data Binding

Single-record data binding refers to binding an HTML element that isn't a table and isn't included in a bound table. The HTML element—for example, a SPAN, BUTTON, or LABEL element—is bound to an individual XML field (*not* to a record). The HTML element then automatically displays the content of the XML field to which you bind it. For example, the following HTML SPAN element is bound to the TITLE field in the XML document that's accessed through the *dsoInventory* data island:

```
<SPAN DATASRC="#dsoInventory" DATAFLD="TITLE"></SPAN>
```

To use single-record data binding as described in this section, the XML document must be organized as a simple record set. I gave a description of a simple record set at the beginning of the section "Using a Single HTML Table to Display a Simple Record Set" on page 302.

Because the HTML element doesn't have multiple parts like a table, however, it can display the field's value for only one record at a time. For example, if you wanted to display the book information in the Inventory Big.xml document (given in Listing 10-3), you could bind a SPAN element to each of the fields of a BOOK record, as in the following HTML page:

```
<HTML>

<HEAD>
   <TITLE>Book Description</TITLE>
</HEAD>

<BODY>

   <XML ID="dsoInventory" SRC="Inventory Big.xml"></XML>

   <H2>Book Description</H2>

   <SPAN STYLE="font-style:italic">Title: </SPAN>
   <SPAN STYLE="font-weight:bold" DATASRC="#dsoInventory"
      DATAFLD="TITLE"></SPAN>
   <BR>
```

```
<SPAN STYLE="font-style:italic">Author: </SPAN>
<SPAN DATASRC="#dsoInventory" DATAFLD="AUTHOR"></SPAN>
<BR>
<SPAN STYLE="font-style:italic">Binding type: </SPAN>
<SPAN DATASRC="#dsoInventory" DATAFLD="BINDING"></SPAN>
<BR>
<SPAN STYLE="font-style:italic">Number of pages: </SPAN>
<SPAN DATASRC="#dsoInventory" DATAFLD="PAGES"></SPAN>
<BR>
<SPAN STYLE="font-style:italic">Price: </SPAN>
<SPAN DATASRC="#dsoInventory" DATAFLD="PRICE"></SPAN>

</BODY>
</HTML>
```

This page, however, would display only the *first* BOOK record in the XML document, as shown here:

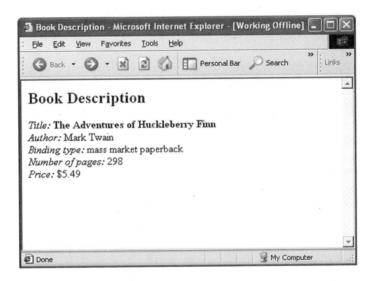

To circumvent this limitation, you need to use the technique for navigating through records described in the next section.

Navigating Through the Records

With single-record data binding, the bound HTML elements can display only one record at a time. The record that they display is known as the *current record*. (Hence, an alternative term for single-record data binding is *current-record binding*.) Initially, the current record is the first (or only) record in the document.

The DSO associated with the XML document provides a set of methods that you can call to navigate through the records. These methods belong to the *recordset* member object of the DSO, and are listed in the following table. Note that the example calls in the last column assume that the HTML page contains an XML data island with the ID *dsoInventory*.

DSO *recordset* method	Changes the current record to	Example call
moveFirst	The first record in the document	`dsoInventory.recordset.moveFirst()`
movePrevious	The previous record	`dsoInventory.recordset.movePrevious()`
moveNext	The next record	`dsoInventory.recordset.moveNext()`
moveLast	The last record in the document	`dsoInventory.recordset.moveLast()`
move	The record with the specified number	`dsoInventory.recordset.move(5)` (Moves to the sixth record. Records are numbered starting with zero.)

> **note**
>
> The *recordset* member object of the DSO conforms to a standard data access technology that Microsoft calls ActiveX Data Objects (ADO). You can use the general-purpose ADO *recordset* object with a variety of different data sources, in addition to the XML DSO described in this chapter. For general information on ADO and the ADO *recordset* object, see the topic "Microsoft ActiveX Data Objects (ADO)" in the MSDN Library on the Web at *http://msdn.microsoft.com/library/*. See also Microsoft's home page for information on ADO at *http://www.microsoft.com/data/ado/*.

You can call any of these methods from a script that you write (as discussed later in the chapter). The easiest way to call one of them, however, is by assigning the method to the ONCLICK attribute of a BUTTON element, as shown here:

```
<BUTTON ONCLICK="dsoInventory.recordset.moveFirst()">
    First Record
</BUTTON>
```

This element creates a push button that displays the text "First Record." When the user clicks the button, the method assigned to the ONCLICK attribute, *dsoInventory.recordset.moveFirst*, gets called.

If the current record is the first one, calling *movePrevious* moves the record set to the beginning-of-file state where no record is available and a bound element will go blank. Likewise, calling *moveNext* when the current record is the last one moves the record set to the end-of-file state, which also makes a bound element go blank.

Fortunately, the *recordset* object provides the BOF property, which is *true* if the record set is at beginning-of-file, and the EOF property, which is *true* if the record set is at end-of-file. You can use these properties to detect these states and make the necessary corrections. For example, the code assigned to the following button quickly redisplays the first record if the record set has moved to the beginning-of-file:

```
<BUTTON ONCLICK="dsoInventory.recordset.movePrevious();
                 if (dsoInventory.recordset.BOF)
                     dsoInventory.recordset.moveNext()">
    Back
</BUTTON>
```

The following code corrects for the end-of-file state:

```
<BUTTON ONCLICK="dsoInventory.recordset.moveNext();
                 if (dsoInventory.recordset.EOF)
                     dsoInventory.recordset.movePrevious()">
    Forward
</BUTTON>
```

Notice that you can assign an entire block of script code to the ONCLICK attribute (or to other event attributes, such as ONMOUSEOVER). In these examples, the code is in Microsoft JScript. Later in the chapter, you'll learn how to write freestanding blocks of script code, which make it easier to include more instructions.

In the following exercise, you'll create an HTML page that displays the XML document in Listing 10-3 one record at a time. The page provides buttons to navigate to the first, previous, next, and last records.

Display a Document One Record at a Time

1　Open a new, empty text file in your text editor, and type in the HTML page shown in Listing 10-7. (You'll find a copy of this listing on the companion CD under the filename Inventory Single.htm.)

Notice that the page contains a data island that links the Inventory Big.xml document, which contains 16 records. (Inventory Big.xml is given in Listing 10-3; you'll also find a copy on the companion CD.)

10

Data Binding

2   Use your text editor's Save command to save the page on your hard disk,
assigning it the filename Inventory Single.htm. Make sure that a copy of the
Inventory Big.xml file is in the same folder in which you save Inventory Single.htm.

Inventory Single.htm

```
<!-- File Name: Inventory Single.htm -->

<HTML>

<HEAD>
   <TITLE>Book Inventory</TITLE>
</HEAD>

<BODY>

   <XML ID="dsoInventory" SRC="Inventory Big.xml"></XML>

   <H2>Book Description</H2>

   <SPAN STYLE="font-style:italic">Title: </SPAN>
   <SPAN DATASRC="#dsoInventory" DATAFLD="TITLE"
      STYLE="font-weight:bold"></SPAN>
   <BR>
   <SPAN STYLE="font-style:italic">Author: </SPAN>
   <SPAN DATASRC="#dsoInventory" DATAFLD="AUTHOR"></SPAN>
   <BR>
   <SPAN STYLE="font-style:italic">Binding type: </SPAN>
   <SPAN DATASRC="#dsoInventory" DATAFLD="BINDING"></SPAN>
   <BR>
   <SPAN STYLE="font-style:italic">Number of pages: </SPAN>
   <SPAN DATASRC="#dsoInventory" DATAFLD="PAGES"></SPAN>
   <BR>
   <SPAN STYLE="font-style:italic">Price: </SPAN>
   <SPAN DATASRC="#dsoInventory" DATAFLD="PRICE"></SPAN>

   <HR>

   <BUTTON ONCLICK="dsoInventory.recordset.movefirst()">
      |&lt; First
   </BUTTON>
   <BUTTON ONCLICK="dsoInventory.recordset.moveprevious();
```

```
                            if (dsoInventory.recordset.BOF)
                                 dsoInventory.recordset.movenext()">
        &lt; Back
    </BUTTON>
    <BUTTON ONCLICK="dsoInventory.recordset.movenext();
                            if (dsoInventory.recordset.EOF)
                                 dsoInventory.recordset.moveprevious()">
        Forward &gt;
    </BUTTON>
    <BUTTON ONCLICK="dsoInventory.recordset.movelast()">
        Last &gt;|
    </BUTTON>

</BODY>

</HTML>
```

Listing 10-7.

3   In Windows Explorer or in a folder window, double-click the name of the file, Inventory Single.htm, that you saved in the previous step: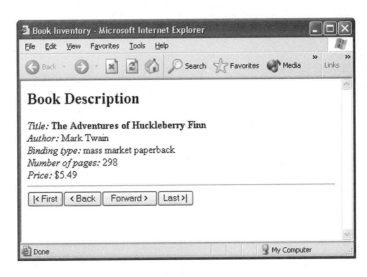

Internet Explorer will open the page and display it, as shown here:

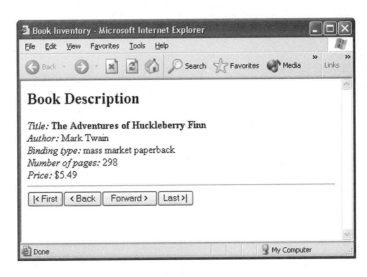

Notice that initially, until the user starts clicking the buttons, Internet Explorer displays only the first record in the document.

Other Data Binding Techniques

In the following sections, you'll learn a variety of additional techniques for binding non-table HTML elements to XML fields. These can be individual HTML elements used for single-record data binding, or they can be HTML elements contained an HTML table that's bound to an XML record. Specifically, you'll learn:

- How to bind other HTML elements to XML fields

- How to render HTML markup contained in XML fields

- How to update the cached XML data

Table 10-1 summarizes important information that you'll need as you read the following sections. It lists the HTML elements you can use for single-record data binding—that is, all bindable HTML elements except the TABLE element. For each element, it describes the purpose of the element, indicates the specific property of the element that is bound to the XML field, indicates whether the element can render any HTML markup contained in the XML field that it's bound to, and shows whether the element can update the contents of the XML field. Much of this information won't make sense until you read the following sections, but I include it here for convenient reference.

HTML element	Purpose of element	Bound property (or properties) of the element	Render HTML contained in XML field?	Update bound XML field?
A	Anchor element; indicates the start or destination of a hyperlink	*href*	No	No
APPLET	Adds a Java applet to the page	*param*	No	Yes
BUTTON	Displays a push button control	*innerText* and *innerHTML*	Yes	No
DIV	Used to format a division of a document, such as a chapter, section, or appendix	*innerText* and *innerHTML*	Yes	No

HTML element	Purpose of element	Bound property (or properties) of the element	Render HTML contained in XML field?	Update bound XML field?
FRAME	Contains an individual frame within a frame set	*src*	No	No
IFRAME	Creates an inline floating frame	*src*	No	No
IMG	Displays an image or video clip	*src*	No	No
INPUT TYPE =BUTTON	Displays a push button control in a form	*innerText* and *innerHTML*	Yes	No
INPUT TYPE =CHECKBOX	Displays a check box control in a form	*checked*	No	Yes
INPUT TYPE =HIDDEN	Stores and submits information to the server rather than displaying a control in a form	*value*	No	Yes
INPUT TYPE =PASSWORD	Same as INPUT TYPE=TEXT, but the element displays a series of asterisks (*) rather than the text that the user types	*value*	No	Yes
INPUT TYPE =RADIO	Displays a radio button in a form	*checked*	No	Yes
INPUT TYPE =TEXT	Lets the user enter a single line of text in a form	*value*	No	Yes
LABEL	Displays a text label	*innerText* and *innerHTML*	Yes	No
LEGEND	Displays a caption that labels a group of related controls in a form	*innerText* and *innerHTML*	Yes	No
MARQUEE	Displays scrolling text	*innerText* and *innerHTML*	Yes	No
SELECT	Displays a list box control	*text* property of the selected list item	No	Yes

continued

Data Binding **10**

continued

HTML element	Purpose of element	Bound property (or properties) of the element	Render HTML contained in XML field?	Update bound XML field?
SPAN	Used to format a block of inline text (for example, text within a P [paragraph] or DIV element)	*innerText* and *innerHTML*	Yes	No
TEXTAREA	Lets the user enter multiple lines of text	*value*	No	Yes

Table 10-1 *The bindable HTML elements (not including the TABLE element).*

Binding to Other HTML Elements

As you have seen, when you bind a SPAN element to an XML field, the element simply displays the field's contents. That's because the SPAN element's *innerText* property—which sets the text that the element displays—is bound to the XML field.

> **note**
>
> In DHTML as implemented by Internet Explorer, each HTML element has a set of properties that you can use to set or retrieve various features of the element through script code. Also, as explained in this section, a property is set automatically from the value of an XML field to which it's bound.

However, Table 10-1 shows that with some of the bindable HTML elements, other properties are bound to the XML field.

> **note**
>
> Binding a SPAN element actually binds both its *innerText* and its *innerHTML* properties. The *innerText* property sets or retrieves the text content of an element, without including HTML markup. The *innerHTML* property sets or retrieves the entire content of the element, including any HTML markup.

For example, with a bound A element (an anchor, used to create a hyperlink), such as the following, the *href* property is bound to the XML field:

```
<A DATASRC="#dsoInventory" DATAFLD="REVIEWS">
   Click here for reviews
</A>
```

The *href* property, like the element's HREF attribute, sets the hyperlink's destination URL. Therefore, the bound A element's destination URL, rather than its text content, is derived from the XML field. (The REVIEWS XML field in the example must, of course, contain a valid URL.)

As another example, with a bound check box type of INPUT element, such as the following, the *checked* property—which changes the element's checked status—is bound to the XML field:

```
<INPUT TYPE="CHECKBOX" DATASRC="#dsoInventory" DATAFLD="INSTOCK">
```

If the INSTOCK XML field is empty or if it contains the text *0* or *false*, the check box is cleared. If it contains any other text, the check box is checked.

As a final example, with an IMG (image) element, the *src* property is bound to the XML field. This property, like the element's SRC attribute, specifies the URL of the file containing the graphics data to display. Listings 10-8 and 10-9 illustrate the techniques for binding an IMG element. (You'll find copies of these listings on the companion CD under the filenames Inventory Image.xml and Inventory Image Table.htm. On the CD you'll also find copies of the referenced graphics files Leaves.bmp, Legend.bmp, and Moby.bmp.)

Inventory Image.xml

```xml
<?xml version="1.0"?>

<!-- File Name: Inventory Image.xml -->

<INVENTORY>
   <BOOK>
      <COVERIMAGE>Leaves.bmp</COVERIMAGE>
      <TITLE>Leaves of Grass</TITLE>
      <AUTHOR>Walt Whitman</AUTHOR>
      <BINDING>hardcover</BINDING>
      <PAGES>462</PAGES>
      <PRICE>$7.75</PRICE>
   </BOOK>
   <BOOK>
      <COVERIMAGE>Legend.bmp</COVERIMAGE>
```

```
        <TITLE>The Legend of Sleepy Hollow</TITLE>
        <AUTHOR>Washington Irving</AUTHOR>
        <BINDING>mass market paperback</BINDING>
        <PAGES>98</PAGES>
        <PRICE>$2.95</PRICE>
    </BOOK>
    <BOOK>
        <COVERIMAGE>Moby.bmp</COVERIMAGE>
        <TITLE>Moby-Dick</TITLE>
        <AUTHOR>Herman Melville</AUTHOR>
        <BINDING>hardcover</BINDING>
        <PAGES>724</PAGES>
        <PRICE>$9.95</PRICE>
    </BOOK>
</INVENTORY>
```

Listing 10-8.

Inventory Image Table.htm

```
<!-- File Name: Inventory Image Table.htm -->

<HTML>

<HEAD>
    <TITLE>Book Inventory</TITLE>
</HEAD>

<BODY>

    <XML ID="dsoInventory" SRC="Inventory Image.xml"></XML>

    <H2>Book Inventory</H2>

    <TABLE DATASRC="#dsoInventory" BORDER="1" CELLPADDING="5">
        <THEAD>
            <TH>Cover</TH>
            <TH>Title</TH>
            <TH>Author</TH>
            <TH>Binding</TH>
            <TH>Pages</TH>
            <TH>Price</TH>
        </THEAD>
```

```
<TR ALIGN="center">
    <TD><IMG DATAFLD="COVERIMAGE"></TD>
    <TD><SPAN DATAFLD="TITLE"
        STYLE="font-style:italic"></SPAN></TD>
    <TD><SPAN DATAFLD="AUTHOR"></SPAN></TD>
    <TD><SPAN DATAFLD="BINDING"></SPAN></TD>
    <TD><SPAN DATAFLD="PAGES"></SPAN></TD>
    <TD><SPAN DATAFLD="PRICE"></SPAN></TD>
</TR>
</TABLE>

</BODY>

</HTML>
```

Listing 10-9.

Listing 10-8 is an XML document that contains a field named COVERIMAGE in each BOOK record. Each COVERIMAGE field contains the URL of a graphics file that stores an image of the book's cover. Listing 10-9 is the same HTML page as the one in Listing 10-2, except that at the beginning of each row is an additional cell (TD element) that contains an IMG element rather than a SPAN. The IMG element is bound to the COVERIMAGE field in the XML document, and therefore displays the cover image for each book, as you can see here:

You can experiment with binding some of the other HTML elements listed in Table 10-1 to learn about their bound properties and how the elements use the data in the XML fields to which you bind them.

Rendering HTML

By default, if an XML field's character data happens to include HTML markup, the HTML element bound to that field treats and displays the markup characters as literal text. Consider, for example, the following SPAN element, which is bound to the AUTHOR-BIO XML field:

```
<SPAN DATASRC="#dsoInventory" DATAFLD="AUTHOR-BIO"></SPAN>
```

If the AUTHOR-BIO field contains an italic (I) element, like this:

```
<AUTHOR-BIO>
Henry James was an American author who lived from 1843 to
1916, and wrote &lt;I>The Bostonians&lt;/I> and many other works of
psychologically realistic fiction.
</AUTHOR-BIO>
```

the SPAN element would treat the HTML markup characters as literal text and would display the field as follows:

Henry James was an American author who lived from 1843 to
1916, and wrote <I>The Bostonians</I> and many other works of
psychologically realistic fiction.

With some of the bindable HTML elements, such as SPANs, you can assign the DATAFORMATAS attribute the value HTML to cause the element to process any HTML markup included in the field's text, rather than simply treating it as literal characters. Assume, for example, that you defined the example SPAN element shown previously like this:

```
<SPAN DATASRC="#dsoInventory" DATAFLD="AUTHOR-BIO"
    DATAFORMATAS="HTML"></SPAN>
```

It would then render the text within the I element in italics, like this:

Henry James was an American author who lived from 1843 to 1916, and wrote
The Bostonians and many other works of psychologically realistic fiction.

Note that without the DATAFORMATAS="HTML" attribute specification, Internet Explorer preserves all white space in the XML element's content. With this attribute setting, however, the browser handles white space in the XML element just as it handles white space contained in text within HTML elements in a page. That is, it replaces sequences of white space characters with a single space character, and it discards leading or trailing white space.

> **note**
>
> Assigning DATAFORMATAS its default value, TEXT, has the same effect as simply omitting the attribute—that is, it causes HTML markup characters to be treated as literal text.

To find out which elements you can use to render HTML via the DATAFORMATAS="HTML" attribute setting, see Table 10-1. These elements have a "Yes" in the next-to-last column (labeled "Render HTML contained in XML field?").

Inserting and rendering HTML in XML fields is useful for modifying the formatting of portions of the text (using I or B elements, for example) and for including HTML elements such as hyperlinks in the text. Although formatting XML text by including HTML markup in the XML violates the basic tenet of separating data and formatting, when you use data binding, this technique might be the only feasible way to modify the formatting or include HTML elements within a field. (In contrast, if you use the other methods discussed in this book for displaying XML, you can generally modify formatting or insert elements within an XML element by including child elements and processing them appropriately.)

When you add HTML markup to an XML field, you can't insert a left angle bracket (<) or an ampersand (&) literally in the text. (Recall that these characters are illegal within an element's character data.) However, you can insert them using the predefined entity references < and &. Another option, which makes the HTML more readable to humans and is especially useful for a large block of HTML, is to include the markup within a CDATA section, as discussed in Chapter 4.

> **note**
>
> Another way to include HTML elements in an XML document is to identify the elements using the *html* namespace prefix, and display the document using a cascading style sheet, as discussed in "Inserting HTML Elements into XML Documents" in Chapter 9.

Updating the Cached XML Data

The XML DSO allows you to modify the XML data in several ways. Before you get too excited about this possibility, however, keep in mind that these techniques modify only the copy of the XML data that the DSO has temporarily cached in memory, not the original XML document on the Web server. Unless you use fairly elaborate techniques to update the original server document (which are beyond the scope of this book), updating the cached XML data has limited usefulness, and I've only briefly summarized it here.

You can allow the user to modify a specific XML field by binding to this field an HTML element that allows updating, such as an INPUT element of the TEXT type. The rightmost column in Table 10-1 indicates which HTML elements allow the user to update the XML field the element is bound to. For example, if rather than binding a SPAN to the TITLE field, you bound a TEXT type INPUT element to this field, as shown here, the user could edit, as well as view, the TITLE contents:

```
<INPUT TYPE="TEXT" DATASRC="#dsoInventory" DATAFLD="TITLE">
```

Also, the *recordset* member object of the DSO provides methods that let you add or remove entire records from the cached record set and to cancel modifications to a record. I've summarized these methods in the following table. Note that the example calls in the last column assume that the HTML page contains an XML data island with the ID *dsoInventory*.

DSO *recordset* method	Effect	Example call
addNew	Adds a new record to the cached record set	dsoInventory.recordset.addNew()
delete	Removes the current record from the cached record set	dsoInventory.recordset.delete()
cancelUpdate	Reverses any changes made to the fields of the current record or discards a newly added record	dsoInventory.recordset.cancelUpdate()

Using a DTD with Data Binding

Each of the example documents you've seen so far in this chapter has been a well-formed XML document without a document type definition (DTD). However, if you're going to display an XML document using data binding, including a DTD and making the document valid can help ensure that you conform to the required symmetric record set organization when you define the document's elements. A DTD will also help ensure that the DSO properly constructs its cached record set from the elements in your document.

Including a DTD is especially useful for a document that has the more complex hierarchical type of record structure that you can display using nested tables. An example is the document in Listing 10-5. In the following exercise, you'll add a DTD to this document to make the document valid and to ensure that the document conforms to the record structure required for data binding.

Note that if the XML document you display with data binding contains any validity errors, no data will be displayed in the bound elements, but you won't see an error message. To see a helpful description of any error in the linked XML document, test that document using the DTD validity-testing page presented in "Checking an XML Document for Validity Using a DTD" on page 396.

caution

When you create an element declaration for a record (such as CATEGORY or BOOK in Listing 10-10), you must include a content model that explicitly lists all the record's fields and nested records. You must not use the ANY content specification, which causes data binding to fail.

Create a Valid XML Document for Data Binding

1   In your text editor, open the Inventory Hierarchy.xml document you created earlier in this chapter. (You'll find the document in Listing 10-5 and on the companion CD.)

2   Just above the document element (INVENTORY), type in the following document type declaration:

```
<!DOCTYPE INVENTORY
    [
    <!ELEMENT INVENTORY (CATEGORY*)>
    <!ELEMENT CATEGORY (CATNAME, BOOK*)>
    <!ELEMENT CATNAME (#PCDATA)>
```

```
<!ELEMENT BOOK (TITLE, AUTHOR, BINDING, PAGES, PRICE)>
<!ELEMENT TITLE (#PCDATA)>
<!ELEMENT AUTHOR (#PCDATA)>
<!ELEMENT BINDING (#PCDATA)>
<!ELEMENT PAGES (#PCDATA)>
<!ELEMENT PRICE (#PCDATA)>
]
>
```

These element declarations can be explained, using the language of record sets and data binding, as follows:

- **<!ELEMENT INVENTORY (CATEGORY*)>** The document contains zero or more CATEGORY records.

- **<!ELEMENT CATEGORY (CATNAME, BOOK*)>** Each CATEGORY record contains one CATNAME field, followed by zero or more nested BOOK records.

- **<!ELEMENT BOOK (TITLE, AUTHOR, BINDING, PAGES, PRICE)>** Each nested BOOK record contains exactly one of each of the following fields, in the order listed: TITLE, AUTHOR, BINDING, PAGES, and PRICE.

- **<!ELEMENT TITLE (#PCDATA)> and the remaining declarations** Each of the fields in a BOOK record contains character data only.

3   To reflect the new filename you're going to assign, change the comment at the beginning of the document from:

```
<!-- File Name: Inventory Hierarchy.xml -->
```

to this:

```
<!-- File Name: Inventory Hierarchy Valid.xml -->
```

4   Use your text editor's Save As command to save a copy of the modified document under the filename Inventory Hierarchy Valid.xml.

Listing 10-10 shows the complete XML document. (You'll find a copy of this listing on the companion CD under the filename Inventory Hierarchy Valid.xml.)

Inventory Hierarchy Valid.xml

```
<?xml version="1.0"?>

<!-- File Name: Inventory Hierarchy Valid.xml -->

<!DOCTYPE INVENTORY
    [
```

```
        <!ELEMENT INVENTORY (CATEGORY*)>
        <!ELEMENT CATEGORY (CATNAME, BOOK*)>
        <!ELEMENT CATNAME (#PCDATA)>
        <!ELEMENT BOOK (TITLE, AUTHOR, BINDING, PAGES, PRICE)>
        <!ELEMENT TITLE (#PCDATA)>
        <!ELEMENT AUTHOR (#PCDATA)>
        <!ELEMENT BINDING (#PCDATA)>
        <!ELEMENT PAGES (#PCDATA)>
        <!ELEMENT PRICE (#PCDATA)>
        ]
>

<INVENTORY>
    <CATEGORY>
        <CATNAME>Middle Ages</CATNAME>
        <BOOK>
            <TITLE>The Canterbury Tales</TITLE>
            <AUTHOR>Geoffrey Chaucer</AUTHOR>
            <BINDING>hardcover</BINDING>
            <PAGES>692</PAGES>
            <PRICE>$18.95</PRICE>
        </BOOK>
        <BOOK>
            <TITLE>Piers Plowman</TITLE>
            <AUTHOR>William Langland</AUTHOR>
            <BINDING>trade paperback</BINDING>
            <PAGES>385</PAGES>
            <PRICE>$10.95</PRICE>
        </BOOK>
    </CATEGORY>
    <CATEGORY>
        <CATNAME>Renaissance</CATNAME>
        <BOOK>
            <TITLE>The Blazing World</TITLE>
            <AUTHOR>Margaret Cavendish</AUTHOR>
            <BINDING>trade paperback</BINDING>
            <PAGES>225</PAGES>
            <PRICE>$8.79</PRICE>
        </BOOK>
        <BOOK>
            <TITLE>Oroonoko</TITLE>
            <AUTHOR>Aphra Behn</AUTHOR>
```

```
        <BINDING>mass market paperback</BINDING>
        <PAGES>295</PAGES>
        <PRICE>$4.95</PRICE>
    </BOOK>
    <BOOK>
        <TITLE>Doctor Faustus</TITLE>
        <AUTHOR>Christopher Marlowe</AUTHOR>
        <BINDING>hardcover</BINDING>
        <PAGES>472</PAGES>
        <PRICE>$15.95</PRICE>
    </BOOK>
</CATEGORY>
<CATEGORY>
    <CATNAME>18th Century</CATNAME>
    <BOOK>
        <TITLE>Gulliver's Travels</TITLE>
        <AUTHOR>Jonathan Swift</AUTHOR>
        <BINDING>hardcover</BINDING>
        <PAGES>324</PAGES>
        <PRICE>$11.89</PRICE>
    </BOOK>
    <BOOK>
        <TITLE>The History of Tom Jones: A Foundling</TITLE>
        <AUTHOR>Henry Fielding</AUTHOR>
        <BINDING>hardcover</BINDING>
        <PAGES>438</PAGES>
        <PRICE>$16.95</PRICE>
    </BOOK>
    <BOOK>
        <TITLE>Love in Excess</TITLE>
        <AUTHOR>Eliza Haywood</AUTHOR>
        <BINDING>trade paperback</BINDING>
        <PAGES>429</PAGES>
        <PRICE>$12.95</PRICE>
    </BOOK>
    <BOOK>
        <TITLE>Tristram Shandy</TITLE>
        <AUTHOR>Laurence Sterne</AUTHOR>
        <BINDING>hardcover</BINDING>
        <PAGES>322</PAGES>
        <PRICE>$9.49</PRICE>
    </BOOK>
```

```
    </CATEGORY>
    <CATEGORY>
        <CATNAME>19th Century</CATNAME>
        <BOOK>
            <TITLE>Dracula</TITLE>
            <AUTHOR>Bram Stoker</AUTHOR>
            <BINDING>hardcover</BINDING>
            <PAGES>395</PAGES>
            <PRICE>$17.95</PRICE>
        </BOOK>
        <BOOK>
            <TITLE>Great Expectations</TITLE>
            <AUTHOR>Charles Dickens</AUTHOR>
            <BINDING>mass market paperback</BINDING>
            <PAGES>639</PAGES>
            <PRICE>$6.95</PRICE>
        </BOOK>
        <BOOK>
            <TITLE>Percival Keene</TITLE>
            <AUTHOR>Frederick Marryat</AUTHOR>
            <BINDING>trade paperback</BINDING>
            <PAGES>425</PAGES>
            <PRICE>$12.89</PRICE>
        </BOOK>
        <BOOK>
            <TITLE>Treasure Island</TITLE>
            <AUTHOR>Robert Louis Stevenson</AUTHOR>
            <BINDING>trade paperback</BINDING>
            <PAGES>283</PAGES>
            <PRICE>$11.85</PRICE>
        </BOOK>
        <BOOK>
            <TITLE>Wuthering Heights</TITLE>
            <AUTHOR>Emily Bronte</AUTHOR>
            <BINDING>hardcover</BINDING>
            <PAGES>424</PAGES>
            <PRICE>$12.95</PRICE>
        </BOOK>
    </CATEGORY>
</INVENTORY>
```

Listing 10-10.

5   In your text editor, open the Inventory Hierarchy.htm page you created earlier in this chapter. (You'll find this document in Listing 10-6 and on the companion CD.)

6   Change the SRC attribute of the page's data island so that it links the new XML document you just created. That is, change it from:

```
<XML ID="dsoInventory" SRC="Inventory Hierarchy.xml"></XML>
```

to this:

```
<XML ID="dsoInventory" SRC="Inventory Hierarchy
Valid.xml"></XML>
```

7   To reflect the new filename you're going to assign, change the comment at the beginning of the page from:

```
<!-- File Name: Inventory Hierarchy.htm -->
```

to this:

```
<!-- File Name: Inventory Hierarchy Valid.htm -->
```

8   Use your text editor's Save As command to save a copy of the modified page under the filename Inventory Hierarchy Valid.htm.

Listing 10-11 shows the complete HTML page. (You'll find a copy of this listing on the companion CD under the filename Inventory Hierarchy Valid.htm.)

Inventory Hierarchy Valid.htm

```
<!-- File Name: Inventory Hierarchy Valid.htm -->

<HTML>

<HEAD>
   <TITLE>Inventory of Classic English Literature</TITLE>
</HEAD>

<BODY>

   <XML ID="dsoInventory" SRC="Inventory Hierarchy Valid.xml">
   </XML>

   <TABLE DATASRC="#dsoInventory" BORDER="1">
      <THEAD>
         <TH>Classic English Literature</TH>
      </THEAD>
```

```
<TR>
    <TD><SPAN DATAFLD="CATNAME"></SPAN></TD>
</TR>
<TR>
    <TD>
        <TABLE DATASRC="#dsoInventory" DATAFLD="BOOK"
            BORDER="0" CELLSPACING="10">
            <THEAD>
                <TH WIDTH="25%">Title</TH>
                <TH WIDTH="25%">Author</TH>
                <TH WIDTH="25%">Binding</TH>
                <TH WIDTH="10%">Pages</TH>
                <TH WIDTH="15%">Price</TH>
            </THEAD>
            <TR ALIGN="CENTER">
                <TD WIDTH="25%">
                    <SPAN DATAFLD="TITLE"
                        STYLE="font-style:italic"></SPAN>
                </TD>
                <TD WIDTH="25%">
                    <SPAN DATAFLD="AUTHOR"></SPAN>
                </TD>
                <TD WIDTH="25%">
                    <SPAN DATAFLD="BINDING"></SPAN>
                </TD>
                <TD WIDTH="10%">
                    <SPAN DATAFLD="PAGES"></SPAN>
                </TD>
                <TD WIDTH="15%">
                    <SPAN DATAFLD="PRICE"></SPAN>
                </TD>
            </TR>
        </TABLE>
    </TD>
</TR>
</TABLE>

</BODY>

</HTML>
```

Listing 10-11.

9   Open the page in Internet Explorer.

It should look like this:

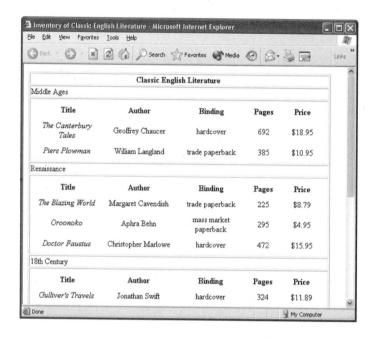

10   If the data doesn't appear, the document must contain a well-formedness or validity error. To locate the error, use the DTD validity-checking page given in "Checking an XML Document for Validity Using a DTD" on page 396.

Binding HTML Elements to XML Attributes

In the example XML documents you've seen so far, none of the elements has included attributes. Attributes add a bit of complexity to data binding, although you can bind to elements that include attributes, as well as to the attributes themselves.

When you use data binding, an attribute is treated essentially as if it were a child element.

With a *record* element, this treatment makes it easy to access (or to simply ignore) an attribute. For example, the following BOOK record contains an attribute named *InStock*:

```
<BOOK InStock="yes">
   <TITLE>The Adventures of Huckleberry Finn</TITLE>
   <AUTHOR>Mark Twain</AUTHOR>
   <BINDING>mass market paperback</BINDING>
```

```
<PAGES>298</PAGES>
<PRICE>$5.49</PRICE>
</BOOK>
```

This record would be treated essentially as if the *InStock* attribute were a field belonging to BOOK, and *InStock*'s value were the content of this field. That is, BOOK would be treated as if it had the following structure:

```
<BOOK>
<InStock>yes</InStock>
<TITLE>The Adventures of Huckleberry Finn</TITLE>
<AUTHOR>Mark Twain</AUTHOR>
<BINDING>mass market paperback</BINDING>
<PAGES>298</PAGES>
<PRICE>$5.49</PRICE>
</BOOK>
```

You could therefore access the attribute value using the usual data binding techniques. For example, the following SPAN element is bound to the attribute and displays its value:

```
<SPAN DATASRC="#dsoInventory" DATAFLD="InStock"></SPAN>
```

(This example assumes that the XML document is linked to the page through a data island with the identifier *dsoInventory*.)

---

note

If a record element has an attribute with the same name as one of the child field elements, in assigning a value to DATAFLD you refer to the child field element by prefacing its name with an exclamation point (!) and you refer to the attribute by using its simple name. For instance, if the BOOK record element in the examples shown in this section had an attribute named PRICE, in addition to the PRICE child element, you would bind to the PRICE child element as in this example:

```
<SPAN DATASRC="#dsoInventory" DATAFLD="!PRICE"></SPAN>

<!-- bind to the element -->
```

And you would bind to the PRICE attribute, as shown in this example:

```
<SPAN DATASRC="#dsoInventory" DATAFLD="PRICE"></SPAN>

<!-- bind to the attribute -->
```

Consider, however, adding an attribute to one of the field elements in an XML document—for example, adding an attribute to the AUTHOR field, as in the following example:

```
<BOOK>
    <TITLE>The Adventures of Huckleberry Finn</TITLE>
    <AUTHOR Born="1835">Mark Twain</AUTHOR>
    <BINDING>mass market paperback</BINDING>
    <PAGES>298</PAGES>
    <PRICE>$5.49</PRICE>
</BOOK>
```

In data binding, the AUTHOR element would be interpreted like this:

```
<AUTHOR><Born>1835</Born>Mark Twain</AUTHOR>
```

As a result, the DSO would store the element as a nested record, not as a field. (Recall that field elements can contain only character data and not child elements.) Therefore, the record set would become a hierarchical record set rather than a simple record set, and you would have to display the nested record using a nested table, as described in the section "Using a Nested Table to Display a Hierarchical Record Set" earlier in the chapter.

You need one more fact, however, to be able to display both the character data (*Mark Twain*) and the attribute of such a nested record: The DSO uses the special name $TEXT to refer to all of the character data within an element, including all text within any child elements but *not* including attribute values. Thus, it would interpret the AUTHOR element as follows:

```
<AUTHOR>
    <Born>1835</Born>
    <$TEXT>Mark Twain</$TEXT>
</AUTHOR>
```

You could use $TEXT as the field name to bind a table cell to the AUTHOR record's character data content.

note

The previous discussion stated that the DSO treats an attribute as if it were a child element. One difference, however, is that $TEXT includes the text of all child elements but *doesn't* include attribute values.

Listing 10-12 contains an HTML page that demonstrates all of the techniques given in this section. (You'll find a copy of this page on the companion CD under the filename Inventory Attribute.htm.) This page displays the Inventory Valid.xml XML document (which you'll find in Listing 5-2 and on the companion CD).

Inventory Attribute.htm

```
<!-- File Name: Inventory Attribute.htm -->

<HTML>

<HEAD>
   <TITLE>Book Inventory</TITLE>
</HEAD>

<BODY>

   <XML ID="dsoInventory" SRC="Inventory Valid.xml"></XML>

   <H2>Book Inventory</H2>

   <TABLE DATASRC="#dsoInventory" BORDER="1" CELLPADDING="5">
      <THEAD>
         <TH>Title</TH>
         <TH>Author</TH>
         <TH>Binding</TH>
         <TH>Pages</TH>
         <TH>Price</TH>
         <TH>In Stock?</TH>
      </THEAD>
      <TR ALIGN="center">
         <TD>
            <TABLE DATASRC="#dsoInventory" DATAFLD="TITLE">
            <TR>
               <TD><SPAN DATAFLD="$TEXT"></SPAN></TD>
            </TR>
            </TABLE>
         </TD>
         <TD>
            <TABLE DATASRC="#dsoInventory" DATAFLD="AUTHOR">
            <TR>
               <TD><SPAN DATAFLD="$TEXT"></SPAN></TD>
               <TD><SPAN DATAFLD="Born"></SPAN></TD>
```

```
            </TR>
          </TABLE>
        </TD>
        <TD><SPAN DATAFLD="BINDING"></SPAN></TD>
        <TD><SPAN DATAFLD="PAGES"></SPAN></TD>
        <TD><SPAN DATAFLD="PRICE"></SPAN></TD>
        <TD><SPAN DATAFLD="InStock"></SPAN></TD>
      </TR>
    </TABLE>

  </BODY>

</HTML>
```

Listing 10-12.

Here's how Internet Explorer displays Listing 10-12:

In this page, the last column of the outer table displays the value of the *InStock* attribute of each BOOK record by simply binding a SPAN element to the attribute, as if the attribute were a field:

```
<TD><SPAN DATAFLD="InStock"></SPAN></TD>
```

Because the AUTHOR child element of BOOK contains an attribute (*Born*), it's interpreted as a nested record rather than as a field, and therefore the page must display it using a nested table:

```
<TD>
   <TABLE DATASRC="#dsoInventory" DATAFLD="AUTHOR">
   <TR>
      <TD><SPAN DATAFLD="$TEXT"></SPAN></TD>
      <TD><SPAN DATAFLD="Born"></SPAN></TD>
   </TR>
   </TABLE>
</TD>
```

The special name $TEXT refers to all of the text within the AUTHOR element, not including the attribute value. This text consists of the author name (for example, Mark Twain).

Note also that because the TITLE element in BOOK *can* include a child element (SUBTITLE), it's also interpreted as a nested record rather than as a field, and must likewise be displayed using a nested table:

```
<TD>
   <TABLE DATASRC="#dsoInventory" DATAFLD="TITLE">
   <TR>
      <TD><SPAN DATAFLD="$TEXT"></SPAN></TD>
   </TR>
   </TABLE>
</TD>
```

Here, $TEXT is used to display all of the record's character data. (There is no way to bind to only the title text without including the subtitle.)

caution

Data binding can become complex if the linked XML file uses namespaces (as discussed in "Using Namespaces" on page 69). You can bind an HTML element to an XML element whose name includes a namespace prefix by simply including the prefix in the DATAFLD value. For instance, if the linked XML document contained an element named *ns:TITLE,* you could bind to it as shown in the following HTML SPAN element:

```
<SPAN DATASRC="#dsoInventory" DATAFLD="ns:TITLE" ></SPAN>
```

The problem, however, is that if an XML document uses namespaces, it must include attributes for declaring those namespaces. And as explained in this section, because the DSO treats attributes essentially like child elements, attributes can significantly change and complicate the structure of the document from the perspective of data binding.

10

Data Binding

Using Scripts with the DSO

The chapter concludes with an example of a more complex script that uses the DSO to work with the associated XML document's record set. The example script uses methods and properties of the DSO *recordset* object to search for books in the Inventory Big.xml document (which you'll find in Listing 10-3 and also on the companion CD). The techniques used to search through and display the XML data are suitable only for an XML document organized as a simple record set. (For a description of a simple record set, see "Using a Single HTML Table to Display a Simple Record Set" on page 302.)

tip

You'll see many more examples of scripts in Chapter 11. The scripts in that chapter use an entirely different programming object (the XML Document Object Model), which lets you work with any type of XML document, not just those structured as record sets.

Listing 10-13 presents the HTML page containing the example script. You'll find it on the companion CD under the filename Inventory Find.htm.

Inventory Find.htm

```
<!-- File Name: Inventory Find.htm -->

<HTML>

<HEAD>

   <TITLE>Book Finder</TITLE>

</HEAD>

<BODY>

   <XML ID="dsoInventory" SRC="Inventory Big.xml"></XML>

   <H2>Find a Book</H2>

   Title text: <INPUT TYPE="TEXT" ID="SearchText"> 
```

```
<BUTTON ONCLICK='FindBooks()'>Search</BUTTON>
<HR>
Results:<P>
<DIV ID=ResultDiv></DIV>

<SCRIPT LANGUAGE="JavaScript">
    function FindBooks ()
        {
        SearchString = SearchText.value.toUpperCase();
        if (SearchString == "")
            {
            ResultDiv.innerHTML = "&ltYou must enter text into "
                            + "'Title text' box.&gt";

            return;
            }

        dsoInventory.recordset.moveFirst();

        ResultHTML = "";
        while (!dsoInventory.recordset.EOF)
            {
            TitleString = dsoInventory.recordset("TITLE").value;

            if (TitleString.toUpperCase().indexOf(SearchString)
                >=0)
                ResultHTML += "<I>"
                            + dsoInventory.recordset("TITLE")
                            + "</I>, "
                            + "<B>"
                            + dsoInventory.recordset("AUTHOR")
                            + "</B>, "
                            + dsoInventory.recordset("BINDING")
                            + ", "
                            + dsoInventory.recordset("PAGES")
                            + " pages, "
                            + dsoInventory.recordset("PRICE")
                            + "<P>";

            dsoInventory.recordset.moveNext();
            }
```

Data Binding

10

```
        if (ResultHTML == "")
            ResultDiv.innerHTML = "&ltno books found&gt";
        else
            ResultDiv.innerHTML = ResultHTML;
        }
    </SCRIPT>

</BODY>

</HTML>
```

Listing 10-13.

The HTML page displays a TEXT type INPUT element, which lets the user enter a single line of search text:

```
<INPUT TYPE="TEXT" ID="SearchText">
```

The page also displays a BUTTON element labeled "Search":

```
<BUTTON ONCLICK='FindBooks()'>Search</BUTTON>
```

When the user clicks the button, the *FindBooks* script function is called, which extracts the search text from the INPUT element, searches the titles of all BOOK records in the XML document for the text, and then displays the matching BOOK records, as shown here:

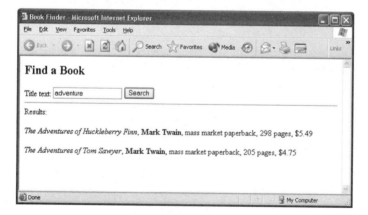

The script function *FindBooks* is contained in its own SCRIPT element and is written in JScript:

```
<SCRIPT LANGUAGE="JavaScript">
   function FindBooks ()
      {
      SearchString = SearchText.value.toUpperCase();
      if (SearchString == "")
         {
         ResultDiv.innerHTML = "&ltYou must enter text into "
                                  + "'Title text' box.&gt";

         return;
         }

      dsoInventory.recordset.moveFirst();

      ResultHTML = "";
      while (!dsoInventory.recordset.EOF)
         {
         TitleString = dsoInventory.recordset("TITLE").value;

         if (TitleString.toUpperCase().indexOf(SearchString)
            >=0)
            ResultHTML += "<I>"
                        + dsoInventory.recordset("TITLE")
                        + "</I>, "
                        + "<B>"
                        + dsoInventory.recordset("AUTHOR")
                        + "</B>, "
                        + dsoInventory.recordset("BINDING")
                        + ", "
                        + dsoInventory.recordset("PAGES")
                        + " pages, "
                        + dsoInventory.recordset("PRICE")
                        + "<P>";

          dsoInventory.recordset.moveNext();
          }

      if (ResultHTML == "")
         ResultDiv.innerHTML = "&ltno books found&gt";
      else
         ResultDiv.innerHTML = ResultHTML;
      }
</SCRIPT>
```

> **tip**
>
> JScript is Microsoft's version of the generic JavaScript scripting language. (In the example SCRIPT block, the LANGUAGE attribute gives the generic language name.) For information on JScript and other Microsoft Web scripting technologies, see the topic "Scripting" in the MSDN Library on the Web at *http://msdn.microsoft.com/library/*.

The *FindBooks* function begins by obtaining the text currently entered into the INPUT element (which has the ID *SearchText*), and then using the JScript method *toUpperCase* to convert the text to uppercase. (*FindBooks* converts all text to uppercase so that the search will be case-insensitive.)

```
SearchString = SearchText.value.toUpperCase();
```

If the user hasn't entered anything into the INPUT, the function displays a message and exits:

```
if (SearchString == "")
   {
   ResultDiv.innerHTML = "&ltYou must enter text into "
                       + "'Title text' box.&gt";
   return;
   }
```

ResultDiv is the ID of a DIV element at the bottom of the page that displays the search results. Assigning text (which can include HTML markup) to its *innerHTML* property causes the DIV to display that text (and to render any HTML markup it contains).

The function then makes the first XML record current, using the *recordset.moveFirst* method that you've seen before:

```
dsoInventory.recordset.moveFirst();
```

Next it blanks the string variable used to store the HTML for the search results (*ResultHTML*):

```
ResultHTML = "";
```

Now *FindBooks* enters a loop that moves through all records in the XML document. It uses the *recordset.EOF* property to stop the loop when end-of-file is reached, and it uses *recordset.moveNext* to move to each new record:

```
while (!dsoInventory.recordset.EOF)
   {
   TitleString = dsoInventory.recordset("TITLE").value;

   if (TitleString.toUpperCase().indexOf(SearchString)
      >=0)
      ResultHTML += "<I>"
                  + dsoInventory.recordset("TITLE")
                  + "</I>, "
                  + "<B>"
                  + dsoInventory.recordset("AUTHOR")
                  + "</B>, "
                  + dsoInventory.recordset("BINDING")
                  + ", "
                  + dsoInventory.recordset("PAGES")
                  + " pages, "
                  + dsoInventory.recordset("PRICE")
                  + "<P>";

   dsoInventory.recordset.moveNext();
   }
```

The loop first obtains the value of the TITLE field in the current record:

```
TitleString = dsoInventory.recordset("TITLE").value;
```

The expression on the right of the equal sign is a shorthand notation for calling the *fields* property of the *recordset* object. Here's the full notation:

```
TitleString = dsoInventory.recordset.fields("TITLE").value;
```

The *fields* property contains a collection of all the fields belonging to the current record. You access a particular field by placing its name in parentheses ("TITLE" in the example), and you obtain the content of this field as a string by appending the *value* property.

The loop then uses the JScript method *indexOf* to determine whether the current record's title contains the search text. If the loop finds the search text, the code inside the *if* statement appends to the *ResultHTML* string the text and HTML markup required to display the current record:

```
if (TitleString.toUpperCase().indexOf(SearchString)
    >=0)
    ResultHTML += "<I>"
              + dsoInventory.recordset("TITLE")
              + "</I>, "
              + "<B>"
              + dsoInventory.recordset("AUTHOR")
              + "</B>, "
              + dsoInventory.recordset("BINDING")
              + ", "
              + dsoInventory.recordset("PAGES")
              + " pages, "
              + dsoInventory.recordset("PRICE")
              + "<P>";
```

Once the loop has exited, the function assigns the HTML markup containing the results to the *innerHTML* property of the DIV element in the BODY of the document that is used to display these results (this DIV element has the identifier *ResultDiv*):

```
if (ResultHTML == "")
    ResultDiv.innerHTML = "&ltno books found&gt";
else
    ResultDiv.innerHTML = ResultHTML;
```

The DIV element immediately renders the HTML markup and displays the results.

Displaying XML Documents Using Document Object Model Scripts

In the previous chapter, you learned about the Data Source Object (DSO) programming model, which lets you use either data binding or a script to display an XML document from within an HTML page. The DSO stores the XML data as a record set, and is thus suitable primarily for displaying those XML documents structured as symmetrical record sets.

In this chapter, you'll learn about an entirely different programming model known as the XML Document Object Model, or DOM. The DOM consists of a set of programming objects that represent the different components of an XML document. The properties and methods of these objects let you use scripts to display the XML document from within an HTML page. Although the DOM requires a bit more work than the DSO (for example, it doesn't allow the simple technique of data binding), it stores the XML data in a hierarchical, treelike data structure that mirrors the hierarchical structure of the XML document. You can thus use the DOM to display any type of XML document—whether or not it's structured as a record set—and you can use it to access any component of an XML document, including elements, attributes, processing instructions, comments, and entity and notation declarations.

note

The W3C uses the term *Document Object Model* or *DOM* to refer to a broader object model that provides access to HTML elements as well as to XML documents. (See "Document Object Model (DOM) Level 1 Specification" at *http://www.w3.org/TR/REC-DOM-Level-1*.) In this book, however, I use the term to refer in particular to the XML DOM provided by Microsoft Internet Explorer, which is tailored specifically to accessing XML documents.

In this chapter, you'll first learn how to link an XML document to an HTML page so that you can access the document using the DOM. You'll then learn about the overall structure of the DOM and the programming objects it provides. The chapter begins presenting the specific DOM programming techniques by showing you how to display a simple XML document with a fixed number of elements. You'll then learn the more general-purpose techniques required to display a document containing an unknown number of elements. After this, you'll learn other ways to access XML elements, as well as the techniques for accessing attributes, entities, and notations. The chapter then gives an exercise in which you'll create a DOM script that you can use to traverse any XML document and to display basic information on each of the document components. The chapter concludes by presenting two HTML page scripts that you can use to check the well-formedness and validity of an XML document using either a document type definition (DTD) or an XML schema.

tip

For further information on the XML DOM as implemented by Internet Explorer, see the topics "DOM Developer's Guide" and "DOM Reference" in the Microsoft XML SDK 4.0 help file, or the same topics in the XML SDK documentation provided by the MSDN (Microsoft Developer Network) Library on the Web at *http://msdn.microsoft.com/library/*.

Linking the XML Document to the HTML Page

To access an XML document using the DOM, you must link the XML document to the HTML page. The easiest way to do this is to insert a data island. Recall that you create a data island by using an HTML element named XML. For example, the following BODY element of an HTML page includes a data island that links the XML document contained in the file Book.xml:

```
<BODY>

    <XML ID="dsoBook" SRC="Book.xml"></XML>

    <!-- other elements in body of page ... -->

</BODY>
```

For more information on data islands, see "The First Step: Linking the XML Document to the HTML Page" in Chapter 10.

As you learned in Chapter 10, the ID that you assign to the data island refers to the document's DSO. You use the *XMLDocument* member of the DSO to access the DOM, as shown in this line of script code:

```
Document = dsoBook.XMLDocument;
```

Specifically, the *XMLDocument* member contains the root object of the DOM, known as the *Document node*. You'll use the Document node to access all the other DOM objects.

Thus, adding a data island to an HTML page causes Internet Explorer to create both a DSO (represented directly by the data island's ID) and a DOM (accessed through the DSO's *XMLDocument* member).

tip

If you want to access more than one XML document from an HTML page, you can insert a data island for each. You can even include more than one data island for a single XML document. (The latter technique might be useful for maintaining several different versions of the XML data if your page modifies the contents of the DOM data cached in memory. This chapter, however, doesn't cover the techniques for modifying DOM data.)

> **note**
>
> When you open an XML document through a data island in an HTML page, Internet Explorer checks the document for well-formedness and also—if the document includes a document type declaration—for validity. If the document contains an error, the DOM nodes will be empty of data and a DOM script will fail in its attempt to display the XML data. However, you won't see a message indicating the specific error in the XML document. To see a helpful description of any well-formedness or validity error in the linked XML document, you can test that document using one of the validity testing pages presented in "Checking an XML Document for Validity" on page 396.

The Structure of the DOM

In the DOM, the programming objects that represent the XML document are known as *nodes*. When Internet Explorer processes a linked XML document and stores it within a DOM, it creates a node for each of the basic components of the XML document, such as the elements, attributes, and processing instructions.

The DOM uses different types of nodes to represent different types of XML components. For example, an element is stored in an Element node and an attribute in an Attribute node. Table 11-1 lists the most important of these node types.

Node type	XML document component that the node object represents	Node name (*nodeName* property)	Node value (*nodeValue* property)
Document	The entire XML document (This is the root node of the DOM node hierarchy. It's used to access all other nodes.)	*#document*	*null*
Element	An element	Element type name (for example, BOOK)	*null* (any character data contained in the element is in one or more child Text nodes)

continued

continued

Node type	XML document component that the node object represents	Node name (*nodeName* property)	Node value (*nodeValue* property)
Text	The text belonging to the element, attribute, or entity declaration represented by this node's parent	*#text*	The parent XML component's text
Attribute	An attribute (as well as other name-value pairs, such as a name and a value in a processing instruction)	Attribute name (for example, *Binding*)	Attribute value (for example, *hardcover*)
ProcessingInstruction	A processing instruction (the XML declaration or other type of processing instruction)	The target of the processing instruction (for example, *xml*)	The entire content of the processing instruction, except the target (for example, *version= "1.0"*)
Comment	A comment	*#comment*	All the text within the comment delimiters
CDATASection	A CDATA section	*#cdata-section*	The content of the CDATA section
DocumentType	The document type declaration	The name of the root element that appears in the DOCTYPE declaration (for example, INVENTORY)	*null*
Entity	An entity declaration in the DTD	The entity name (for example, *image*)	*null* (the value of an internal entity is in a child Text node)
Notation	A notation declaration in the DTD	The notation name (for example, BMP)	*null* (notation's system identifier is in a child Attribute node named SYSTEM)

Table 11-1. *The basic types of nodes used to represent different XML document components. Each of these node types is a programming object that provides properties and methods for accessing the associated component.*

> **note**
>
> In the Microsoft XML DOM documentation (cited in the Tip on page 356), each of the node names listed in the first column of Table 11-1 is prefaced with IXMLDOM—for example, IXMLDOMDocument, IXMLDOMElement, and IXMLDOMText. (These are the names of the programming interfaces for each node type.) Note also that the common node properties and methods (described later in this chapter) are listed under the name IXMLDOMNode.

You can obtain each of the node names (listed in the third column) from the node's *nodeName* property. The names beginning with a # character are standard names for nodes representing XML components not named in the document. (For example, a comment is not given a name in an XML document. Therefore, the DOM uses the standard name *#comment*.) The other node names derive from the names assigned to the corresponding components in the XML document. (For example, the Element node representing an element of type BOOK would also be named BOOK.)

You can obtain each of the node values (listed in the last column) from the node's *nodeValue* property. Notice that for certain types of nodes (namely, Document, Element, DocumentType, Entity, and Notation nodes), *nodeValue* is always set to *null*, indicating that a node of that type doesn't have a value (either because the corresponding document component doesn't have a value, or because the DOM stores the component's value in a child Text or Attribute node). You'll learn more about many of the node types listed in Table 11-1 later in the chapter.

> **note**
>
> For a type of node that has a value, such as an Attribute node, if the corresponding document component contains no text (for instance, an attribute is assigned an empty string), *nodeValue* is set to an empty string, not to *null*.

The DOM organizes the XML document's nodes in a treelike hierarchical structure that mirrors the hierarchical structure of the document itself. It creates a single Document node that represents the entire XML document and serves as the root of this hierarchy. Note that the logical hierarchical structure of the XML elements, of which the document element is the root, is only a branch of the hierarchical structure of DOM nodes, which encompasses the entire document.

Consider, for instance, the example XML document in Listing 11-1. (You'll find a copy of this listing on the companion CD under the filename Inventory Dom.xml.) This document contains an XML declaration, a comment, and a root element that includes child elements as well as attributes. The following figure shows the hierarchical organization of the nodes that the DOM creates to represent this document. For each component of the example document, the figure indicates the type of node used to represent the component (for example, Document, Comment, and Element) as well as the node's name (given in parentheses—for example, *#document*, *#comment*, and INVENTORY).

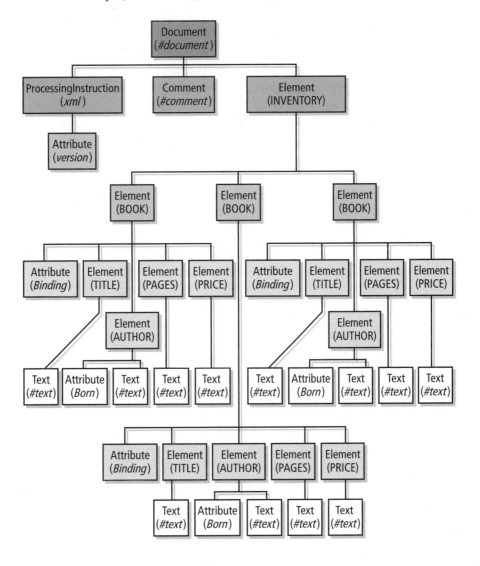

Inventory Dom.xml

```xml
<?xml version="1.0"?>

<!-- File Name: Inventory Dom.xml -->

<INVENTORY>
    <BOOK Binding="mass market paperback">
        <TITLE>The Adventures of Huckleberry Finn</TITLE>
        <AUTHOR Born="1835">Mark Twain</AUTHOR>
        <PAGES>298</PAGES>
        <PRICE>$5.49</PRICE>
    </BOOK>
    <BOOK Binding="trade paperback">
        <TITLE>The Marble Faun</TITLE>
        <AUTHOR Born="1804">Nathaniel Hawthorne</AUTHOR>
        <PAGES>473</PAGES>
        <PRICE>$10.95</PRICE>
    </BOOK>
    <BOOK Binding="hardcover">
        <TITLE>Moby-Dick</TITLE>
        <AUTHOR Born="1819">Herman Melville</AUTHOR>
        <PAGES>724</PAGES>
        <PRICE>$9.95</PRICE>
    </BOOK>
</INVENTORY>
```

Listing 11-1.

Each node, as a programming object, provides properties and methods that let you access, display, manipulate, and obtain information on the corresponding XML component. For example, for some types of nodes the *nodeName* and *nodeValue* properties (shown in Table 11-1) provide the component's name and value.

All types of nodes share a common set of properties and methods. These properties and methods are designed for working with nodes in general. Table 11-2 lists some of the more useful common properties. You'll find more information and examples for many of these properties later in the chapter.

Property	Description	Example
attributes	A NamedNodeMap collection of all this node's Attribute child nodes (or *null* if the node type can't have Attribute children, such as a Document or Comment node)	`AttributeNode =` `Element.attributes.getNamedItem ("Binding");`
childNodes	A NodeList collection of all this node's nonattribute child nodes	`FirstChildNode = Element.childNodes (0);`
dataType	The data type of this node (applies only to certain types of Attribute nodes)	`AttributeType = Attribute.dataType;`
firstChild	This node's first nonattribute child node	`FirstChildNode = Element.firstChild;`
lastChild	This node's last nonattribute child node	`LastChildNode = Element.lastChild;`
nextSibling	The following node at the same level as this node (that is, the following node with the same parent as this node)	`NextElement = Element.nextSibling;`
nodeName	This node's name	`ElementName = Element.nodeName;`
nodeType	A numeric code indicating the type of this node	`NodeTypeCode = Node.nodeType;`
nodeTypeString	A string containing the type of this node, in lowercase (for example, "element" or "attribute")	`NodeTypeString = Node.nodeTypeString;`
nodeValue	The value of this node (or *null* if the node type doesn't have a value, such as a Document or Element node)	`AttributeValue = Attribute.nodeValue;`
ownerDocument	The root Document node of the document containing this node	`Document = Node.ownerDocument;`
parentNode	The node of which this note is a child (always set to *null* for a Document or Attribute node)	`ParentElement = Element.parentNode;`
previousSibling	The previous node at the same level as this node (that is, the previous node with the same parent as this node)	`PreviousElement = Element.previousSibling;`

Document Object Model Scripts 11

continued

continued

Property	Description	Example
text	The entire text content of this node and of all descendent Element nodes	`AllCharacterData = Element.text;`
xml	The entire XML content of this node and all its descendent nodes	`XMLContent = Element.xml;`

Table 11-2. *Useful common properties provided by all node types.*

Besides the common properties and methods, each type of node provides additional properties and methods designed for working with the particular XML component that the node type represents. For example, the Document node provides the *parseError* property, which contains a description of the error status of the document. Only a Document node has this property. Later in the chapter, you'll see tables describing useful node-specific properties and methods for some of the node types discussed.

> **tip**
>
> A property will contain the value *null* if that property doesn't apply to the particular node. For example, if a node represents a type of XML component that can't have attributes (such as a Document or Comment node) its *attributes* property will be *null*. If a node represents a type of XML component that doesn't have a data type (only certain attributes have a data type), its *dataType* property will be *null*. If a node doesn't have a nonattribute child node, its *firstChild* property will be *null*. And if the node is of a type that doesn't have values (such as a Document or Element node), its *nodeValue* property will be *null*.

Notice in Table 11-2 that every node has a set of properties that allow you to navigate through the node hierarchy—that is, to access other nodes from the current node. For instance, with the document in Listing 11-1, if the variable *Document* contains the root Document node, the following code would display the content of the comment near the beginning of the document, which the DOM stores as the second child node of the Document node:

```
alert (Document.childNodes(1).nodeValue);
```

This line would display a message box containing the text "File Name: Inventory Dom.xml". (This code is explained later in the chapter.)

In the previous section, you saw how to access the root Document node through the *XMLDocument* member of the DSO obtained from the XML data island. The Document node is the gateway to the XML document. You use it to access all other nodes. In the following sections, you'll learn the specific ways to access nodes.

Accessing and Displaying XML Document Elements

In this section, you'll learn the basic techniques for using an HTML page and the DOM to display the contents of an XML document's elements. Listings 11-2 and 11-3 demonstrate these techniques. (You'll find copies of these listings on the companion CD under the filenames Book.xml and DomDemo Fixed.htm.)

Book.xml

```
<?xml version="1.0"?>

<!-- File Name: Book.xml -->

<BOOK>
    <TITLE>The Adventures of Huckleberry Finn</TITLE>
    <AUTHOR>Mark Twain</AUTHOR>
    <BINDING>mass market paperback</BINDING>
    <PAGES>298</PAGES>
    <PRICE>$5.49</PRICE>
</BOOK>
```

Listing 11-2.

DomDemo Fixed.htm

```
<!-- File Name: DomDemo Fixed.htm -->

<HTML>

<HEAD>

    <TITLE>Book Description</TITLE>

    <SCRIPT LANGUAGE="JavaScript" FOR="window" EVENT="ONLOAD">
        Document = dsoBook.XMLDocument;
        title.innerText=
            Document.documentElement.childNodes(0).text;
```

```
      author.innerText=
          Document.documentElement.childNodes(1).text;
      binding.innerText=
          Document.documentElement.childNodes(2).text;
      pages.innerText=
          Document.documentElement.childNodes(3).text;
      price.innerText=
          Document.documentElement.childNodes(4).text;
  </SCRIPT>

</HEAD>

<BODY>

  <XML ID="dsoBook" SRC="Book.xml"></XML>

  <H2>Book Description</H2>

  <SPAN STYLE="font-style:italic">Title: </SPAN>
  <SPAN ID="title" STYLE="font-weight:bold"></SPAN>
  <BR>
  <SPAN STYLE="font-style:italic">Author: </SPAN>
  <SPAN ID="author"></SPAN>
  <BR>
  <SPAN STYLE="font-style:italic">Binding: </SPAN>
  <SPAN ID="binding"></SPAN>
  <BR>
  <SPAN STYLE="font-style:italic">Number of pages: </SPAN>
  <SPAN ID="pages"></SPAN>
  <BR>
  <SPAN STYLE="font-style:italic">Price: </SPAN>
  <SPAN ID="price"></SPAN>

</BODY>

</HTML>
```

Listing 11-3.

Listing 11-2 contains a simple XML document that describes a single book. Its root element, BOOK, contains five child elements (TITLE, AUTHOR, BINDING, PAGES, and PRICE), each containing character data describing one feature of the book.

Listing 11-3 contains an HTML page that displays the content of each of the child elements in the XML document. Here's how this page looks in Internet Explorer:

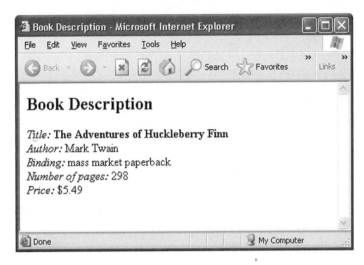

The XML document is linked to the page through the following data island:

```
<XML ID="dsoBook" SRC="Book.xml"></XML>
```

The page displays the XML document by means of the following block of script code, which is contained in the page's HEAD element:

```
<SCRIPT LANGUAGE="JavaScript" FOR="window" EVENT="ONLOAD">
    Document = dsoBook.XMLDocument;
    title.innerText=
        Document.documentElement.childNodes(0).text;
    author.innerText=
        Document.documentElement.childNodes(1).text;
    binding.innerText=
        Document.documentElement.childNodes(2).text;
    pages.innerText=
        Document.documentElement.childNodes(3).text;
    price.innerText=
        Document.documentElement.childNodes(4).text;
</SCRIPT>
```

The *FOR="window"* and *EVENT="ONLOAD"* attribute specifications cause the browser to execute the code in the SCRIPT element when it first opens the window for the page, before it displays the contents of the page.

The script first obtains the Document node that represents the entire document and that forms the root of the hierarchy of the DOM nodes. It does this by using the DSO member *XMLDocument*, as described previously in the chapter:

```
Document = dsoBook.XMLDocument;
```

The script then accesses and displays the character data contained in each of the child elements of the root element (TITLE, AUTHOR, BINDING, PAGES, and PRICE). For example, it displays contents of the first child element (TITLE), as follows:

```
title.innerText=
    Document.documentElement.childNodes(0).text;
```

Here's a part-by-part explanation of the expression on the right side of the equal sign:

- *Document* contains the Document node at the root of the DOM node hierarchy.

- *documentElement* is a property of the Document node. It contains an Element node representing the root element of the XML document—in this example, BOOK.

note

The *documentElement* property is one of the node-specific properties provided by a Document type node. Table 11-3 lists some other useful properties, as well as methods, provided specifically by Document nodes. Keep in mind that with a Document node you can also use any of the common node properties listed in Table 11-2.

■ *childNodes* is a property of the Element node for the root element. It contains a collection of all the nonattribute child nodes of the root Element node. In this example, it contains the Element nodes for the five child XML elements: TITLE, AUTHOR, BINDING, PAGES, and PRICE. The expression *childNodes(0)* references the first of these child nodes (the one for the TITLE element).

note

In the example page (Listing 11-3), you *could* use the expression *Document.childNodes(2)* to obtain the Element node for the root element. (*Document.childNodes(0)* is the node for the XML declaration and *Document.childNodes(1)* is the node for the comment.) However, an advantage of using the Document node's *documentElement* property is that its value doesn't depend on the position of the root element within the XML document. For example, if you were to remove the comment at the beginning of the document, or if you were to add a document type declaration, *Document.childNodes(2)* would no longer represent the root element.

■ *text* is a property of the Element node returned by *childNodes(0)*. It provides the complete text content of this node as well as the text belonging to any descendent Element nodes it might have. In this example, TITLE has no descendent elements, so *text* contains only TITLE's own text, *The Adventures of Huckleberry Finn*.

note

The *childNodes* and *text* properties are among the common node properties given in Table 11-2.

Document node property	Description	Example
async	Assigning *false* to the *async* property causes a subsequent call to the *load* method (described later in the table) to load the XML document synchronously (that is, the call won't return until the document is fully loaded). The default property value is *true*.	`Document.async = false;`
doctype	The DocumentType node representing the document type declaration	`DocumentType = Document.doctype;`
documentElement	The Element node representing the root element of the XML document	`RootElement = Document.documentElement;`

parseError	An object that contains information on the first well-formedness or validity error that the processor encountered when it loaded and processed the XML document, or a code indicating that the document is error-free	`ErrorCode =`
		`Document.parseError.errorCode;`
		`if (ErrorCode ! = 0)`
		`    /* report and handle error...*/`
		`else`
		`    /* document is error-free */`

schemas	If you assign an XML SchemaCache object to this property, the document will be validated against the associated XML schema when the *load* method (described later in the table) is subsequently called.	`XMLSchemaCache = new ActiveXObject`
		`    ("Msxml2.XML SchemaCache.4.0");`
		`XMLSchemaCache.add`
		`    (XMLNamespaceName,`
		`    "Book Schema.xsd");`
		`Document.schemas = XMLSchemaCache;`

url	The URL of the XML document	`URL = Document.url;`

Document node method	Description	Example
getElementsByTagName (type-name)	Returns a NodeList collection of all elements in the document that have the specified type name. If you pass "*", it returns all elements.	`AuthorElementCollection =` `Document.getElementsByTagName("AUTHOR");`
nodeFromID (id-value)	Returns the node representing the element whose ID type attribute has the value that you pass. (For information on ID attributes, see "Specifying a Tokenized Type" in Chapter 5.)	`Element =` `Document.nodeFromID ("S021");`

Table 11-3. *Useful properties and methods provided by Document nodes. The available properties also include the common node properties listed in Table 11-2.*

The TITLE element's character data that derives from the expression on the right side of the equal sign (*The Adventures of Huckleberry Finn*) is assigned to the *innerText* property of the HTML SPAN element that has the identifier *title*:

```
title.innerText=
    Document.documentElement.childNodes(0).text;
```

This SPAN element is defined within the BODY of the HTML page, as follows:

```
<SPAN ID="title" STYLE="font-weight:bold"></SPAN>
```

Assigning the character data to the SPAN's *innerText* property causes the SPAN to display that text, using the cascading style sheet property setting defined within its start-tag (*font-weight:bold*).

> **tip**
>
> In the Dynamic HTML (DHTML) model supported by Internet Explorer, each HTML element has a set of properties that you can use to set or retrieve various features of the element through script code. The *innerText* property sets or retrieves the text content of an HTML element. For information on working with DHTML as implemented in Internet Explorer, see the topic "HTML and Dynamic HTML" in the MSDN Library on the Web at *http://msdn.microsoft.com/library/*.

Document Object Model Scripts 11

Using a NodeList Object

As I explained earlier in the chapter, the *childNodes* node property contains a collection of the current node's nonattribute child nodes. (As you'll learn later, you access attribute child nodes through the node's *attributes* property.) The specific type of collection that *childNodes* contains is known as a NodeList object.

To extract a specific child node from a NodeList object, you can call its *item* method, passing it the 0-based index of the child node you want to retrieve. For example, the following method call obtains the first child node belonging to *Element*:

```
FirstNode = Element.childNodes.item(0);
```

However, because *item* is the default method for a NodeList object, you can omit it, as you've seen in previous examples in this chapter:

```
FirstNode = Element.childNodes(0);
```

Table 11-4 lists the property and the methods provided by a NodeList object.

NodeList property	Description	Example
length	The number of nodes contained in the collection	`NodeCount = Element.childNodes.length;`

NodeList method	Description	Example
item (0-based-index) (default method)	Returns the node at the position indicated by the index you pass, where 0 indicates the first node	`SecondChild = Element.childNodes.item (1);` or `SecondChild = Element.childNodes (1);`
reset ()	Sets the internal pointer to the position before the first node in the collection, so the next call to *nextNode* returns the first node	`Element.childNodes.reset ();`
nextNode ()	Returns the next node in the collection, as marked by the internal pointer	`Element.childNodes.reset (); FirstNode = Element.childNodes.nextNode ();`

Table 11-4. *The property and methods provided by a NodeList collection object. A NodeList object is supplied by the* childNodes *node property.*

Retrieving an Element's Character Data

The script in Listing 11-3 used the *text* property of each child element (TITLE, AUTHOR, BINDING, PAGES, and PRICE) as a shortcut for obtaining the element's character data. For instance, here's the statement used to retrieve the character data of the TITLE element:

```
title.innerText=
    Document.documentElement.childNodes(0).text;
```

The *text* property provides the text content of the element represented by the current node, plus the text content of any descendent elements. It works fine for extracting an element's character data if the element has no child elements (such as TITLE). However, if the element contains one or more child elements as well as character data, as in the following example, the *text* property returns all the text (in this example, "Moby-Dick Or, The Whale").

```
<TITLE>Moby-Dick <SUBTITLE>Or, The Whale</SUBTITLE></TITLE>
```

To obtain only the character data of the TITLE element, you need to access its child Text node.

Recall from Table 11-1 that an Element node's *nodeValue* property is always set to *null*. If the element contains character data, this text is stored in a child Text node and you can obtain it from the Text node's *nodeValue* property. For example, if *Element* contains the node for the "Moby-Dick" TITLE element shown in the preceding example, the following expression would supply TITLE's character data (*Moby-Dick*) without including the character data belonging to SUBTITLE:

```
Element.firstChild.nodeValue
```

(Because TITLE's character data comes before its subelement, it is represented by the first child node and you can therefore retrieve it using the *firstChild* property.)

If an element's character data is interspersed with child elements, comments, or processing instructions, each separate block of character data is represented by its own child Text node. For instance, the following ITEM element would have three child nodes that would occur in this order: a Text node representing the first block of character data, an Element node representing the child element SUB-ITEM, and another Text node representing the second block of character data.

```
<ITEM>
    character data block 1
    <SUB-ITEM>sub-item text</SUB-ITEM>
    character data block 2
</ITEM>
```

Table 11-5 lists a useful property and method provided by Text nodes.

Text node property	Description	Example
length	The number of characters in the node's text	`CharacterCount = Text.length;`

Text node method	Description	Example
substringData (char-offset, num-chars)	Returns a string containing the specified number of characters from the node's text content, starting at the specified character offset	`SubString = Text.substringData (2, 3);` (Returns the third, fourth, and fifth characters from the Text element's content)

Table 11-5. *A useful property and method provided by Text nodes. The available properties also include the common node properties listed in Table 11-2.*

Displaying a Variable Number of XML Elements

So far, you've learned how to display an XML document that has a known number of elements. If a document has an unknown number of elements, using the DOM to display it is a bit more complex.

For example, with an XML document such as Inventory.xml (given in Listing 10-1 and on the companion CD) or Inventory Big.xml (given in Listing 10-3 and on the companion CD), you generally would not know in advance how many BOOK elements the document contains. And if the number of BOOK elements changes, you of course would like your script to keep working.

Listing 11-4 presents an HTML page that uses the DOM to display Inventory.xml in a way that is independent of the number of BOOK elements contained in the document. (You'll find this listing on the companion CD under the filename DomDemo Variable.htm.) Here's how the page looks in Internet Explorer:

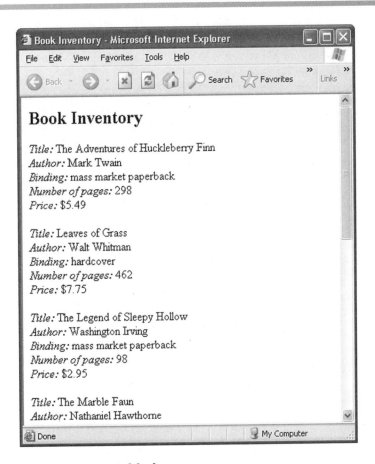

DomDemo Variable.htm

```
<!-- File Name: DomDemo Variable.htm -->

<HTML>

<HEAD>

    <TITLE>Book Inventory</TITLE>

    <SCRIPT LANGUAGE="JavaScript" FOR="window" EVENT="ONLOAD">
        HTMLCode = "";
        Document = dsoInventory.XMLDocument;

        for (i=0;
             i < Document.documentElement.childNodes.length;
             i++)
        {
```

```
        HTMLCode +=
        "<SPAN STYLE='font-style:italic'>Title: </SPAN>"
        + Document.documentElement.childNodes(i).childNodes(0).text
        + "<BR>"
        + "<SPAN STYLE='font-style:italic'>Author: </SPAN>"
        + Document.documentElement.childNodes(i).childNodes(1).text
        + "<BR>"
        + "<SPAN STYLE='font-style:italic'>Binding: </SPAN>"
        + Document.documentElement.childNodes(i).childNodes(2).text
        + "<BR>"
        + "<SPAN STYLE='font-style:italic'>Number of pages: "
        + "</SPAN>"
        + Document.documentElement.childNodes(i).childNodes(3).text
        + "<BR>"
        + "<SPAN STYLE='font-style:italic'>Price: </SPAN>"
        + Document.documentElement.childNodes(i).childNodes(4).text
        + "<P>";
        }

        DisplayDIV.innerHTML=HTMLCode;
    </SCRIPT>

</HEAD>

<BODY>

    <XML ID="dsoInventory" SRC="Inventory.xml"></XML>

    <H2>Book Inventory</H2>

    <DIV ID="DisplayDIV"></DIV>

</BODY>

</HTML>
```

Listing 11-4.

The script in the example page uses the *length* property to determine the number of BOOK elements contained within the root element. (The *length* property is a member of the NodeList collection object provided by the *childNodes* property of the root element node. See Table 11-4.) The script contains a *for* loop that is executed once for each BOOK element and includes the code to display each of these elements:

```
for (i=0;
     i < Document.documentElement.childNodes.length;
     i++)
{
/* code to display a BOOK element... */
}
```

Because the number of BOOK elements is unknown, the page can't use a fixed set of SPAN elements in its BODY to display the data (as did the previous example page in Listing 11-3). Rather, for each BOOK element, the script dynamically generates the entire block of HTML markup necessary to display the element:

```
for (i=0;
     i < Document.documentElement.childNodes.length;
     i++)
{
HTMLCode +=
"<SPAN STYLE='font-style:italic'>Title: </SPAN>"
+ Document.documentElement.childNodes(i).childNodes(0).text
+ "<BR>"
+ "<SPAN STYLE='font-style:italic'>Author: </SPAN>"
+ Document.documentElement.childNodes(i).childNodes(1).text
+ "<BR>"
+ "<SPAN STYLE='font-style:italic'>Binding: </SPAN>"
+ Document.documentElement.childNodes(i).childNodes(2).text
+ "<BR>"
+ "<SPAN STYLE='font-style:italic'>Number of pages: "
+ "</SPAN>"
+ Document.documentElement.childNodes(i).childNodes(3).text
+ "<BR>"
+ "<SPAN STYLE='font-style:italic'>Price: </SPAN>"
+ Document.documentElement.childNodes(i).childNodes(4).text
+ "<P>";
}
```

The script stores all of these blocks of HTML markup in the variable *HTMLCode*. After the *for* loop, when all blocks have been generated and stored in *HTMLCode*, the script assigns the HTML markup to the *innerHTML* property of the DIV element in the BODY of the page (this element has the ID *DisplayDIV*):

```
DisplayDIV.innerHTML=HTMLCode;
```

The DIV element then immediately renders the HTML and displays the results, which you saw in the previous figure.

To convince yourself that the page works regardless of the number of BOOK elements the XML document contains, you might edit the data island in this page so that it displays Inventory Big.xml, which contains twice as many BOOK elements as Inventory.xml:

```
<XML ID="dsoInventory" SRC="Inventory Big.xml"></XML>
```

Using Other Ways to Access Elements

The example scripts you've seen so far have accessed Element nodes by traversing the node hierarchy using the *childNodes* or the *firstChild* node property to move from one node to an adjoining node. Keep in mind that you can use the *lastChild*, *previousSibling*, *nextSibling*, and *parentNode* node properties in analogous ways. Table 11-2 describes all these properties.

> **note**
>
> The *childNodes*, *firstChild*, and *lastChild* properties allow you to access only nonattribute child nodes, while the *previousSibling* and *nextSibling* properties let you access any type of sibling node. For a Document or Attribute node, the *parentNode* property is always set to *null*.

Another way to access XML elements is to use the *getElementsByTagName* property to extract all elements that have a particular type name (such as TITLE). This method is available for a Document node, as described in Table 11-3, as well as for an Element node, as described in Table 11-6. If you call the method for a Document node, it returns a collection of Element nodes for all elements in the document that have the specified type name. For example, the following statement obtains a collection of nodes for all elements in the document that have the name BOOK:

```
NodeList = Document.getElementsByTagName("BOOK");
```

If you call *getElementsByTagName* for an Element node, as shown in the following example, it returns a collection of nodes for all matching elements that are descendents of the Element node:

```
NodeList = Element.getElementsByTagName("AUTHOR");
```

tip

If you pass the value "*" to *getElementsByTagName*, it returns a collection of nodes for all elements (all elements in the document if you call the method for a Document node and all descendent elements if you call it for an Element node).

Element node method	Description	Example
getAttribute (attr-name)	Returns the value of the element's attribute that has the specified name.	```AttValue = Element.getAttribute ("InStock");```
getAttributeNode (attr-name)	Returns the Attribute node representing the element's attribute that has the specified name.	```Attribute = Element.getAttributeNode ("InStock");```
getElementsByTagName (type-name)	Returns a NodeList collection of Element nodes for all of this element's descendent elements that have the specified type name. If you pass "*", it returns nodes for all descendent elements.	```AuthorElementCollection = Element.getElementsByTagName ("AUTHOR");```

Table 11-6. *Useful methods provided by Element nodes. With Element nodes you can also use any of the common node properties listed in Table 11-2.*

note

If the type name of the elements you want to retrieve includes a namespace prefix, you'll need to include that prefix in the value you pass to *getElementsByTagName*, as in the following example:

```
NodeList = Document.getElementsByTagName("inventory:BOOK");
```
For information on namespaces, see "Using Namespaces" on page 69.

The *getElementsByTagName* method supplies the Element nodes in the form of a NodeList collection object. You can therefore access the individual nodes using any of the techniques discussed in "Using a NodeList Object" on page

372. For example, the following script code displays (in an "alert" message box) the text content of all Element nodes in the NodeList object returned by *getElementsByTagName*:

```
for (i=0; i < NodeList.length; ++i)
   alert (NodeList(i).text);
```

The HTML page in Listing 11-5 demonstrates the use of the *getElementsByTagName* method for the Document node. (You'll find a copy of this listing on the companion CD under the filename GetElements.htm.) The page displays a TEXT type INPUT control that lets you enter an element name. When you click the Show Elements button, the *ShowElements* script function uses the *getElementsByTagName* method for the Document node to find and display the XML markup for all elements in the document that have the element name you entered (if there are any). Note that the script uses the *xml* property of each Element node to display the element's XML markup content. The page is initially linked to the Inventory.xml document, although you can edit the data island in order to display elements within another XML document. Here's how Internet Explorer displays the page after you enter AUTHOR into the INPUT control and click the button:

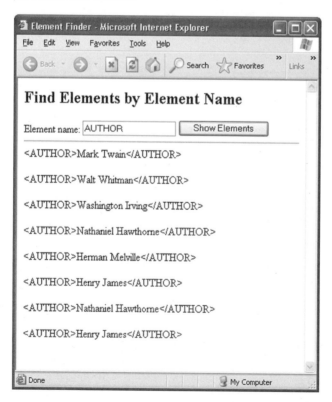

GetElements.htm

```
<!-- File Name: GetElements.htm -->

<HTML>

<HEAD>

    <TITLE>Element Finder</TITLE>

    <SCRIPT LANGUAGE="JavaScript">
        function ShowElements()
            {
            /* make sure user has entered text into the
                'Element name' box: */
            if (ElementName.value == "")
                {
                ResultDiv.innerText = "<You must enter an element "
                    + "name into 'Element name' box.>";
                return;
                }

            /* get a NodeList collection of all matching Element
                nodes in the document: */
            Document = dsoXML.XMLDocument;
            NodeList =
                Document.getElementsByTagName (ElementName.value);

            /* store the XML markup for each Element node
                in ResultHTML: */
            ResultHTML = "";
            for (i=0; i < NodeList.length; ++i)
                ResultHTML += NodeList(i).xml + "\n\n";

            /* assign the stored results to the innerText property
                of the DIV: */
            if (ResultHTML == "")
                ResultDiv.innerText = "<no matching elements found>";
            else
                ResultDiv.innerText = ResultHTML;
            }
```

```
        </SCRIPT>

    </HEAD>

    <BODY>

        <XML ID="dsoXML" SRC="Inventory.xml"></XML>

        <H2>Find Elements by Element Name</H2>
        Element name: <INPUT TYPE="TEXT" ID="ElementName"> 
        <BUTTON ONCLICK="ShowElements()">Show Elements</BUTTON>
        <HR>
        <DIV ID=ResultDiv></DIV>

    </BODY>

</HTML>
```

Listing 11-5.

Accessing and Displaying XML Document Attribute Values

An attribute contained in an XML element is represented by a child Attribute node. However, you can't access child Attribute nodes using the *childNodes*, *firstChild*, or *lastChild* Element node property, which you can use to access other types of child nodes. Rather, you must use the *attributes* property of the Element node.

> **note**
>
> The DOM uses Attribute nodes to represent not only attributes, but also several other types of XML components that consist of name-value pairs—namely:
>
> - A name and a value in a processing instruction (such as *version="1.0"* in the XML declaration)
>
> - The keyword SYSTEM followed by a system identifier in a document type declaration, external entity declaration, or notation declaration
>
> - The keyword NDATA followed by a notation name in an unparsed entity declaration

Consider the example XML document in Listing 11-6. (You'll find a copy of this listing on the companion CD under the filename Inventory Attributes.xml.)

Inventory Attributes.xml

```
<?xml version="1.0"?>

<!-- File Name: Inventory Attributes.xml -->

<INVENTORY>
    <BOOK Binding="mass market paperback" InStock="yes"
        Review="***">
        <TITLE>The Adventures of Huckleberry Finn</TITLE>
        <AUTHOR Born="1835">Mark Twain</AUTHOR>
        <PAGES>298</PAGES>
        <PRICE>$5.49</PRICE>
    </BOOK>
    <BOOK Binding="hardcover" InStock="no">
        <TITLE>Leaves of Grass</TITLE>
        <AUTHOR Born="1819">Walt Whitman</AUTHOR>
        <PAGES>462</PAGES>
        <PRICE>$7.75</PRICE>
    </BOOK>
    <BOOK Binding="mass market paperback" InStock="yes"
        Review="****">
        <TITLE>The Legend of Sleepy Hollow</TITLE>
        <AUTHOR>Washington Irving</AUTHOR>
        <PAGES>98</PAGES>
        <PRICE>$2.95</PRICE>
    </BOOK>
</INVENTORY>
```

Listing 11-6.

The BOOK elements in this document each have either two or three attributes. The following script expression obtains the Element node for the first BOOK element:

```
Document.documentElement.childNodes(0)
```

(This and the following examples in this section assume that *Document* contains the Document node for the XML document.)

The *attributes* property of this Element node provides a NamedNodeMap collection of Attribute nodes for all attributes belonging to the first BOOK element:

```
NamedNodeMap = Document.documentElement.childNodes(0).attributes
```

A NamedNodeMap collection object is somewhat different from a NodeList collection object supplied by the *childNodes* node property. Table 11-7 lists the property and some of the useful methods provided by NamedNodeMap objects.

NamedNodeMap property	Description	Example
length	The number of nodes contained in the collection	`AttributeCount = Element.attributes.length;`

NamedNodeMap method	Description	Example
getNamedItem (att-name)	Returns the node that has the specified name, or *null* if the attribute isn't found	`Attribute = Element.attributes.getNamedItem ("Binding");`
item (0-based-index) (default method)	Returns the node at the position indicated by the index, where 0 indicates the first node	`SecondAttribute = Element.attributes.item (1);` or `SecondAttribute = Element.attributes (1);`
reset ()	Sets the internal pointer to the position before the first node in the collection, so the next call to *nextNode* returns the first node	`Element.attributes.reset ();`
nextNode ()	Returns the next node in the collection, as marked by the internal pointer	`Element.attributes.reset (); FirstAttribute = Element.attributes.nextNode ();`

Table 11-7. *The property and some useful methods provided by NamedNodeMap collection objects. A NamedNodeMap object is supplied by the* attributes *node property.*

You can use the NamedNodeMap object's *length* property and its default *item* method to traverse the collection and extract the individual Attribute nodes. For instance, the following script code displays the name and value of each attribute in the first BOOK element of the example document:

```
NamedNodeMap = Document.documentElement.childNodes(0).attributes;
for (i=0; i<NamedNodeMap.length; ++i)
```

```
alert ("node name: " + NamedNodeMap(i).nodeName + "\n"
    + "node value: " + NamedNodeMap(i).nodeValue);
```

Each name-value pair is displayed in an "alert" message box. Here's how the first one looks:

Notice that the *nodeName* property of an Attribute node contains the attribute name, while the *nodeValue* property contains the attribute value.

note

An Attribute node actually has a child Text node that contains the attribute's value. However, this node is unnecessary because you can easily obtain the attribute's value directly from the Attribute node's *nodeValue* property. Consequently, I've ignored this type of child Text node in this chapter.

You can also retrieve a specific Attribute node from a NamedNodeMap object by calling the NamedNodeMap's *getNamedItem* method. For instance, the following script code displays the value of the *Binding* attribute in the first BOOK element of the example document:

```
NamedNodeMap = Document.documentElement.childNodes(0).attributes;
Attribute = NamedNodeMap.getNamedItem("Binding");
if (Attribute == null)
    alert ("attribute not found");
else
    alert (Attribute.nodeValue);
```

Here's the resulting "alert" message box:

Accessing XML Entities and Notations

As I explained in Chapter 6, you use an unparsed entity declaration to incorporate an external data file into an XML document. (All unparsed entities are of the general external type.) The way you use an unparsed entity is to assign its name to an attribute that has the ENTITY or ENTITIES type, as a means of associating the external entity file with a particular XML element. The XML processor doesn't access an unparsed entity file. Rather, it merely makes the description of the entity and its notation available to the application, which can obtain and use the information appropriately.

This section presents an XML document and an HTML page that demonstrate the basic steps for using the DOM to extract from an XML document the information on an entity as well as the notation that describes the entity's format. Listing 11-7 contains the example XML document and Listing 11-8 contains the example HTML page. (You'll find copies of these two listings on the companion CD under the filenames Inventory Entity.xml and Inventory Entity.htm.)

Inventory Entity.xml

```
<?xml version="1.0"?>

<!-- File Name: Inventory Entity.xml -->

<!DOCTYPE INVENTORY
    [
    <!NOTATION TXT SYSTEM "plain text file">
    <!ENTITY rev_huck SYSTEM "Review of Huckleberry Finn.txt"
        NDATA TXT>
    <!ENTITY rev_leaves SYSTEM "Review of Leaves of Grass.txt"
        NDATA TXT>
    <!ENTITY rev_legend SYSTEM "Review of Sleepy Hollow.txt"
        NDATA TXT>

    <!ELEMENT INVENTORY (BOOK)*>
    <!ELEMENT BOOK (TITLE, AUTHOR, BINDING, PAGES, PRICE)>
    <!ATTLIST BOOK    Review ENTITY #IMPLIED>
    <!ELEMENT TITLE (#PCDATA)>
    <!ELEMENT AUTHOR (#PCDATA)>
    <!ELEMENT BINDING (#PCDATA)>
    <!ELEMENT PAGES (#PCDATA)>
    <!ELEMENT PRICE (#PCDATA)>
    ]
>
```

```
<INVENTORY>
   <BOOK Review="rev_huck">
      <TITLE>The Adventures of Huckleberry Finn</TITLE>
      <AUTHOR>Mark Twain</AUTHOR>
      <BINDING>mass market paperback</BINDING>
      <PAGES>298</PAGES>
      <PRICE>$5.49</PRICE>
   </BOOK>
   <BOOK Review="rev_leaves">
      <TITLE>Leaves of Grass</TITLE>
      <AUTHOR>Walt Whitman</AUTHOR>
      <BINDING>hardcover</BINDING>
      <PAGES>462</PAGES>
      <PRICE>$7.75</PRICE>
   </BOOK>
   <BOOK Review="rev_legend">
      <TITLE>The Legend of Sleepy Hollow</TITLE>
      <AUTHOR>Washington Irving</AUTHOR>
      <BINDING>mass market paperback</BINDING>
      <PAGES>98</PAGES>
      <PRICE>$2.95</PRICE>
   </BOOK>
</INVENTORY>
```

Listing 11-7.
Inventory Entity.htm

```
<!-- File Name: Inventory Entity.htm -->

<HTML>

<HEAD>

   <TITLE>Get Entity Information</TITLE>

   <SCRIPT LANGUAGE="JavaScript" FOR="window" EVENT="ONLOAD">
     Document = dsoInventory.XMLDocument;
     Attribute =
         Document.documentElement.childNodes(0).attributes(0);
     if (Attribute.dataType == "entity")
     {
     DisplayText = "'" + Attribute.nodeName
        + "' attribute has ENTITY type" + "\n";
     DisplayText += "attribute value = "
```

```
        + Attribute.nodeValue + "\n";
    Entity =
    Document.doctype.entities.getNamedItem(Attribute.nodeValue);
    DisplayText += "entity file = "
        + Entity.attributes.getNamedItem("SYSTEM").nodeValue
        + "\n";
    NotationName =
        Entity.attributes.getNamedItem("NDATA").nodeValue;
    DisplayText += "entity notation = " + NotationName + "\n";
    Notation =
        Document.doctype.notations.getNamedItem(NotationName);
    DisplayText += "notation URI or description = "
        + Notation.attributes.getNamedItem("SYSTEM").nodeValue
        + "\n";
    alert (DisplayText);
    location.href =
        Entity.attributes.getNamedItem("SYSTEM").nodeValue;
    }
  </SCRIPT>

</HEAD>

<BODY>

  <XML ID="dsoInventory" SRC="Inventory Entity.xml"></XML>

</BODY>

</HTML>
```

Listing 11-8.

Each BOOK element in the example XML document contains an ENTITY type attribute named *Review*, which is assigned the name of an unparsed entity that contains a review of the particular book. The example HTML page includes a script that demonstrates the basic steps a DOM script must perform to extract all of the information about an entity when it encounters an attribute that has the ENTITY or ENTITIES type. Specifically, the script extracts information on the unparsed entity assigned to the *Review* attribute within the first BOOK element. It displays this information in an "alert" message box that looks like this:

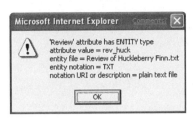

Here's a brief explanation of the basic steps that the script performs:

1 The script obtains the Attribute node for the *Review* attribute in the first BOOK element:

```
Attribute
    Document.documentElement.childNodes(0).attributes(0);
```

2 The script uses the *dataType* node property (see Table 11-2) to determine whether the attribute has the ENTITY type:

```
if (Attribute.dataType == "entity")
{
/* obtain entity information ... */
}
```

The script performs the remaining steps only if the attribute does have the ENTITY type. That is, the remaining steps are included in the *if* statement, and are executed only when the *if* condition is true.

3 The script obtains the Entity node for the DTD declaration of the entity assigned to the attribute:

```
Entity =
Document.doctype.entities.getNamedItem(Attribute.nodeValue);
```

The Document property *doctype* (explained in Table 11-3) provides a DocumentType node representing the document type declaration. The DocumentType property *entities* provides a NamedNodeMap collection of Entity nodes for all entity declarations in the DTD. The Entity node for the specific entity assigned to the attribute is obtained by passing the entity's name (*Attribute.nodeValue*) to the NamedNodeMap's *getNamedItem* method, which you saw in Table 11-7.

4 The script obtains the entity's system identifier, which specifies the URI of the file containing the entity data. The system identifier is stored as the value of an Attribute node named SYSTEM:

```
DisplayText += "entity file = "
    + Entity.attributes.getNamedItem("SYSTEM").nodeValue
    + "\n";
```

5   The script obtains the name of the entity's notation, which is stored as the value of an Attribute named NDATA:

```
NotationName =
    Entity.attributes.getNamedItem("NDATA").nodeValue;
```

6   The script obtains the Notation node for the declaration of the entity's notation:

```
Notation =
    Document.doctype.notations.getNamedItem(NotationName);
```

The DocumentType property *notations* provides a NamedNodeMap collection of Notation nodes for all notation declarations in the DTD. The Notation node for the entity's notation is obtained by passing the notation's name (*NotationName*) to the NamedNodeMap's *getNamedItem* method.

7   The script gets the notation's system identifier, which contains the notation's URI or—as in this example—its description. The system identifier is stored as the value of an Attribute node named SYSTEM:

```
DisplayText += "notation URI or description = "
    + Notation.attributes.getNamedItem("SYSTEM").nodeValue
    + "\n";
```

8   The script displays all of the stored results in an "alert" message box:

```
alert (DisplayText);
```

9   The script concludes by having Internet Explorer open and display the entity file containing the review. It does this by assigning the file's URI (obtained as explained in step 4) to the HTML page's *location.href* property, which sets the URL of the file currently displayed in the browser:

```
location.href =
    Entity.attributes.getNamedItem("SYSTEM").nodeValue;
```

The *location.href* property is part of the DHTML object model.

Traversing an Entire XML Document

In the following exercise, you'll create an HTML page that includes a script for traversing the entire DOM hierarchy of nodes for an XML document, starting with the root Document node. For each node, the script displays the node's name, type, and value. The script indents each block of node information to indicate its level in the hierarchy. You can use this page to display the nodes for any XML document, and to learn a great deal about how the DOM structures the nodes for different types of XML documents and document components.

Create the Node-Traversing Page

1   Open a new, empty text file in your text editor, and type in the HTML page
     shown in Listing 11-9. (You'll find a copy of this listing on the companion CD
     under the filename ShowNodes.htm).

2   Use your text editor's Save command to save the document on your hard
     disk, assigning it the filename ShowNodes.htm.

ShowNodes.htm

```
<!-- File Name: ShowNodes.htm -->

<HTML>

<HEAD>

    <TITLE>Show DOM Nodes</TITLE>

    <SCRIPT LANGUAGE="JavaScript" FOR="window" EVENT="ONLOAD">
        /* get Document node: */
        Document = dsoXML.XMLDocument;

        /* start by passing the Document node to DisplayNodes: */
        DisplayDIV.innerText = DisplayNodes (Document, 0);

        function DisplayNodes (Node, IndentLevel)
           {
           /* declare local variables for recursion: */
           var i;
           var DisplayString = "";

           /* build up the indentation for this level: */
           Indent = "";
           IndentDelta = "        ";
           for (i=0; i < IndentLevel; ++i)
               Indent += IndentDelta;

           /* display the current node's properties: */
           DisplayString += Indent + "nodeName: "
                          + Node.nodeName + "\n"
                          + Indent + "nodeTypeType: "
                          + Node.nodeType + "\n"
```

```
                            + Indent + "nodeTypeString: "
                            + Node.nodeTypeString + "\n"
                            + Indent + "nodeValue: "
                            + Node.nodeValue + "\n\n";

            /* display each of the node's attribute child
            nodes: */
            Indent += IndentDelta;
            for (i=0;
                 Node.attributes != null
                 && i < Node.attributes.length;
                 ++i)
                DisplayString += Indent + "nodeName: "
                                + Node.attributes(i).nodeName +
                                "\n"
                                + Indent + "nodeTypeType:    "
                                + Node.attributes(i).nodeType +
                                "\n"
                                + Indent + "nodeTypeString: "
                                + Node.attributes(i).nodeTypeString
                                + "\n"
                                + Indent + "nodeValue: "
                                + Node.attributes(i).nodeValue
                                + "\n\n";

            /* display each of the node's nonattribute child
               nodes: */
            for (i=0; i < Node.childNodes.length; ++i)
                DisplayString +=
                    DisplayNodes (Node.childNodes(i), IndentLevel
                    + 1);

            /* return the string containing the results: */
            return DisplayString;
            }
        </SCRIPT>

    </HEAD>

    <BODY>

        <XML ID="dsoXML" SRC="Inventory Dom.xml"></XML>
```

```
<H2>XML Document Object Model (DOM) Nodes</H2>

<DIV ID="DisplayDIV"></DIV>

</BODY>

</HTML>
```

Listing 11-9.

The script begins by passing the Document node to the *DisplayNodes* function, which returns display information on that node and on all its child nodes. The script assigns the display information to the *innerText* property of the *DisplayDIV* DIV element in the BODY of the page, which then displays this information:

```
DisplayDIV.innerText = DisplayNodes (Document, 0);
```

The second *DisplayNodes* parameter indicates the level of indentation used for displaying the node information.

The *DisplayNodes* function has the following form:

```
function DisplayNodes (Node, IndentLevel)
```

This function performs the following main steps:

▪ It stores the appropriate number of space characters in the *Indent* variable, which is used to create an indentation at the beginning of each line of node information. The number of space characters is determined by the value of the *IndentLevel* parameter passed to *DisplayNodes*:

```
/* build up the indentation for this level: */
Indent = "";
IndentDelta = "    ";
for (i=0; i < IndentLevel; ++i)
    Indent += IndentDelta;
```

▪ It stores display information on the current node—that is, the node passed to the *DisplayNodes* function through the *Node* parameter (initially, the Document node):

```
/* display the current node's properties: */
DisplayString += Indent + "nodeName: "
                + Node.nodeName + "\n"
                + Indent + "nodeTypeType: "
                + Node.nodeType + "\n"
```

```
+ Indent + "nodeTypeString: "
+ Node.nodeTypeString + "\n"
+ Indent + "nodeValue: "
+ Node.nodeValue + "\n\n";
```

tip

If you want to see additional properties for each node, you can add them to the preceding block of code. You can use any of the common node properties given in Table 11-2. However, don't use any of the node-specific properties (such as those given in Table 11-3 for Document nodes) because they aren't available for all node types.

■ It stores display information on the current node's child Attribute nodes. The indentation is increased by one level to indicate that these are child nodes of the current node:

```
/* display each of the node's attribute child nodes: */
Indent += IndentDelta;
for (i=0;
     Node.attributes != null
     && i < Node.attributes.length;
     ++i)
    DisplayString += Indent + "nodeName: "
                    + Node.attributes(i).nodeName + "\n"
                    + Indent + "nodeTypeType:    "
                    + Node.attributes(i).nodeType + "\n"
                    + Indent + "nodeTypeString: "
                    + Node.attributes(i).nodeTypeString
                    + "\n"
                    + Indent + "nodeValue: "
                    + Node.attributes(i).nodeValue
                    + "\n\n";
```

note

DisplayNodes doesn't display the superfluous child Text node of an Attribute node, because it's more convenient to obtain the attribute's value directly from the *nodeValue* property of the Attribute node itself.

■ The *DisplayNodes* function stores display information on each of the node's nonattribute child nodes by calling itself for each of these nodes. These are known as *recursive* function calls:

```
/* display each of the node's nonattribute child
    nodes: */
for (i=0; i < Node.childNodes.length; ++i)
    DisplayString += DisplayNodes
        (Node.childNodes(i), IndentLevel + 1);
```

■ The *DisplayNodes* function concludes by returning the string containing all of the node information:

```
/* return the string containing the results: */
return DisplayString;
```

3   Open the page in Internet Explorer: ShowNodes.htm

Notice that the *nodeTypeString* property contains the node type in all lowercase letters. (For instance, "Document" and "ProcessingInstruction" become "document" and "processinginstruction".)

Initially, the page displays the Inventory Dom.xml XML document (given in Listing 11-1 and provided on the companion CD). The first part of the display results looks like this:

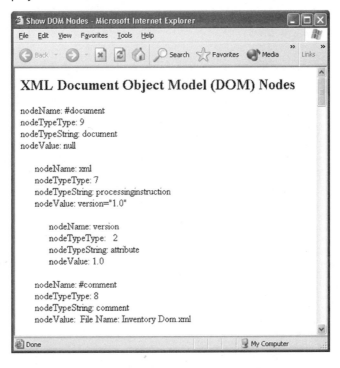

4   To view the node structure of other XML documents, edit the page's data island. For example, to view the nodes in Inventory Valid Entity.xml (given in Listing 6-1 and provided on the companion CD), you would edit the data island so that it reads like this:

```
<XML ID="dsoXML" SRC="Inventory Valid Entity.xml"></XML>
```

Checking an XML Document for Validity

The final sections of this chapter present two HTML pages that you can use to check the validity of your XML documents. The first page checks an XML document's validity against a document type definition (DTD) contained in or referenced by the document. The second page checks a document's validity against an XML schema contained in a separate file. Creating valid XML documents using DTDs was covered in Chapters 5 and 6, and creating valid XML documents using XML schemas was covered in Chapter 7. The topic of checking documents for validity was postponed until the current chapter because the techniques require using a script and the Document object of the DOM.

Checking an XML Document for Validity Using a DTD

The DTD validity-testing HTML page contains a script that opens an XML document and uses DOM properties to report any errors that it contains. If the document doesn't have a document type declaration, the page reports only well-formedness errors. If the document includes a document type declaration, the page reports both well-formedness and validity errors. You can use this page to test any XML document. (But keep in mind that if you want to check merely the well-formedness of a document—perhaps one without a DTD—you can do so by simply opening the document directly in Internet Explorer.)

How to Use the DTD Validity-Testing Page

1   In your text editor, open the DTD validity-testing page, Validity Test DTD.htm. (You'll find this file on the companion CD and in Listing 11-10 in the next section.)

2   Edit the data island in the BODY of the page so that its SRC attribute is assigned the URL of the XML document you want to test. For example, to test the document Raven.xml, you would edit the data island to read like this:

```
<XML ID="dsoTest" SRC="Raven.xml"></XML>
```

Typically, the XML document is contained in the same folder as the validity-testing page, so you need enter only the XML document's filename, as in the example above.

3   Use your text editor's Save command to save the modified page.

4   Open the page in Internet Explorer:  Validity Test DTD.htm

The page will display a message box indicating the error status of the document. If the document contains no well-formedness or validity errors, the message box appears like this:

Microsoft Internet Explorer

parseError.errorCode: 0
parseError.filepos: 0
parseError.line: 0
parseError.linepos: 0
parseError.reason:
parseError.srcText:
parseError.url:

OK

If, however, the document contains one or more well-formedness or validity errors, the message box will display the first error encountered, like this:

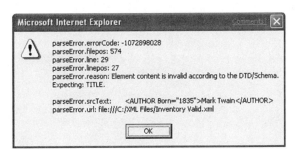

Microsoft Internet Explorer

parseError.errorCode: -1072898028
parseError.filepos: 574
parseError.line: 29
parseError.linepos: 27
parseError.reason: Element content is invalid according to the DTD/Schema. Expecting: TITLE.

parseError.srcText: <AUTHOR Born="1835">Mark Twain</AUTHOR>
parseError.url: file:///C:/XML Files/Inventory Valid.xml

OK

How the DTD Validity-Testing Page Works

When Internet Explorer loads an XML document that's contained in or referenced by a data island in an HTML page, the processor automatically checks the document for well-formedness and—if the document contains a document type declaration—for validity. After the processor loads the document (or attempts to load the document; it will quit if it encounters an error), it assigns information on the document's error status to the *parseError* property of the Document node for that document. The *parseError* property will contain either a code indicating that the document is error-free, or complete information on the first well-formedness or validity error that was encountered. The DTD validity-testing page presented here contains a script that uses *parseError* to display error information on the XML document that's linked to the page through the data island.

Document Object Model Scripts 11

> **tip**
>
> In the full-featured DOM scripts that you write, you can use the information in the *parseError* property to determine whether the XML document contains an error. If an error is found, your script can display a helpful error message rather than attempting to display the document's data (an attempt that would fail because the DOM hierarchy would contain no data).

The DTD validity-testing page is given in Listing 11-10. (You'll find a copy of this listing on the companion CD under the filename Validity Test DTD.htm.)

Validity Test DTD.htm

```
<!-- File Name: Validity Test DTD.htm -->

<HTML>

<HEAD>
   <TITLE>DTD Validity Tester</TITLE>

   <SCRIPT LANGUAGE="JavaScript" FOR="window" EVENT="ONLOAD">
      Document = dsoTest.XMLDocument;
      message = "parseError.errorCode: "
            + Document.parseError.errorCode + "\n"
            + "parseError.filepos: "
            + Document.parseError.filepos + "\n"
            + "parseError.line: " + Document.parseError.line
            + "\n"
            + "parseError.linepos: "
            + Document.parseError.linepos + "\n"
            + "parseError.reason: "
            + Document.parseError.reason + "\n"
            + "parseError.srcText: "
            + Document.parseError.srcText + "\n"
            + "parseError.url: " + Document.parseError.url;
      alert (message);
   </SCRIPT>

</HEAD>

<BODY>
```

```
<!-- set SRC to the URL of the XML document you want to
check: -->
<XML ID="dsoTest" SRC="Inventory Valid.xml"></XML>

<H2>DTD Validity Tester</H2>

</BODY>

</HTML>
```

Listing 11-10.

The HTML page contains a script that it runs when the browser first opens the window for the page:

```
<SCRIPT LANGUAGE="JavaScript" FOR="window" EVENT="ONLOAD">
   /* script code ... */
</SCRIPT>
```

The script first obtains the Document node for the XML document that is linked through the data island:

```
Document = dsoTest.XMLDocument;
```

By the time the script receives control, the Internet Explorer XML processor has already loaded—or attempted to load—the XML document, and the document's error status is contained in the Document node's *parseError* property. The *parseError* property is a programming object with its own set of properties. The script concludes by displaying all of the *parseError* properties:

```
message = "parseError.errorCode: "
        + Document.parseError.errorCode + "\n"
        + "parseError.filepos: "
        + Document.parseError.filepos + "\n"
        + "parseError.line: " + Document.parseError.line
        + "\n"
        + "parseError.linepos: "
        + Document.parseError.linepos + "\n"
        + "parseError.reason: "
        + Document.parseError.reason + "\n"
        + "parseError.srcText: "
        + Document.parseError.srcText + "\n"
        + "parseError.url: " + Document.parseError.url;
alert (message);
```

The *parseError* properties fully describe the XML document's error status. If the document is error-free, *parseError.errorCode* is set to zero and the other properties are set to either zero or blank. If the document has one or more errors, *parseError.errorCode* contains the numeric code for the first error, and the other properties describe this error.

Checking an XML Document for Validity Using an XML Schema

This section presents an HTML page that checks a document for validity with respect to an XML schema. The page contains a script that opens both an XML document and an XML schema file, and checks whether the XML document is well-formed and whether it conforms to the schema. The page reports any well-formedness errors in the XML document as well as any failure of the XML document to conform to the constraints defined in the XML schema. Internet Explorer itself reports any errors contained in the XML schema file.

> ## caution
>
> To use the XML validity-testing page presented here, MSXML version 4.0 must be installed on the computer. For information on MSXML, see *"XML Step by Step*, Internet Explorer, and MSXML" in the Introduction.

How to Use the XML Schema Validity-Testing Page

1 In your text editor, open the XML schema validity-testing page, Validity Test Schema.htm. (You'll find this file on the companion CD and in Listing 11-11 in the next section.)

2 Edit the values of the three variables at the beginning of the script as follows:

Variable to edit	Set to this value
XMLFileURL	The URL of the XML document
XMLNamespaceName	If the XML document's root element belongs to a namespace (a default namespace or one assigned through a namespace prefix), then set *XMLNamespaceName* to the corresponding namespace name. Otherwise, set it to an empty string. For information on namespaces, see "Using Namespaces" on page 69.
SchemaFileURL	The URL of the XML schema file

Typically, the validity-testing page, the XML document, and the XML schema file are all located in the same folder; in this case you would need to assign *XMLFileURL* and *SchemaFileURL* just the simple filenames. For example, to test the validity of the Book Instance.xml document against the Book Schema.xsd XML schema (assuming that the Book Instance.xml document element doesn't belong to a namespace and that all three files are in the same folder), you would set the variables as follows:

```
var XMLFileURL = "Book Instance.xml";
var XMLNamespaceName = "";
var SchemaFileURL = "Book Schema.xsd";
```

3   Use your text editor's Save command to save the modified page.

4   Open the page in Internet Explorer:  Validity Test Schema.htm

You'll now see one of the following three messages:

■ If the XML document is well formed and conforms to the schema, you'll see the following message box:

Microsoft Internet Explorer

parseError.errorCode: 0
parseError.filepos: 0
parseError.line: 0
parseError.linepos: 0
parseError.reason:
parseError.srcText:
parseError.url:

OK

■ If the XML document contains a well-formedness or validity error, you'll see a message box similar to the following one:

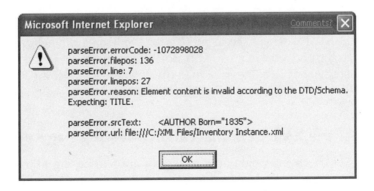

Microsoft Internet Explorer

parseError.errorCode: -1072898028
parseError.filepos: 136
parseError.line: 7
parseError.linepos: 27
parseError.reason: Element content is invalid according to the DTD/Schema. Expecting: TITLE.

parseError.srcText: <AUTHOR Born="1835">
parseError.url: file:///C:/XML Files/Inventory Instance.xml

OK

Document Object Model Scripts 11

- If the XML schema itself contains an error—either a well-formedness error or a violation of one of the rules of the XML Schema definition language—the message box will not appear. Rather, Internet Explorer will display an error icon at the left end of its status bar. Double-clicking this icon:

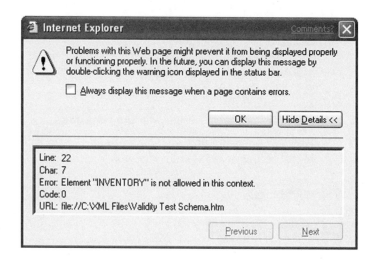

will display an error message such as the following one:

(If you check the Always Display This Message When A Page Contains Errors option, from then on the error message will appear automatically and you won't need to double-click the error icon in the status bar to display the message.)

note

If the XML schema contains an error and you have a debugger installed, such as the one provided with Microsoft Visual Studio .NET, you might see a different type of error message than the one described here.

How the XML Schema Validity-Testing Page Works

The XML schema validity-testing page is given in Listing 11-11. (You'll find a copy of this listing on the companion CD under the filename Validity Test Schema.htm.)

Validity Test Schema.htm

```
<!-- File Name: Validity Test Schema.htm -->

<HTML>

<HEAD>

    <TITLE>XML Schema Validity Tester</TITLE>

    <SCRIPT LANGUAGE="JavaScript" FOR="window" EVENT="ONLOAD">

        /* set XMLFileURL to the URL of the XML document: */
        var XMLFileURL = "Inventory Instance.xml";

        /* if the XML document's root element belongs to a
            namespace, set XMLNamespaceName to the namespace name;
            otherwise, set it to an empty string: */
        var XMLNamespaceName = "";

        /* set SchemaFileURL to the URL of the XML schema file: */
        var SchemaFileURL = "Inventory Schema.xsd";

        /* create a new, empty Document node: */
        Document = new ActiveXObject ("Msxml2.DOMDocument.4.0");

        /* store the URL of the XML schema file in a new
            XMLSchemaCache object, and then assign that object to
            the Document node's 'schemas' property: */
        XMLSchemaCache =
            new ActiveXObject ("Msxml2.XMLSchemaCache.4.0");
        XMLSchemaCache.add (XMLNamespaceName, SchemaFileURL);
        Document.schemas = XMLSchemaCache;

        /* cause subsequent call to 'load' method to load the XML
            document synchronously: */
        Document.async = false;

        /* load the XML document into the Document node: */
        Document.load (XMLFileURL);

        /* display error information: */
        message = "parseError.errorCode: "
```

11

```
        + Document.parseError.errorCode + "\n"
        + "parseError.filepos: "
        + Document.parseError.filepos + "\n"
        + "parseError.line: " + Document.parseError.line
        + "\n"
        + "parseError.linepos: "
        + Document.parseError.linepos + "\n"
        + "parseError.reason: "
        + Document.parseError.reason + "\n"
        + "parseError.srcText: "
        + Document.parseError.srcText + "\n"
        + "parseError.url: " + Document.parseError.url;
      alert (message);

  </SCRIPT>

</HEAD>

<BODY>

  <H2>XML Schema Validity Tester</H2>

</BODY>

</HTML>
```

Listing 11-11.

Unlike the previous HTML pages you've seen in the book, the XML schema validity-testing page *doesn't* link the XML document to the page by using a data
island. Rather, the script in this page creates a new, empty Document node:

```
/* create a new, empty Document node: */
Document = new ActiveXObject ("Msxml2.DOMDocument.4.0");
```

Next, it uses the Document node's *schemas* property to indicate the URL of the
XML schema file that should be used to validate the XML document when it's
loaded and processed:

```
/* store the URL of the XML schema file in a new
   XMLSchemaCache object, and then assign that object to
   the Document node's 'schemas' property: */
XMLSchemaCache =
   new ActiveXObject ("Msxml2.XMLSchemaCache.4.0");
```

```
XMLSchemaCache.add (XMLNamespaceName, SchemaFileURL);
Document.schemas = XMLSchemaCache;
```

It then sets the Document node's *async* property to *false* to cause the document to be loaded synchronously (explained later):

```
/* cause subsequent call to 'load' method to load the XML
   document synchronously: */
Document.async = false;
```

Finally, it calls the Document node's *load* method to load the XML document from the document file:

```
/* load the XML document into the Document node: */
Document.load (XMLFileURL);
```

The *schemas* and *async* properties and the *load* method are briefly described in Table 11-3. Because the script provides the URL of an XML schema file via the Document node's *schemas* property before calling *load*, the Internet Explorer XML processor checks the validity of the XML document against that schema when it loads and processes the XML document. And because the script sets the Document node's *async* property to *false* before calling *load*, the document is loaded synchronously. That is, the call to *load* doesn't return until the XML document is completely loaded, eliminating the need to check whether the document is fully loaded before accessing the error information or the document data. (When you load an XML document using a data island, as in the DTD validity-checking page presented previously, Internet Explorer automatically causes the document to be loaded synchronously.)

note

The schema validity-testing page can't use a data island to load the XML document because, with that technique, by the time the script gains access to the Document node, the XML document has already been fully or partially loaded, and the script would be unable to use Document node properties to control the way the loading is performed. In particular, it would be unable to supply an XML schema that the processor uses to validate the document when it loads it.

As when a document is loaded through a data island, document error information is stored in the Document node's *parseError* member object. The script displays this information as explained for the DTD validity-testing script in the earlier section "How the DTD Validity-Testing Page Works."

CHAPTER 12

Displaying XML Documents Using XSLT Style Sheets

In this chapter, you'll learn the final method covered in this book for displaying XML documents in the Microsoft Internet Explorer browser: Extensible Stylesheet Language Transformations (XSLT) style sheets. Like a cascading style sheet (CSS), explained in Chapters 8 and 9, an XSLT style sheet is linked to an XML document and tells the browser how to display the XML data, allowing you to open the XML document directly in the browser without using an intermediary HTML page.

For displaying XML, however, an XSLT style sheet is considerably more powerful and flexible than a CSS. Although a CSS allows you to fully specify the formatting of each XML element, the browser merely copies the text in its original XML document order to the displayed output. An XSLT style sheet, however, gives you complete control over the output. Specifically, XSLT allows you to precisely select the XML data you want to display, to present that data in any order or arrangement, and to freely modify or add information. XSLT gives you access to almost all XML document components (such as elements, attributes, comments, and processing instructions), it lets you easily sort and filter the XML data, it allows you to include loop and conditional structures and use variables as in a programming language, and it provides a set of useful built-in functions you can use to work with the information.

The basic form of XSLT style sheet described in this chapter selectively transforms an XML document to an HTML page, which the browser then renders and displays (hence the word *transformations* in XSLT). An XSLT style sheet thus lets you take full advantage of feature-rich HTML elements—such as headings, paragraphs, line breaks, tables, images, and hyperlinks—to display your data.

Using XSLT Style Sheets

On top of all this, you lose nothing by linking an XSLT style sheet to your XML document rather than a CSS, because in an XSLT style sheet you can use any of the CSS properties to format the HTML elements that display the XML data. You can easily use CSS properties to format individual HTML elements in the output by including STYLE attributes in the elements' start-tags. You'll see many examples of this technique throughout the chapter. You can also embed an entire cascading style sheet within the output HTML page or even link a separate CSS file to that page.

A final advantage of XSLT is that an XSLT style sheet is an XML document itself, so its basic syntax will already be familiar to you (assuming you've read the previous chapters!).

Learning how to create an XSLT style sheet, however, can be a bit more difficult than simply using a CSS, because of the vast array of features provided by XSLT and because writing an XSLT style sheet requires knowledge of HTML. This chapter provides only an introduction to XSLT, which could form the topic of an entire book. The features the chapter describes are based on two World Wide Web Consortium (W3C) specifications. The first is the XSL Transformations (XSLT) Version 1.0 recommendation (at *http://www.w3.org/TR/xslt*), which defines the general structure and components of an XSLT style sheet. The second specification is the XML Path Language (XPath) Version 1.0 recommendation (at *http://www.w3.org/TR/xpath*), which defines the expressions that you use in an XSLT style sheet to select and match elements and other components belonging to the XML document. For more information on XSLT and XPath as implemented by Internet Explorer, see the topics "XSLT Developer's Guide," "XSLT Reference," "XPath Developer's Guide," and "XPath Reference," in the Microsoft XML SDK 4.0 help file, or the same topics in the XML SDK documentation provided by the MSDN (Microsoft Developer Network) Library on the Web at *http://msdn.microsoft.com/library/*.

caution

The technique for using XSLT style sheets explained in this chapter requires that the XML document be displayed using Internet Explorer version 6.0.

Using an XSLT Style Sheet—the Basics

There are two basic steps for using an XSLT style sheet to display an XML document:

1. **Create the XSLT style sheet file.** XSLT is an application of XML. That is, an XSLT style sheet is a well-formed XML document that conforms to the XSLT rules. Like any XML document, an XSLT style sheet consists of plain text, and you can create it using your favorite text editor. The following sections explain how to write various types of XSLT style sheets.

2. **Link the XSLT style sheet to the XML document.** Although you use XML to create both the XML document and the XSLT style sheet, they are kept in separate files: an XML document file (with the .xml extension) and an XSLT style sheet file (with the .xsl extension). You link the XSLT style sheet to the XML document by including in this document an *xml-stylesheet* processing instruction, which has the following general form:

    ```
    <?xml-stylesheet type="text/xsl" href=XSLTFilePath?>
    ```

    Here, *XSLTFilePath* is a quoted URL indicating the location of the style sheet file. You can use a fully qualified URL, such as this:

    ```
    <?xml-stylesheet type="text/xsl"
        href="http://www.mjyOnline.com/Inventory.xsl"?>
    ```

    More often, however, you use a partial URL that specifies a location relative to the location of the XML document containing the *xml-stylesheet* processing instruction, such as this:

    ```
    <?xml-stylesheet type="text/xsl" href="Inventory.xsl"?>
    ```

    (A relative URL is more common because you typically store a style sheet file in the folder where you store the XML document, or in one of its subfolders.)

    You must place the *xml-stylesheet* processing instruction at the beginning of the XML document, following the XML declaration and the document type declaration (if included).

    If you've linked an XSLT style sheet to an XML document, you can open that document directly in Internet Explorer, and the browser will display the XML document using the transformation instructions in the style sheet. Unlike cascading style sheets, if you link more than one XSLT style sheet to an XML document, the browser will use the first one and ignore the others. If you link both a CSS and an XSLT style sheet to an XML document, the browser will use only the XSLT style sheet. (If you link neither a CSS nor an XSLT style sheet to an XML document, Internet Explorer will display the document using its default, built-in XSLT style sheet. This style sheet displays the XML source as a collapsible/expandable tree, as shown in "Display the XML Document Without a Style Sheet" in Chapter 2.)

> **note**
>
> When you open an XML document with a linked XSLT style sheet directly in Internet Explorer, the browser will display an error message for any well-formedness error it finds in the XML document or in the linked style sheet. It will also display a message for any violation of the XSLT rules that it discovers in the style sheet. As explained in Chapter 5, however, Internet Explorer *won't* check the validity of the XML document against a document type definition (DTD) that is contained in or referenced by the document. To check a document's validity, you can use one of the validity-testing pages presented in "Checking an XML Document for Validity" on page 396.

Using a Single XSLT Template

Rather than containing rules, as in a CSS, an XSLT style sheet includes one or more *templates*. The templates tell the browser how to display the XML document by providing instructions for selectively transforming the XML document's elements, attributes, and other components into an HTML page that the browser renders and displays. Each template contains the information for transforming—and thereby displaying—a particular component or set of components of the XML document.

XSLT represents an XML document's components as a treelike hierarchy of nodes. This hierarchy is similar, although not identical, to the node hierarchy created by the Document Object Model (DOM) that was discussed in Chapter 11. XSLT provides a node for representing each of the following types of components found in an XML document: an element, the character data contained in an element (represented by a *text node*), an attribute, a comment, a processing instruction, and the entire XML document (represented by the XSLT *root node*).

> **note**
>
> XSLT also provides nodes for any namespaces used in the XML document. This type of node isn't covered in this chapter. For instructions on referencing namespaces that are used in the XML document, see "Referencing Namespaces in XSLT," later in the chapter.
>
> Unlike the DOM, XSLT *doesn't* provide nodes for accessing an XML declaration or a document type declaration in the document prolog.

In this section, you'll learn how to create a simple XSLT style sheet that includes only a single template, which contains the information for transforming and displaying the content of the entire document. Listing 12-1 provides an example of such a style sheet. This style sheet is linked to the XML document in Listing 12-2. (You'll find copies of both listings on the companion CD under the filenames XsltDemo01.xsl and XsltDemo01.xml.)

XsltDemo01.xsl

```xml
<?xml version="1.0"?>

<!-- File Name: XsltDemo01.xsl -->

<xsl:stylesheet
    version="1.0"
    xmlns:xsl="http://www.w3.org/1999/XSL/Transform">

    <xsl:template match="/">  <!-- match the XSLT root node -->
        <HTML>
        <HEAD>
            <TITLE>Book Description</TITLE>
        </HEAD>
        <BODY>
        <H2>Book Description</H2>
        <SPAN STYLE="font-style:italic">Author: </SPAN>
        <xsl:value-of select="BOOK/AUTHOR"/><BR/>
        <SPAN STYLE="font-style:italic">Title: </SPAN>
        <xsl:value-of select="BOOK/TITLE"/><BR/>
        <SPAN STYLE="font-style:italic">Price: </SPAN>
        <xsl:value-of select="BOOK/PRICE"/><BR/>
        <SPAN STYLE="font-style:italic">Binding type: </SPAN>
        <xsl:value-of select="BOOK/BINDING"/><BR/>
        <SPAN STYLE="font-style:italic">Number of pages: </SPAN>
        <xsl:value-of select="BOOK/PAGES"/>
        </BODY>
        </HTML>
    </xsl:template>

</xsl:stylesheet>
```

Listing 12-1.

XsltDemo01.xml

```
<?xml version="1.0"?>

<!-- File Name: XsltDemo01.xml -->

<?xml-stylesheet type="text/xsl" href="XsltDemo01.xsl"?>

<BOOK>
   <TITLE>Moby-Dick</TITLE>
   <AUTHOR>
      <FIRSTNAME>Herman</FIRSTNAME>
      <LASTNAME>Melville</LASTNAME>
   </AUTHOR>
   <BINDING>hardcover</BINDING>
   <PAGES>724</PAGES>
   <PRICE>$9.95</PRICE>
</BOOK>
```

Listing 12-2.

Here's how Internet Explorer displays the XML document, following the instructions in the style sheet:

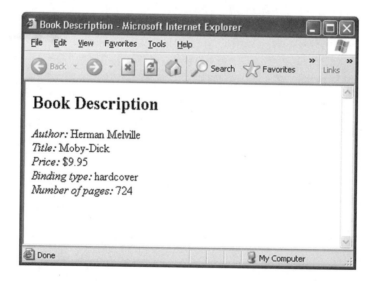

Every XSLT style sheet must have the following document element:

```
<xsl:stylesheet
    version="1.0"
    xmlns:xsl="http://www.w3.org/1999/XSL/Transform">

    <!-- one or more elements... -->

</xsl:stylesheet>
```

Recall that the document element of an XML document, also known as the root element, is the top-level XML element that contains all the other elements. The *xsl:stylesheet* document element serves not only to contain the other elements, but also to identify the document as an XSLT style sheet. You *must* include the *version="1.0"* attribute specification within the element's start-tag to identify the XSLT version.

The *xsl:stylesheet* element is one of the special-purpose XSLT elements used in a style sheet. All of the XSLT elements belong to the namespace named *http://www.w3.org/1999/XSL/Transform*. You should declare this namespace within the start-tag of the *xsl:stylesheet* root element so that you can use the defined namespace prefix within any of the style sheet's elements. The conventional namespace prefix is *xsl*, which you'll see in the XSLT specification and in the Microsoft XSLT documentation. You can, however, use a different namespace prefix if you wish, as long as you use the prescribed namespace name. For information on namespaces, see "Using Namespaces" on page 69.

The *xsl:stylesheet* root element of an XSLT style sheet can contain one or more templates, each of which is defined by means of an *xsl:template* element. The document element in Listing 12-1 contains only a single template, which has the following form:

```
    <xsl:template match="/">

        <!-- child elements... -->

    </xsl:template>
```

You use the *xsl:template* element's *match* attribute to indicate the specific XML document component or set of components that the template is designed to transform. You do this by assigning *match* a value known as a *location path*, which specifies—or *matches*—the XSLT node or nodes that represent the component or components to be transformed. The location path in this example (/) matches the XSLT root node, which represents the entire XML document.

> **note**
>
> Keep in mind that a location path consisting of the root operator (/) does *not* match the node for the document (or root) element of the XML document. Rather, it matches the XSLT root node representing the entire document, of which the document element is an immediate child. (The XSLT root node is thus equivalent to the root Document node of the Document Object Model, discussed in Chapter 11.)

When Internet Explorer processes a style sheet, it first looks for a template that matches the XSLT root node. If it finds such a template, it then carries out the transformation instructions contained in that template. In the example style sheet, the template matching the XSLT root node is the sole template and it therefore contains instructions for transforming the complete XML document. As you'll learn later, a style sheet sometimes divides the task of transforming the document among several templates, each of which matches a particular XML document component or set of components and transforms the corresponding branch or branches of the document. For information on the way the browser applies the templates contained in a style sheet, see the following sidebar "How Internet Explorer Applies XSLT Templates."

How Internet Explorer Applies XSLT Templates

The simple style sheet in Listing 12-1 contains a single template that matches the XSLT root node. It's permissible, however, for a style sheet to omit the template matching the XSLT root node, to have several templates, or even to have no templates at all. It's important to understand how the browser transforms the document in each situation.

In all cases, the browser begins by "applying a template" to the XSLT root node. The following are the steps that it takes when it applies a template to the root node or to any other node:

1   It looks for a template defined in the style sheet that matches the node.

2   If it finds a matching template, it turns over the transformation of the node to that template. That is, it executes the transformation instructions contained in the template.

3   If it doesn't find a matching template, it uses the appropriate built-in template. A built-in template is one whose behavior is defined by the XSLT specification, rather than in an *xsl:template* element that you include in your style sheet. The particular built-in template the browser uses depends upon the type of the node that is being transformed, as follows:

■   The built-in template for the XSLT root node applies a template to each child node of the root node—that is, for each child node it performs steps 1 through 3. The child nodes of the root node include the document element node, and possibly one or more comment or processing instruction nodes.

■   The built-in template for an element node applies a template to each child node of the element node—that is, it performs steps 1 through 3 for each of these nodes. The possible child nodes of an element node include a text node, which represents any character data contained directly within the element, as well as nested element nodes, comment nodes, and processing instruction nodes.

■   The built-in template for a text node displays the text—that is, it outputs the character data associated with the text node's parent element node.

The built-in template for an attribute node also displays the associated text (in this case, the attribute's value). However, if an element has an attribute, the attribute node is *not* considered to be a child of the element node; therefore, the built-in template for an element node does *not* apply a template to the attribute node. The browser applies a template to an attribute node only if one of the templates that you write explicitly selects the attribute node within an *xsl:apply-templates* element, as explained later in the chapter.

■   The built-in template for a comment or processing instruction node does nothing—that is, it *doesn't* display the node's text content. (These types of nodes don't have child nodes.)

For instance, when the browser processes the example style sheet in Listing 12-1, it immediately finds a template matching the XSLT root node and simply turns over control to that template. If that style sheet also contained a template matching the BOOK element node, that template would never be used (unless the root node template contained an *xsl:apply-templates* element that selected the BOOK element node, as explained later in the chapter).

If the example style sheet contained *only* a template matching the BOOK node,

continued

12

Using XSLT Style Sheets

continued

```
<xsl:template match="BOOK">

    <!-- template contents... -->

</xsl:template>
```

the browser would begin, as always, by applying a template to the XSLT root node. Because it would not find a template in the style sheet matching the XSLT root node, it would use its built-in template for a root node, which would apply a template to each child of the root node. For the first child node—the one representing the *<!-- File Name: XsltDemo01.xsl -->* comment—the browser wouldn't find a matching template and would use its built-in template, which would do nothing. For the second child node—the one representing the BOOK document element—the browser would find the matching template in the style sheet and would turn over handling of the BOOK node and all its children to that template. The browser would not look for any additional templates (unless the BOOK template contained an *xsl:apply-templates* element).

You can deduce from the three steps outlined in this sidebar what the browser would do if the linked XSLT style sheet contained just an empty *xsl:stylesheet* element with *no* templates. You're right: The browser would display all of the character data found in the XML document's elements, but would not display any attribute values or the content of any comments or processing instructions.

The following is the complete template in the example style sheet:

```
<xsl:template match="/">  <!-- match the XSLT root node -->
    <HTML>
    <HEAD>
        <TITLE>Book Description</TITLE>
    </HEAD>
    <BODY>
    <H2>Book Description</H2>
    <SPAN STYLE="font-style:italic">Author: </SPAN>
    <xsl:value-of select="BOOK/AUTHOR"/><BR/>
    <SPAN STYLE="font-style:italic">Title: </SPAN>
    <xsl:value-of select="BOOK/TITLE"/><BR/>
    <SPAN STYLE="font-style:italic">Price: </SPAN>
    <xsl:value-of select="BOOK/PRICE"/><BR/>
```

```
<SPAN STYLE="font-style:italic">Binding type: </SPAN>
<xsl:value-of select="BOOK/BINDING"/><BR/>
<SPAN STYLE="font-style:italic">Number of pages: </SPAN>
<xsl:value-of select="BOOK/PAGES"/>
</BODY>
</HTML>
</xsl:template>
```

The transformation instructions contained in a template consist of two kinds of XML elements:

- *Literal result elements.* These are XML elements that represent HTML elements. Examples of this kind of XML element from the preceding template are:

  ```
  <TITLE>Book Description</TITLE>
  ```

  which defines the output page's title,

  ```
  <H2>Book Description</H2>
  ```

  which displays a second-level heading,

  ```
  <SPAN STYLE="font-style:italic">Author: </SPAN>
  ```

  which displays a block of italicized text (*Author:*), and,

  ```
  <BR/>
  ```

  which creates a line break. The template also contains literal result elements that represent the standard HTML elements that define the page's heading (HEAD), the page's body (BODY), and the entire page (HTML).

  Literal result elements are all standard HTML elements entered as well-formed XML. The browser simply copies each literal result element directly to the HTML output that it renders and displays.

note

When the browser copies a literal result element to the output, it always copies the element's start-tag, any character data contained in the element, and the element's end-tag. If the literal result element contains a child element, it will copy that child element if it is also a literal result element, but it will process the child element if it is an XSLT element (described next). For instance, the BODY literal result element in the example style sheet contains several child elements. Its H2 child element is copied to the output because it's also a literal result element. However, each of its *xsl:value-of* child elements is processed because it is an XSLT element.

caution

Each literal result element must be a well-formed XML element as well as a standard HTML element. (Don't forget that an XSLT style sheet is an XML document.) Therefore, you can't use HTML shortcuts that aren't allowed in XML, such as overlapping elements or omitting the end-tag when you haven't used an empty-element tag. For example, to specify an HTML break element, you can't simply enter <BR> as you can in an HTML page. Rather, you must use a well-formed XML empty-element tag, <BR/>.

tip

In the example XSLT style sheet, notice the use of the STYLE attribute specifications in many of the literal result elements. Using the STYLE attribute is one of the ways to apply CSS property settings to the HTML output elements that are displayed in the browser. You could also embed an entire cascading style sheet within the output HTML page by inserting a literal result STYLE element within the literal result HEAD element in the template. Or, you could attach an external cascading style sheet by inserting an appropriate LINK element within the HEAD element. For an introduction to these techniques, see the topic "2.1 A brief CSS2 tutorial for HTML" in the W3C page "2 Introduction to CSS2" at *http://www.w3.org/TR/REC-CSS2/intro.html*.

■   *XSLT elements.* Examples of XSLT elements from the preceding style sheet are the *xsl:value-of* elements, such as the following:

```
<xsl:value-of select="BOOK/AUTHOR"/>
```

The browser distinguishes an XSLT element from a literal result element representing HTML because the former has a namespace prefix (*xsl* in the examples) that points to the namespace named *http://www.w3.org/1999/XSL/Transform*. XSLT elements contain instructions for selecting or modifying the XML data or for performing other tasks. Accordingly, the browser processes them rather than simply copying them to the output.

The *xsl:value-of* XSLT element inserts the text content of the specified XML element or other type of node into the HTML output that the browser renders and displays. The text content of an element consists of a concatenation of any character data contained directly within the element plus any character data in child elements. You specify the particular XML element or other node by assigning a location path to the *select* attribute of the *xsl:value-of* element. In the preceding example *xsl:value-of* element, *select* is assigned the location path BOOK/AUTHOR, which causes this element to output the text content of the XML document's AUTHOR element. The text content of the AUTHOR element consists of the character data belonging to its two child elements, FIRSTNAME and LASTNAME.

A location path specifies a particular element or other type of node (or set of nodes, as you'll see later) by indicating its location in the XML document's node hierarchy. The location path in the example, BOOK/AUTHOR, designates the AUTHOR element that is a child of the BOOK element. The slash character (/) is known as the *child operator,* and each of the parts of a location path that are separated with child operators (BOOK and AUTHOR in the example) are known as *location steps*. Notice that a location path is quite similar to a file path that an operating system uses to designate the location of a file or folder.

The critical concept to understand here is that the location path in a *select* attribute value is relative to the current *context node*. Each location within the instructions in an XSLT template has a context node. Because the example template matches the XSLT root node (through its *match="/"* attribute specification), the context node within this template is the XSLT root node. Thus, within this template, the location path BOOK/AUTHOR indicates the AUTHOR element, within the BOOK element, *within the XSLT root node*. The BOOK/AUTHOR location path is thus analogous to a relative file path, which gives the location of a file in relation to the current working folder. (As you'll learn later in the chapter, you can also use an *absolute* location path, which fully designates the location of a node or set of nodes within the document, and isn't relative to the current context node.)

The overall result of the elements in the example template is to display a text label for each of the child elements of the XML root element (AUTHOR, TITLE, PRICE, BINDING, and PAGES), plus the text content of each of these elements. Notice that the order of the *xsl:value-of* elements in the template determines the order in which the browser displays these elements. Thus, even in this simple style sheet, you can already see that an XSLT style sheet is more flexible than a CSS, which always displays elements in the order they occur in the document.

The following figure shows how the browser transforms the XML document to the output HTML page that it renders and displays. It illustrates the transformation generated by the first eight lines within the example template given in this section. The solid line indicates the copying of literal result elements from the XML document directly to the output HTML page, while the dashed lines indicate the processing of an XSLT element (namely, the *xsl:value-of* element, which extracts the text content from the AUTHOR element and inserts it into the output HTML page).

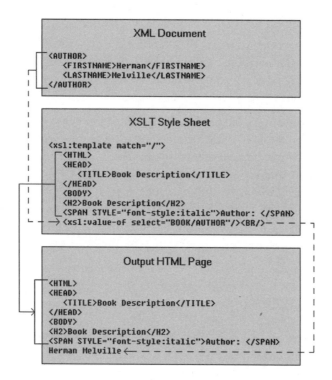

tip

For information on working with HTML and Dynamic HTML (DHTML) as implemented in Internet Explorer, see the topic "HTML and Dynamic HTML" in the MSDN Library on the Web at *http://msdn.microsoft.com/library/*. To read the official specification for the latest version of HTML 4, see the following Web site, provided by the W3C: *http://www.w3.org/TR/html4/*.

Displaying a Variable Number of Elements

The example XML document given in the previous section (Listing 12-2) contained only a single BOOK element. If, however, a document contained several BOOK elements, the technique you learned in the previous section would display only the first one. Consider, for example, an XML document with the following document element:

```
<INVENTORY>
   <BOOK>
      <TITLE>The Adventures of Huckleberry Finn</TITLE>
      <AUTHOR>
```

```
        <FIRSTNAME>Mark</FIRSTNAME>
        <LASTNAME>Twain</LASTNAME>
    </AUTHOR>
    <BINDING>mass market paperback</BINDING>
    <PAGES>298</PAGES>
    <PRICE>$5.49</PRICE>
  </BOOK>
  <BOOK>
    <TITLE>The Adventures of Tom Sawyer</TITLE>
    <AUTHOR>
        <FIRSTNAME>Mark</FIRSTNAME>
        <LASTNAME>Twain</LASTNAME>
    </AUTHOR>
    <BINDING>mass market paperback</BINDING>
    <PAGES>205</PAGES>
    <PRICE>$4.75</PRICE>
  </BOOK>
  <BOOK>
    <TITLE>The Ambassadors</TITLE>
    <AUTHOR>
        <FIRSTNAME>Henry</FIRSTNAME>
        <LASTNAME>James</LASTNAME>
    </AUTHOR>
    <BINDING>mass market paperback</BINDING>
    <PAGES>305</PAGES>
    <PRICE>$5.95</PRICE>
  </BOOK>
</INVENTORY>
```

Assume that the style sheet used to display this document contains the following template:

```
<xsl:template match="/">  <!-- match the XSLT root node -->
   <HTML>
   <HEAD>
      <TITLE>Book Inventory</TITLE>
   </HEAD>
   <BODY>
   <H2>Book Inventory</H2>
   <SPAN STYLE="font-style:italic">Author: </SPAN>
   <xsl:value-of select="INVENTORY/BOOK/AUTHOR"/><BR/>
   <SPAN STYLE="font-style:italic">Title: </SPAN>
   <xsl:value-of select="INVENTORY/BOOK/TITLE"/><BR/>
```

```
        <SPAN STYLE="font-style:italic">Price: </SPAN>
        <xsl:value-of select="INVENTORY/BOOK/PRICE"/><BR/>
        <SPAN STYLE="font-style:italic">Binding type: </SPAN>
        <xsl:value-of select="INVENTORY/BOOK/BINDING"/><BR/>
        <SPAN STYLE="font-style:italic">Number of pages: </SPAN>
        <xsl:value-of select="INVENTORY/BOOK/PAGES"/>
        </BODY>
        </HTML>
</xsl:template>
```

This template uses the technique discussed in the previous section. Notice that the location path assigned to each *select* attribute starts with the document element, which in this case is INVENTORY (for example, INVENTORY/BOOK/AUTHOR).

Each location path, however, describes a collection of three different elements. In XSLT, a collection of elements or other nodes is known as a *node-set*. For example, the location path INVENTORY/BOOK/AUTHOR describes a node-set consisting of all three AUTHOR elements. The *xsl:value-of* element uses only the *first* element in the node-set assigned to its *select* attribute. The style sheet would thus display the content of only the first BOOK element, as shown here:

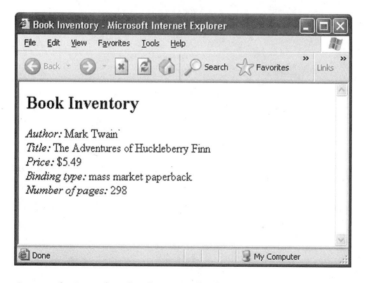

One technique for displaying *all* of the elements or other types of nodes in a node-set is to use the *xsl:for-each* element, which repeats the output from the elements contained within it, once for each node in a specified node-set. The XSLT style sheet in Listing 12-3 demonstrates this technique. This style sheet is linked to the XML document in Listing 12-4. (You'll find copies of both listings on the companion CD under the filenames XsltDemo02.xsl and XsltDemo.xml.)

XsltDemo02.xsl

```
<?xml version="1.0"?>

<!-- File Name: XsltDemo02.xsl -->

<xsl:stylesheet
    version="1.0"
    xmlns:xsl="http://www.w3.org/1999/XSL/Transform">

    <xsl:template match="/">
        <HTML>
        <HEAD>
            <TITLE>Book Inventory</TITLE>
        </HEAD>
        <BODY>
        <H2>Book Inventory</H2>
        <xsl:for-each select="INVENTORY/BOOK">
            <SPAN STYLE="font-style:italic">Title: </SPAN>
            <xsl:value-of select="TITLE"/><BR/>
            <SPAN STYLE="font-style:italic">Author: </SPAN>
            <xsl:value-of select="AUTHOR"/><BR/>
            <SPAN STYLE="font-style:italic">Binding type: </SPAN>
            <xsl:value-of select="BINDING"/><BR/>
            <SPAN STYLE="font-style:italic">Number of pages: </SPAN>
            <xsl:value-of select="PAGES"/><BR/>
            <SPAN STYLE="font-style:italic">Price: </SPAN>
            <xsl:value-of select="PRICE"/><P/>
        </xsl:for-each>
        </BODY>
        </HTML>
    </xsl:template>

</xsl:stylesheet>
```

Listing 12-3.

XsltDemo.xml

```
<?xml version="1.0"?>

<!-- File Name: XsltDemo.xml -->

<?xml-stylesheet type="text/xsl" href="XsltDemo02.xsl"?>
```

```
<INVENTORY>
   <BOOK>
      <TITLE>The Adventures of Huckleberry Finn</TITLE>
      <AUTHOR>
         <FIRSTNAME>Mark</FIRSTNAME>
         <LASTNAME>Twain</LASTNAME>
      </AUTHOR>
      <BINDING>mass market paperback</BINDING>
      <PAGES>298</PAGES>
      <PRICE>$5.49</PRICE>
   </BOOK>
   <BOOK>
      <TITLE>The Adventures of Tom Sawyer</TITLE>
      <AUTHOR>
         <FIRSTNAME>Mark</FIRSTNAME>
         <LASTNAME>Twain</LASTNAME>
      </AUTHOR>
      <BINDING>mass market paperback</BINDING>
      <PAGES>205</PAGES>
      <PRICE>$4.75</PRICE>
   </BOOK>
   <BOOK>
      <TITLE>The Ambassadors</TITLE>
      <AUTHOR>
         <FIRSTNAME>Henry</FIRSTNAME>
         <LASTNAME>James</LASTNAME>
      </AUTHOR>
      <BINDING>mass market paperback</BINDING>
      <PAGES>305</PAGES>
      <PRICE>$5.95</PRICE>
   </BOOK>
   <BOOK>
      <TITLE>The Awakening</TITLE>
      <AUTHOR>
         <FIRSTNAME>Kate</FIRSTNAME>
         <LASTNAME>Chopin</LASTNAME>
      </AUTHOR>
      <BINDING>mass market paperback</BINDING>
      <PAGES>195</PAGES>
      <PRICE>$4.95</PRICE>
   </BOOK>
   <BOOK>
```

```
      <TITLE>Billy Budd</TITLE>
      <AUTHOR>
         <FIRSTNAME>Herman</FIRSTNAME>
         <LASTNAME>Melville</LASTNAME>
      </AUTHOR>
      <BINDING>mass market paperback</BINDING>
      <PAGES>195</PAGES>
      <PRICE>$4.49</PRICE>
   </BOOK>
   <BOOK>
      <TITLE>A Connecticut Yankee in King Arthur's Court</TITLE>
      <AUTHOR>
         <FIRSTNAME>Mark</FIRSTNAME>
         <LASTNAME>Twain</LASTNAME>
      </AUTHOR>
      <BINDING>mass market paperback</BINDING>
      <PAGES>385</PAGES>
      <PRICE>$5.49</PRICE>
   </BOOK>
   <BOOK>
      <TITLE>Joan of Arc</TITLE>
      <AUTHOR>
         <FIRSTNAME>Mark</FIRSTNAME>
         <LASTNAME>Twain</LASTNAME>
      </AUTHOR>
      <BINDING>trade paperback</BINDING>
      <PAGES>465</PAGES>
      <PRICE>$6.95</PRICE>
   </BOOK>
   <BOOK>
      <TITLE>Leaves of Grass</TITLE>
      <AUTHOR>
         <FIRSTNAME>Walt</FIRSTNAME>
         <LASTNAME>Whitman</LASTNAME>
      </AUTHOR>
      <BINDING>hardcover</BINDING>
      <PAGES>462</PAGES>
      <PRICE>$7.75</PRICE>
   </BOOK>
   <BOOK>
      <TITLE>The Legend of Sleepy Hollow</TITLE>
      <AUTHOR>
```

```
            <FIRSTNAME>Washington</FIRSTNAME>
            <LASTNAME>Irving</LASTNAME>
        </AUTHOR>
        <BINDING>mass market paperback</BINDING>
        <PAGES>98</PAGES>
        <PRICE>$2.95</PRICE>
    </BOOK>
    <BOOK>
        <TITLE>The Marble Faun</TITLE>
        <AUTHOR>
            <FIRSTNAME>Nathaniel</FIRSTNAME>
            <LASTNAME>Hawthorne</LASTNAME>
        </AUTHOR>
        <BINDING>trade paperback</BINDING>
        <PAGES>473</PAGES>
        <PRICE>$10.95</PRICE>
    </BOOK>
    <BOOK>
        <TITLE>Moby-Dick</TITLE>
        <AUTHOR>
            <FIRSTNAME>Herman</FIRSTNAME>
            <LASTNAME>Melville</LASTNAME>
        </AUTHOR>
        <BINDING>hardcover</BINDING>
        <PAGES>724</PAGES>
        <PRICE>$9.95</PRICE>
    </BOOK>
    <BOOK>
        <TITLE>Passing</TITLE>
        <AUTHOR>
            <FIRSTNAME>Nella</FIRSTNAME>
            <LASTNAME>Larsen</LASTNAME>
        </AUTHOR>
        <BINDING>trade paperback</BINDING>
        <PAGES>165</PAGES>
        <PRICE>$5.95</PRICE>
    </BOOK>
    <BOOK>
        <TITLE>The Portrait of a Lady</TITLE>
        <AUTHOR>
            <FIRSTNAME>Henry</FIRSTNAME>
            <LASTNAME>James</LASTNAME>
```

```
        </AUTHOR>
        <BINDING>mass market paperback</BINDING>
        <PAGES>256</PAGES>
        <PRICE>$4.95</PRICE>
    </BOOK>
    <BOOK>
        <TITLE>Roughing It</TITLE>
        <AUTHOR>
            <FIRSTNAME>Mark</FIRSTNAME>
            <LASTNAME>Twain</LASTNAME>
        </AUTHOR>
        <BINDING>mass market paperback</BINDING>
        <PAGES>324</PAGES>
        <PRICE>$5.25</PRICE>
    </BOOK>
    <BOOK>
        <TITLE>The Scarlet Letter</TITLE>
        <AUTHOR>
            <FIRSTNAME>Nathaniel</FIRSTNAME>
            <LASTNAME>Hawthorne</LASTNAME>
        </AUTHOR>
        <BINDING>trade paperback</BINDING>
        <PAGES>253</PAGES>
        <PRICE>$4.25</PRICE>
    </BOOK>
    <BOOK>
        <TITLE>The Turn of the Screw</TITLE>
        <AUTHOR>
            <FIRSTNAME>Henry</FIRSTNAME>
            <LASTNAME>James</LASTNAME>
        </AUTHOR>
        <BINDING>trade paperback</BINDING>
        <PAGES>384</PAGES>
        <PRICE>$3.35</PRICE>
    </BOOK>
</INVENTORY>
```

Listing 12-4.

The template in the style sheet of Listing 12-3 contains the following *for-each* element:

```
<xsl:for-each select="INVENTORY/BOOK">
    <SPAN STYLE="font-style:italic">Title: </SPAN>
```

```
      <xsl:value-of select="TITLE"/><BR/>
      <SPAN STYLE="font-style:italic">Author: </SPAN>
      <xsl:value-of select="AUTHOR"/><BR/>
      <SPAN STYLE="font-style:italic">Binding type: </SPAN>
      <xsl:value-of select="BINDING"/><BR/>
      <SPAN STYLE="font-style:italic">Number of pages: </SPAN>
      <xsl:value-of select="PAGES"/><BR/>
      <SPAN STYLE="font-style:italic">Price: </SPAN>
      <xsl:value-of select="PRICE"/><P/>
</xsl:for-each>
```

The *xsl:for-each* element has two main effects:

- The browser carries out the instructions within the *xsl:for-each* element once for every XML element (or other type of node) that is contained in the node-set described by the location path assigned to the *xsl:for-each* element's *select* attribute. In this example, the instructions are repeated once for each BOOK element within the INVENTORY document element. The location path assigned to the *xsl:for-each* element's *select* attribute works just like a location path assigned to the *xsl:value-of* element's *select* attribute, except that you typically assign a location path that describes a node-set that includes more than one node.

- Each time the browser carries out the instructions within the *xsl:for-each* element, one of the nodes contained in the node-set assigned to the *select* attribute becomes the current context node within the scope of the *xsl:for-each* element. The nodes become the current context node in the order of their appearance in the XML document. In the example style sheet, each BOOK element (within the INVENTORY element, within the XSLT root node) would become the current context node in turn, as shown here:

```
<xsl:stylesheet
   version="1.0"
   xmlns:xsl="http://www.w3.org/1999/XSL/Transform">

   <xsl:template match="/">

      <!-- Here, the context node is the XSLT root node (/). -->

      <xsl:for-each select="INVENTORY/BOOK">
```

```
      <!-- Here, the context node is one of the
           /INVENTORY/BOOK elements. -->

    </xsl:for-each>
  </xsl:template>
</xsl:stylesheet>
```

Hence, within the *xsl:for-each* element, each of the child elements of a BOOK element is accessed by a location path containing just the element name, as in this example:

```
<xsl:value-of select="TITLE"/>
```

The final result is that the output contains the data from all the BOOK elements found in the document, regardless of how many of these elements the document contains. Here's the result displayed in Internet Explorer, showing the first three BOOK elements. (Scrolling down would reveal the remaining elements.)

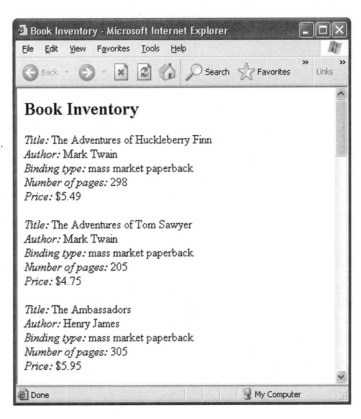

Using Functions in XSLT Style Sheets

The XSLT and XPath specifications provide a large set of useful *functions* that you can call from within your style sheets. An XSLT or XPath function is a built-in software module that performs a task and returns a value.

An example of a useful function is *sum*. If all the nodes in a node-set contain numeric values, you can pass a location path describing this node-set to the *sum* function and it will return the sum of those values. To display the sum in your output, you can assign the returned value to the *select* attribute of the *xsl:value-of* element. For example, in the XsltDemo02.xsl style sheet given in Listing 12-3, you could display the grand total of the page counts of all the books at the end of the list of book descriptions by adding the following instructions immediately after the *xsl:for-each* element:

```
TOTAL PAGE COUNT:
<xsl:value-of select="sum(INVENTORY/BOOK/PAGES)"/>
```

If one or more of the values of the nodes in the node-set you pass to *sum* can't be converted to a numeric value, *sum* returns the string "NaN," meaning "not a number."

Describing additional XSLT and XPath functions is beyond the scope of this chapter. However, you'll find complete descriptions of all available functions in the documentation sources cited in the chapter introduction.

Using Multiple Templates

Another way to display a repeated XML element is to create a separate template that matches that element, and then invoke that template by using the *xsl:apply-templates* element. The example XSLT style sheet in Listing 12-5 uses this technique. (You'll find a copy of this style sheet on the companion CD under the filename XsltDemo03.xsl.) This style sheet is designed to be linked to the XML document in Listing 12-4, XsltDemo.xml; you would link the style sheet by modifying that XML document's *xml-stylesheet* instruction to read as follows:

```
<?xml-stylesheet type="text/xsl" href="XsltDemo03.xsl"?>
```

XsltDemo03.xsl

```
<?xml version="1.0"?>

<!-- File Name: XsltDemo03.xsl -->
```

```
<xsl:stylesheet
  version="1.0"
  xmlns:xsl="http://www.w3.org/1999/XSL/Transform">

  <xsl:template match="/">
    <HTML>
    <HEAD>
      <TITLE>Book Inventory</TITLE>
    </HEAD>
    <BODY>
    <H2>Book Inventory</H2>
    <xsl:apply-templates select="INVENTORY/BOOK" />
    </BODY>
    </HTML>
  </xsl:template>

  <xsl:template match="BOOK">
    <SPAN STYLE="font-style:italic">Title: </SPAN>
    <xsl:value-of select="TITLE"/><BR/>
    <SPAN STYLE="font-style:italic">Author: </SPAN>
    <xsl:value-of select="AUTHOR"/><BR/>
    <SPAN STYLE="font-style:italic">Binding type: </SPAN>
    <xsl:value-of select="BINDING"/><BR/>
    <SPAN STYLE="font-style:italic">Number of pages: </SPAN>
    <xsl:value-of select="PAGES"/><BR/>
    <SPAN STYLE="font-style:italic">Price: </SPAN>
    <xsl:value-of select="PRICE"/><P/>
  </xsl:template>

</xsl:stylesheet>
```

Listing 12-5.

The example style sheet includes two templates. One template contains instructions for displaying the entire document (the one with the *match*="/" setting, specifying the XSLT root node). The other template contains instructions for displaying a BOOK element (the template with *match*="*BOOK*"). The browser begins by processing the template that matches the XSLT root node:

```
<xsl:template match="/">
  <HTML>
  <HEAD>
    <TITLE>Book Inventory</TITLE>
```

```
            </HEAD>
            <BODY>
            <H2>Book Inventory</H2>
            <xsl:apply-templates select="INVENTORY/BOOK" />
            </BODY>
            </HTML>
        </xsl:template>
```

The *xsl:apply-templates* element tells the browser that for every BOOK element within the INVENTORY root element, it should apply a template. As explained in the sidebar "How Internet Explorer Applies XSLT Templates" on page 414, when the browser applies a template to a particular element or other type of node, it begins by looking for a matching template explicitly defined in the style sheet. If it finds a matching template, it executes its instructions. If it doesn't find a matching template, it uses a built-in template that's appropriate for the type of the node. (See the referenced sidebar for a description of the exact actions of the different built-in templates.)

As you learned earlier in the chapter, the browser automatically applies a template to the XSLT root node (and if it doesn't find a template matching the root node, its built-in template automatically applies a template to all child nodes of the XSLT root node). With the *xsl:apply-templates* element, you can *force* the browser to apply a template to a designated set of nodes. You specify this node-set by assigning a location path to the *xsl:apply-templates* element's *select* attribute.

By assigning the location path INVENTORY/BOOK to the *select* attribute of the *xsl:apply-templates* element, the example style sheet causes the browser to apply a template to every BOOK element. Because the style sheet contains a template that matches BOOK elements—that is, a template whose *match* attribute is set to the value BOOK—the browser invokes this template for each BOOK element. The template, shown below, contains the same display instructions you saw within the example *xsl:for-each* element given in the previous section, and the output is the same as that shown in the figure at the end of the previous section.

```
<xsl:template match="BOOK">
    <SPAN STYLE="font-style:italic">Title: </SPAN>
    <xsl:value-of select="TITLE"/><BR/>
    <SPAN STYLE="font-style:italic">Author: </SPAN>
    <xsl:value-of select="AUTHOR"/><BR/>
    <SPAN STYLE="font-style:italic">Binding type: </SPAN>
    <xsl:value-of select="BINDING"/><BR/>
    <SPAN STYLE="font-style:italic">Number of pages: </SPAN>
```

```
   <xsl:value-of select="PAGES"/><BR/>
   <SPAN STYLE="font-style:italic">Price: </SPAN>
   <xsl:value-of select="PRICE"/><P/>
</xsl:template>
```

Within the template, the context node is the BOOK element that is currently being processed. Thus, each of the child elements of BOOK is accessed by a location path containing just the element name, as in this example:

```
<xsl:value-of select="TITLE"/>
```

> **note**
>
> If you omit the *select* attribute from an *xsl:apply-templates* element, the browser applies a template to each child node of the current context node. With the example *xsl:apply-templates* element, omitting the *select* attribute would actually have the same effect as assigning to *select* the value that is assigned in the example, INVENTORY/BOOK. To understand why, see the sidebar "How Internet Explorer Applies XSLT Templates" on page 414.

One advantage of using separate templates for processing different sets of nodes, rather than employing one or more *xsl:for-each* constructs all within a single template, is that separate templates allow you to break up your code into smaller and more manageable modules (just as it can be advantageous to break up program source code into separate functions in a language such as C).

Using Other Select and Match Expressions

As explained previously in this chapter, you assign a location path to the *select* attribute of the *xsl:value-of*, *xsl:for-each*, and *xsl:apply-templates* elements, as well as to the *match* attribute of the *xsl:template* element, to select or match a particular set of elements or other types of nodes within the XML document. Each of the simple location paths you've seen so far has consisted of a single element name, several element names separated with slash (/) characters, or just a slash character. Table 12-1 describes some additional expressions you can use within location paths to achieve a finer level of control over selecting and matching elements or to select or match other types of nodes, such as attributes, comments, and processing instructions.

The examples in Table 12-1, and the discussion that follows the table, refer to the following XML document:

```xml
<?xml version="1.0"?>
<!-- Example XML document for Table 12-1. -->
<?xml-stylesheet type="text/xsl" href="XsltDemo02.xsl"?>
<INVENTORY>
    <BOOK InStock="yes" Bestseller="yes">
        <TITLE>The Adventures of Huckleberry Finn</TITLE>
        <AUTHOR>
            <FIRSTNAME>Mark</FIRSTNAME>
            <LASTNAME>Twain</LASTNAME>
        </AUTHOR>
        <BINDING>mass market paperback</BINDING>
        <PAGES>298</PAGES>
        <PRICE>$5.49</PRICE>
    </BOOK>
    <BOOK InStock="no" Bestseller="no">
        <TITLE>The Adventures of Tom Sawyer</TITLE>
        <AUTHOR>
            <FIRSTNAME>Mark</FIRSTNAME>
            <LASTNAME>Twain</LASTNAME>
        </AUTHOR>
        <BINDING>mass market paperback</BINDING>
        <PAGES>205</PAGES>
        <PRICE>$4.75</PRICE>
    </BOOK>
    <BOOK InStock="yes" Bestseller="yes">
        <TITLE>The Ambassadors</TITLE>
        <AUTHOR>
            <FIRSTNAME>Henry</FIRSTNAME>
            <LASTNAME>James</LASTNAME>
        </AUTHOR>
        <BINDING>mass market paperback</BINDING>
        <PAGES>305</PAGES>
        <PRICE>$5.95</PRICE>
    </BOOK>
</INVENTORY>
```

Location path expression	Meaning or use	Example (selects or matches)
name	Every element with the specified *name*	BOOK (Every BOOK element)
/ (*within* a location path)	The child operator, which is used to separate location steps	AUTHOR/LASTNAME (Every LASTNAME element that's a child of an AUTHOR element)
/ (at the *beginning* of a location path)	The XSLT root node	/INVENTORY/BOOK (Every BOOK element that's a child of an INVENTORY element that's a child of the XSLT root node)
//	The recursive descent operator, which indicates that the following expression refers to descendant nodes at any level	BOOK//FIRSTNAME (Every FIRSTNAME element that's a descendant of a BOOK element) //BOOK (Every BOOK element that's a descendant of the XSLT root node—that is, every BOOK element in the document)
. (Can be used in a *select* value only)	The context node	.//BOOK (Every BOOK element that's a descendant of the context node) `<xsl:value-of select="."/>` (Outputs the value of the context node)
.. (Can be used in a *select* value only)	The parent node of the context node	../AUTHOR (Every AUTHOR element that's a child of the context node's parent node)
*	Every element	BOOK/* (Every element that's a child of a BOOK element) /* (The document element, which is the only element that can be a child of the XSLT root node)
@*name*	Every attribute with the specified *name*	BOOK/@InStock (Every *InStock* attribute belonging to a BOOK element)
@*	Every attribute	BOOK/@* (Every attribute belonging to a BOOK element)

comment()	Every comment	/comment() (Every comment that's a child of the XSLT root node) You could display the text of these comments as follows:
		 `<xsl:for-each select="/comment()">`
		 `  <xsl:value-of select="."/>`
		 `</xsl:for-each>`

continued

continued

Location path expression	Meaning or use	Example (selects or matches)

processing-instruction()	Every processing instruction	`/processing-instruction()` (Every processing instruction that's a child of the XSLT root node) You could display the text of these processing instructions (not including the targets) as follows:
		`<xsl:for-each select="/processing-instruction()">`
		    `<xsl:value-of select="."/>`
		`</xsl:for-each>`

text()	Every text node. (Any character data contained directly in an element is stored in a child text node.)	`TITLE/text()` (Every text node that's a child of a TITLE element)
node()	Every node	`/node()` (Every node that's a child of the XSLT root node)
|	Combines separate location paths into a compound location path	`TITLE | AUTHOR` (Every TITLE or AUTHOR element) `* | @*` (Every element or attribute node)

Table 12-1. *Useful expressions you can use in a location path assigned to a* select *or* match *attribute.*

note

The expressions for referencing attributes (@*name* and @*) are discussed in "Accessing XML Attributes," later in the chapter.

A location path that begins with a slash (/) is known as an *absolute* location path, and fully specifies the location of a set of nodes. An absolute location path you assign to a *select* attribute has essentially the same meaning as one you assign to a *match* attribute. (A location path beginning with two slashes (//) is also absolute in the sense that it is independent of the context node, although it doesn't fully specify the location of the node-set.)

All other location paths are termed *relative*. A relative location path you assign to a *select* attribute specifies the location of the node-set relative to the current context node. In the following template, for example, the location path TITLE that's assigned to the *select* attribute of the *xsl:value-of* element selects the TITLE element that is a child of the current context node within the *xsl:for-each* element. The context node is the BOOK element (within the INVENTORY element, within the XSLT root node) that is currently being processed.

```
<xsl:template match="/">
    <!-- context node is XSLT root node (/) -->
    <xsl:for-each select="INVENTORY/BOOK">
        <!-- context node is the current /INVENTORY/BOOK element -->
        <xsl:value-of select="TITLE"/><BR/>
    </xsl:for-each>
</xsl:template>
```

In contrast, a relative location path you assign to a *match* attribute in an *xsl:template* element doesn't specify a location relative to a specific context node. Rather, the location it specifies can be anywhere within the document. Consider, for instance, the following XML document element:

```
<BOOK>
    <TITLE>XML Step by Step, Second Edition</TITLE>
    <PREVIOUS>
        <TITLE>XML Step by Step, First Edition</TITLE>
    </PREVIOUS>
</BOOK>
```

The following template would match a TITLE element wherever it occurs in the document. Specifically, it would match the TITLE element that's a child of BOOK, as well as the one that's a child of PREVIOUS (and the template would therefore be invoked whenever the browser applied a template to either of these TITLE elements):

```
<xsl:template match="TITLE">
    <!-- template elements... -->
</xsl:template>
```

If you wanted a template that matched only the TITLE element within PREVIOUS, you could set the *match* attribute equal to the relative location path PREVIOUS/TITLE, as in this example:

```
<xsl:template match="PREVIOUS/TITLE">
    <!-- template elements... -->
</xsl:template>
```

This template would match a TITLE element that is a child of a PREVIOUS element located anywhere in the document. (Similarly, if you wanted a template that matched only the TITLE element that's an immediate child of BOOK, you would set its *match* attribute to the relative location path BOOK/TITLE.)

Filtering and Sorting XML Data

In the next two sections, you'll learn the basics of using an XSLT style sheet to filter or sort XML data. Following that, you'll see some example style sheets that demonstrate both filtering and sorting.

Filtering

As you've seen, the location path that you assign to the *select* attribute (of the *xsl:value-of*, *xsl:for-each*, or *xsl:apply-templates* element) or to the *match* attribute (of the *xsl:template* element) selects or matches a set of elements or other types of nodes within the XML document. You've learned how to use various expressions and operators within a location path to accurately narrow down the set of nodes that is selected or matched.

In this section, you'll learn how to further restrict the set of selected or matched nodes by including a *filter clause,* also known as a *predicate,* within a location path. A filter clause is contained within square brackets ([]) and can be placed immediately following any of the location steps within a location path. (Recall that the location steps are the individual parts of a location path that are separated with slash (/) characters.) For example, the location path assigned to the *select* attribute in the following *xsl:for-each* element specifies that each of the selected nodes must be a BOOK element, must be contained within an INVENTORY element within the current context node, and (because of the filter clause) must have a child BINDING element containing the text "trade paperback":

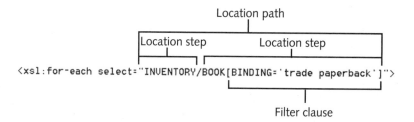

Here's the same *xsl:for-each* element shown in its containing template:

```
<xsl:template match="/">
   <!-- other elements... -->
   <xsl:for-each
      select="INVENTORY/BOOK[BINDING='trade paperback']">
      <xsl:value-of select="TITLE"/><BR/>
   </xsl:for-each>
   <!-- other elements... -->
</xsl:template>
```

This example template refers to the XsltDemo.xml XML document given in Listing 12-4. Its result would be to display a list of the titles of just the trade paperback books.

> ## note
>
> Unless otherwise noted, the examples in this section refer to the XsltDemo.xml example document in Listing 12-4. Also, the *xsl:for-each* and *xsl:apply-templates* examples are assumed to be contained within a template in which the context node is the XSLT root node (/):
>
> ```
> <xsl:template match="/">
>     <!-- The xsl:for-each and xsl:apply-templates examples
>     are assumed to be located here. -->
> </xsl:template>
> ```

You could also use this same filter clause with a *select* attribute in an *xsl:apply-templates* element:

```
<xsl:apply-templates
    select="INVENTORY/BOOK[BINDING='trade paperback']"/>
```

This element would cause the browser to apply a template to each of the BOOK elements that stores a trade paperback book. If you included the following matching template, the output would be the same as that generated by the *xsl:for-each* example given previously:

```
<xsl:template match="BOOK">
    <xsl:value-of select="TITLE"/><BR/>
</xsl:template>
```

An alternative approach would be to use the *xsl:apply-templates* element to apply a template to all BOOK elements:

```
<xsl:apply-templates select="INVENTORY/BOOK"/>
```

and place the filter clause in the value assigned to the *match* attribute of the matching template:

```
<xsl:template match="BOOK[BINDING='trade paperback']">
    <xsl:value-of select="TITLE"/><BR/>
</xsl:template>
```

Note that with this alternative approach, the browser would apply a template to *every* BOOK element. For a trade paperback BOOK element, it would use the matching template. However, for a BOOK element that stores a different type of book (such as a hardcover), the browser would be unable to find a matching template (unless you added a matching template to the style sheet). It would therefore use its built-in template, which would display the entire text content of the element. To prevent the browser from doing this, you could add a "do nothing" template that matches all non-trade paperback books:

```
<xsl:template match="BOOK[BINDING!='trade paperback']">
</xsl:template>
```

The not-equal operator (!=) is another of the comparison operators you can use in a filter clause. Table 12-2 provides a complete list of these operators.

Comparison operator	Meaning
=	Equal
!=	Not equal
&lt;	Less than
<=	Less than or equal
>	Greater than
>=	Greater than or equal

Table 12-2. *The XSLT comparison operators*

You can use any of the last four operators to test the value of elements (or attributes) that contain numeric values. For instance, the *xsl:for-each* element in the following example would select every BOOK element that has a child PAGES element containing a numeric value greater than 300:

```
<xsl:for-each select="INVENTORY/BOOK/PAGES[. > 300]">
   <xsl:value-of select="."/><BR/>
</xsl:for-each>
```

This example would display a list of page counts for all books that have more than 300 pages. Notice the use of the context node operator (.) in the filter clause to test the value of the preceding element itself (PAGES) rather than a child of that element.

tip

If you wanted to be able to use the PRICE elements found in the XsltDemo.xml XML document (Listing 12-4) in numeric comparisons in filter clauses and elsewhere, you would have to store the prices as pure decimal numbers, without including the dollar sign ($) characters. (The dollar signs prevent the values from being converted to numbers.) Storing the PRICE elements as decimal numbers would also let you use the *sum* function, described earlier in the chapter, to sum PRICE values. If you want, you can always add a dollar sign to the output used to display a price value.

note

You must enter the "less than" and the "less than or equal" operators using the < predefined entity because a literal left angle bracket (<) is illegal in an attribute value.

Keep in mind that the filter clause doesn't need to be at the end of the entire location path. Rather, it can be placed at the end of one of the preceding location steps. For example, the location path in the following *xsl:for-each* start-tag selects every TITLE element that is a child of a BOOK element that also has a BINDING child element containing "trade paperback." In other words, it selects the TITLE elements for trade paperback books.

```
<xsl:for-each
    select="INVENTORY/BOOK[BINDING='trade paperback']/TITLE">
```

If an element has more than one child element that matches the name given in the filter clause, the element will be selected if *any* of the child elements meets the filter criteria. For example, consider an XML document with the following document element:

```
<CATALOG>
    <SHIRT>
        <DESCRIPTION>short-sleeve Henley</DESCRIPTION>
        <COLOR>red</COLOR>
        <COLOR>green</COLOR>
        <COLOR>blue</COLOR>
    </SHIRT>
    <SHIRT>
        <DESCRIPTION>pocket T-shirt</DESCRIPTION>
```

```
        <COLOR>white</COLOR>
        <COLOR>black</COLOR>
    </SHIRT>

    <!-- other elements... -->

</CATALOG>
```

The location path in the following start-tag would select the first SHIRT element in the example because one of its COLOR child elements contains "green:"

```
<xsl:for-each select="CATALOG/SHIRT[COLOR='green']">
```

To select only SHIRT elements in which *all* child COLOR elements contain "green," you could use the filter clause given in the following start-tag:

```
<xsl:for-each select="CATALOG/SHIRT[not(COLOR!='green')]">
```

(This location path wouldn't select either of the SHIRT elements in the example document.)

The *not* is a Boolean operator you can use in a filter clause to reverse the true or false value of the expression in the parentheses that follow the *not* operator.

You can test the value of a *specific* child element by including a number in square brackets ([]) following the element name, where [1] refers to the first child element with the specified name. For example, the location path in the following start-tag selects SHIRT elements in which the second COLOR child element contains "green:"

```
<xsl:for-each select="CATALOG/SHIRT[COLOR[2]='green']">
```

(This location path would select the first SHIRT element in the example document.)

If a location step yields a node-set containing more than one node (a common situation), you can select an individual node by appending a filter clause that contains just the number of the node you want to select, where [1] selects the first node in the set. For instance, the location path in the following start-tag selects all the child elements of the *first* BOOK element within INVENTORY:

```
<xsl:for-each select="INVENTORY/BOOK[1]/*">
```

And the following *xsl:value-of* element displays the text content of the second BOOK element within INVENTORY. (Without the filter clause, the *xsl:value-of* element would display the content of the first BOOK element.)

```
<xsl:value-of select="INVENTORY/BOOK[2]"/>
```

A final type of filter clause contains just an element name. It indicates that the preceding node must have at least one child element with the specified name, without regard to the child elements' content. For example, consider an XML document that contains the following document element:

```
<STOCK>
   <MEDIASET>
     <BOOK>XML Step by Step</BOOK>
     <CD>companion CD</CD>
   </MEDIASET>
   <MEDIASET>
     <BOOK>Visual Basic--Game Programming</BOOK>
     <FLOPPY>companion disk</FLOPPY>
   </MEDIASET>

   <!-- other elements... -->

</STOCK>
```

The location path in the following start-tag would select just the first MEDIASET element because it is the only one that contains a child CD element:

```
<xsl:for-each select="STOCK/MEDIASET[CD]">
```

Sorting

In this chapter, you've seen two XSLT elements that you can use to select and process repeated elements or other types of nodes: *xsl:for-each* and *xsl:apply-templates*. The nodes are normally processed in the order in which they occur in the XML document. You can, however, include one or more *xsl:sort* elements as children of the *xsl:for-each* or *xsl:apply-templates* element to control the order in which the nodes are processed, thereby sorting the displayed XML data. For example, the following *xsl:for-each* element causes the browser to display a list of authors and book titles, to sort the list by the authors' last names (the primary sort key), and to sort authors with the same last name by their first names (the secondary sort key):

```
<xsl:for-each select="INVENTORY/BOOK">

   <xsl:sort
      select="AUTHOR/LASTNAME"
      data-type="text"
      order="ascending"/>
   <xsl:sort
      select="AUTHOR/FIRSTNAME"
      data-type="text"
      order="ascending"/>
```

```
<xsl:value-of select="AUTHOR"/>
<SPAN STYLE="font-style:italic">
   <xsl:value-of select="TITLE"/>
</SPAN>
<BR/>


</xsl:for-each>
```

(This example refers to the XsltDemo.xml XML document in Listing 12-4.)

The first *xsl:sort* child element included in *xsl:for-each* or *xsl:apply-templates* specifies the primary sort key, the second *xsl:sort* element the secondary sort key, and so on for any additional sort keys you want to use. Within an *xsl:for-each* element, the *xsl:sort* element(s) must be placed before any other child elements.

You assign the *select* attribute of the *xsl:sort* element a location path, relative to the current context node *within* the *xsl:for-each* or *xsl:apply-templates* element, that specifies the element (or attribute) to be used as the sort key. (The default value of the *select* attribute is the context node operator (.), which causes the sort to be performed using the entire text value of the current context node as the sort key.) You set the *data-type* attribute to *text* to specify an alphabetical sort (the default), or to *number* to specify a numeric sort. (With a numeric sort, the sort key values are treated as numbers and are sorted in the order of the sizes of the numbers. For example, with a numeric sort 95 would come before 105, but with an alphabetical sort 105 would come before 95.) You assign the *order* attribute the value *ascending* (the default) or *descending* to specify the sort order.

Example Style Sheets That Filter and Sort

This section presents two example XSLT style sheets, given in Listings 12-6 and 12-7. Each filters and sorts the BOOK elements that it displays. You'll find copies of these listings on the companion CD under the filenames XsltDemo04.xsl and XsltDemo05.xsl.

XsltDemo04.xsl

```
<?xml version="1.0"?>

<!-- File Name: XsltDemo04.xsl -->

<xsl:stylesheet
   version="1.0"
   xmlns:xsl="http://www.w3.org/1999/XSL/Transform">
```

```
<xsl:template match="/">
  <HTML>
  <HEAD>
     <TITLE>Book Inventory</TITLE>
  </HEAD>
  <BODY>
  <H2>Book Inventory</H2>
  <H3>Trade Paperback Books</H3>
  <xsl:for-each
     select="INVENTORY/BOOK[BINDING='trade paperback']">
     <xsl:sort
        select="AUTHOR/LASTNAME"
        data-type="text"
        order="ascending"/>
     <xsl:sort
        select="AUTHOR/FIRSTNAME"
        data-type="text"
        order="ascending"/>
     <xsl:sort
        select="PAGES"
        data-type="number"
        order="descending"/>

     <SPAN STYLE="font-style:italic">Author: </SPAN>
     <xsl:value-of select="AUTHOR"/><BR/>
     <SPAN STYLE="font-style:italic">Title: </SPAN>
     <xsl:value-of select="TITLE"/><BR/>
     <SPAN STYLE="font-style:italic">Binding type: </SPAN>
     <xsl:value-of select="BINDING"/><BR/>
     <SPAN STYLE="font-style:italic">Number of pages: </SPAN>
     <xsl:value-of select="PAGES"/><BR/>
     <SPAN STYLE="font-style:italic">Price: </SPAN>
     <xsl:value-of select="PRICE"/><P/>
  </xsl:for-each>
  </BODY>
  </HTML>
</xsl:template>

</xsl:stylesheet>
```

Listing 12-6.

XsltDemo05.xsl

```xml
<?xml version="1.0"?>

<!-- File Name: XsltDemo05.xsl -->

<xsl:stylesheet
    version="1.0"
    xmlns:xsl="http://www.w3.org/1999/XSL/Transform">

    <xsl:template match="/">
        <HTML>
        <HEAD>
            <TITLE>Book Inventory</TITLE>
        </HEAD>
        <BODY>
        <H2>Book Inventory</H2>
        <H3>Trade Paperback Books</H3>
        <xsl:apply-templates
            select="INVENTORY/BOOK[BINDING='trade paperback']">
            <xsl:sort
                select="AUTHOR/LASTNAME"
                data-type="text"
                order="ascending"/>
            <xsl:sort
                select="AUTHOR/FIRSTNAME"
                data-type="text"
                order="ascending"/>
            <xsl:sort
                select="PAGES"
                data-type="number"
                order="descending"/>
        </xsl:apply-templates>
        </BODY>
        </HTML>
    </xsl:template>

    <xsl:template match="BOOK">
        <SPAN STYLE="font-style:italic">Author: </SPAN>
        <xsl:value-of select="AUTHOR"/><BR/>
        <SPAN STYLE="font-style:italic">Title: </SPAN>
        <xsl:value-of select="TITLE"/><BR/>
        <SPAN STYLE="font-style:italic">Binding type: </SPAN>
```

```
        <xsl:value-of select="BINDING"/><BR/>
        <SPAN STYLE="font-style:italic">Number of pages: </SPAN>
        <xsl:value-of select="PAGES"/><BR/>
        <SPAN STYLE="font-style:italic">Price: </SPAN>
        <xsl:value-of select="PRICE"/><P/>
    </xsl:template>

</xsl:stylesheet>
```

Listing 12-7.

Both style sheets are designed to be linked to the XML document in Listing 12-4 (XsltDemo.xml). They both use the following *select* attribute specification to cause the browser to display only the trade paperback books:

```
select="INVENTORY/BOOK[BINDING='trade paperback']"
```

And they both use the following *xsl:sort* elements to sort the BOOK elements:

```
<xsl:sort
    select="AUTHOR/LASTNAME"
    data-type="text"
    order="ascending"/>
<xsl:sort
    select="AUTHOR/FIRSTNAME"
    data-type="text"
    order="ascending"/>
<xsl:sort
    select="PAGES"
    data-type="number"
    order="descending"/>
```

These three *xsl:sort* elements cause the browser to sort the BOOK elements in ascending alphabetical order by the authors' last names, then in ascending alphabetical order by the authors' first names, and then in descending numerical order by the numbers of pages in the books (so that a particular author's books are arranged from longest to shortest).

The following is the first part of the output, which is the same for both style sheets:

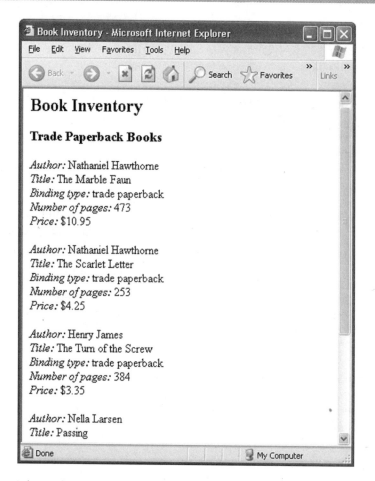

The style sheet in Listing 12-6 uses an *xsl:for-each* element to display the multiple BOOK elements. In this style sheet, the *select* attribute specification is added to the *xsl:for-each* start-tag, and the *xsl:sort* elements are inserted at the beginning of the *xsl:for-each* element's content. This causes the transformation instructions within *xsl:for-each* to be applied once for each trade paperback book, in the specified sort order.

The style sheet in Listing 12-7 uses an *apply-templates* element, together with a separate matching template, to display the multiple BOOK elements. In this style sheet, the *select* attribute specification is added to the *xsl:apply-templates* start-tag, and the *xsl:sort* elements are placed within the *xsl:apply-templates* element. This causes the browser to apply a template to each BOOK element that stores a trade paperback book, in the specified sort order. For each of these BOOK elements, the browser finds and applies the matching template defined in the style sheet:

```
<xsl:template match="BOOK">

    <!-- display current BOOK element... -->

</xsl:template>
```

Although the filter clause could be added to the *match* attribute of the *xsl:template* element rather than the *select* attribute of the *xsl:apply-templates* element, the browser would then apply a template to *all* BOOK elements. For the BOOK elements that don't match the filter criteria in the *xsl:template* element (the non-trade paperback books), the browser would use its built-in template, which would display all the BOOK elements' text, creating extraneous output (unless you explicitly defined another template to match the non-trade paperback books).

Accessing XML Attributes

Technically, in XSLT an attribute is not considered to be a child of the element that contains it. However, in a location path or in a filter clause within a location path, you can reference an attribute as if it were a child of the element that contains it by entering the attribute name prefaced with the at sign (@), which indicates that the name refers to an attribute rather than to an element.

For example, the location path in the following start-tag selects every BOOK element with an attribute named *InStock* that has the value *yes*. In other words, it selects only the books that are in stock:

```
<xsl:for-each select="INVENTORY/BOOK[@InStock='yes']">
```

And the location path in the following *xsl:for-each* start-tag selects every BOOK element that has an attribute named *InStock*, regardless of the attribute's value:

```
<xsl:for-each select="INVENTORY/BOOK[@InStock]">
```

You can use the *xsl:value-of* element to extract the value of an attribute in the same way you use it to extract the text content of an element. For example, the following *xsl:value-of* element outputs the value of the *Born* attribute belonging to the AUTHOR element:

```
<xsl:value-of select="AUTHOR/@Born"/>
```

The location path in the following *xsl:for-each* start-tag selects *every* attribute belonging to the AUTHOR element:

```
<xsl:for-each select="AUTHOR/@*"/>
```

note

The attribute expressions @*name* and @* are also described in Table 12-1.

The style sheet in Listing 12-8 demonstrates the techniques for accessing attributes belonging to elements in the XML document. This style sheet is linked to the XML document in Listing 12-9, and it displays all in-stock books in the book inventory. (You'll find copies of these listings on the companion CD under the filenames XsltDemo06.xsl and XsltDemo06.xml.)

XsltDemo06.xsl

```xml
<?xml version="1.0"?>

<!-- File Name: XsltDemo06.xsl -->

<xsl:stylesheet
    version="1.0"
    xmlns:xsl="http://www.w3.org/1999/XSL/Transform">

    <xsl:template match="/">
      <HTML>
      <HEAD>
        <TITLE>Books in Stock</TITLE>
      </HEAD>
      <BODY>
      <H2>Books In Stock</H2>
      <TABLE BORDER="1" CELLPADDING="5">
        <THEAD>
          <TH>Title</TH>
          <TH>Author</TH>
          <TH>Binding Type</TH>
          <TH>Number of Pages</TH>
          <TH>Price</TH>
        </THEAD>
        <xsl:for-each select="INVENTORY/BOOK[@InStock='yes']">
          <TR ALIGN="CENTER">
            <TD>
              <xsl:value-of select="TITLE"/>
            </TD>
            <TD>
              <xsl:value-of select="AUTHOR"/> <BR/>
              (born <xsl:value-of select="AUTHOR/@Born"/>)
```

```
                    </TD>
                    <TD>
                       <xsl:value-of select="BINDING"/>
                    </TD>
                    <TD>
                       <xsl:value-of select="PAGES"/>
                    </TD>
                    <TD>
                       <xsl:value-of select="PRICE"/>
                    </TD>
                 </TR>
             </xsl:for-each>
          </TABLE>
          </BODY>
          </HTML>
       </xsl:template>

</xsl:stylesheet>
```

Listing 12-8.

XsltDemo06.xml

```
<?xml version="1.0"?>

<!-- File Name: XsltDemo06.xml -->

<?xml-stylesheet type="text/xsl" href="XsltDemo06.xsl"?>

<INVENTORY>
   <BOOK InStock="yes">
      <TITLE>The Adventures of Huckleberry Finn</TITLE>
      <AUTHOR Born="1835">Mark Twain</AUTHOR>
      <BINDING>mass market paperback</BINDING>
      <PAGES>298</PAGES>
      <PRICE>$5.49</PRICE>
   </BOOK>
   <BOOK InStock="no">
      <TITLE>Leaves of Grass</TITLE>
      <AUTHOR Born="1819">Walt Whitman</AUTHOR>
      <BINDING>hardcover</BINDING>
      <PAGES>462</PAGES>
      <PRICE>$7.75</PRICE>
```

```
   </BOOK>
   <BOOK InStock="yes">
      <TITLE>The Marble Faun</TITLE>
      <AUTHOR Born="1804">Nathaniel Hawthorne</AUTHOR>
      <BINDING>trade paperback</BINDING>
      <PAGES>473</PAGES>
      <PRICE>$10.95</PRICE>
   </BOOK>
   <BOOK InStock="yes">
      <TITLE>Moby-Dick</TITLE>
      <AUTHOR Born="1819">Herman Melville</AUTHOR>
      <BINDING>hardcover</BINDING>
      <PAGES>724</PAGES>
      <PRICE>$9.95</PRICE>
   </BOOK>
</INVENTORY>
```

Listing 12-9.

Each BOOK element in the XML document contains an *InStock* attribute set to *yes* or *no* to indicate whether the book is in stock. Each AUTHOR element has a *Born* attribute giving the birth year of the author.

Rather than displaying the value of the *InStock* attribute, the style sheet uses the attribute in a filter clause to eliminate all out-of-stock books from the set of BOOK elements that it displays:

```
<xsl:for-each select="INVENTORY/BOOK[@InStock='yes']">

   <!-- display each BOOK element... -->

</xsl:for-each>
```

The style sheet displays the BOOK elements within an HTML table rather than in a list of SPAN elements as in the previous examples. It displays the value of the *Born* attribute, following the value of the AUTHOR element, by using the *xsl:value-of* element. The following elements create the table cell displaying these values:

```
<TD>
   <xsl:value-of select="AUTHOR"/> <BR/>
   (born <xsl:value-of select="AUTHOR/@Born"/>)
</TD>
```

Here's the way the Internet Explorer displays the document:

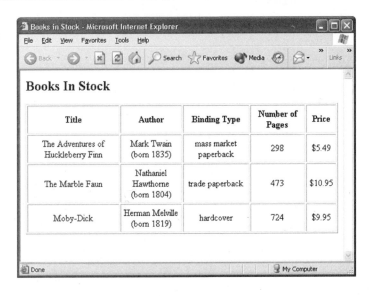

Adding an Attribute to a Literal Result Element

You can add an attribute with a known, constant value to a literal result element by simply entering the attribute specification into the element start-tag that appears in the style sheet. You've seen many examples in the style sheets shown in this chapter, such as the STYLE attribute in the following literal result SPAN element:

```
<SPAN STYLE="font-style:italic">
    <xsl:value-of select="TITLE"/>
</SPAN>
```

If, however, you want to obtain the attribute's value from the XML file, you need to use the *xsl:attribute* element. For example, consider an XML document with the following document element, in which the COLORCODE elements indicate the color that should be used for displaying each book's title:

```
<BOOKLIST>
    <BOOK>
        <TITLE>The Ambassadors</TITLE>
        <COLORCODE>red</COLORCODE>
    </BOOK>
    <BOOK>
        <TITLE>The Awakening</TITLE>
```

continued

Using XSLT Style Sheets   12

continued

```
        <COLORCODE>green</COLORCODE>
    </BOOK>
    <BOOK>
        <TITLE>The Marble Faun</TITLE>
        <COLORCODE>blue</COLORCODE>
    </BOOK>

    <!-- other BOOK elements... -->

</BOOKLIST>
```

You could use the *xsl:template* element as follows to insert a STYLE attribute into each literal result SPAN element that is copied to the output. The color part of each attribute's value is obtained from the content of the corresponding COLORCODE element in the XML document (*red*, *green*, or *blue*):

```
<xsl:for-each select="BOOKLIST/BOOK">
    <SPAN>
        <xsl:attribute name="STYLE">
            color: <xsl:value-of select="COLORCODE"/>
        </xsl:attribute>
        <xsl:value-of select="TITLE"/><BR/>
    </SPAN>
</xsl:for-each>
```

The result of this example would be to display the first book title in red, the second in green, and the third in blue.

You can add one or more *xsl:attribute* elements to a literal result element in addition to adding attributes with known values to the literal result element's start-tag. The *xsl:attribute* element or elements must come before any other child elements or any character data belonging to the literal result element.

You'll probably discover quite a few other uses for the *xsl:attribute* element. For example, if an XML document contains the addresses of image files, you could use *xsl:attribute* to assign these addresses to the SRC attributes of literal result IMG elements that are displayed in the output, thereby showing the images. And if an XML document contains the URLs of Web sites, you could use *xsl:attribute* to assign these URLs to the HREF attributes of hyperlink (A) elements, thereby providing hyperlinks to the sites.

Referencing Namespaces in XSLT

The section "Using Namespaces" on page 69 explained how to use namespaces in XML documents. When you write an XSLT style sheet, if an element or attribute in the XML document belongs to a namespace, you must identify that namespace when you reference the element or attribute in a location path assigned to a *select* or *match* attribute. This applies to an XML element or attribute that has an explicit namespace prefix, as well as to an element that's in the scope of a default namespace. (Unlike a CSS, an XSLT style sheet provides a way to reference default namespaces.) You reference a namespace in an XSLT style sheet by declaring and using a namespace prefix that refers to the namespace name used in the XML document.

To illustrate, Listing 12-10 contains an XSLT style sheet that displays the contents of the example XML document given in Listing 3-5. The style sheet first displays a list of the books in the collection and then a list of the CDs. It's able to display the books and CDs in separate lists because the ITEM elements for books and the ITEM elements for CDs are in separate namespaces. (You'll find copies of Listings 12-10 and 3-5 on the companion CD under the filenames Collection Default XSLT.xsl and Collection Default.xml.) To display the XML document in Listing 3-5 using this style sheet, add the following *xml-stylesheet* processing instruction to the document just above the start-tag of the COLLECTION root element:

```
<?xml-stylesheet type="text/xsl"
   href="Collection Default XSLT.xsl"?>
```

Collection Default XSLT.xsl

```
<?xml version="1.0"?>

<!-- File Name: Collection Default XSLT.xsl -->

<xsl:stylesheet
   version="1.0"
   xmlns:xsl="http://www.w3.org/1999/XSL/Transform"
   xmlns:book="http://www.mjyOnline.com/books"
   xmlns:cd="http://www.mjyOnline.com/cds">

   <xsl:template match="/">
      <HTML>
      <HEAD>
         <TITLE>Collection Inventory</TITLE>
```

```
        </HEAD>
        <BODY>
        <H2>Collection Inventory</H2>
        <H3>Books</H3>
        <xsl:for-each select="book:COLLECTION/book:ITEM">
            <xsl:value-of select="book:TITLE"/><BR/>
            <xsl:value-of select="book:AUTHOR"/><BR/>
            <xsl:value-of select="book:PRICE"/><BR/>
            <xsl:value-of select="@Status"/><BR/><BR/>
        </xsl:for-each>
        <H3>CDs</H3>
        <xsl:for-each select="book:COLLECTION/cd:ITEM">
            <xsl:value-of select="cd:TITLE"/><BR/>
            <xsl:value-of select="cd:COMPOSER"/><BR/>
            <xsl:value-of select="cd:PRICE"/><BR/><BR/>
        </xsl:for-each>
        </BODY>
        </HTML>
    </xsl:template>

</xsl:stylesheet>
```

Listing 12-10.

The example style sheet globally declares (in the *xsl:stylesheet* start-tag) two namespace prefixes that it can use to reference the two namespaces found in the XML document:

```
<xsl:stylesheet
    version="1.0"
    xmlns:xsl="http://www.w3.org/1999/XSL/Transform"
    xmlns:book="http://www.mjyOnline.com/books"
    xmlns:cd="http://www.mjyOnline.com/cds">
```

The style sheet uses the *book* namespace prefix to refer to the XML elements that belong to the default namespace named *http://www.mjyOnline.com/books*, and it uses the *cd* namespace prefix to refer to the XML elements that belong to the explicit namespace named *http://www.mjyOnline.com/cds*. (In the style sheet, you can use any namespace prefixes you want, provided that the namespace names match those in the XML document.) Here's an example of how the style sheet uses the *book* namespace prefix:

```
<xsl:value-of select="book:TITLE"/>
```

And here's an example of how it uses the *cd* namespace prefix:

```
<xsl:value-of select="cd:TITLE"/>
```

Using Conditional Structures

This final section introduces the XSLT conditional elements, which allow you to selectively include transformation instructions in your style sheet based on conditions such as the value of an element or attribute.

The simplest conditional element is *xsl:if*, which allows you to include or exclude a block of instructions based on a single test. Assume, for example, that the following template is in a style sheet linked to the XsltDemo06.xml XML document given in Listing 12-9. This template displays a simple list of the book titles. The *xsl:if* element within the template displays "out of stock!" to the left of the title for any BOOK element whose *InStock* attribute is set to *no*:

```
<xsl:template match="/">
   <!-- other elements... -->

   <xsl:for-each select="INVENTORY/BOOK">
      <SPAN STYLE="font-style:italic">
         <xsl:if test="@InStock = 'no'">out of stock! </xsl:if>
         <xsl:value-of select="TITLE"/>
      </SPAN>
      <BR/>
   </xsl:for-each>

   <!-- other elements... -->
</xsl:template>
```

You assign to the *test* attribute of the *xsl:if* element an expression that evaluates to true or false (that is, a Boolean expression). If the expression is true, the browser uses the transformation instructions contained within the *xsl:if* element. If the expression is false, the browser skips the instructions. You can assign *test* the same types of comparison expressions that are used in filter clauses (described in "Filtering" on page 438), and you can use any of the comparison operators listed in Table 12-2.

You can branch to one of several alternative blocks of instructions by using the *xsl:choose*, *xsl:when*, and *xsl:otherwise* elements, which work like an *if-else* or *switch* construct in a programming language such as C. The following template contains an example. If this template were in a style sheet attached to the XsltDemo06.xml XML document, it would display a list of all book titles, indicating the size category of each book by displaying one, two, or three asterisks to the title's left. (One asterisk indicates a length less than or equal to 300 pages, two asterisks a length greater than 300 but less than or equal to 500, and three asterisks a length greater than 500.)

```
<xsl:template match="/">
   <!-- other elements... -->

   <xsl:for-each select="INVENTORY/BOOK">
      <SPAN STYLE="font-style:italic">
         <xsl:choose>
            <xsl:when test="PAGES &lt;= 300">*</xsl:when>
            <xsl:when test="PAGES &lt;= 500">**</xsl:when>
            <xsl:otherwise>***</xsl:otherwise>
         </xsl:choose>
         <xsl:value-of select="TITLE"/>
      </SPAN>
      <BR/>
   </xsl:for-each>

   <!-- other elements... -->
</xsl:template>
```

When these three conditional elements are arranged as in the example, the browser uses the instructions contained in the first *xsl:when* element with a *test* attribute that evaluates to true. If none of the *xsl:when* elements have true *test* values, it uses the instructions contained in the *xsl:otherwise* element at the end (if it's included). In the example, the "instructions" consist of only one to three asterisk characters to be copied to the output.

Web Addresses for Further Information

The following Web sites provide a wealth of supplemental information on XML and its related technologies. I've also included these addresses in the previous chapters, each in the appropriate context. You'll find a copy of this appendix in the Resource Links folder on the companion CD, under the filename Appendix.htm. (If you wish, you can use the CD installation program to copy this file to your hard drive, as explained in "Using the Companion CD" in the introduction.) You can visit any of these Web sites by opening Appendix.htm in your Web browser and simply clicking a link, rather than having to type the address into the browser.

General Information on XML

- The Microsoft Developer Network (MSDN) Library furnishes extensive documentation on XML as supported by Microsoft products under the topic "XML and Web Services" at *http://msdn.microsoft.com/library/*.

- The World Wide Web Consortium (W3C) offers a wide variety of information, standards, and services for Web authors at *http://www.w3.org/*. It provides a diverse collection of XML resources at *http://www.w3.org/XML/*. And it publishes the latest version of the official XML specification at *http://www.w3.org/TR/REC-xml*.

- The online reference work *The XML Cover Pages* includes comprehensive information on XML and other markup languages at *http://www.oasis-open.org/cover/*.

Internet Explorer and MSXML

- You can download the latest version of Microsoft Internet Explorer at *http://www.microsoft.com/windows/ie/*.

- You can download the latest version of MSXML from the MSDN Library on the Web at *http://msdn.microsoft.com/library/*.

XML Applications

- *The XML Cover Pages* Web site provides a comprehensive list of current and proposed XML applications, as well as detailed descriptions of each application, at *http://www.oasis-open.org/cover/xml.html#applications*.

- Jon Bosak, who chaired the XML Working Group, has created XML versions of the complete works of William Shakespeare, as well as the Old Testament, New Testament, Koran, and Book of Mormon. You can download these documents from *http://www.ibiblio.org/bosak/*.

- The W3C publishes the latest version of the XHTML specification at *http://www.w3.org/TR/xhtml1*.

Namespaces

- For information on using namespaces in XML with Internet Explorer and MSXML, see the topic "Using Namespaces in Documents" in the XML SDK documentation provided by the MSDN Library on the Web at *http://msdn.microsoft.com/library/*.

- The W3C publishes the "Namespaces in XML" specification at *http://www.w3.org/TR/REC-xml-names/*.

URIs and URNs

- For information on URIs, see the following page on the W3C Web site: *http://www.w3.org/Addressing/*.

- For information on URN syntax, go to *http://www.ietf.org/rfc/rfc2141.txt*.

XML Schemas

- For information on XML schemas as supported by Internet Explorer and MSXML 4.0, see the topic "XML Schemas" in the XML SDK documentation provided by the MSDN Library on the Web at *http://msdn.microsoft.com/library/*.

- You'll find the complete text of the W3C XML Schema specification in the following three pages on the Web: "XML Schema Part 0: Primer" at *http://www.w3.org/TR/xmlschema-0/*, "XML Schema Part 1: Structures" at *http://www.w3.org/TR/xmlschema-1/*, and "XML Schema Part 2: Datatypes" at *http://www.w3.org/TR/xmlschema-2/*.

Cascading Style Sheets (CSS)

- To learn about the CSS features supported by Internet Explorer, see the topic "Cascading Style Sheets" in the MSDN Library on the Web at *http://msdn.microsoft.com/library/*.

- For a list of all the Internet Explorer color names that you can use for assigning colors in a cascading style sheet, see the topic "Color Table" in the MSDN Library on the Web at *http://msdn.microsoft.com/library/*.

- The W3C publishes the specification for Cascading Style Sheets Level 1 (CSS1) at *http://www.w3.org/TR/REC-CSS1*.

- The W3C publishes the specification for Cascading Style Sheets Level 2 (CSS2) at *http://www.w3.org/TR/REC-CSS2*.

- For an introduction to the techniques for using cascading style sheets with HTML, see the topic "2.1 A brief CSS2 tutorial for HTML" in the W3C page "2 Introduction to CSS2" at *http://www.w3.org/TR/REC-CSS2/intro.html*.

Data Binding and the
Data Source Object (DSO)

▨ For information on using data binding and the DSO with Internet Explorer, see the topics "Binding the XML Data Source Object to Data," "Use the C++ XML Data Source Object," and "Use the Master/Detail Feature with the C++ XML Data Source Object" in the XML SDK documentation provided by the MSDN Library on the Web at *http://msdn.microsoft.com/library/*.

ActiveX Data Objects (ADO) and the
ADO *recordset* Object

▨ For general information on ADO and the ADO *recordset* object, see the topic "Microsoft ActiveX Data Objects (ADO)" in the MSDN Library on the Web at *http://msdn.microsoft.com/library/*.

▨ The Microsoft home page for information on ADO is located at *http://www.microsoft.com/data/ado/*.

HTML and Dynamic HTML (DHTML)

▨ For information on working with HTML and DHTML as implemented in Internet Explorer, see the topic "HTML and Dynamic HTML" in the MSDN Library on the Web at *http://msdn.microsoft.com/library/*.

▨ To read the official specification for the latest version of HTML 4, see the following Web site, provided by the W3C: *http://www.w3.org/TR/html4/*.

Microsoft JScript

▨ For information on JScript and other Microsoft Web scripting technologies, see the topic "Scripting" in the MSDN Library on the Web at *http://msdn.microsoft.com/library/*.

The Document Object Model (DOM)

- For information on the XML DOM as implemented by Internet Explorer, see the topics "DOM Developer's Guide" and "DOM Reference" in the XML SDK documentation provided by the MSDN Library on the Web at *http://msdn.microsoft.com/library/*.

- The W3C publishes the "Document Object Model (DOM) Level 1 Specification Version 1.0" at *http://www.w3.org/TR/REC-DOM-Level-1*.

Extensible Stylesheet Language Transformations (XSLT) and XPath

- For information on XSLT and XPath as implemented by Internet Explorer, see the topics "XSLT Developer's Guide," "XSLT Reference," "XPath Developer's Guide," and "XPath Reference" in the XML SDK documentation provided by the MSDN Library on the Web at *http://msdn.microsoft.com/library/*.

- The W3C publishes the XSL Transformations (XSLT) Version 1.0 specification at *http://www.w3.org/TR/xslt*.

- The W3C publishes the XML Path Language (XPath) Version 1.0 specification at *http://www.w3.org/TR/xpath*.

Author's Web Site

- You can contact me through my Web site at *http://www.mjyOnline.com*. At this site, you'll also find book corrections, reader questions and answers on XML, links to additional XML resources on the Web, a list of recommended books on XML and its related technologies, and information on my background and some of my other books.

Index

Symbols

A

F

I

Biography

Michael J. Young has been writing books for computer users and developers since 1986. His more than two dozen titles include *Visual Basic—Game Programming for Windows*, the best-selling *Running Microsoft Office* series, and *Microsoft Office XP Inside Out*, all from Microsoft Press. (He wrote the Office books together with Michael Halvorson.) His developer books have covered MS-DOS, Windows, C, C++, Visual Basic, Java, XML, animation, game, and graphics programming. He is the author of the popular first edition of *XML Step by Step*, which won the top award, "Distinguished Technical Communication," in the 2000-2001 International Technical Publications Competition of the Society for Technical Communication. Books planned for the future will center on the use and programming of Microsoft Office, as well as XML, Java, and other Web publishing topics. Michael graduated from Stanford University with a degree in philosophy. He later studied computer science at several California colleges, completing coursework through the first year of graduate studies. Currently, he lives and works in Taos, New Mexico. You can contact him and find out more about what he does through his Web site at *http://www.mjyOnline.com*.

Get a **Free**
e-mail newsletter, updates,
special offers, links to related books,
and more when you

register on line!

Register your Microsoft Press® title on our Web site and you'll get a FREE subscription to our e-mail newsletter, *Microsoft Press Book Connections.* You'll find out about newly released and upcoming books and learning tools, online events, software downloads, special offers and coupons for Microsoft Press customers, and information about major Microsoft® product releases. You can also read useful additional information about all the titles we publish, such as detailed book descriptions, tables of contents and indexes, sample chapters, links to related books and book series, author biographies, and reviews by other customers.

Registration is easy. Just visit this Web page and fill in your information:

http://www.microsoft.com/mspress/register

Microsoft·

- -

MICROSOFT LICENSE AGREEMENT

Book Companion CD

user manual, in "online" documentation, and/or in other Microsoft-provided materials. Any supplemental software code provided to you as part of the Support Services shall be considered part of the SOFTWARE PRODUCT and subject to the terms and conditions of this EULA. With respect to technical information you provide to Microsoft as part of the Support Services, Microsoft may use such information for its business purposes, including for product support and development. Microsoft will not utilize such technical information in a form that personally identifies you.

- **Software Transfer.** You may permanently transfer all of your rights under this EULA, provided you retain no copies, you transfer all of the SOFTWARE PRODUCT (including all component parts, the media and printed materials, any upgrades, this EULA, and, if applicable, the Certificate of Authenticity), **and** the recipient agrees to the terms of this EULA.

- **Termination.** Without prejudice to any other rights, Microsoft may terminate this EULA if you fail to comply with the terms and conditions of this EULA. In such event, you must destroy all copies of the SOFTWARE PRODUCT and all of its component parts.

3. **COPYRIGHT.** All title and copyrights in and to the SOFTWARE PRODUCT (including but not limited to any images, photographs, animations, video, audio, music, text, SAMPLE CODE, REDISTRIBUTABLES, and "applets" incorporated into the SOFTWARE PRODUCT) and any copies of the SOFTWARE PRODUCT are owned by Microsoft or its suppliers. The SOFTWARE PRODUCT is protected by copyright laws and international treaty provisions. Therefore, you must treat the SOFTWARE PRODUCT like any other copyrighted material **except** that you may install the SOFTWARE PRODUCT on a single computer provided you keep the original solely for backup or archival purposes. You may not copy the printed materials accompanying the SOFTWARE PRODUCT.

4. **U.S. GOVERNMENT RESTRICTED RIGHTS.** The SOFTWARE PRODUCT and documentation are provided with RESTRICTED RIGHTS. Use, duplication, or disclosure by the Government is subject to restrictions as set forth in subparagraph (c)(1)(ii) of the Rights in Technical Data and Computer Software clause at DFARS 252.227-7013 or subparagraphs (c)(1) and (2) of the Commercial Computer Software—Restricted Rights at 48 CFR 52.227-19, as applicable. Manufacturer is Microsoft Corporation/One Microsoft Way/Redmond, WA 98052-6399.

5. **EXPORT RESTRICTIONS.** You agree that you will not export or re-export the SOFTWARE PRODUCT, any part thereof, or any process or service that is the direct product of the SOFTWARE PRODUCT (the foregoing collectively referred to as the "Restricted Components"), to any country, person, entity, or end user subject to U.S. export restrictions. You specifically agree not to export or re-export any of the Restricted Components (i) to any country to which the U.S. has embargoed or restricted the export of goods or services, which currently include, but are not necessarily limited to, Cuba, Iran, Iraq, Libya, North Korea, Sudan, and Syria, or to any national of any such country, wherever located, who intends to transmit or transport the Restricted Components back to such country; (ii) to any end user who you know or have reason to know will utilize the Restricted Components in the design, development, or production of nuclear, chemical, or biological weapons; or (iii) to any end user who has been prohibited from participating in U.S. export transactions by any federal agency of the U.S. government. You warrant and represent that neither the BXA nor any other U.S. federal agency has suspended, revoked, or denied your export privileges.

DISCLAIMER OF WARRANTY

NO WARRANTIES OR CONDITIONS. MICROSOFT EXPRESSLY DISCLAIMS ANY WARRANTY OR CONDITION FOR THE SOFTWARE PRODUCT. THE SOFTWARE PRODUCT AND ANY RELATED DOCUMENTATION ARE PROVIDED "AS IS" WITHOUT WARRANTY OR CONDITION OF ANY KIND, EITHER EXPRESS OR IMPLIED, INCLUDING, WITHOUT LIMITATION, THE IMPLIED WARRANTIES OF MERCHANTABILITY, FITNESS FOR A PARTICULAR PURPOSE, OR NONINFRINGEMENT. THE ENTIRE RISK ARISING OUT OF USE OR PERFORMANCE OF THE SOFTWARE PRODUCT REMAINS WITH YOU.

LIMITATION OF LIABILITY. TO THE MAXIMUM EXTENT PERMITTED BY APPLICABLE LAW, IN NO EVENT SHAI MICROSOFT OR ITS SUPPLIERS BE LIABLE FOR ANY SPECIAL, INCIDENTAL, INDIRECT, OR CONSEQUENTIAL DAMAGES WHATSOEVER (INCLUDING, WITHOUT LIMITATION, DAMAGES FOR LOSS OF BUSINESS PROFITS, BUSINESS INTERRUPTION, LOSS OF BUSINESS INFORMATION, OR ANY OTHER PECUNIARY LOSS) ARISING OUT THE USE OF OR INABILITY TO USE THE SOFTWARE PRODUCT OR THE PROVISION OF OR FAILURE TO PROVIDE SUPPORT SERVICES, EVEN IF MICROSOFT HAS BEEN ADVISED OF THE POSSIBILITY OF SUCH DAMAGES. IN ANY CASE, MICROSOFT'S ENTIRE LIABILITY UNDER ANY PROVISION OF THIS EULA SHALL BE LIMITED TO THE GREATER OF THE AMOUNT ACTUALLY PAID BY YOU FOR THE SOFTWARE PRODUCT OR US$5.00; PROVIDED, HOWEVER, IF YOU HAVE ENTERED INTO A MICROSOFT SUPPORT SERVICES AGREEMENT, MICROSOFT'S ENTIR LIABILITY REGARDING SUPPORT SERVICES SHALL BE GOVERNED BY THE TERMS OF THAT AGREEMENT. BECAUSE SOME STATES AND JURISDICTIONS DO NOT ALLOW THE EXCLUSION OR LIMITATION OF LIABILITY, THE ABOVE LIMITATION MAY NOT APPLY TO YOU.

MISCELLANEOUS

This EULA is governed by the laws of the State of Washington USA, except and only to the extent that applicable law man governing law of a different jurisdiction.

Should you have any questions concerning this EULA, or if you desire to contact Microsoft for any reason, please conta Microsoft subsidiary serving your country, or write: Microsoft Sales Information Center/One Microsoft Way/Redmond, 98052-6399.